John Wiley & Sons

Founded in 1807, John Wiley & Sons is the oldest independent publishing company in the United States. With offices in North America, Europe, Australia, and Asia, Wiley is globally committed to developing and marketing print and electronic products and services for our customers' professional and personal knowledge and understanding.

The Wiley Finance series contains books written specifically for finance and investment professionals as well as sophisticated individual investors and their financial advisors. Book topics range from portfolio management to e-commerce, risk management, financial engineering, valuation and financial instrument analysis, as well as much more.

For a list of available titles, please visit our Web site at www.WileyFinance.com.

financial statement analysis

A Practitioner's Guide

Third Edition

University Edition

MARTIN FRIDSON
FERNANDO ALVAREZ

John Wiley & Sons, Inc.

In memory of my father, Harry Yale Fridson, who introduced me to accounting, economics, and logic, as well as the fourth discipline essential to the creation of this book—hard work!

M. F.

For Shari, Virginia, and Armando.

F. A.

"With a solid understanding of accepted accounting standards, one must peel through the fog generated by audited accounting numbers to get a clear picture of any company's financial health. Certainly, Fridson and Alvarez show us how to do just that. What I like best about the book is the authors' ability to provide examples of real-life debacles discussed in the business press that could have been foreseen using the techniques explained in the book and having a healthy dose of skepticism. Their approach to analyzing financial statements should be commended."

—Ivan Brick
Professor and Chair, Finance and Economics Department, Rutgers Business School

"This book should be required reading for the seasoned investor and novice alike. Fridson and Alvarez show, in a very readable format, that diligent analysis still can make a difference. Finally a book that covers not just the basics, but all the subtleties and everything that management doesn't want you to know."

—Robert S. Franklin, CFA
Portfolio Manager, Neuberger Berman, LLC

"Read it, digest it, and review it frequently. Fridson and Alvarez take you through financial statement analysis with many salient examples that expose hidden agendas and help with assessing the true value of securities."

—Ron Habakus
Director of High Yield Investments, Brown Brothers Harriman

"Fridson and Alvarez clearly show why the most successful financial analysts approach their jobs with healthy doses of cynicism. Well written, insightful, and with numerable real life war stories, this book is required reading for all high yield bond analysts at AIG."

—Gordon Massie
Managing Director, High Yield Bonds
American International Group Global Investment Advisors

"Fridson and Alvarez give financial analysts, accountants, investors, auditors and all other finance professionals something to chew over. They succeed in illustrating the use of financial statement analysis with many astonishing real life examples. This book starts where others stop. Clearly, a must read that brings the reader beyond the pure number crunching!"

—Marc J.K. De Ceuster
Professor at the University of Antwerp (Belgium) and Director of Risk Management at Deloitte & Touche

"Alvarez and Fridson have a real gift for expressing the concepts of finance in down-to-earth, understandable ways. The situations they choose, and the skillful way they lay out each example, make all the subtle relationships come to. They are real artists with spreadsheets that are easy for the reader to follow, and easy to adapt to new situations. For instant financial empowerment, buy this book and let Alvarez and Fridson ramp up your financial modeling skills."

—John Edmunds
Director of the Stephen D. Cutler Investment Management Center at Babson College

preface to third edition

This third edition of *Financial Statement Analysis*, like its predecessors, seeks to equip its readers for practical challenges of contemporary business. Once again, the intention is to acquaint readers who have already acquired basic accounting skills with the complications that arise in applying textbook-derived knowledge to the real world of extending credit and investing in securities. Just as a swiftly changing environment necessitated extensive revisions and additions in the second edition, new concerns and challenges for users of financial statements have accompanied the dawn of the twenty-first century.

For one thing, corporations have shifted their executive compensation plans increasingly toward rewarding senior managers for "enhancing shareholder value." This lofty-sounding concept has a dark side. Chief executive officers who are under growing pressure to boost their corporations' share prices can no longer increase their bonuses by goosing reported earnings through financial reporting tricks that are transparent to the stock market. They must instead devise more insidious methods that gull investors into believing that the reported earnings gains are real. In response to this trend, we have expanded our survey of revenue recognition gimmicks designed to deceive the unwary.

Another innovation that demands increased vigilance by financial analysts is the conversion of stock market proceeds into revenues. In terms of accounting theory, this kind of transformation is the equivalent of alchemy. Companies generate revenue by selling goods or services, not by selling their own shares to the public.

During the Internet stock boom of the late 1990s, however, clever operators found a way around that constraint. Companies took the money they raised in initial public offerings, bought advertising on one another's websites, and recorded the shuttling of dollars as sales. Customers were superfluous to the revenue recognition process. In another variation on the theme, franchisers sold stock, lent the proceeds to franchisees, then immediately had the cash returned under the rubric of fees. By going out for a short stroll and coming back, the proceeds of a financing mutated into revenues.

The artificial nature of these revenues becomes apparent when readers combine an understanding of accounting principles with a corporate finance perspective. We facilitate such integration of disciplines throughout *Financial Statement Analysis,* making excursions into economics and business management as well. In addition, we encourage analysts to consider the institutional context in which financial reporting occurs. Organizational pressures result in divergences from elegant theories, both in the conduct of financial statement analysis and in auditors' interpretations of accounting principles. The issuers of financial statements also exert a strong influence over the creation of the financial principles, with powerful politicians sometimes carrying their water.

A final area in which the new edition offers a sharpened focus involves success stories in the critical examination of financial statements. Wherever we can find the necessary documentation, we show not only how a corporate debacle *could have been* foreseen through application of basis analytical techniques, but how practicing analysts actually did detect the problem before it became widely recognized. Readers will be encouraged by these examples, we hope, to undertake genuine, goal-oriented analysis, instead of simply going through the motions of calculating standard financial ratios. Moreover, the case studies should persuade them to stick to their guns when they spot trouble, despite management's predictable litany. ("Our financial statements are consistent with Generally Accepted Accounting Principles. They have been certified by one of the world's premier auditing firms. We will not allow a band of greedy short-sellers to destroy the value created by our outstanding employees.") Typically, as the vehemence of management's protests increases, conditions deteriorate and accusations of aggressive accounting give way to revelations of fraudulent financial reporting.

As for the plan of *Financial Statement Analysis,* readers should not feel compelled to tackle its chapters in the order we have assigned to them. To aid those who want to jump in somewhere in the middle of the book, the third edition provides increased cross-referencing and an expanded Glossary. Words that are defined in the Glossary are shown in **bold faced type** in the text. Although skipping around will be the most efficient approach for many analysts, a logical flow does underlie the sequencing of the material.

In Part I ("Reading between the Lines"), we show that financial statements do not simply represent unbiased portraits or corporations' financial performance and explain why. The section explores the complex motivations of issuing firms and their managers. We also study the distortions produced by the organizational context in which the analyst operates.

Part II ("The Basic Financial Statements") takes a hard look at the information disclosed in the balance sheet, income statement, and statement of cash flows. Under close scrutiny, terms such as *value* and *income* begin to look muddier than they appear when considered in the abstract. Even *cash flow*, a concept commonly thought to convey redemptive clarification, is vulnerable to stratagems designed to manipulate the perceptions of investors and creditors.

In Part III ("A Closer Look at Profits"), we zero in on the lifeblood of the capitalist system. Our scrutiny of profits highlights the manifold ways in which earnings are exaggerated or even fabricated. By this point in the book, the reader should be amply imbued with the healthy skepticism necessary for a sound, structured approach to financial statement analysis.

Application is the theme of Part IV ("Forecasts and Security Analysis"). For both credit and equity evaluation, forward-looking analysis is emphasized over seductive but ultimately unsatisfying retrospection. Tips for maximizing the accuracy of forecasts are included and real-life projections by professional securities analysts are dissected. We cast a critical eye on standard financial ratios and valuation models, however widely accepted they may be.

Financial markets continue to evolve, but certain phenomena appear again and again in new guises. In this vein, companies never lose their resourcefulness in finding new ways to skew perceptions of their performance. By studying their methods closely, analysts can potentially anticipate the variations on old themes that will materialize in years to come.

MARTIN FRIDSON
FERNANDO ALVAREZ

acknowledgments

Mukesh Agarwal
John Bace
Mitchell Bartlett
Richard Bernstein
Richard Byrne
Richard Cagney
George Chalhoub
Sanford Cohen
Margarita Declet
Sylvan Feldstein
David Fitton
Thomas Flynn III
Daniel Fridson
Igor Fuksman
Ryan Gelrod
Kenneth Goldberg
Susannah Gray
Evelyn Harris
David Hawkins
Avi Katz
Rebecca Keim
James Kenney
Andrew Kroll
Les Levi
Ross Levy
Jennie Ma
Michael Marocco

Eric Matejevich
John Mattis
Pat McConnell
Oleg Melentyev
Krishna Memani
Ann Marie Mullan
Kingman Penniman
Richard Rolnick
Clare Schiedermayer
Gary Schieneman
Bruce Schwartz
Devin Scott
Elaine Sisman
Charles Snow
Vladimir Stadnyk
John Thieroff
Scott Thomas
John Tinker
Kivin Varghese
Sharyl Van Winkle
David Waill
Steven Waite
Douglas Watson
Burton Weinstein
Stephen Weiss
David Whitcomb
Mark Zand

contents

Reading between the Lines

CHAPTER 1

The Adversarial Nature of Financial Reporting

Financial statement analysis is an essential skill in a variety of occupations including investment management, corporate finance, commercial lending, and the extension of credit. For individuals engaged in such activities, or who analyze financial data in connection with their personal investment decisions, there are two distinct approaches to the task.

The first is to follow a prescribed routine, filling in boxes with standard financial ratios, calculated according to precise and inflexible definitions. It may take little more effort or mental exertion than this to satisfy the formal requirements of many positions in the field of financial analysis. Operating in a purely mechanical manner, though, will not provide much of a professional challenge. Neither will a rote completion of all of the "proper" standard analytical steps ensure a useful, or even a nonharmful, result. Some individuals, however, will view such problems as only minor drawbacks.

This book is aimed at the analyst who will adopt the second and more rewarding alternative, the relentless pursuit of accurate financial profiles of the entities being analyzed. Tenacity is essential because financial statements often conceal more than they reveal. To the analyst who pursues this proactive approach, producing a standard spreadsheet on a company is a means rather than an end. Investors derive but little satisfaction from the knowledge that an untimely stock purchase recommendation was supported by the longest row of figures available in the software package. Genuinely valuable analysis begins *after* all the usual questions have been answered. Indeed, a superior analyst adds value by raising questions that are not even on the checklist.

Some readers may not immediately concede the necessity of going beyond an analytical structure that puts all companies on a uniform, objective scale. They may recoil at the notion of discarding the structure altogether when a sound assessment depends on factors other than comparisons of standard financial ratios. Comparability, after all, is a cornerstone of **generally accepted accounting principles (GAAP)**. It might therefore seem to follow that financial statements prepared in accordance with GAAP necessarily produce fair and useful indications of relative value.

The corporations that issue financial statements, moreover, would appear to have a natural interest in facilitating convenient, cookie-cutter analysis. These companies spend heavily to disseminate information about their financial performance. They employ investor-relations managers, they communicate with existing and potential shareholders via interim financial reports and press releases, and they dispatch senior management to periodic meetings with securities analysts. Given that companies are so eager to make their financial results known to investors, they should also want it to be easy for analysts to monitor their progress. It follows that they can be expected to report their results in a transparent and straightforward fashion . . . or so it would seem.

THE PURPOSE OF FINANCIAL REPORTING

Analysts who believe in the inherent reliability of GAAP numbers and the good faith of corporate managers misunderstand the essential nature of financial reporting. Their conceptual error connotes no lack of intelligence, however. Rather, it mirrors the standard accounting textbook's idealistic but irrelevant notion of the purpose of financial reporting. Even Howard Schilit (see the MicroStrategy discussion, later in this chapter), an acerbic critic of financial reporting as it is actually practiced, presents a high-minded view of the matter:

> *The primary goal in financial reporting is the dissemination of financial statements that accurately measure the profitability and financial condition of a company.*[1]

Missing from this formulation is an indication of *whose* primary goal is accurate measurement. Schilit's words are music to the ears of the financial statements users listed in this chapter's first paragraph, but they are not the ones doing the financial reporting. Rather, the issuers are for-profit companies, generally organized as corporations.[2]

A corporation exists for the benefit of its shareholders. Its objective is not to educate the public about its financial condition, but to maximize its shareholders' wealth. If it so happens that management can advance that objective through "dissemination of financial statements that accurately measure the profitability and financial condition of the company," then in principle, management should do so. At most, however, reporting financial results in a transparent and straightforward fashion is a means unto an end.

Management may determine that a more direct method of maximizing shareholder wealth is to reduce the corporation's *cost of capital.* Simply stated, the lower the interest rate at which a corporation can borrow or the higher the price at which it can sell stock to new investors, the greater is the wealth of its shareholders. From this standpoint, the best kind of financial statement is not one that represents the corporation's condition most fully and most fairly, but rather one that produces the highest possible credit rating (see Chapter 13) and price-earnings multiple (see Chapter 14). If the highest ratings and multiples result from statements that measure profitability and financial condition *inaccurately,* the logic of fiduciary duty to shareholders obliges management to publish that sort, rather than the type held up as a model in accounting textbooks. The best possible outcome is a cost of capital lower than the corporation deserves on its merits. This admittedly perverse argument can be summarized in the following maxim, presented from the perspective of issuers of financial statements:

The purpose of financial reporting is to obtain cheap capital.

Attentive readers will raise two immediate objections. First, they will say, it is fraudulent to obtain capital at less than a fair rate by presenting an unrealistically bright financial picture. Second, some readers will argue that misleading the users of financial statements is not a sustainable strategy over the long run. Stock market investors who rely on overstated historical profits to project a corporation's future earnings will find that results fail to meet their expectations. Thereafter, they will adjust for the upward bias in the financial statements by projecting lower earnings than the historical results would otherwise justify. The outcome will be a stock valuation no higher than accurate reporting would have produced. Recognizing that the practice would be self-defeating, corporations will logically refrain from overstating their financial performance. By this reasoning, the users of financial statements can take the numbers at face value, because corporations that act in their self-interest will report their results honestly.

The inconvenient fact that confounds these arguments is that financial statements do *not* invariably reflect their issuers' performance faithfully. In lieu of easily understandable and accurate data, users of financial statements often find numbers that conform to GAAP yet convey a misleading impression of profits. Worse yet, outright violations of the accounting rules come to light with distressing frequency. Not even the analyst's second line of defense, an affirmation by independent auditors that the statements have been prepared in accordance with GAAP, assures that the numbers are reliable. A few examples from recent years indicate how severely an overly trusting user of financial statements can be misled.

Mercury Plunges

In January 1997, Mercury Finance's controller was reported to have disappeared[3] after the company reduced its 1996 earnings to $56.7 million from an originally reported $120.7 million. The used-car loan company's co-founder and chief executive officer, John Brincat, contended that the irregularities necessitating the restatements were apparently "the result of unauthorized entries being made to the accounting records of the company by the principal accounting officer," the missing James A. Doyle.[4] On January 28, the day before the earnings revision, Mercury's stock closed at $14.875 a share. When trading in the shares reopened on January 31, the price plunged to $2.125.

As the story developed, controller Doyle's attorney denied that his client had disappeared. Rather, "He decided with the advice of counsel to no longer participate in the charade taking place at Mercury Finance."[5] Speaking through his lawyer, Doyle added that he was cooperating with a federal investigation of the company.

Thickening the plot was the provision in CEO Brincat's management contract whereby he was not entitled to any bonus in any year in which earnings per share rose by less than 20%. Doyle had no such bonus arrangement, leading some observers to wonder what motive he would have had to falsify the financials. Additional earnings revisions announced along with the 1996 restatement indicated that Mercury did not, after all, achieve the 20% target in 1994 or 1995, even though Brincat received bonuses of $1.4 million and $1.6 million, respectively, for those years.[6] In any case, Brincat resigned as chief executive officer on February 3. A year later he stepped down from the company's board and agreed to repay part of his 1994–1996 bonuses.

Also in February 1998, Mercury announced that it would file for bankruptcy. By then, the company had revised its originally reported 1996 profit of $120.7 million to a net loss. In hindsight, the financial statements had incorporated unrealistic assumptions about the percentage of Mercury's low-income borrowers who would fail to keep up their loan payments. The auditors had certified the results, despite the telltale warning sign that the statements showed Mercury earning more than double the historical average return on equity (see Chapter 13) of other companies in its business.

Securities analyst Charles Mills of Anderson & Strudwick likened such improbably superior performance to a human running a two-minute mile.[7]

MicroStrategy Changes Its Mind

On March 20, 2000, MicroStrategy announced that it would restate its 1999 revenue, originally reported as $205.3 million, to around $150 million. The company's shares promptly plummeted by $140 to $86.75 a share, slashing chief executive officer Michael Saylor's paper wealth by over $6 billion. The company explained that the revision had to do with recognizing revenue on the software company's large, complex projects.[8] MicroStrategy and its auditors initially suggested that the company had been obliged to restate its results in response to a recent (December 1999) **Securities and Exchange Commission** (SEC) advisory on rules for booking software revenues. After the SEC objected to that explanation, the company conceded that its original accounting was inconsistent with accounting principles published way back in 1997 by the American Institute of Certified Public Accountants.

Until MicroStrategy dropped its bombshell, the company's auditors had put their seal of approval on the company's revenue recognition policies. That was despite questions raised about MicroStrategy's financials by accounting expert Howard Schilit six months earlier and by reporter David Raymond in an issue of *Forbes ASAP* distributed on February 21.[9] It was reportedly only after reading Raymond's article that an accountant in the auditor's national office contacted the local office that had handled the audit, ultimately causing the firm to retract its previous certification of the 1998 and 1999 financials.[10]

No Straight Talk from Lernout & Hauspie

On November 16, 2000, the auditor for Lernout & Hauspie Speech Products (L&H) withdrew its clean opinion of the company's 1998 and 1999 financials. The action followed a November 9 announcement by the Belgian producer of speech-recognition and translation software that an internal investigation had uncovered accounting errors and irregularities that would require restatement of results for those two years and the first half of 2000. Two weeks later, the company filed for bankruptcy.

Prior to November 16, 2000, while investors were relying on the auditor's opinion that Lernout & Hauspie's financial statements were consistent with generally accepted accounting principles, several events cast doubt on that opinion. In July 1999, short-seller David Rocker criticized transactions such as L&H's arrangement with Brussels Translation Group (BTG). Over a two-year period, BTG paid L&H $35 million to develop translation software. L&H then bought BTG and the translation product along with it. The net effect was that instead of booking a $35 million research and development expense, L&H recognized $35 million of revenue.[11] In August 2000, certain Korean companies that L&H claimed as customers said that they in fact did no business with the corporation. In September, the Securities and Exchange Commission and Europe's Easdaq stock market began to investigate L&H's accounting practices.[12] Along the way, Lernout & Hauspie's stock fell from a high of $72.50 in March 2000 to $7 before being suspended from trading in November. In retrospect, uncritical reliance on the company's financials, based on the auditor's opinion and a presumption that management wanted to help analysts get the true picture, was a bad policy.

THE FLAWS IN THE REASONING

As the preceding deviations from GAAP demonstrate, neither fear of antifraud statutes nor enlightened self-interest invariably deters corporations from cooking the books. The reasoning by which these two forces ensure honest accounting rests on hidden assumptions. None of the assumptions can stand up to an examination of the organizational context in which financial reporting occurs.

To begin with, corporations can push the numbers fairly far out of joint before they run afoul of GAAP, much less open themselves to prosecution for fraud. When major financial reporting violations come to light, as in most other kinds of white-collar crime, the real scandal involves what is *not* forbidden. In practice, generally accepted accounting principles countenance a lot of measurement that is decidedly inaccurate, at least over the short run.

For example, corporations routinely and unabashedly smooth their earnings. That is, they create the illusion that their profits rise at a consistent rate from year to year. Corporations engage in this behavior, with the blessing of their auditors, because the appearance of smooth growth receives a higher price-earnings multiple from stock market investors than the jagged reality underlying the numbers.

Suppose that, in the last few weeks of a quarter, earnings threaten to fall short of the programmed year-over-year increase. The corporation simply "borrows" sales (and associated profits) from the next quarter by offering customers special discounts to place orders earlier than they had planned. *Higher*-than-trendline growth, too, is a problem for the earnings-smoother. A sudden jump in profits, followed by a return to a more ordinary rate of growth, produces volatility, which is regarded as an evil to be avoided at all costs. Management's solution is to run up expenses in the current period by scheduling training programs and plant maintenance that, while necessary, would ordinarily be undertaken in a later quarter.

These are not tactics employed exclusively by fly-by-night companies. Blue chip corporations openly acknowledge that they have little choice but to smooth their earnings, given Wall Street's allergy to surprises. Officials of General Electric have indicated that when a division is in danger of failing to meet its annual earnings goal, it is accepted procedure to make an acquisition in the waning days of the reporting period. According to an executive in the company's financial services business, he and his colleagues hunt for acquisitions at such times, saying, "Gee, does somebody else have some income? Is there some other deal we can make?"[13] The freshly acquired unit's profits for the full quarter can be incorporated into GE's, helping to ensure the steady growth so prized by investors.

Why do auditors not forbid such gimmicks? They hardly seem consistent with the ostensible purpose of financial reporting, namely, the accurate portrayal of a corporation's earnings. The explanation is that sound principles of accounting theory represent only one ingredient in the stew from which financial reporting standards emerge.

Along with accounting professionals, the issuers and users of financial statements also have representation on the **Financial Accounting Standards Board** (FASB), the rule-making body that operates under authority delegated by the Securities and Exchange Commission. When FASB identifies an area in need of a new standard, its professional staff typically defines the theoretical issues in a matter of a few months. Issuance of the new standard may take several years, however, as the corporate issuers of financial statements pursue their objectives on a decidedly less abstract plane.

From time to time, highly charged issues such as executive stock options and mergers lead to fairly testy confrontations between FASB and the corporate world. The compromises that emerge from these dustups fail to satisfy theoretical purists. On the other hand, rule-making by negotiation heads off all-out assaults by the corporations' allies in Congress. If the lawmakers were ever to get sufficiently riled up, they might drastically curtail FASB's authority. Under extreme circumstances, they might even replace FASB with a new rule-making body that the corporations could more easily bend to their will.

There is another reason that enlightened self-interest does not invariably drive corporations toward candid financial reporting. The corporate executives who lead the battles against FASB have their own agenda. Just like the investors who buy their corporations' stock, managers seek to maximize their wealth. If producing bona fide economic profits advances that objective, it is rational for a chief executive officer (CEO) to try to do so. In some cases, though, the CEO can achieve greater personal gain by taking advantage of the compensation system through financial reporting gimmicks.

Suppose, for example, the CEO's year-end bonus is based on growth in earnings per share. Assume also that for financial reporting purposes, the corporation's **depreciation** schedules assume an average life of eight years for fixed assets. By arbitrarily amending that assumption to nine years (and obtaining the auditors' consent to the change), the corporation can lower its annual depreciation expense. This is strictly an accounting change; the actual cost of replacing equipment worn down through use does not decline. Neither does the corporation's tax deduction for depreciation expense rise nor, as a consequence, does cash flow [14] (see Chapter 4). Investors recognize that bona fide profits (see Chapter 5) have not increased, so the corporation's stock price does not change in response to the new accounting policy. What *does* increase is the CEO's bonus, as a function of the artificially contrived boost in earnings per share.

This example explains why a corporation may alter its accounting practices, making it harder for investors to track its performance, even though the shareholders' enlightened self-interest favors straightforward, transparent financial reporting. The underlying problem is that corporate executives sometimes put their own interests ahead of their shareholders' welfare. They beef up their bonuses by overstating profits, while shareholders bear the cost of reductions in price–earnings ratios to reflect deterioration in the quality of reported earnings.[15]

The logical solution for corporations, it would seem, is to align the interests of management and shareholders. Instead of calculating executive bonuses on the basis of earnings per share, the board should reward senior management for increasing shareholders' wealth by causing the stock price to rise. Such an arrangement gives the CEO no incentive to inflate reported earnings through gimmicks that transparently produce no increase in bona fide profits and therefore no rise in the share price.

Following the logic through, financial reporting ought to have moved closer to the ideal of accurate representation of corporate performance as companies have increasingly linked executive compensation to stock price appreciation. In reality, though, no such trend is discernible. If anything, the preceding examples of Mercury Finance, MicroStrategy, and Lernout & Hauspie suggest that corporations are becoming more creative and more aggressive in their financial reporting.

Aligning management and shareholder interests, it turns out, has a dark side. Corporate executives can no longer increase their bonuses through financial reporting tricks that are readily detectable by investors. Instead, they must devise better-hidden gambits that fool the market and artificially elevate the stock price. Financial statement analysts must work harder than ever to spot corporations' subterfuges.

SMALL PROFITS AND BIG BATHS

Certainly, financial statement analysts do not have to fight the battle single-handedly. The Securities and Exchange Commission and the Financial Accounting Standards Board prohibit corporations from going too far in prettifying their profits to pump up their share prices. These regulators refrain from indicating exactly how far is too far, however. Inevitably, corporations hold diverse opinions on matters such as the extent to which they must divulge bad news that might harm their stock market valuations. For some, the standard of disclosure appears to be that if nobody happens to ask about a specific event, then declining to volunteer the information does not constitute a lie.

The picture is not quite that bleak in every case, but the bleakness extends pretty far. A research team led by Harvard economist Richard Zeckhauser has compiled evidence that lack of perfect candor is widespread.[16] Zeckhauser et al. focus on instances in which a corporation reports quarterly earnings that are only slightly higher or slightly lower than its earnings in the corresponding quarter of the preceding year.

Suppose that corporate financial reporting followed the accountants' idealized objective of depicting performance accurately. By the laws of probability, corporations' quarterly reports would include about as many cases of earnings that barely exceed year-earlier results as cases of earnings that fall just shy of year-earlier profits. Instead, Zeckhauser et al. find that corporations post small increases far more frequently than they post small declines. The strong implication is that when companies are in danger of showing slightly negative earnings comparisons, they locate enough discretionary items to squeeze out marginally improved results.

On the other hand, suppose a corporation suffers a quarterly profit decline too large to erase through discretionary items. Such circumstances create an incentive to "take a big bath" by maximizing the reported setback. The reasoning is that investors will not be much more disturbed by a 30% drop in earnings than by a 20% drop. Therefore, management may find it expedient to accelerate certain future expenses into the current quarter, thereby ensuring positive reported earnings in the following period. It may also be a convenient time to recognize long-run losses in the value of assets such as outmoded production facilities and **goodwill** created in unsuccessful acquisitions of the past. In fact, the corporation may take a larger write-off on those assets than the principle of accurate representation would dictate. Reversals of the excess write-offs offer an artificial means of stabilizing reported earnings in subsequent periods.

Zeckhauser and his associates corroborate the big bath hypothesis by showing that large earnings declines are more common than large increases. By implication, managers do not passively record the combined results of their own skill and business factors beyond their control, but intervene in the calculation of earnings by exploiting the latitude in accounting rules. The researchers' overall impression is that corporations regard financial reporting as a technique for propping up stock prices, rather than a means of disseminating objective information.[17]

If corporations' gambits escape detection by investors and lenders, the rewards can be vast. For example, an interest-cost savings of one-half of a percentage point on $1 billion of borrowings equates to $5 million (pretax) per year. If the corporation is in a 34% tax bracket and its stock trades at 15 times earnings, the payoff for risk-concealing financial statements is $49.5 million in the cumulative value of its shares.

Among the popular methods for pursuing such opportunities for wealth enhancement, aside from the big bath technique studied by Zeckhauser, are:

- Maximizing growth expectations.
- Downplaying contingencies.

MAXIMIZING GROWTH EXPECTATIONS

Imagine a corporation that is currently reporting annual net earnings of $20 million. Assume that five years from now, when its growth has leveled off somewhat, the corporation will be valued at 15 times earnings. Further assume that the company will pay no dividends over the next five years and that investors in growth stocks currently seek returns of 25% (before considering capital gains taxes).

Based on these assumptions, plus one additional number, the analyst can place an aggregate value on the corporation's outstanding shares. The final required input is the expected growth rate of earnings. Suppose the corporation's earnings have been growing at a 30% annual rate and appear likely to continue increasing at the same rate over the next five years. At the end of that period, earnings (rounded) will be $74 million annually. Applying a multiple of 15 times to that figure produces a valuation at the end of the fifth year of $1.114 billion. Investors seeking a 25% rate of return will pay $365 million today for that future value.

These figures are likely to be pleasing to a founder/chief executive officer who owns, for sake of illustration, 20% of the outstanding shares. The successful entrepreneur is worth $73 million on paper, quite possibly up from zero just a few years ago. At the same time, the newly minted multimillionaire is a captive of the market's expectations.

Suppose investors conclude for some reason that the corporation's potential for increasing its earnings has declined from 30% to 25% per annum. That is still well above average for Corporate America. Nevertheless, the value of corporation's shares will decline from $365 million to $300 million, keeping previous assumptions intact.

Overnight, the long-struggling founder will see the value of his personal stake plummet by $13 million. Financial analysts may shed few tears for him. After all, he is still worth $60 million on paper. If they were in his shoes, however, how many would accept a $13 million loss with perfect equanimity? Most would be sorely tempted, at the least, to avoid incurring a financial reverse of comparable magnitude via every means available to them under GAAP.

That all-too-human response is the one typically exhibited by owner-managers confronted with falling growth expectations. Many, perhaps, most, have no intention to deceive. It is simply that the entrepreneur is by nature a self-assured optimist. A successful entrepreneur, moreover, has had this optimism vindicated. Having taken his company from nothing to $20 million of earnings against overwhelming odds, he believes he can lick whatever short-term problems have arisen. He is confident that he can get the business back onto a 30% growth curve, and perhaps he is right. One thing is certain—if he were not the sort who believed he could beat the odds one more time, he would never have built a company worth $300 million.

Financial analysts need to assess the facts more objectively. They must recognize that the corporation's predicament is not unique, but on the contrary, quite common. Almost invariably, senior managers try to dispel the impression of decelerating growth, since that perception can be so costly to them. Simple mathematics, however, tends to make false prophets of corporations that extrapolate high growth rates indefinitely into the future. Moreover, once growth begins to level off (see Exhibit 1.1), restoring it to the historical rate requires overcoming several powerful limitations.

EXHIBIT 1.1   The Inevitability of Deceleration

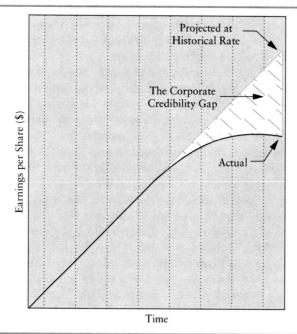

Shifting investors' perceptions upward through the Corporate Credibility Gap between actual and management-projected growth is a potentially valuable but inherently difficult undertaking for a company. Liberal financial reporting practices can make the task somewhat easier. In this light, analysts should read financial statements with a skeptical eye.

Limits to Continued Growth

Saturation   Sales of a hot new consumer product can grow at astronomical rates for a time. Eventually, however, everybody who cares to will own one (or two, or some other finite number that the consumer believes is enough). At that point, potential sales will be limited to replacement sales plus growth in population, that is, the increase in the number of potential purchasers.

Entry of Competition   Rare is the company with a product or service that cannot either be copied or encroached on by a "knockoff" sufficiently similar to tap the same demand, yet different enough to fall outside the bounds of patent and trademark protection.

Increasing Base   A corporation that sells 10 million units in Year I can register a 40% increase by selling just 4 million additional units in Year 2. If growth continues at the same rate, however, the corporation will have to generate 59 million new unit sales to achieve a 40% gain in Year 10.

In absolute terms, it is arithmetically possible for volume to increase indefinitely. On the other hand, a growth rate far in excess of the gross domestic product's annual increase is nearly impossible to sustain over any extended period. By definition, a product that experiences higher-than-GDP growth captures a larger percentage of GDP each year. As the numbers get larger, it becomes increasingly difficult to switch consumers' spending patterns to accommodate continued high growth of a particular product.

Market Share Constraints   For a time, a corporation may overcome the limits of growth in its market and the economy as a whole by expanding its sales at the expense of competitors. Even when growth is achieved by market share gains rather than by expanding the overall demand for a product, however, the firm must eventually bump up against a ceiling on further growth at a constant rate. For example, suppose a producer with a 10% share of market is currently growing at 25% a year while total demand for the product is expanding at only 5% annually. By Year 14, this supergrowth company will require a 115% market share to maintain its rate of increase. (Long before confronting this mathematical impossibility, the corporation's growth will likely be curtailed by the antitrust authorities.)

Basic economics and compound-interest tables, then, assure the analyst that all growth stories come to an end, a cruel fate that must eventually be reflected in stock prices. Financial reports, however, frequently tell a different tale. It defies common sense yet almost has to be told, given the stakes. Users of financial statements should acquaint themselves with the most frequently heard corporate versions of "Jack and the Beanstalk," in which earnings—in contradiction to a popular saw—do grow to the sky.

Commonly Heard Rationalizations for Declining Growth

"Our Year-over-Year Comparisons Were Distorted"   Recognizing the sensitivity of investors to any slowdown in growth, companies faced with earnings deceleration commonly resort to certain standard arguments to persuade investors that the true, underlying profit trend is still rising at its historical rate (see Exhibit 1.2). Freak weather conditions may be blamed for supposedly anomalous, below-trendline earnings. Alternatively, the company may

EXHIBIT 1.2   "Our Year-over-Year Comparisons Were Distorted"

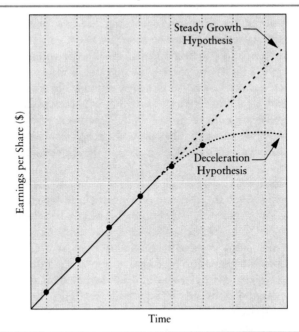

Is the latest earnings figure an outlier or does it signal the start of a slowdown in growth? Nobody will know for certain until more time has elapsed, but the company will probably propound the former hypothesis as forcefully as it can.

allege that shipments were delayed (never canceled, merely delayed) because of temporary production problems caused, ironically, by the company's explosive growth. (What appeared to be a negative for the stock price, in other words, was actually a positive. Orders were coming in faster than the company could fill them—a high-class problem indeed.) Widely publicized macroeconomic events such as the Y2K problem[18] receive more than their fair share of blame for earnings shortfalls. However plausible these explanations may sound, analysts should remember that in many past instances, short-term supposed aberrations have turned out to be advance signals of earnings slowdowns.

"New Products Will Get Growth Back on Track"   Sometimes, a corporation's claim that its obviously mature product lines will resume their former growth path becomes untenable. In such instances, it is a good idea for management to have a new product or two to show off. Even if the products are still in development, some investors who strongly wish to believe in the corporation will remain steadfast in their faith that earnings will continue growing at the historical rate. (Such hopes probably rise as a function of owning stock on margin at a cost well above the current market.) A hard-headed analyst, though, will wait to be convinced, bearing in mind that new products have a high failure rate.

"We're Diversifying Away from Mature Markets" If a growth-minded company's entire industry has reached a point of slowdown, it may have little choice but to redeploy its earnings into faster-growing businesses. Hunger for growth, along with the quest for cyclical balance, is a prime motivation for the corporate strategy of diversification.

Diversification reached its zenith of popularity during the "conglomerate" movement of the 1960s. Up until that time, relatively little evidence had accumulated regarding the actual feasibility of achieving high earnings growth through acquisitions of companies in a wide variety of growth industries. Many corporations subsequently found that their diversification strategies worked better on paper than in practice. One problem was that they had to pay extremely high price-earnings multiples for growth companies that other conglomerates also coveted. Unless earnings growth accelerated dramatically under the new corporate ownership, the acquirer's return on investment was fated to be mediocre. This constraint was particularly problematic for managers who had no particular expertise in the businesses they were acquiring. Still worse was the predicament of a corporation that paid a big premium for an also-ran in a "hot" industry. Regrettably, the number of industry leaders available for acquisition was by definition limited.

By the 1980s, the stock market had rendered its verdict. The price-earnings multiples of widely diversified corporations carried a "conglomerate discount." One practical problem was the difficulty security analysts encountered in trying to keep tabs on companies straddling many different industries. Instead of making 2 + 2 equal 5, as they had promised, the conglomerates' managers presided over corporate empires that traded at cheaper prices than their constituent companies would have sold for in aggregate had they been listed separately.

Despite this experience, there are periodic attempts to revive the notion of diversification as a means of maintaining high earnings growth indefinitely into the future. In one variant, management makes lofty claims about the potential for "cross-selling" one division's services to the customers of another. It is not clear, though, why paying premium acquisition prices to assemble the two businesses under the same corporate roof should prove more profitable than having one independent company pay a fee to use the other's mailing list. Battle-hardened analysts wonder whether such corporate strategies rely as much on the vagaries of mergers-and-acquisitions accounting (see Chapter 10) as they do on bona fide **synergy.**

All in all, users of financial statements should adopt a "show-me" attitude toward a story of renewed growth through diversification. It is often nothing more than a variant of the myth of above-average growth forever. Multi-industry corporations bump up against the same arithmetic that limits earnings growth for "focused" companies.

DOWNPLAYING CONTINGENCIES

A second way to mold disclosure to suit the issuer's interests is by downplaying extremely significant contingent liabilities. Thanks to the advent of class action suits, the entire net worth of even a multi-billion-dollar corporation may be at risk in litigation involving environmental hazards or product liability. Understandably, an issuer of financial statements would prefer that securities analysts focus their attention elsewhere.

At one time, analysts tended to shunt aside claims that ostensibly threatened major corporations with bankruptcy. They observed that massive lawsuits were often settled for small fractions of the original claims. Furthermore, the outcome of a lawsuit often hinged on facts that emerged only when the case finally came to trial (which by definition never happened if the suit was settled out of court). Considering also the susceptibility of juries to emotional appeals, securities analysts of bygone days found it extremely difficult to incorporate legal risks into earnings forecasts that relied primarily on **micro-** and **macroeconomic** variables. At most, a contingency that had the potential of wiping out a corporation's equity became a qualitative factor in determining the multiple assigned to a company's earnings.

Manville Corporation's 1982 bankruptcy marked a watershed in the way analysts have viewed legal contingencies. To their credit, specialists in the building-products sector had been asking detailed questions about Manville's exposure to asbestos-related personal injury suits for a long time before the company filed. Many investors nevertheless seemed to regard the corporation's August 26, 1982, filing under Chapter 11 of the Bankruptcy Code as a sudden calamity. Manville's stock plunged by 35% on the day following its filing.

In part, the surprise element was a function of disclosure. The corporation's last quarterly report to the Securities and Exchange Commission prior to its bankruptcy had implied a total cost of settling asbestos-related claims of about $350 million. That was less than half of Manville's $830 million of shareholders' equity. On August 26, by contrast, Manville estimated the potential damages at no less than $2 billion.

For analysts of financial statements, the Manville episode demonstrated the plausibility of a scenario previously thought inconceivable. A bankruptcy at an otherwise financially sound company, brought on solely by legal claims, had become a nightmarish reality. Intensifying the shock was that the problem had lain dormant for many years. Manville's bankruptcy resulted from claims for diseases contracted decades earlier through contact with the company's products. The long-tailed nature of asbestos liabilities was underscored by a series of bankruptcy filings over succeeding years. Prominent examples, each involving a billion dollars or more of assets, included Walter Industries (1989), National Gypsum (1990), USG Corporation (1993 and again in 2001), Owens Corning (2000), and Armstrong World Industries (2000).

Bankruptcies connected with asbestos exposure, silicone gel breast implants, and assorted environmental hazards (see Chapter 13) have heightened analysts' awareness of legal risks. Even so, analysts still miss the forest for the trees in some instances, concentrating on the minutiae of financial ratios of corporations facing similarly large contingent liabilities. They can still be lulled by companies' matter-of-fact responses to questions about the gigantic claims asserted against them.

Thinking about it from the issuer's standpoint, one can imagine several reasons why the investor-relations officer's account of a major legal contingency is likely to be considerably less dire than the economic reality. To begin with, the corporation's managers have a clear interest in downplaying risks that threaten the value of their stock and options. Furthermore, as parties to a highly contentious lawsuit, the executives find themselves in a conflict. It would be difficult for them to testify persuasively in their company's defense while simultaneously acknowledging to investors that the plaintiffs' claims have merit and might, in fact, prevail. (Indeed, any such public admission could compromise the corporation's case. Candid disclosure therefore may not be a viable option.) Finally, it would hardly represent aberrant behavior if, on a subconscious level, management were to deny the real possibility of a company-wrecking judgment. It must be psychologically very difficult for managers to acknowledge that their company may go bust for reasons seemingly outside their control. Filing for bankruptcy may prove to be the only course available to the corporation, notwithstanding an excellent record of earnings growth and a conservative balance sheet.

For all these reasons, analysts must take particular care to rely on their independent judgment when a potentially devastating contingent liability looms larger than their conscientiously calculated financial ratios. It is not a matter of sitting in judgment on management's honor and forthrightness. If corporate executives remain in denial about the magnitude of the problem, they are not deliberately misleading analysts by presenting an overly optimistic picture. Moreover, the managers may not provide a reliable assessment even if they soberly face the facts. In all likelihood, they have never worked for a company with a comparable problem. They consequently have little basis for estimating the likelihood that the worst-case scenario will be fulfilled. Analysts who have seen other corporations in similar predicaments have more perspective on the matter, as well as greater objectivity. Instead of relying entirely on the company's periodic updates on a huge class action suit, analysts should also speak to representatives of the plaintiffs' side. Their views, while by no means unbiased, will expose logical weaknesses in management's assertions that the liability claims will never stand up in court.

THE IMPORTANCE OF BEING SKEPTICAL

By now, the reader presumably understands why this chapter is entitled "The Adversarial Nature of Financial Reporting." The issuer of financial statements has been portrayed in an unflattering light, invariably choosing the accounting option that will tend to prop up its stock price, rather than generously assisting the analyst in deriving an accurate picture of its financial condition. Analysts have been warned not to partake of the optimism that drives all great business enterprises, but instead to maintain an attitude of skepticism bordering on distrust. Some readers may feel they are not cut out to be financial analysts if the job consists of constant naysaying, of posing embarrassing questions, and of being a perennial thorn in the side of companies that want to win friends among investors, customers, and suppliers.

Although pursuing relentless antagonism can indeed be an unpleasant way to go through life, the stance that this book recommends toward issuers of financial statements implies no such acrimony. Rather, analysts should view the issuers as adversaries in the same manner that they temporarily demonize their opponents in a friendly pickup basketball game. On the court, the competition can be intense, which only adds to the fun. Afterward, everyone can have a fine time going out together for pizza and beer. In short, financial analysts and investor-relations officers can view their work with the detachment of litigators who engage in every legal form of shin-kicking out of sheer desire to win the case, not because the litigants' claims necessarily have intrinsic merit.

Too often, financial writers describe the give-and-take of financial reporting and analysis in a highly moralistic tone. Typically, the author exposes a tricky presentation of the numbers and reproaches the company for greed and chicanery. Viewing the production of financial statements as an epic struggle between good and evil may suit a crusading journalist, but financial analysts need not join the ethics police to do their job well.

An alternative is to learn to understand the gamesmanship of financial reporting, perhaps even to appreciate on some level the cleverness of issuers who constantly devise new stratagems for leading investors off the track. Outright fraud cannot be countenanced, but disclosure that shades economic realities without violating the law requires truly impressive ingenuity. By regarding the interaction between issuers and users of financial statements as a game, rather than a morality play, analysts will find it easier to view the action from the opposite side. Just as a chess master anticipates an opponent's future moves, analysts should consider which gambits they themselves would use if they were in the issuer's seat.

"Oh no!" some readers must be thinking at this point. "First the authors tell me that I must not simply plug numbers into a standardized spreadsheet. Now I have to engage in role-playing exercises to guess what tricks will be embedded in the statements before they even come out. I thought this book was supposed to make my job easier, not more complicated."

In reality, this book's goal is to make the reader a better analyst. If that goal could be achieved by providing shortcuts, the authors would not hesitate to do so. Financial reporting occurs in an institutional context that obliges conscientious analysts to go many steps beyond conventional calculation of financial ratios. Without the extra vigilance advocated in these pages, the user of financial statements will become mired in a system that provides excessively simple answers to complex questions, squelches individuals who insolently refuse to accept reported financial data at face value, and inadvisably gives issuers the benefit of the doubt.

These systematic biases are inherent in selling stocks. Within the universe of investors are many large, sophisticated financial institutions that utilize the best available techniques of analysis to select securities for their portfolios. Also among the buyers of stocks are individuals who, not being trained in financial statement analysis, are poorly equipped to evaluate annual and quarterly earnings reports. Both types of investors are important sources of financing for industry, and both benefit over the long term from the returns that accrue to capital in a market economy. The two groups cannot be sold stocks in the same way, however.

What generally sells best to individual investors is a "story." Sometimes the story involves a new product with seemingly unlimited sales potential. Another kind of story portrays the recommended stock as a play on some current economic trend, such as declining interest rates or a step-up in defense spending. Some stories lie in the realm of rumor, particularly those that relate to possible corporate takeovers. The chief characteristics of most stories are the promise of spectacular gains, superficially sound logic, and a paucity of quantitative verification.

No great harm is done when an analyst's stock purchase recommendation, backed up by a thorough study of the issuer's financial statements, is translated into soft, qualitative terms for laypersons' benefit. Not infrequently, though, a story originates among stockbrokers or even in the executive offices of the issuer itself. In such an instance, the zeal with which the story is disseminated may depend more on its narrative appeal than on the solidity of the supporting analysis.

Individual investors' fondness for stories undercuts the impetus for serious financial analysis, but the environment created by institutional investors is not ideal, either. Although the best investment organizations conduct rigorous and imaginative research, many others operate in the mechanical fashion derided earlier in this chapter. They reduce financial statement analysis to the bare bones of forecasting earnings per share, from which they derive a price-earnings multiple. In effect, the less conscientious investment managers assume that as long as a stock stacks up well by this single measure, it represents an attractive investment. Much Wall Street research, regrettably, caters to these institutions' tunnel vision, sacrificing analytical comprehensiveness to the operational objective of maintaining up-to-the-minute earnings estimates on vast numbers of companies.

Investment firms, moreover, are not the only workplaces in which serious analysts of financial statements may find their style crimped. The credit departments of manufacturers and wholesalers have their own set of institutional hazards.

Consider, to begin with, the very term "credit approval process." As the name implies, the vendor's bias is toward extending rather than refusing credit. Up to a point, this is as it should be. In Exhibit 1.3, "neutral" Cutoff Point A, where half of all applicants are approved and half are refused, represents an unnecessarily high credit standard. Any company employing it would turn away many potential customers who posed almost no threat of delinquency. Even Cutoff Point B, which allows more business to be written but produces no credit losses, is less than optimal. Credit managers who seek to maximize profits aim for Cutoff Point C. It represents a level of credit extension at which losses on receivables occur but are slightly more than offset by the profits derived from incremental customers.

To achieve this optimal result, a credit analyst must approve a certain number of accounts that will eventually fail to pay. In effect, the analyst is required to make "mistakes" that could be avoided by rigorously obeying

EXHIBIT 1.3 The Bias toward Favorable Credit Evaluations

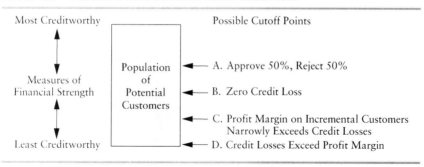

the conclusions derived from the study of applicants' financial statements. The company makes up the cost of such mistakes by avoiding mistakes of the opposite type (rejecting potential customers who will not fail to pay).

Trading off one type of error for another is thoroughly rational and consistent with sound analysis, so long as the objective is truly to maximize profits. There is always a danger, however, that the company will instead maximize sales at the expense of profits. That is, the credit manager may bias the system even further, to Cutoff Point D in Exhibit 1.3. Such a problem is bound to arise if the company's salespeople are paid on commission and their compensation is not tightly linked to the collection experience of their customers. The rational response to that sort of incentive system is to pressure credit analysts to approve applicants whose financial statements cry out for rejection.

A similar tension between the desire to book revenues and the need to make sound credit decisions exists in commercial lending. At a bank or a finance company, an analyst of financial statements may be confronted by special pleading on behalf of a loyal, long-established client that is under allegedly temporary strain. Alternatively, the lending officer may argue that a loan request ought to be approved, despite substandard financial ratios, on the grounds that the applicant is a young, struggling company with the potential to grow into a major client. Requests for exceptions to established credit policies are likely to increase in both number and fervor during periods of slack demand for loans.

When considering pleas of mitigating circumstances, the credit analyst should certainly take into account pertinent qualitative factors that the financial statements fail to capture. At the same time, the analyst must bear in mind that qualitative credit considerations come in two flavors, favorable and unfavorable. It is also imperative to remember that the cold, hard statistics show that companies in the "temporarily" impaired and start-up categories have a higher-than-average propensity to default on their debt.

Every high-risk company seeking a loan can make a plausible soft case for overriding the financial ratios. In aggregate, though, a large percentage of such borrowers will fail, proving that many of their seemingly valid qualitative arguments were specious. This unsentimental truth was driven home by a massive 1989–1991 wave of defaults on high-yield bonds that had been marketed on the strength of supposedly valuable assets not reflected on the issuers' balance sheets. Bond investors had been told that the bold dreams and ambitions of management would suffice to keep the companies solvent. Another large default wave in 2001 involved early-stage telecommunications ventures for which there was scarcely any financial data from which to calculate ratios. The rationale advanced for lending to these nascent companies was the supposedly limitless demand for services made possible by miraculous new technology.

To be sure, defaults also occur among companies that satisfy established quantitative standards. The difference is that analysts can test financial ratios against a historical record to determine their reliability as predictors of bankruptcy (see Chapter 13). No comparable testing is feasible for the highly idiosyncratic, qualitative factors that weakly capitalized companies cite when applying for loans. Analysts are therefore on more solid ground when they rely primarily on the numbers than when they try to discriminate among companies' soft arguments.

CONCLUSION

A primary objective of this chapter has been to supply an essential ingredient that is missing from many discussions of financial statement analysis. Aside from accounting rules, cash flows, and definitions of standard ratios, analysts must consider the motivations of corporate managers, as well as the dynamics of the organizations in which they work. Neglecting these factors will lead to false assumptions about the underlying intent of issuers' communications with users of financial statements.

Moreover, analysts may make incorrect inferences about the quality of their own work if they fail to understand the workings of their own organizations. If a conclusion derived from thorough financial analysis is deemed "wrong," it is important to know whether that judgment reflects a flawed analysis or a higher-level decision to override analysts' recommendations. Senior managers sometimes subordinate financial statement analysis to a determination that idle funds must be put to work or that loan volume must be increased. At such times, organizations rationalize their behavior by persuading themselves that the principles of interpreting financial statements have fundamentally changed. Analysts need not go to the extreme of resigning in protest, but they will benefit if they can avoid getting caught up in the prevailing delusion.

To be sure, organizational behavior has not been entirely overlooked up until now in the literature of financial statement analysis. Typically, academic studies depict issuers as profit-maximizing firms, inclined to overstate their earnings if they can do so legally and if they believe it will boost their equity market valuation. This model lags behind the portrait of the firm now prevalent in other branches of finance.[19] Instead of a monolithic organization that consistently pursues the clear-cut objective of share price maximization, the corporation is now viewed more realistically as an aggregation of individuals with diverse motivations.

Using this more sophisticated model, an analyst can unravel an otherwise vexing riddle concerning corporate reporting. Overstating earnings would appear to be a self-defeating strategy in the long term, since it has a tendency to catch up with the perpetrator. Suppose, for example, a corporation depreciates assets over a longer period than can be justified by physical wear-and-tear and the rate of technological change in manufacturing methods. When the time comes to replace the existing equipment, the corporation will face two unattractive options. The first is to penalize reported earnings by writing off the remaining undepreciated balance on equipment that is obsolete and hence of little value in the resale market. Alternatively, the company can delay the necessary purchase of more up-to-date equipment, thereby losing ground competitively and reducing future earnings. Would the corporation not have been better off if it had refrained from overstating its earnings in the first place, an act that probably cost it some measure of credibility among investors?

If the analyst considers the matter from the standpoint of management, a possible solution to the riddle emerges. The day of reckoning, when the firm must "pay back" the reported earnings "borrowed" via underdepreciation, may be beyond the planning horizon of senior management. A chief executive officer who intends to retire in five years, and who will be compensated in the interim according to a formula based on reported earnings growth, may have no qualms about exaggerating current results at the expense of future years' operations. The long-term interests of the firm's owners, in other words, may not be consistent with the short-term interests of their agents, the salaried managers.

Plainly, analysts cannot be expected to read minds or to divine the true motives of management in every case. There is a benefit, however, in simply being cognizant of objectives other than the ones presupposed by introductory accounting texts. If nothing else, the awareness that management may have something up its sleeve will encourage readers to trust their instincts when some aspect of a company's disclosure simply does not ring true. In a given instance, management may judge that its best chance of minimizing analysts' criticism of an obviously disastrous corporate decision lies in stubbornly defending the decision and refusing to change course. Even though the chief executive officer may be able to pull it off with a straight face, however, the blunder remains a blunder. Analysts who remember that managers may be pursuing their own agendas will be ahead of the game. They will be properly skeptical that management is genuinely making tough choices designed to yield long-run benefits to shareholders, but which individuals outside the corporation cannot envision.

Armed with the attitude that the burden of proof lies with those making the disclosures, the analyst is now prepared to tackle the basic financial statements. Methods for uncovering the information they conceal, as well as that which they reveal, constitute the heart of the next three chapters. From that elementary level right on up to making investment decisions with the techniques presented in the final two chapters, it will pay to maintain an adversarial stance at all times.

QUESTIONS

1. Given their fiduciary duty to shareholders, are corporate managers acting responsibly when they do not take advantage of this flexibility?
2. How can the firm lower the rate it must pay to obtain financing?
3. How can the new way of looking at the firm explain why firms would overstate earnings (i.e., reporting depreciation for a period longer than can be justified in light of the rate of technological change in its industry's manufacturing methods)?
4. How did the Manville Corporation's 1982 bankruptcy change the way analysts view legal considerations?
5. Why do corporations seem to have an interest in facilitating cookie-cutter analysis?
6. How does the flexibility of present accounting standards allow a company to lower outsiders' perceptions of its riskiness without making the sacrifices necessary to bring reality into line with those perceptions?
7. How has the firm traditionally been portrayed? How is the firm viewed now?
8. How would a company's managers reduce a sudden jump in profits? Why would they want to do so?

9. In addition to accounting rules, cash flows, and analytical techniques, what must a complete financial analysis include?
10. In what way should the analyst consider the issuers of financial statements as adversaries?
11. Many companies strike a balance at a point near the ideal of fair and reasonable disclosure. Why should analysts harbor no illusions about the premises under which many issuers of financial statements operate?
12. Since a corporation exists for the benefit of its shareholders, what can be said about the purpose of financial reporting?
13. Since analysts cannot read minds or divine the true motives of management in every case, what is the benefit of being cognizant of objectives other than the ones presupposed by the exposition found in introductory accounting texts?
14. Thinking about it from the issuer's standpoint, what are some of the reasons why the firm's account of a major legal contingency is likely to be less dire than the economic reality?
15. Using a numerical example, demonstrate the dramatic change on the value of a firm brought about by lowering the earnings growth expectations from 30% to 25%.
16. What are some of the commonly heard rationalizations for declining growth?
17. What are some of the institutional hazards found in the credit departments of manufacturers and wholesalers?
18. What are some of the tensions that exist between the desire to book credit and the need to make sound credit decisions that exist in commercial lending?
19. What are the powerful limitations to continued growth faced by companies?
20. What are the systematic biases inherent in selling stocks?
21. List three ways corporations can use financial reporting to enhance value.
22. What are two possible objections to the purpose of financial reporting?
23. What are two assumptions that misconstrue the motives that frequently underlie financial reporting?
24. What are two distinct approaches to financial statement analysis?
25. What do basic economics and compound-interest tables assure the analyst about all growth stories?
26. What is another reason why candid reporting is not consistent with management self-interest?
27. What is the "big bath" hypothesis, and how was it corroborated?
28. What is the cornerstone of GAAP?

29. What is the dark side of aligning management and shareholder interests?
30. What is the environment created by institutional investors, and why is it far from ideal?
31. What is the fallacy of "cross selling" in the context of rationalizations for declining growth?
32. What is the real scandal involving major financial reporting violations when they come to light?
33. What led Charles Mills to liken the return on equity of Mercury Finance to a human running a two-minute mile?
34. What point did the Manville bankruptcy bring home to analysts?
35. What role did disclosure play in this bankruptcy?
36. What two types of investors are important sources of financing for industry? Why are they sold stocks in different ways?
37. What events cast doubt on the auditor's opinion that Lernout & Hauspie's financial statements were consistent with generally accepted accounting principles?
38. What's the implication of the finding that corporations post small increases in quarterly profits more frequently than they post small declines?
39. Why are the many steps that go beyond the conventional calculation of ratios the trademark of the better financial analysts?
40. Why don't auditors forbid gimmicks to smooth earnings?
41. Why is tenacity so essential to the analysis of financial statements?
42. Why should analysts maintain an attitude of skepticism bordering on distrust?
43. In the past why did securities analysts find it difficult to incorporate legal risks into their earnings forecasts?

The Basic
Financial Statements

2

The Balance Sheet

The balance sheet is a remarkable invention, yet it has two fundamental shortcomings. First, although it is in theory useful to have a summary of the values of all the assets owned by an enterprise, these values frequently prove elusive in practice. Second, many kinds of things have value and could be construed, at least by the layperson, as assets. Not all of them can be assigned a specific value and recorded on a balance sheet, however. For example, proprietors of service businesses are fond of saying, "Our assets go down the elevator every night." Everybody acknowledges the value of a company's "human capital"—the skills and creativity of its employees—but no one has devised a means of valuing it precisely enough to reflect it on the balance sheet. Accountants do not go to the opposite extreme of banishing all intangible assets from the balance sheet, but the dividing line between the permitted and the prohibited is inevitably an arbitrary one.[1]

During the late 1990s, doctrinal disputes over accounting for assets intensified as intellectual capital came to represent growing proportions of many major corporations' perceived value. A study conducted on behalf of Big Five accounting firm Arthur Andersen showed that between 1978 and 1999, book value fell from 95% to 71% of the stock market value of public companies in the United States.[2] Increasingly, investors were willing to pay for things other than the traditional assets that GAAP (generally accepted accounting principles) had grown up around, including buildings, machinery, inventories, receivables, and a limited range of capitalized expenditures.

At the extreme, start-up Internet companies with negligible physical assets attained gigantic **market capitalizations.** Their valuations derived from "business models" purporting to promise vast profits far in the future. Building up subscriber bases through heavy consumer advertising was an expensive proposition, but one day, investors believed, a large, loyal following would translate into rich revenue streams.

Much of the dot-coms' stock market value disappeared during the "tech wreck" of 2000, but the perceived mismatch between the information-intensive New Economy and traditional notions of assets persisted. Prominent accounting theorists argued that financial reporting practices rooted in an era more dominated by heavy manufacturing grossly understated the value created by research and development outlays, which GAAP was resistant to capitalizing. They observed further that traditional accounting generally permitted assets to rise in value only if they were sold. "Transactions are no longer the basis for much of the value created and destroyed in today's economy, and therefore traditional accounting systems are at a loss to capture much of what goes on," argued Baruch Lev of New York University. As examples, he cited the rise in value resulting from a drug passing a key clinical test and from a computer software program being successfully beta-tested. "There's no accounting event because no money changes hands," Lev noted.[3]

THE VALUE PROBLEM

The problems of value that accountants wrestle with have also historically plagued philosophers, economists, tax assessors, and the judiciary. Moral philosophers over the centuries grappled with the notion of a "fair" price for merchants to charge. Early economists attempted to derive a product's intrinsic value by calculating the units of labor embodied in it. Several distinct approaches have evolved for assessing real property. These include capitalization of rentals, inferring a value based on sales of comparable properties, and estimating the value a property would have if put to its "highest and best" use. Similar theories are involved when the courts seek to value the assets of bankrupt companies, although vigorous negotiations among the different classes of creditors play an essential role in the final determination.

With commendable clarity of vision, the accounting profession has cut through the thicket of valuation theories by establishing historical cost as the basis of its system. The cost of acquiring or constructing an asset has the great advantage of being an objective and verifiable figure. As a benchmark for value, it is, therefore, compatible with accountants' traditional principle of conservatism.

Whatever its strengths, however, the historical cost system also has disadvantages that are apparent even to the beginning student of accounting. As noted, basing valuation on transactions means that no asset can be reflected on the balance sheet unless it has been involved in a transaction. The most familiar difficulty that results from this convention involves goodwill.

Company A has value above and beyond its tangible assets, in the form of well-regarded brand names and close relationships with merchants built up over many years. None of this intangible value appears on Company A's balance sheet, however, for it has never figured in a transaction. When Company B acquires Company A at a premium to book value, though, the intangibles are suddenly recognized. To the benefit of users of financial statements, Company A's assets are now more fully reflected. On the negative side, Company A's balance sheet now says it is more valuable than Company C, which has equivalent tangible and intangible assets but has never been acquired.

Liabilities, too, can become distorted under historical cost accounting. Long-term debt obligations floated at rates of 5% or lower during the 1950s and 1960s remained outstanding during the late 1970s and early 1980s, when rates on new corporate bonds soared to 15% and higher. The economic value of the low-coupon bonds, as evidenced by market quotations, plunged to as little as 40 cents on the dollar. At that point, corporations that had had the foresight (or simply the luck) to lock in low rates for 30 years or more enjoyed a significant cost advantage over their competitors. A company in this position could argue with some validity that its low-cost debt constituted an asset rather than a liability. On its books, however, the company continued to show a $1,000 liability for each $1,000 face amount of bonds. Consequently, its balance sheet did not reflect the value that an acquirer, for example, might capture by locking in a cheap cost of capital for an extended period.

ISSUES OF COMPARABILITY

Although some would regard the prohibition of adjusting debt figures to the market as artificial, they might at least find it tolerable if it applied in every instance. Consider what happens, however, in an acquisition. Statement of Financial Accounting Standards (SFAS) 141 ("Business Combinations") makes it mandatory to revalue the acquired company's debt to current market if its value differs significantly from face value as a consequence of a shift in interest rates since the debt was issued. Here again, as in the case of first-time recognition of goodwill, the historical cost principle makes comparable companies appear quite dissimilar. The equally large "hidden asset value" of another company with low-cost debt will not be reflected on its balance sheet, simply because it has never been acquired.

The lack of comparability arising from the revaluation of the liability persists long after the acquisition is consummated. By contrast, the footnote detailing the adjustment eventually disappears from the acquired firm's annual report. In later years, readers receive no hint that the company's debts have been reduced—not in fact, but through one of accounting's convenient fictions.

Critics of historical-cost accounting deplore the quirks that give rise to such distortions, arguing that corporations should be made to report the true economic value of their assets. Such criticisms assume, however, that there *is* a true value. If so, determining it is a job better left to metaphysicians than to accountants. In the business world, it proves remarkably difficult to establish values with which all the interested parties concur.

The difficulties a person may encounter in the quest for true value are numerous. Consider, for example, a piece of specialized machinery, acquired for $50,000. On the day the equipment is put into service, even before any controversies surrounding depreciation rates arise, value is already a matter of opinion. The company that made the purchase would presumably not have paid $50,000 if it perceived the machine to be worth a lesser amount. A secured lender, however, is likely to take a more conservative view. For one thing, the lender will find it difficult in the future to monitor the value of the collateral through "comparables," since only a few similar machines (perhaps none, if the piece is customized) are produced each year. Furthermore, if the lender is ultimately forced to foreclose, there may be no ready purchaser of the machinery for $50,000, since its specialized nature makes it useful to only a small number of manufacturers. All of the potential purchasers, moreover, may be located hundreds of miles away, so that the machinery's value in a liquidation would be further reduced by the costs of transporting and reinstalling it.

The problems encountered in evaluating one-of-a-kind industrial equipment might appear to be eliminated when dealing with actively traded commodities such as crude oil reserves. Even this type of asset, however, resists precise, easily agreed on valuation. Since oil companies frequently buy and sell reserves "in the ground," current transaction prices are readily available. These transactions, however, are based on estimates of eventual production from unique geologic formations, for there is no means of directly measuring oil reserves. Even when petroleum engineers employ the most advanced technology, their estimates rely heavily on judgment and inference. It is not unheard of, moreover, for a well to begin to produce at the rate predicted by the best scientific methods, only to peter out a short time later, ultimately yielding just a fraction of its estimated reserves. With this degree of uncertainty, recording the true value of oil reserves is not a realistic objective for accountants. Users of financial statements can, at best, hope for informed guesses, and there is considerable room for honest people (not to mention rogues with vested interests) to disagree.

"INSTANTANEOUS" WIPEOUT OF VALUE

Because the value of many assets is so subjective, balance sheets are prone to sudden, arbitrary revisions. To cite one dramatic example, on July 27, 2001, JDS Uniphase, a manufacturer of components for telecommunications networks, reduced the value of its goodwill by $44.8 billion. It was the largest write-off in corporate history up to that time.

This drastic decline in economic value did not occur in one day. Several months earlier, JDS had warned investors to expect a big write-off arising from declining prospects at businesses that the company had acquired during the telecommunications euphoria of the late 1990s.[4] If investors had relied entirely on JDS's balance sheet, however, they would have perceived the loss of value as a sudden event.

Shortly before JDS Uniphase's action, Nortel Networks took a $12.3 billion goodwill write-off and several major companies in such areas as Internet software and optical fiber quickly followed suit. High-tech companies had no monopoly on "instantaneous" evaporation of book value, however. In the fourth quarter of 2000, Sherwin-Williams recognized an impairment charge of $352.0 million ($293.6 million after taxes). Most of the write-off represented a reduction of goodwill that the manufacturer of paint and related products had created through a string of acquisitions. Even after the huge hit, goodwill represented 18.8% of Sherwin-Williams's assets and accounted for 47.9% of shareholders' equity.

Both Old Economy and New Economy companies, in short, are vulnerable to a sudden loss of stated asset value. Therefore, users of financial statements should not assume that balance sheet figures invariably correspond to the current economic worth of the assets they represent. A more reasonable expectation is that the numbers have been calculated in accordance with GAAP. The trick is to understand the relationship between these accounting conventions and reality.

If this seems a daunting task, the reader may take encouragement from the success of the bond rating agencies (see Chapter 13) in sifting through the financial reporting folderol to get to the economic substance. The multibillion-dollar goodwill write-offs in 2001 did not, as one might have expected, set off a massive wave of rating downgrades. As in many previous instances of companies writing down assets, Moody's and Standard & Poor's did not equate changes in accounting values with reduced protection for lenders. To be sure, if a company wrote off a billion dollars worth of goodwill, its ratio of assets to liabilities declined. Its ratio of *tangible* assets to liabilities did not change, however. The rating agencies monitored both ratios, but had customarily attached greater significance to the version that ignored intangible assets such as goodwill.

HOW GOOD IS GOODWILL?

By maintaining a skeptical attitude to the value of intangible assets throughout the New Economy excitement of the late Nineties, Moody's and Standard & Poor's were bucking the trend. The more stylish view was that balance sheets constructed according to GAAP seriously understated the value of corporations in dynamic industries as computer software and e-commerce. Their earning power, so the story went, derived from inspired ideas and improved methods of doing business, not from the bricks and mortar for which conventional accounting was designed. To adapt to the economy's changing profile, proclaimed the heralds of the New Paradigm, the accounting rule makers had to allow all sorts of items traditionally expensed to be capitalized onto the asset side of the balance sheet. Against that backdrop, analysts who questioned the value represented by goodwill, an item long deemed legitimate under GAAP, look conservative indeed.

In reality, the stock market euphoria that preceded Uniphase's mind-boggling write-off illustrated in classic fashion the reasons for rating agency skepticism toward goodwill. Through stock-for-stock acquisitions, the sharp rise in equity prices during the late 1990s was transformed into increased balance sheet values, despite the usual assumption that fluctuations in a company's stock price do not alter its stated net worth. It was a form of financial alchemy as remarkable as the transmutation of proceeds from stock sales into revenues described in Chapter 3.

The link between rising stock prices and escalating goodwill is illustrated by the fictitious example in Exhibit 2.1. In Scenario I, the shares of Associated Amalgamator Corporation ("Amalgamator") and United Consolidator Inc. ("Consolidator") are both trading at multiples of 1.0 times book value per share. Shareholders' equity is $200 million at Amalgamator and $60 million at Consolidator, equivalent to the companies' respective market capitalizations. Amalgamator uses stock held in its treasury to acquire Consolidator for $80 million. The purchase price represents a premium of 33⅓% above the prevailing market price.

Let us now examine a key indicator of credit quality. Prior to the acquisition, Amalgamator's ratio of total assets to total liabilities (see Chapter 13) is 1.25 times whereas the comparable figure for Consolidator is 1.18 times. The stock-for-stock acquisition introduces no new hard assets (e.g., cash, inventories or factories). Neither does the transaction eliminate any existing liabilities. Logically, then, Consolidator's 1.18 times ratio should drag down Amalgamator's 1.25 times ratio, resulting in a figure somewhere in between for the combined companies.

In fact, though, the total-assets-to-total-liabilities ratio after the deal is 1.25 times. By paying a premium to Consolidator's tangible asset value,

EXHIBIT 2.1   Pro Forma Balance Sheets, December 31, 20XX ($000 omitted)

	Associated Amalgamator Corporation	United Consolidator Inc.	Purchase Price	Combined Companies Pro Forma
Scenario I				
Tangible assets	$,1000	$400		$1,400
Intangible assets	0	0		20
Total assets	1,000	400		1,420
Liabilities	800	340		1,140
Shareholders' equity (SE)	200	60	80	280
Total liabilities and SE	$1,000	$400		$1,420
Tangible assets/total liabilities	1.25	1.18		1.23
Total assets/total liabilities	1.25	1.18		1.25
Market capitalization	200	60		280
Scenario II				
Tangible assets	$1,000	$400		$1,400
Intangible assets	0	0		60
Total assets	1,000	400		1,460
Liabilities	800	340		1,140
Shareholders' equity (SE)	200	60	120	320
Total liabilities and SE	$1,000	$400		$1,460
Total assets/total liabilities	1.25	1.18		1.28
Tangible assets/total liabilities	1.25	1.18		1.23
Market capitalization	300	90		520*

Amalgamator creates $20 million of goodwill. This intangible asset represents just 1.4% of the combined companies' total assets, but that suffices to enable Amalgamator to acquire a company with a weaker debt-quality ratio without showing any deterioration on that measure.

If this outcome seems perverse, consider Scenario II. As the scene opens, an explosive stock market rally has driven up both companies' shares to 150% of book value. The ratio of total assets to total liabilities, however, remains at 1.25 times for Amalgamator and 1.18 times for Consolidator. Conservative bond buyers take comfort from the fact that the assets remain on the books at historical cost less depreciation, unaffected by euphoria on the stock exchange that may dissipate at any time without notice.

As in Scenario I, Amalgamator pays a premium of 33⅓% above the prevailing market price to acquire Consolidator. The premium is calculated on a higher market capitalization, however. Consequently, the purchase price rises from $80 million to $120 million. Instead of creating $20 million of goodwill, the acquisition gives rise to a $60 million intangible asset.

When the conservative bond investors calculate the combined companies' ratio of total assets to total liabilities, they make a startling discovery. Somehow, putting together a company boasting a 1.25 times ratio with another sporting a 1.18 times ratio has produced an entity with a ratio of 1.28 times. Moreover, a minute of experimentation with the numbers will show that the ratio would be higher still if Amalgamator had bought Consolidator at a higher price. Seemingly, the simplest way for a company to improve its credit quality is to make stock-for-stock acquisitions at grossly excessive prices.

Naturally, this absurd conclusion embodies a fallacy. In reality, the receivables, inventories, and machinery available to be sold to satisfy creditors' claims are no greater in Scenario II than in Scenario I. Given that the total-assets-to-total-liabilities ratio is lower at Consolidator than at Amalgamator, the combined companies' ratio logically must be lower than at Amalgamator. Common sense further states that Amalgamator cannot truly have better credit quality if it overpays for Consolidator than if it acquires the company at a fair price.

As it happens, there is a simple way out of the logical conundrum. Let us exclude goodwill in calculating the ratio of assets to liabilities. As shown in the exhibit, Amalgamator's ratio of *tangible* assets to total liabilities following its acquisition of Consolidator is 1.23 times in both Scenario I and Scenario II. This is the outcome that best reflects economic reality. To ensure that they reach this commonsense conclusion, credit analysts must follow the rating agencies' practice of calculating balance sheet ratios both with and without goodwill and other intangible assets, giving greater emphasis to the latter version.

Calculating ratios on a tangibles-only basis is not equivalent to saying that the intangibles have no value. Amalgamator will likely recoup all or most of the $60 million accounted for as goodwill if it turns around and sells Consolidator tomorrow. Such a transaction is hardly likely, however. A sale several years hence, after stock prices have fallen from today's lofty levels, is a more plausible scenario. Under such conditions, the full $60 million probably will not be recoverable.

Even leaving aside the possibility of a plunge in stock prices, it makes eminent sense to eliminate or sharply downplay the value of goodwill in a balance-sheet-based analysis of credit quality. Unlike inventories or accounts receivable, goodwill is not an asset that can be readily sold or *factored* to raise cash. Neither can a company enter into a **sale-leaseback** of its goodwill, as it can with its plant and equipment. In short, goodwill is not a separable asset that management can either convert into cash or use to raise cash to extricate itself from a financial tight spot. Therefore, the relevance of goodwill to an analysis of asset protection is questionable.

On the whole, the rating agencies appear to have shown sound judgment during the 1990s by resisting the New Economy's siren song. While enthusiasm mounted for all sorts of intangible assets, they continued to gear their analysis to tangible-assets-only versions of key balance sheet ratios. By and large, therefore, companies did not alter the way they were perceived by Moody's and Standard & Poor's when they suddenly took an axe to their intangible assets.

More generally, asset write-offs do not cause ratings to fall. Occasionally, to be sure, the announcement of a write-off coincides with the disclosure of a previously unrevealed impairment of value, ordinarily arising from operating problems. That sort of development may trigger a downgrade. In addition, a write-off sometimes coincides with a decision to close down certain operations. The associated severance costs (payments to terminated employees) may represent a substantial cash outlay that does weaken the company's financial position. Finally, a write-off can put a company in violation of a debt covenant (see Chapter 12). Nervous lenders may exploit the technical default by canceling the company's credit lines, precipitating a liquidity crisis. In and of itself, however, adjusting the balance sheet to economic reality does not represent a reduction in credit protection measures.

LOSING VALUE THE OLD-FASHIONED WAY

Goodwill write-offs by technology companies such as Uniphase make splashy headlines in the financial news, but they by no means represent the only way in which balance sheet assets suddenly and sharply decline in value. In the "Old Economy," where countless manufacturers earn slender margins on low-tech industrial goods, companies are vulnerable to long-run erosion in profitability. Common pitfalls include fierce price competition and a failure, because of near-term pressures to conserve cash, to invest adequately in modernization of plants and equipment. As the rate of return on their fixed assets declines, producers of basic commodities such as paper, chemicals, and steel must eventually face up to the permanent impairment of their reported asset values.

In the case of a chronically low rate-of-return company, it is not feasible to predict precisely the magnitude of a future reduction in accounting values. Indeed, there is no guarantee that a company will fully come to grips with its overstated net worth, especially on the first round. To estimate the expected order of magnitude of future write-offs, however, an analyst can adjust the shareholders' value shown on the balance sheet to the rate of return typically being earned by comparable corporations.

To illustrate, suppose Company Z's average net income over the past five years has been $24 million. With most of the company's modest earnings being paid out in dividends, shareholders' equity has been stagnant at around $300 million. Assume further that during the same period, the average return of companies in the Standard & Poor's 400 index of industrial corporations has been 14%.

Does the figure $300 million accurately represent Company Z's equity value? If so, the implication is that investors are willing to own the company's shares and accept a return of only 8% ($24 million divided by $300 million), even though a 14% return is available on other stocks. There is no obvious reason why investors would voluntarily make such a sacrifice, however. Therefore, Company Z's book value is almost certainly overstated.

A reasonable estimate of the low-profit company's true equity value would be the amount that produces a return on equity equivalent to the going rate:

$$\frac{\text{Company Z average earnings stream}}{X} = \frac{\text{Average return on equity}}{\text{for U.S. corporations}}$$

$$\frac{\$24 \text{ million}}{X} = 14\%$$

$$X = \$171 \text{ million}$$

Although useful as a general guideline, this method of adjusting the shareholders' equity of underperforming companies neglects important subtleties. For one thing, Company Z may be considered riskier than the average company. In that case, shareholders would demand a return higher than 14% to hold its shares. Furthermore, cash flow (see Chapter 4) may be a better indicator of the company's economic performance than net income. This would imply that the adjustment ought to be made to the ratio of cash flow to market capitalization, rather than return on equity. Furthermore, investors' rate-of-return requirements reflect expected future earnings, rather than past results. Depending on the outlook for its business, it might be reasonable to assume that Company Z will either realize higher profits in the next five years than in the past five or see its profits plunge further. By the same token, securities analysts may expect the peer group of stocks that represent alternative investments to produce a return higher or lower than 14% in coming years. The further the analyst travels in search of true value, it seems, the murkier the notion becomes.

TRUE EQUITY IS ELUSIVE

What financial analysts are actually seeking, but are unable to find in the financial statements, is equity as economists define it. In scholarly studies, the term *equity* generally refers not to accounting book value, but to the present value of future cash flows accruing to the firm's owners. Consider a firm that is deriving huge earnings from a trademark that has no accounting value because it was developed internally rather than acquired. The present value of the profits derived from the trademark would be included in the economist's definition of equity, but not in the accountant's, potentially creating a gap of billions of dollars between the two.

The contrast between the economist's and the accountant's notion of equity is dramatized by the phenomenon of negative equity. In the economist's terms, equity of less than zero is synonymous with bankruptcy. The reasoning is that when a company's liabilities exceed the **present value** of all future income, it is not rational for the owners to continue paying off the liabilities. They will stop making payments currently due to lenders and trade creditors, which will in turn prompt the holders of the liabilities to try to recover their claims by forcing the company into bankruptcy. Suppose on the other hand, that the present value of a highly successful company's future income exceeds the value of its liabilities by a substantial margin. If the company runs into a patch of bad luck, recording net losses for several years running and writing off selected operations, the book value of its assets may fall below the value of its liabilities. In accounting terms, the result is negative shareholders' equity. The economic value of the assets, however, may still exceed the stated value of the liabilities. Under such circumstances, the company has no reason to consider either suspending payments to creditors or filing for bankruptcy.

Negative shareholders' equity can also arise from a **leveraged recapitalization,** a type of transaction that gained a considerable vogue in the 1980s. The analytical relevance of leveraged recaps does not arise solely from the insight they provide into the differences between economic and accounting-based equity. One day, they may be of more than historical interest. If stock prices ever become as depressed as they were in the early 1980s, the massive stock repurchases with borrowed funds may easily make a comeback.

A leveraged recap is ostensibly designed to remedy a corporation's low stock market valuation. Another, unadvertised purpose may be to fend off a hostile takeover. Suppose that several large shareholders, who are sympathetic (or even identical to) the corporation's incumbent management, retain their stock as the total number of outstanding shares declines sharply. The small group of shareholders will materially increase its proportional ownership. If all goes well, the leveraged recap will kill two birds with one stone, solidifying the insiders' control of the company while boosting the share price to appease shareholders who were disposed to support the hostile bid.

In the fictitious example shown in Exhibit 2.2, Sluggard Corporation's stock is languishing at a modest 9.3 times earnings, or $25 a share. Restive shareholders are urging management to improve Sluggard's operating performance, explore the possibility of selling the company at a premium to its present stock price, or step aside in favor of others who can do a better job of enhancing shareholder value. A dissident group has even nominated its own slate of directors, who are committed to divesting unprofitable operations and replacing the current chief executive officer.

Management counters by asserting that the real problem is with the stock market. Fickle, short-term-oriented investors are not attributing appropriate value to Sluggard's excellent long-term business prospects. Under current market conditions, says the CEO, shareholders cannot realize full value on their investment by engineering the sale of Sluggard to a bigger company.

To satisfy shareholders' legitimate desire for better stock performance, while preserving Sluggard's ability to capitalize on its outstanding opportunities as an independent company, management and the board announce a bold financial transaction. The company will tender for 32 million of its 45 million outstanding shares at a 25% premium to the current market price, or $30 a share. To pay for the $960 million stock repurchase, Sluggard has arranged an interim credit line, which it plans to refinance through a long-term bond offering. The greatly increased debt load that will result will raise interest expense from $68 million to $183 million annually, on a pro forma basis. After-tax income will consequently drop from $121 million to $46 million. That decline will be more than offset, however, by the reduction in shares outstanding. Earnings per share, management concludes, will rise from $2.69 to $3.54.

To be sure, the market may lower Sluggard's price-earnings ratio to reflect the increase in financial risk indicated by a sharply higher ratio of long-term debt to capital and a significantly reduced pretax interest coverage ratio (see Chapter 13). Under reasonable assumptions, however, the company's stock should continue to trade at the tender price of $30 a share

EXHIBIT 2.2 Leveraged Recapitalization (Illustration)

Sluggard Corpooration
Condensed Balance Sheet and Income Statement
December 31, 20XX
($000 omitted)

	Before Recapitalization	Transaction	Pro Forma
Current assets	$ 500	$ 0	$ 500
Fixed assets	1,500	0	1,500
Total assets	2,000	0	2,000
Current liabilities	250	0	250
Long-term debt	850	+960	1,810
Shareholders' equity	900	(960)	(60)
Total liabilities and equity	2,000		2,000
Earnings before interest and taxes	252	0	252
Interest expense	68	+115	183
Pretax income	184		69
Income tax	63		23
Net income	$ 121		$ 46
Shares outstanding (milions)	45		13
Shareholders' equity per share	$20		$(4.62)
Market price per share	$25		$30
Purchase price per share	30		N.A.
Interest rate on new borrowing	12.0%		
Numbers of shares purchased (millions)	32		
Earnings per share	$2.69		$3.54
Return on shareholders' equity	13.4%		N.M.
Pretax interest coverage	3.7X		1.4X
Long-term debt as a percentage of total capital	48.6%		103.4%
Price-earnings ratio (at market price)	9.3X		8.5X

after the tender offer is completed. Accordingly, the currently disgruntled stockholders will get a chance to sell some of their shares at a big premium to the current market and also enjoy a longer-run boost to the share price. Furthermore, for the next few years, Sluggard plans to devote the cash generated from its operations to debt repayment. That should take care of the biggest concern raised by management's plan, namely, the heightened risk of financial strain posed by sharply increased interest costs.

Based on the bankruptcies of many prominent companies that underwent leveraged buyouts or leveraged recapitalizations in the 1980s, investors' worries about Sluggard's expanded debt load are by no means unfounded. In the period of the leveraged recaps' greatest popularity, in fact, many veteran financial analysts perceived the leveraged recaps to be bankrupt from inception. The only instances in which they had previously observed negative shareholders' equity, comparable to the −$60 million figure shown in Exhibit 2.2, involved moribund companies that had wiped out their retained earnings through repeated losses. Typically, those companies were approaching negative equity in the economic, as well as the accounting sense.

The leveraged recaps presented a very different case, however. Their negative shareholders' equity figures arose from the conventions of **double-entry-bookkeeping**. Unlike other kinds of asset purchases, a company's purchase of its own stock does not simply result in one type of asset (cash) being replaced by another (such as inventory or plant and equipment) on the balance sheet. Instead, the entry that offsets the reduction in cash is a reduction in shareholders' equity. In the illustration, Sluggard pays a premium over book value, with the consequence that a buyback of less than 100% of the shares costs more than the stated shareholders' equity.

Despite the resulting negative shareholders' equity that arises, Sluggard is by no means faced with an immediate prospect of bankruptcy. The company's pretax earnings continue to cover expense, albeit by a slimmer margin than formerly. Moreover, Sluggard is continuing to earn a profit, which the stock market is capitalizing at $30 a share times 13 million shares, or $390 million. This is a plain demonstration that in economists' terms, the company continues to have a substantially positive equity, whatever the financial statements show.

PROS AND CONS OF A
MARKET-BASED EQUITY FIGURE

Relying on market capitalization is the practical means by which financial analysts commonly estimate the economists' more theoretically rigorous definition of equity as the present value of expected future cash flows.

Monumental difficulties confront anyone who instead attempts to arrive at the figure through conventional financial reporting systems. The problem is that traditional accounting favors items that can be objectively measured. Unfortunately, future earnings and cash flows are unobservable. Moreover, calculating present value requires selecting a **discount rate** representing the company's **cost of capital.** Determining the cost of capital is a notoriously controversial subject in the financial field, complicated by thorny tax considerations and risk adjustments. The figures needed to calculate economists' equity are not, in short, the kind of numbers accountants like to deal with. Their ideal value is a price on an invoice that can be independently verified by a canceled check.

Market capitalization has additional advantages beyond its comparative ease of calculation. For one thing, it represents the consensus of large numbers of analysts and investors who constantly monitor companies' future earnings prospects as the basis for their evaluations. In addition, an up-to-the-minute market capitalization can be calculated on any day that the stock exchange is open. This represents a considerable advantage over the shareholders' equity shown on the balance sheet, which is updated only once every three months. Market capitalization adjusts instantaneously to news such as a surprise product launch by a competitor, an explosion that halts production at a key plant, or a sudden hike in interest rates by the Federal Reserve. In contrast, these events may never be reflected in book value in a discrete, identifiable manner. Ardent advocates of market capitalization cannot conceive any more accurate estimate of true equity value.

Against these advantages, however, the analyst must weigh several drawbacks to relying on market capitalization to estimate a company's actual equity value. For one thing, although the objectivity of a price quotation established in a competitive market is indeed a benefit, it is obtainable only for corporations with publicly traded stocks. For privately owned companies, the proponents of market capitalization typically generate a proxy for true equity through reference to industry-peer public companies. For example, to calculate the equity of a privately owned paper producer, an analyst might multiply the publicly traded peer group's average price-earnings ratio (see Chapter 14) by the private company's earnings. By failing to capture the impact of company-specific events, however, this approach sacrifices one of the great merits of using market capitalization as a gauge of actual equity value.

Even if analysts rely on market capitalization exclusively in connection with publicly traded companies, they will still encounter pitfalls. Consider the case of Intel, a leading manufacturer of computer components. On May 13, 2000, Intel's market capitalization of $407.5 billion was the third largest among the 30 companies represented in the Dow Jones Industrial

Average. The following day, the Dow plummeted by 618 points, a decline of 5.7%. Intel had the dubious distinction of losing more market value on March 14 than any other company in the Dow Industrials. If the stock market was a reliable guide, then Intel's equity contracted by 8.8%, or a staggering $35.7 billion, in a single day. Collectively, the Dow Industrials' value fell by $227.2 billion.

Whatever theoretical arguments can be advanced in favor of regarding market capitalization as a company's true equity value, short-run changes of the magnitude experienced by Intel on May 14, 2000, raise a caution. Such incidents justify a bit of skepticism about the assertion that the aggregate market price of a company's shares represents its correct value at every moment. To an observer who is not wedded to a belief that securities prices are perfect reflections of underlying value, sudden swings in market capitalization sometimes reveal more about the dynamics of the market than they do about short-run changes in companies' earnings prospects.

An inference along those lines is supported by extensive academic research conducted under the rubric of "behavioral finance." In contrast to more traditional financial economists, the behavioralists doubt that investors invariably process information accurately and act on it according to rules of rationality, as defined by economists. Empirical studies by adherents of behavioral finance show that instead of faithfully tracking companies' intrinsic values, market prices frequently overreact to news events. Even though investors supposedly evaluate stocks on the basis of expected future dividends (see Chapter 14), the behavioralists find that the stock market is far more volatile than the variability of dividends can explain.[5]

To be sure, these conclusions remain controversial. Traditionalists have challenged the empirical studies that underlie them, producing a vigorous debate. Nevertheless, the findings of behavioral finance lend moral support to analysts who find it hard to believe that the one-day erasure of $35.7 billion of Intel's market capitalization must automatically be a truer representation of the company's change in equity value than a figure derived from financial statement data.

Market capitalization, then, is a useful tool, but not one to be heeded blindly. In the end, "true" equity remains an elusive number. Instead of striving for theoretical purity on the matter, analysts should adopt a flexible attitude, using the measure of equity value most useful to a particular application.

For example, historical-cost-based balance sheet figures are the ones that matter in estimating the risk that a company will violate a loan covenant requiring maintenance of a minimum ratio of debt to net worth (see Chapter 12). The historical cost figures are less relevant to a liquidation analysis aimed at gauging creditors' asset protection. That is, if a company were sold to pay off its debts, the price it would fetch would probably reflect the market's current valuation of its assets more nearly than the carrying cost of those assets.

Neither measure, however, could be expected to equate precisely to the proceeds that would actually be realized in a sale of the company. Between the time that a sale was decided on and executed, its market capitalization might change significantly, purely as a function of the stock market's dynamics. By the same token, the current balance sheet values of certain assets could be overstated through tardy recognition of impairments in value, or understated reflecting the prohibition on writing up an asset that has not changed hands.

UNDISCLOSED HAZARDS

Yet another complication in the quest for true equity involves disclosure. Despite the pitfalls previously discussed, analysts can feel comfortable in relying on market capitalization for certain applications, provided they believe that all material information affecting companies' equity values is available for investors to assess. In practice, though, companies' equity values can be significantly altered by items that are either undisclosed or disclosed only in a limited fashion.

Early in 1994, analysts were largely caught off guard by problems involving financial derivatives. (The collective term for these instruments reflects that their valuations derive from the values of other assets, e.g., commodities, indexes of securities.) For years, corporations had used derivatives such as swaps and structured financings to hedge against swings in interest rates, currency exchange rates, and other cost factors.

As time went on, some corporate treasurers sought to capitalize further on expertise gained through hedging. Instead of merely trying to control risk, they hoped to profit by correctly predicting the direction of interest rates or the future relationship among various commodity prices. If their predictions proved wrong, trading losses would result.

Provided the companies understood and limited the risks incurred in these transactions, they did not act irresponsibly. Often, the trading was profitable, producing a welcome supplement to earnings generated in more traditional activities.

As a comparatively new phenomenon, though, derivatives trading did not generate highly detailed mandatory disclosure. Typically, corporations divulged the scale, but not the terms or riskiness of the transactions. Some types of derivative were merely aggregated with the general cash accounts.

Just as accounting rule makers were urging companies to expand their derivatives disclosure, while also considering new mandatory reporting on the subject, a sudden burst of interest rate volatility socked several major corporations with huge trading losses. Procter & Gamble took a one-time charge of $102 million on two interest rate swaps it had entered into in the United States and Germany. Air Products & Chemicals charged off $60 million on five swap contracts, acknowledging that with hindsight, its risk analysis had been faulty. Dell Computer sustained a $26.3 million loss on derivatives and other investments related to interest rates. (All figures are on an aftertax basis.)

The shock of these announcements probably moved companies toward greater conservatism in their use of derivatives. Additionally, the surprise losses strengthened the hand of those calling for fuller disclosure. SFAS 133 ("Accounting for Derivative and Similar Instruments and Hedging Activities") now requires all derivatives to be recorded as either assets or liabilities at fair value. As the values change, the resulting gains or losses may be recognized immediately or deferred, depending on whether the derivative qualifies for classification as a hedge.

At the same time, the incidents underscored the misfortunes that can befall even meticulous and thoughtful analysts. Users of financial statements can process only the information they have, and they do not always have the information they need.

While FASB was able to bring about fuller disclosure of derivatives, the accounting rule makers did not and could not resolve the larger issue for all time. Innovation in the financial markets is unlikely to abate, meaning that it will remain a challenge for accounting rule makers to keep pace. To recognize possible undisclosed hazards, therefore, analysts must stay abreast of new types of transactions. Where feasible, users of financial statements should also solicit as much detail as management will disclose regarding risks not spelled out in the balance sheet or footnotes.

THE COMMON FORM BALANCE SHEET

As the technology companies' huge 2001 write-offs demonstrate, deterioration in a company's financial position may catch investors by surprise because it occurs gradually and is reported suddenly. It is also possible for an increase in financial risk to sneak up on analysts even though it is reported as it occurs. Many companies alter the mix of their assets, or their methods of financing them, in a gradual fashion. To spot these subtle, yet frequently significant, changes, it is helpful to prepare a common form balance sheet.

EXHIBIT 2.3 Lowe's Companies Inc. Consolidated Balance Sheet in Thousands

	January 28, 2000	Percent Total
Assets		
Current Assets:		
Cash and cash equivalents	$ 491,122	5.4
Short-term investments	77,670	0.9
Accounts receivable—net	147,901	1.6
Merchandise inventory	2,812,361	31.2
Deferred income taxes	53,145	0.6
Other current assets	127,342	1.4
Total current assets	3,709,541	41.2
Property, less accumulated depreciation	5,177,222	57.5
Long-term investments	31,114	0.3
Other assets	94,446	1.0
Total assets	$9,012,323	100.0
Liabilities and Shareholders' Equity		
Current Liabilities:		
Short-term borrowings	$ 92,475	1.0
Current maturities of long-term debt	59,908	0.7
Accounts payable	1,566,946	17.4
Employee retirement plans	101,946	1.1
Accrued salaries and wages	164,003	1.8
Other current liabilities	400,676	4.5
Total current liabilities	2,385,954	26.5
Long-term debt, excluding current maturities	1,726,579	19.2
Deferred income taxes	199,824	2.2
Other long-term liabilities	4,495	—
Total liabilities	$4,316,852	47.9
Shareholders' Equity:		
Preferred stock—$5 par value, none issued	—	
Common stock—$.50 Par value; issued and outstanding		
January 28, 2000 382,359		
January 29, 1999 374,388	$ 191,179	2.1
Capital in excess of par value	1,755,616	19.5
Retained earnings	2,761,964	30.6
Unearned compensation-restricted stock awards	(12,868)	(0.1)
Accumulated other comprehensive income (loss)	(420)	N.M.
Total shareholders' equity	4,695,471	52.1
Total liabilities and shareholders' equity	$9,012,323	100.0

Calculations are subject to rounding error.

Source: Lowe's Companies Inc., Form 10-K405, April 26, 2000.

Also known as the percentage balance sheet, the common form balance sheet converts each asset into a percentage of total assets and each liability or component of equity into a percentage of total liabilities and shareholders' equity. Exhibit 2.3 applies this technique to the 2000 balance sheet of Lowe's Companies, Inc., a home improvement retailer.

The analyst can view a company's common form balance sheets over several quarters to check, for example, whether inventory is increasing significantly as a percentage of total assets. An increase of that sort might signal involuntary inventory buildup resulting from an unanticipated slowdown in sales. Similarly, a rise in accounts receivable as a percentage of assets may point to increasing reliance on the extension of credit to generate sales or a problem in collecting on credit previously extended. Over a longer period, a rise in the percentage of assets represented by property, plant, and equipment can signal that a company's business is becoming more capital-intensive. By implication, fixed costs are probably rising as a percentage of revenues, making the company's earnings more volatile.

CONCLUSION

By closely examining the underlying values reflected in the balance sheet, this chapter emphasizes the need for a critical, rather than a passive, approach to financial statement analysis. The discussions of return on equity, goodwill, and leveraged recapitalizations underscore the chapter's dominant theme, the elusiveness of "true" value. Mere tinkering with the conventions of historical cost cannot bring accounting values into line with equity as economists define it and, more to the point, as financial analysts would ideally like it to be. Market capitalization probably represents a superior approach in many instances. Under certain circumstances, however, serious questions can be raised about the validity of a company's stock price as a standard of value. In the final analysis, users of financial statements cannot retreat behind the numbers derived by any one method. They must instead exercise judgment to draw sound conclusions.

QUESTIONS

1. Explain some of the unique difficulties encountered in assessing the value of oil reserves.
2. How can looking at the ratio of total-assets-to-total-liabilities mislead the analyst?

3. How does "negative equity" dramatize the contrast between the economist's and the accountant's notion of equity?
4. How does disclosure complicate the quest for a true measure of equity?
5. How does the case of Intel present pitfalls to those analysts who rely on using market capitalization as a measure of equity?
6. How does the thorny issue of determining the cost of capital affect the use of market capitalizations as a reliable measure of equity?
7. How were the rating agencies bucking the trend regarding the value of intangible assets?
8. Under what circumstances, if any, can a firm claim that a liability should be considered an asset?
9. Use a numerical example to illustrate how an analyst can adjust the balance sheet's shareholders' value to the rate of return typically being earned by corporations.
10. Users of financial statements can rely on "the numbers" derived by any one method. True or False? Discuss.
11. Using the example of a piece of specialized machinery, illustrate some of the difficulties encountered in the quest for "true" value.
12. What are some of the approaches used by non-accountants to establish the value of assets?
13. What are the advantages and disadvantages of using market capitalization as a measure of equity?
14. What are the subtleties that this method of adjustment neglects?
15. What are the two fundamental shortcomings of using the Balance Sheet to summarize the values of all assets owned by an enterprise?
16. What did Baruch Lev have to say about traditional accounting systems?
17. What do critics of accounting practices deplore and what is their implicit assumption which, in fact, nullifies this criticism?
18. What impact did the use of derivatives have on analysts in early 1994?
19. What is a "leveraged recapitalization," and how is it related to the notion of negative equity?
20. What is a major difference between inventories (or accounts receivables) and goodwill?
21. What is one of the inferences drawn from "behavioral finance" regarding market capitalization as a measure of equity?
22. What is the "Common Form" Balance Sheet, also known as the percentage balance sheet, and what are its uses?
23. What is the difficulty encountered in valuing a piece of specialized equipment that is not present when trying to value an actively traded commodity such as oil reserves?

24. What is the fallacy embodied in the conclusion that a company can improve its credit quality by making stock-for-stock acquisitions at excessive prices?
25. What is the main advantage of using historical cost as the basis of a system to value assets? What are some of its disadvantages?
26. What is the main emphasis of this chapter?
27. What is the startling discovery that conservative bond investors make when calculating the ratio of total-assets-to-total-liabilities of the combined company after one firm purchases another using treasury stock?
28. What is the trick that will allow investors to understand sudden changes in value in both the Old Economy and New Economy?
29. What is this chapter's dominant theme?
30. What moved companies toward greater conservatism in their use of derivatives?
31. What role does financial innovation play in the challenge to accounting rule makers?
32. What were the doctrinal disputes over accounting for assets that intensified during the late 1990s?
33. Why would investors who relied solely on JDS's balance sheet have perceived the reduction in value of $44.8 billion in July 2001 as a sudden event?

3

The Income Statement

The goal of analyzing an income statement is essentially to determine whether the story it tells is good, bad, or indifferent. To accomplish this objective, the analyst draws a few initial conclusions, then puts the income statement into context by comparing it with income statements of earlier periods, as well as statements of other companies. These steps are described in the section of this chapter entitled "Making the Numbers Talk."

Simple techniques of analysis can extract a great deal of information from an income statement, but the quality of the information is no less a concern than the quantity. A conscientious analyst must determine how accurately the statement reflects the issuer's revenues, expenses, and earnings. This deeper level of scrutiny requires an awareness of imperfections in the accounting system that can distort economic reality.

The section entitled "How Accurate Are the Numbers?" documents the indefatigability of issuers in devising novel gambits for exploiting these vulnerabilities. Analysts must be equally resourceful. In particular, students of financial statements must keep up with the innovations of the past few years in transforming rising stock values into revenues of dubious quality.

MAKING THE NUMBERS TALK

By observing an income statement in its raw form, the reader can make several useful, albeit limited, observations. Boston Beer's 2000 income statement (Exhibit 3.1) shows, for example, that the company was profitable rather than unprofitable. The statement also provides some sense of the firm's cost structure. Selling, general, and administrative expenses (SG&A) were the largest component of total costs. These outlays exceeded cost of goods sold (COGS), an item that includes materials and labor directly involving in brewing.

EXHIBIT 3.1   Boston Beer Annual Income Statement ($000 omitted)

	2000
Sales	$190,554
Cost of goods sold	77,741
Gross profit	112,813
Selling, general, and administrative expense	90,377
Operating income before depreciation	22,436
Depreciation, depletion, and amortization	6,316
Operating profit	16,120
Nonoperating income/expense	2,930
Pretax income	19,050
Total income taxes	7,811
Net income	$ 11,239

Source: Compustat.

A conspicuous feature of Boston Beer's income statement is the absence of interest expense, reflecting the company's debt-free balance sheet. This characteristic eliminates one source of earnings volatility—fluctuations in interest rates.[1] (Note that even if a company confines its borrowings to fixed-rate debt, its interest expense is variable in the sense that the company may replace maturing debt with higher-cost or lower-cost debt as a consequence of changes in interest rates.) For most beverage producers (and for companies in the industrial sector, generally), rising and falling interest rates have only a limited effect on the earnings. They are not invariably debt-free, but interest expense typically represents a minor portion of their total costs. Changes in interest rates have a dramatic impact, however, on banks and finance companies which have cost structures heavily concentrated in interest expense.

One of the most powerful tools for advancing beyond basic conclusions about a company's cost structure is the percentage income statement. In this format, each income statement item is expressed as a percentage of the "top line" (sales or revenues), which is represented as 100%. Recasting the figures in this way permits the analyst to compare a company's income statement in a meaningful way with its income statement from an earlier year or with an industry peer company's income statement. The percentage income statement's facilitation of comparisons gives rise to its other name, the "common form income statement."

Exhibit 3.2 converts Boston Beer's 2000 income statement to percentages and compares the year's results with the company's 1999 figures.

EXHIBIT 3.2 Boston Beer Annual Income Statement ($000 omitted)

	2000		1999	
	Amount	Percentage	Amount	Percentage
Sales	$190,554	100.0%	$176,781	100.0%
Cost of goods sold	77,741	40.8	72,490	41.0
Gross profit	112,813	59.2	104,291	59.0
Selling, general, and administrative expense	90,377	47.4	81,509	46.1
Operating income before depreciation	22,436	11.8	22,782	12.9
Depreciation, depletion, and amortization	6,316	3.3	5,907	3.3
Operating profit	16,120	8.5	16,875	9.5
Interest expense	0		148	.01
Nonoperating income/expense	2,930	1.5	2,363	1.3
Pretax income	19,050	10.0	19,090	10.8
Total income taxes	7,811	4.1	8,010	4.5
Net income	$ 11,239	5.9%	$ 11,080	6.3%

Source: Compustat.

The potential for enriched analytical insight is readily apparent. Most significantly, selling, general, and administrative expense increased from 46.1% to 47.4% of sales.

In encountering a period-over-period variance of this type, an analyst must investigate further to determine what it signifies. Several possible explanations for this change leap to mind. For one thing, competition may be intensifying, forcing the company to step up advertising and promotion outlays. Alternatively, the growth of overhead costs such as salaries of headquarters staff may be increasing faster than sales. In any event, it is imperative for the analyst to understand the underlying trend to judge whether the deterioration in margins is temporary or likely to continue (or worsen) in future periods.

The Management's Discussion and Analysis (MD&A) section of the annual report may provide some insight into the matter. Another potentially useful source is the company's investor relations officer. Realistically, though, commentary emanating from within a corporation usually reflects the inveterate optimism of can-do managers. After decades of exposure to the exhortations of motivational speakers, corporate executives typically exude confidence that they will turn the situation around, right up to the steps of the bankruptcy court. Accordingly, analysts should solicit other views of the situation from the company's customers, suppliers, competitors, and lenders, as well as from analysts who have followed the company over a lengthy period.

Besides facilitating comparisons between a company's present and past results, the percentage income statement can highlight important facts about a company's competitive standing. Exhibit 3.3 displays the 2000 performance of Boston Beer alongside that of Anheuser-Busch, producer of the leading brand, Budweiser. Despite their vast difference in size, the two companies can be compared head-to-head through the common form approach. The contrast is sharp, with cost of goods sold accounting for 55.4% of the sales dollar at Anheuser-Busch, but only 40.8% at Boston Beer. Despite Boston Beer's substantial advantage in gross margin, however, Anheuser-Busch achieves a far higher operating margin—20.3% versus 8.5%. With its much greater unit volume, Anheuser-Busch can spread its advertising and other marketing costs across a larger revenue base. Consequently, SG&A expenses represent a dramatically lower portion of its sales dollar (17.7%) than in Boston Beer's case (47.4%). The SG&A edge enables Anheuser-Busch to overcome the handicap of a 2.8% interest component and bring 12.7% of sales down to the bottom line. That is more than double the net margin achieved by Boston Beer (5.9%).

EXHIBIT 3.3   Boston Beer and Anheuser-Busch Comparative Percentage Income Statements 2000

	Boston Beer	Anheuser-Busch
Sales	100.0%	100.0%
Cost of goods sold	40.8	55.4
Gross profit	59.2	44.6
Selling, general, and administrative expense	47.4	17.7
Operating income before depreciation	11.8	26.9
Depreciation, depletion, and amortization	3.3	6.6
Operating profit	8.5	20.3
Interest expense		2.8
Nonoperating income/expense	1.5	1.9
Pretax income	10.0	19.4
Total income taxes	4.1	6.8
Net income	5.9%	12.7%

Source: Compustat.

Contrasting operating strategies explain the large difference between the two companies in percentage of sales represented by product costs (COGS). Anheuser-Busch's income statement reflects the heavy costs of doing business the traditional way. The company sells beer produced in breweries that it owns and operates. Boston Beer, on the other hand, relies largely on contract brewing, a strategy of utilizing the excess capacity of breweries owned by other companies.

Naturally, the total cost of producing a barrel of beer is the same, whether the brewery sells it under its own label or sells it to another company under a contract brewing arrangement. Nevertheless, it is not surprising that contract brewing can prove economical to Boston Beer. The brewery owner's fixed costs, including occupancy, depreciation, and interest expense, will be incurred whether the brewery operates at 60% or 90% of capacity. If the company has idle capacity, it can increase its profit by utilizing it to produce incremental volume, even if it sells the beer at a price only slightly higher than its variable cost. Accordingly, a company following Boston Beer's strategy can potentially negotiate terms under which its share of fixed costs is less than proportionate to its share of the brewery's output. Its total cost per barrel can therefore be lower than the total cost per barrel to a brewery's owner-operator (see "Behind the Numbers—Fixed versus Variable Costs," later in this chapter).

Boston Beer's management maintains that contract brewing promotes quality control by allowing it to select breweries that use traditional methods. Management adds that brewing in several locations enables the company to hold down its distribution costs. Moreover, according to Boston Beer, multiple production facilities permit it to deliver fresher beer to its customers than competing "craft" brewers, which distribute the output of single breweries over large territories. By not emphasizing ownership of its brewing operations, Boston Beer not only limits its product costs, but also expends half as much of its sales dollar (3.3% versus 6.6%) on depreciation of fixed assets as Anheuser-Busch.

While Boston Beer sources most of its product through contract brewing, it also brews some beer in its own facilities. Its Boston Brewery supplies limited quantities of beer for the local market. In addition, effective March 1, 1997, the company acquired, through its wholly owned subsidiary, Samuel Adams Brewery Company, Ltd., all of the equipment of an independent brewer located in Cincinnati, Ohio. Pursuant to the agreement, Samuel Adams Brewery also completed acquisition of the Cincinnati brewer's land and buildings as of November 15, 2000.

Boston Beer's management contended that the deviation from its general approach of contract brewing enhanced its brewing flexibility. A percentage income statement comparison between the company's results in 2000 and at the time of its 1994 initial public offering (Exhibit 3.4) suggests, though, that the change in operating strategy had a financial impact. Depreciation of fixed property quadrupled from 0.8% to 3.3% of sales over the period. The rise in this essentially fixed cost slightly increased the operating leverage, and therefore, the inherent volatility of Boston Beer's earnings. Over the five-year period, though, the company managed to reduce cost of goods sold as a percentage of sales, producing a net improvement in operating margin from 7.7% to 8.5%.

The contrasting cost structures of Boston Beer and Anheuser-Busch highlight a potential pitfall of using the percentage income statement. Even though the two companies participate in the same business, a line-by-line comparison of their cost ratios does not definitively answer the question of which company is more efficient. An analyst cannot infer that Boston Beer is able to record a lower ratio of COGS to sales because it purchases its ingredients more economically or uses its labor more efficiently than Anheuser-Busch. Even a comparatively inefficient operator relying on contract brewing would be expected to have lower product costs, in percentage terms, than an integrated company that produces in-house all of the beer it sells.

EXHIBIT 3.4   Boston Beer Annual Income Statement ($000 omitted)

	2000		1994	
	Amount	Percentage	Amount	Percentage
Sales	$190,554	100.0%	$114,833	100.0%
Cost of goods sold	77,741	40.8	51,926	45.2
Gross profit	112,813	59.2	62,907	54.8
Selling, general, and administrative expense	90,377	47.4	53,096	46.2
Operating income before depreciation	22,436	11.8	9,811	8.5
Depreciation, depletion, and amortization	6,316	3.3	925	0.8
Operating profit	16,120	8.5	8,886	7.7
Interest expense			233	0.2
Nonoperating income/expense	2,930	1.5	432	0.4
Pretax income	19,050	10.0	9,085	7.9
Total income taxes	7,811	4.1	0	0.0
Net income	$ 11,239	5.9%	$ 9,085	7.9%

Source: Compustat.

A similar problem arises with companies ostensibly competing in the same industry, but producing substantially different product lines. For example, some pharmaceutical manufacturers also manufacture and market medical devices, nonprescription health products, toiletries, and beauty aids. The more widely diversified manufacturers can be expected to have higher percentage product costs, as well as lower percentage research and development expenses, than industry peers that focus exclusively on prescription drugs. Analysts must take care not to mistake a difference that is actually a function of business strategy as evidence of inferior or superior managerial skills. A subtler explanation may be available at the modest cost of contacting some long-established industry watchers. All the while, analysts must watch for evidence that the reported numbers are somehow distorting the company's true financial performance, the subject of the next section of this chapter.

HOW REAL ARE THE NUMBERS?

Many individuals are attracted to business careers not only by monetary rewards but by the opportunity, lacking in many other professions, to be measured against an objective standard. The personal desire to improve the bottom line, that is, a company's net profit, challenges a businessperson in much the same way that an athlete is motivated by the quantifiable goal of breaking a world record. The income statement is the stopwatch against which a company runs; net profit is the corporation's record of wins and losses for the season.

The analogy between business and athletics extends to the fact, which is apparent to any close observer, that superior skills and teamwork alone do not win championships. A baseball manager can intimidate the umpire by heatedly protesting a call on the basepaths, hoping thereby to have the next close ruling go in his team's favor. A corporation has the power to fire its auditor, and may use that power to influence accounting decisions that are matters of judgment, rather than clear-cut reporting standards. A baseball team's front office can shorten the right-field fence in its home stadium to favor a lineup stocked with left-handed power hitters; a corporation's management can select the accounting method that shows its results in the most favorable light. Collectively, the team owners can urge the Rules Committee to lower the pitching mound if they believe that a predictable increase in base hits and runs will boost attendance. Similarly, a group of corporations can try to block the introduction of new accounting standards that might reduce their reported earnings.

Attempts to transform the yardstick become most vigorous when the measure of achievement becomes more important to participants than the accuracy of the measure itself. Regrettably, this is often the case when corporations seek to motivate managers by linking their compensation to the attainment of specific financial goals. Executives whose bonuses rise in tandem with earnings per share have a strong incentive not only to generate bona fide earnings, but also to use every lawful means of inflating the figures through accounting sleight of hand.

It would take many more pages than are allotted to this chapter to detail all the ways that companies can manipulate the accounting rules to inflate their earnings. Instead, the following examples should convey to the reader the thought process involved in this rule bending. Equipped with an understanding of how the rule benders think, users of financial statements will be able to detect other ruses they are sure to encounter.

Not All Sales Are Final

"Take care of the top line and the bottom line will take care of itself." So goes a business bromide, which underscores the importance of revenues (the top line) to net income (the bottom line). The point is that if a company wants to cure an earnings problem, it should concentrate on bringing in more sales.

Generally, this is sound advice, as long as the needed sales are brought in by the salesforce. A company can compound its problems, however, if the financial staff makes up the shortfall in revenues through accounting gimmicks. Some revenue-inflating tricks are achievable within GAAP boundaries, whereas others clearly fall outside the law. They all produce similar ill effects, however. Enhancements to reported sales boost reported earnings without increasing cash flow commensurately.

Often, a company's earnings and cash flow diverge to an extent that becomes unsustainable. The eventual result is an abrupt adjustment to the financial statements of previous periods. In the process, earnings and cash flow come back into alignment, but management's credibility plummets. Even when no such shock occurs, the practice of pumping up revenues through discretionary accounting decisions represents a hazard for analysts. At a minimum, it reduces the comparability of a company's financial statements from one period to the next.

The revenue recognition practices of International Business Machines came in for criticism when competition heated up in the computer business during the late 1980s. Management responded by becoming more accommodating in its marketing practices. The company stretched out payment periods, offered to make partial refunds if prices were subsequently reduced, and allowed customers to try out equipment without making any initial payments. For additional variations on the theme of aggressive revenue recognition, see Chapter 6.

Additional Reasons to Be Skeptical about Revenues

Unfortunately for analysts, companies do not always spell out in the Notes to Financial Statements the means by which they have artificially inflated their revenues. A company might lower the credit standards it applies to prospective customers without simultaneously raising the percentage of reserves it establishes for losses on receivables. The result would be a rise in both revenues and earnings, in the current period, with the corresponding increase in credit losses not becoming apparent until a later period. Alternatively, a manufacturer may institute short-term discounts that encourage its dealers or wholesalers to place orders earlier than they otherwise would. In this case, sales and earnings will be higher in the current quarter than they would be in the absence of the incentives, but the difference will represent merely a shifting of revenues from a later to an earlier period. Analysts will face disappointment if they regard such inflated quarterly sales as indicative of the future.

Although the current-period income statement may offer no clues that these gambits have been used, several techniques can help the analyst detect artificial expansion of revenues. On a retrospective basis, a surge in credit losses or an unexpected shortfall in revenues may indicate that revenues were inflated in an earlier period with the techniques described in the preceding paragraph. (Hindsight of this kind is not without value; an analyst who finds a historical pattern of hyperbolized sales will be appropriately skeptical about future income statements that look surprisingly strong.) On a current basis, analysts should take notice if a company posts a substantially greater sales increase than its competitors. If discussions with the company and other industry sources fail to elicit a satisfactory explanation (such as the introduction of a successful new product), artificial methods may be the root of the matter. Industry sources can also provide direct testimony about tactics being used to shift revenues from future periods to the present.

Making the Most of Depreciation and Amortization

Along with provisions for credit losses, another major expense category that can be controlled through assumptions is depreciation. As a check against possible abuses, analysts should compare a company's ratio of depreciation to property, plant, and equipment with the ratios of its industry peers. An unusually low ratio may indicate that management is being unrealistic in acknowledging the pace of wear and tear on fixed assets. Understatement of expenses and overstatement of earnings would result.

Knowing that astute analysts will compare their depreciation policies with competitors' practices, companies commonly represent accounting changes in this area as efforts to get into line with industry norms. They do not ordinarily stress another plausible motive, a desire to pump up earnings. Verbs such as *extend* and *liberalize* are considered expendable in the press releases disclosing revisions in depreciable lives.

Depreciation Assumptions—Fort Howard and Weirton Steel   Fort Howard produced a typical announcement of a change in depreciation assumptions in April 1992:

> *During the first quarter of 1992, the company prospectively changed its estimates of the depreciable lives of certain machinery and equipment. These changes were made to better reflect the estimated periods during which such assets will remain in service. As a result, the lives over which the company depreciates the cost of its operating equipment and other capital assets will more closely approximate industry norms. For the three months ended March 31, 1992, the change had the effect of reducing depreciation expense by $9.9 million and reducing net loss by $6.1 million.*

In the same month, Weirton Steel described a change in accounting for depreciation even more tersely. The company did not alter the depreciable lives of the assets, but instead switched its accounting method:

> *Weirton reported a change in depreciation method (accounting principle) effective January 1, 1992, for its steelmaking facilities from the straight-line method to a production-variable method, which adjusts straight-line depreciation to reflect production levels.*

In explaining the change, the company did not emphasize a yearning for conformity with its fellow steelmakers. Nevertheless, Weirton was not the first in its group to abandon straight-line depreciation (already a less conservative technique than the various accelerated methods), for the still more liberal production-variable approach. During the first quarter of 1992,

Weirton's switch in depreciation accounting had the convenient effect of reducing its net loss by nearly half.

A method that "adjusts straight-line depreciation to reflect production levels" may sound innocuous. Analysts should keep in mind, however, that the adjustment is far more likely to be downward than upward. As demand falls, the plant will incur more idle time and the company will record less depreciation expense. The same will be true if the facility turns unprofitable and temporarily shuts down, while lower-cost, more technologically advanced facilities owned by competitors continue to operate. Under these conditions, the book value of the plant will decline more slowly, even as approaching obsolescence.

Extraordinary and Nonrecurring Items

To most individuals who examine a company's income statement, the document is less important for what it tells about the past than for what it implies about future years.[2] Last year's earnings, for example, have no direct impact on a company's stock price, which represents a discounting of a future stream of earnings (see Chapter 14). An equity investor is therefore interested in a company's income statement from the preceding year primarily as a basis for forecasting future earnings. Similarly, a company's creditors already know whether they were paid the interest that came due in the previous year before the income statement arrives. Their motivation for studying the document is to form an opinion about the likelihood of payment in the current year and in years to come.

In addition to recognizing that readers of its income statement will view the document primarily as an indicator of the future, a company knows that creating more favorable expectations about the future can raise its stock price and lower its borrowing cost. It is therefore in the company's interest to persuade readers that a major development that hurt earnings last year will not adversely affect earnings in future years. One way of achieving this is to suggest that any large loss suffered by the company was somehow outside the normal course of business, anomalous and, by implication, unlikely to recur.

To create the desired impression that a loss was alien to the company's normal pattern of behavior, the loss can be shown on a separate line on the income statement and labeled an "extraordinary item." Note that an extraordinary item is reported on an aftertax basis, below the line of income (or loss) from continuing operations. This presentation creates the strongest possible impression that the loss was outside the ordinary course of business. It maximizes the probability that analysts of the income statement will give it little weight in forecasting future performance.

Because the effect created by a "below-the-line" treatment is so strong, the accounting rules carefully limit its use. To qualify as extraordinary under the relevant Accounting Principles Board opinion, events must be "distinguished by their unusual nature and by the infrequency of their occurrence."[3] These criteria are not easily satisfied. According to the opinion, *unusual nature* means that "the underlying event or transaction should possess a high degree of abnormality and be of a type clearly unrelated to, or only incidentally related to, the ordinary and typical activities of the entity, taking into account the environment in which the entity operates." Lest the *extraordinary* label be employed indiscriminately, the opinion prohibits its use for several types of events considered unusual in nature under the strict standard being applied. Among these are:

- Write-offs of receivables and inventories.
- Gains or losses on foreign currency translation (even when they result from major devaluations or revaluations).
- Gains or losses on disposal of a segment of a business or the sale or abandonment of property, plant, or equipment.

Not even the September 11, 2001, terrorist attacks on the Pentagon and World Trade Center qualified as an extraordinary event under FASB's stringent criteria. After tentatively deciding that companies could break out costs arising from the disaster as below-the-line items, the task force on the subject voted not to allow the practice. The chairman of the task force, FASB research director Timothy S. Lucas, noted that even the airlines, which were plainly hurt by the events, would have difficulty separating the impact of the attacks from other revenue and earnings pressures during the period.[4]

Considering the exacting tests that an item must meet to be considered extraordinary, analysts may consider themselves on solid ground if they largely disregard any such item in forecasting future earnings. The APB opinion, after all, adds that "infrequency of occurrence" means that the event or transaction in question must be "of a type not reasonably expected to recur in the foreseeable future." Occasionally, one would suppose, an event meeting this strict standard might be followed just a few years later by an event at the same company, radically different in nature but also qualifying for classification as extraordinary and below-the-line reporting. On even rarer occasions, an extraordinary event might be followed the very next year by a qualifying event of a similar nature, even though such a recurrence was "not reasonably expected," to quote the accounting standard. Judging by the highly restrictive language of the APB opinion, however, it would be extremely surprising if any company ever booked an extraordinary item more than twice in a matter of several years.

Improbable though it might seem, however, a search of Standard & Poor's Compustat database identified 42 companies that recorded extraordinary gains or losses in at least four of the eight years ended 1998. Among the companies that repeatedly experienced events of an allegedly infrequent and unusual nature were such blue chips as Bell Atlantic, Fannie Mae, GTE, Maytag, Ralston Purina, Sears Roebuck, Sunoco, Time Warner, and U.S. West. BellSouth recorded seven extraordinary items during the period. Six were losses, including whacks of $1.6 billion in 1991 and $2.2 billion in 1994. In light of actual experience, analysts cannot simply project a company's future earnings as though an extraordinary event had never occurred, however fervently management might wish them to do precisely that.

Actually, companies lean on analysts to be even more accommodating when they evaluate past results to forecast future performance. Corporate officials not only encourage users of their financial statements to disregard losses that qualify for the label extraordinary, but also ask them to ignore certain hits to earnings simply because management pronounces them aberrant. To steer analysts toward the true (that is, higher trajectory) trend of earnings deemed official by management fiat, companies break out the supposed aberrations from their other operating earnings. The accounting rules prohibit them from displaying such carve-outs "above the line" (that is, on a pretax basis) and from using the label extraordinary. Accordingly they employ designations such as "nonrecurring" or "unusual." These terms have no official standing under GAAP, but they foster the impression that the highlighted items are exceptional in nature. Sometimes, losses that fail to meet the criteria of extraordinary items appear under the more neutral heading, "special charges." Even this terminology, however, leaves the impression that the company has put the problem behind itself. The semantics are so appealing to corporate managers that each year, more than a quarter of all companies filing with the Securities and Exchange Commission take a nonrecurring charge. As recently as 1970, only one percent of companies did so.[5]

In recent years, "restructuring" has become a catchall for charges that companies wish analysts to consider outside the normal course of business, but which do not qualify for below-the-line treatment. The term has a positive connotation, implying that the corporation has cast off its money-losing operations and positioned itself for significantly improved profitability. If abused, the segregation of restructuring charges can create too rosy a picture of past performance. It can entrap the unwary analyst by downplaying the significance of failed business initiatives, which have a bearing on management's judgment. Additionally, the losses associated with a restructuring may be blamed on the company's previous chief executive officer, provided they are booked early in the successor CEO's tenure. Within a year's time, the new kingpin may be able to take credit for a turnaround, based on an improvement in earnings relative to a large loss that can be conveniently attributed to the predecessor regime.

Even more insidiously, companies sometimes write off larger sums than warranted by their actual economic losses on a failed business. Corporate managers commonly perceive that the damage to their stock price will be no greater if they take (for sake of argument) a $1.5 billion write-off than if they write off $1.0 billion. The benefit of exaggerating the damage is that in subsequent years, the overcharges can be reversed in small amounts that do not generate any requirement for specific disclosure. Management can use these gains to supplement and smooth the corporation's bona fide operating earnings.

The most dangerous trap that users of financial statements must avoid, however, is inferring that the term restructuring connotes finality. Some corporations have a bad habit of remaking themselves year after year. For such companies, the analyst's baseline for forecasting future profitability should be earnings after, rather than before, restructuring charges.

Procter & Gamble is a case in point. As of April 2001, the consumer goods company had booked restructuring charges in seven consecutive quarters, aggregating to $1.3 billion. Moreover, management indicated that it planned to continue taking these ostensibly nonrecurring charges until mid-2004, ultimately charging off approximately $4 billion.

P&G defended its reporting by saying that Securities and Exchange Commission accounting rules precluded it from taking one huge charge at the outset of the restructuring program launched in June 1999. Instead, the company was required to record the charges in the periods in which it actually incurred them. Granting the point, the SEC did not compel Procter & Gamble to segregate the costs of closing factories and laying off workers from its other operating expenses. Indeed, the arguments were stronger for treating the chargeoffs as normal costs of operating in P&G's highly competitive consumer goods business, where countless products fail or become obsolete over time.

Abstract issues of accounting theory, however, had little impact on brokerage house securities analysts' treatment of P&G's earnings record. All 14 analysts who followed the company and submitted earnings per share forecasts to Thomson Financial/First Call excluded the restructuring charges from their calculations. P&G management was bound to like Wall Street's interpretation of the numbers. Including all of the ostensibly unusual gains and losses, operating income declined in all four quarters of 2000. Leaving out all the items deemed aberrant by management, net income rose in all quarters but the first. The latter interpretation surely gave investors a more optimistic view of P&G's prospects than the sourpuss GAAP numbers.[6]

Naturally, companies encourage analysts to *include* special items in their earnings calculations when they happen to be gains, rather than losses. They evidently reason that turnabout is fair play and judging by the results, many securities analysts apparently agree. The 14 Wall Street analysts mentioned earlier unanimously chose to include in their "core net earnings" figures the gains that Procter & Gamble classified as nonrecurring or extraordinary, even as they excluded the extraordinary and nonrecurring losses.

By characterizing the extraordinary as standard, Coca-Cola has steered analysts toward a net income surrogate that suggests steadier year-over-year increases than its business can deliver in reality. In particular, management has encouraged investors to treat gains on sales of interests in bottlers as part of its normal stream of earnings. These inherently temporary boosts to profits "are an integral part of the soft drink business," according to the company.[7]

The difference in perceptions is by no means negligible. Beverage analyst Marc Cohen of Goldman Sachs has estimated that excluding non-operating items, Coca-Cola's earnings increased by 11% in 1996. That would have been a highly respectable number for most long-established companies, but it was well below the 18% to 20% annual advance that management was promising investors. Including nonrecurring and extraordinary items earnings per share, as management preferred to present the numbers, EPS rose by 19%.

Coca-Cola's 1996 dependence on out-of-the-ordinary-course-of-events items was not an isolated event. In the first quarter of 1997, Coca-Cola maintained its targeted upper-teens growth rate, at least by its own reckoning, when $0.08 of total EPS of $0.40 represented a gain on the sale of Coca-Cola & Schweppes Bottlers. Oppenheimer analyst Roy Burry went so far as to say that with so many such discretionary items at its disposal, Coca-Cola's management had absolute control over the earnings it would report through the end of 1998, despite the vagaries of weather and competitors' initiatives.

Notwithstanding the creative methods employed by Procter & Gamble and Coca-Cola, the award for ingenuity rewriting history with the help of special items should probably go to Brooke Group. In 1990, the diversified company booked a special gain of $433 million. The gain arose from a reversal of a previously recognized loss generated by Brooke's 50.1% interest in New Valley Corporation (formerly Western Union). By reducing its voting interest in New Valley to less than a majority, Brooke contrived to deconsolidate the company and erase the red ink retroactively.

Redefining Pro Forma Earnings

As highlighted by the P&G and Coca-Cola examples, companies encourage investors to focus on favorably constructed profit measures. The term core net earnings has enjoyed a vogue in recent years. Like above-the-line nonrecurring events, such numbers have no official status under GAAP. Companies' press releases, however, are not subject to GAAP. As time has gone on, corporations have devoted increasing energy to diverting analysts' attention to unofficial numbers that present their results in a better light than FASB-mandated net income. Companies helpfully package their preferred versions of earnings so that analysts can save themselves the trouble of tearing the numbers apart on their own and potentially obtaining more revealing data.

In the boldest innovation in this area, corporate managers have shanghaied the venerable term **pro forma.** Traditionally, the Latin phrase was used in the realm of financial statements exclusively in reference to illustrations of the impact of major discontinuities. The technique came into play when a company announced an acquisition, divestment, or change in accounting policy. Management displayed the company's recent results, along with a pro forma statement incorporating its estimate of what the numbers would have looked like if the discontinuity had occurred prior to the beginning of the period. The purpose of providing pro forma results was to help analysts to project future financial results accurately when some event outside the ordinary course of business caused the unadjusted historical results to convey a misleading impression.

By contrast, many companies now routinely issue press releases highlighting so-called pro forma quarterly earnings. The adjustments to GAAP earnings are not prompted by significant discontinuities. Instead, the companies add back standard expenses that they incur every quarter. This is a dramatic departure from traditional practice, but it does not violate any law or regulation. The right to report non-GAAP-conforming figures in an earnings release is protected by the constitutional guarantee of freedom of the press. According to a Securities and Exchange Commission spokesperson, regulators rarely object to a nonstandardized format employed in a press release unless it appears to be intentionally misleading or fraudulent. As an example of its rare intervention in such matters, the SEC fined Sony Corporation $1 million in 1998 for playing up the box office success of certain of its recent film releases "without tempering those statements with any specific disclosures of the losses sustained by Sony Pictures."[8]

Companies have become quite aggressive in encouraging analysts to judge their performance by the new-style pro forma figures. Their zeal is understandable, considering that the alternative numbers may create an impression of substantially higher profits than the GAAP earnings. As an example of how wide the disparity can be, online merchant Amazon.com reported an actual net loss of $317 million in 2000's second quarter, but its earnings release for the period headlined positive operating profit on sales of books and records. After deducting GAAP-mandated expenses such as amortization of goodwill and other intangibles, the cost of stock options, and costs associated with investments, mergers, and acquisitions, the company declared its pro forma EPS to be −$0.33. That was far closer to the positive-earnings zone that management was under pressure to reach than the GAAP figure of −$0.91.

Amazon.com was by no means alone in publishing an earnings release featuring the new-fashioned pro forma figures. Other companies following the same practice included Cisco Systems, Disney Internet Group, and Yahoo! Publication of pro forma earnings was so widespread, in fact, that Patrick E. Hopkins, assistant professor of accounting of Indiana University's Kelley School of Business, likened it to "creation of a de facto GAAP."[9] Amazon.com went a step further than many other companies, however, by publishing its pro forma earnings in its SEC financial filings, as well as its press releases. That envelope-pushing action required a disclaimer in which the company explained that the pro forma results did not conform to GAAP and were provided solely for informational purposes.

Quarterly pro forma earnings would present fewer stumbling blocks to analysts if all companies were obliged to calculate them according to a standard accounting method, as is the case with GAAP earnings. When it comes to computing pro forma earnings, though, corporations make their own rules. Consequently, they eliminate the company-to-company comparability that accounting standards are designed to achieve. To cite an example, in its fiscal year ending July 31, 2000, Cisco added back $51 million of payroll taxes on exercises of employee stock options in calculating its pro forma earnings per share. Disney Internet Group, on the other hand, made no similar adjustment to its GAAP earnings.

In another innovation of the late 1990s, many Internet companies did EBITDA (earnings before interest, taxes, depreciation, and amortization) one better by adding back marketing expenses to their GAAP income. The result was a pro forma earnings variant called EBITDAM. Such liberties by dot-com companies led short-seller Michael Murphy to coin the acronym

"IAAP" (for "Inter-nut Accepted Accounting Principles").[10] Computer software producers got into the act by omitting amortization of purchased research and development from the expenses considered in calculating pro forma earnings. Using that technique and other adjustments, Veritas Software turned a GAAP loss of $103.1 million in the second quarter of 1999 into a pro forma profit of $29.2 million. The Software and Information Industry Association added an air of legitimacy to the process when, in January 1999, the trade organization issued guidelines for beefing up pro forma results by adding back amortization of software patents and other intangibles.[11] Quest Communications International fused several different adjustments in its earnings release for the third quarter of 2001 by reporting its pro forma normalized recurring earnings before interest, taxes, depreciation, and amortization. Newsletter author Carol Levenson facetiously dubbed the new profit measure PENREBITDA.[12]

Gabelli Asset Management's earnings release for the three months ending March 31, 1999, its first quarter after the mutual fund company went public, informed investors that pro forma earnings for the period were $9.3 million. The figure excluded a $30.9 million (aftertax) charge to cover a $50 million lump-sum payment that chairman and chief executive officer Mario Gabelli was scheduled to receive in 2002. Again, there was no suggestion of a securities law violation. Indeed, for analysts attempting to project Gabelli Asset Management's future earnings, there was a clear need to be able to separate the $30.9 million charge from the rest of the results. Entirely omitting the word "loss" from the company's eight-page press release struck some analysts as aggressive, however. "The right way to do it," said portfolio manager James K. Schmidt of John Hancock Financial Industries Fund, "would have been to show the loss but give me the information I need to figure out the operating results."[13]

The divergences in methodology that inevitably accompany departures from GAAP have affected the reporting of aggregate corporate profits, as well as individual companies' results. Both Standard & Poor's and Thomson Financial/First Call compute "operating earnings" for the S&P 500 index of major stocks. Unlike operating income, a concept addressed by FASB standards, operating earnings is a number that subjectively excludes many above-the-line one-time events that lack any standing under GAAP. S&P takes a comparatively tough line in deciding whether to exclude losses that companies characterize as nonrecurring. First Call, on the other hand, tends to follow the comparatively liberal standards of Wall Street securities analysts. Loews Corporation's performance in the second quarter of 2001 provided a dramatic demonstration of the potential for wide disparities at the individual company level. By First Call's calculation, the diversified company posted operating earnings per share of $1.14. S&P, which was more inclined to regard management-designated "special items" as costs occurred in the ordinary course of business, put the figure at a loss of $7.18 a share. Naturally, First Call and S&P do not disagree so sharply in every instance. Taking into account all 500 companies in the index, however, First Call calculated that operating earnings fell by 17%, year-over-year, in 2001's first quarter, whereas S&P put the decline at 33%.[14]

Divergent computational methods also produced a gap in gauging how attractively the stock market was priced. According to First Call's numbers, the S&P 500 was valued at 22.2 times trailing-12-months operating earnings in August 2001. Using S&P's figures, the market index's valuation was materially richer 24.2 times. By the way, both calculations of the market's multiple were far below the figure derived by using GAAP net income as the basis for measurement. Excluding only below-the-line items (those that met the comparatively strict test to qualify as extraordinary items), the S&P's multiple was a record-high 36.8 times. The gaping difference between that figure and ratios based on the more loosely defined operating earnings graphically explain why companies prefer investors to base their valuation judgments on the latter. Stocks look cheaper when their multiples are geared to management-generated pro forma earnings that lie outside the jurisdiction of FASB's rules.

Notwithstanding the many problems that can arise from abusing the practice, making adjustments to reported earnings is neither wrongheaded nor inherently misleading. In fact, analysts who hope to forecast future financial results accurately *must* apply common sense and set aside genuinely out-of-the-ordinary-course-of-business events. The need for analysts to inject their own judgment applies, whether GAAP requires a particular item to be reported above or below the line. Even FASB officials acknowledge, at least unofficially, that it can be useful to consider earnings stripped of nonrecurring events. Getting carried away with adjustments can produce false judgments about companies' earnings potential, however. "The statement of income presented according to GAAP," FASB Chairman Edmund L. Jenkins contends, "is still the best predictor of future cash flows."[15]

On a bright note, one of the largest and therefore most contentious expenses typically added back in pro forma earnings calculations has been eliminated with the abolition of **pooling-of-interests** accounting for mergers in 2001 (see Chapter 10). As a quid pro quo for making purchase accounting mandatory, FASB ended the requirement to amortize goodwill. (Companies remained obligated to write down this intangible asset to the extent that it became impaired.) For many companies, FASB's change in the accounting rules for mergers substantially narrowed the gap between reported earnings and pro forma figures. Perhaps in a calmer environment, companies will not press analysts as strenuously as in recent years to conform to their highly customized versions of earnings. Analysts may then find it easier to rely on their common sense in adjusting reported earnings to obtain maximum analytical insight.

Go to the Source

Although analysts must exercise judgment when considering pro forma earnings, there is one rule they should follow without fail. They must make sure to examine the actual SEC filings, instead of trying to save time by relying solely on company communications. The consequences of failing to check the filings are illustrated by an incident involving telecommunications services provider I.D.T.

On October 14, 1999, I.D.T. issued a press release highlighting record revenues in its fiscal fourth quarter and year ended July 31. For the third quarter, according to the press release, earnings per share were $0.15. On November 4, I.D.T. filed its SEC annual report on Form 10-K. The filing showed higher expenses in several categories than the press release had indicated, resulting in a per share loss of $0.18. TheStreet.com reported the discrepancy between the press release and the 10-K, but investors did not seem to care. I.D.T.'s stock barely budged in response to the SEC filing, whereas the shares had jumped by 3.6% in response to the press release that subsequently proved inaccurate.

According to the company, the mistake was unintentional. I.D.T. spokesperson Norman Rosenberg explained that figures supplied by a subsidiary, Net2Phone, contained an error that was not discovered until after publication of the press release. Surely, then, the company must have put out a corrected press release for the benefit of investors who relied on that document instead of verifying the results in an SEC document released three weeks later? No, management took the position that because Net2Phone did not issue a corrected press release, I.D.T. could not do so. I.D.T., however, had voting control of the subsidiary. Therefore, *New York Times* reporter Gretchen Morgenson asked Rosenberg, could I.D.T. not have required Net2Phone to publish a corrected release? "Technically, we could have done it," the company spokesperson conceded. "Nobody here felt like forcing them to do it."[16]

The net result was that I.D.T.'s stock rose when the company released the incorrect numbers, but did not react significantly to the disclosure of the correct numbers. In all likelihood, few investors bothered to examine the 10-K. If analysts skip that essential step, they run the risk of basing their valuations on similar mistaken numbers. Recognizing the dissimilar stock market reactions to the correct and incorrect numbers in I.D.T.'s case, dishonest managers might even publish intentionally overstated numbers in their press releases, rectifying the "error" in their subsequent SEC filings.

Capitalizing into Insignificance

A final point worth remembering about pro forma alternatives to GAAP earnings is that even if analysts remove the items that management has added back, they may still derive an unrealistically high impression of a company's future earnings capacity. An older, but not obsolete, device for beefing up reported income is capitalization of selected expenditures. The practice has a legitimate basis in the accounting objective of matching revenues and expenses by period. A current-year outlay that will generate revenues in future years should not be expensed immediately and in full. Rather, a portion should be written off each year as the value created by the outlay diminishes. As with many other basically sound accounting practices, however, problems arise in the execution.

The rule makers, to be sure, have tried to prevent obvious abuses. They have barred altogether the capitalization of certain outlays that have undoubted future-year benefits, including advertising and research and development. Despite such pronouncements, however, a fair amount of discretion remains for the issuers of financial statements. Even the most respectable companies use this latitude to their advantage at times. Firms exploit it to inflate their earnings artificially for as long as possible. Eventually, however, those earnings are offset by huge write-offs of previously capitalized, but in fact worthless, assets.

To avoid being surprised by such nasty events, analysts should be wary of companies that report lower ratios of depreciation to property, plant, and equipment (PP&E) than their industry peers. The implication is that the company is recognizing the wear and tear on its assets more slowly than the norm. A comparatively high ratio of PP&E to sales or cost of goods sold is another sign of potential trouble.

Transforming Stock Market Proceeds into Revenues

At the same time that corporate managers have been supplementing their traditional tactics with new adjustments to earnings, they have also concentrated in recent years on applying their ingenuity to revenues. This focus makes eminent sense for corporations that want to present the best possible, if not necessarily most accurate, profile to investors. If a company achieves its revenue objectives, its battle for profitability is more than half won. To be sure, success also depends on controlling expenses. Without a robust top line, however, the company cannot economize its way to a respectable bottom line.

Garnering sales is not only a vital task, but a tough job as well. Competitors are forever striving to snatch away revenues by introducing superior products or devising means of lowering prices to customers. From the standpoint of maximizing value to consumers and promoting economic efficiency, management's optimal response to this challenge is to upgrade its own products and generate cost savings that it can pass along to customers. Stepping up expenditures on advertising or expanding the sales force can also lead to increased revenues. Along with effective execution of product design or marketing plans, however, another option exists. Management can boost sales through techniques that more properly fall into the category of corporate finance.

Increasing the rate of revenue increases through mergers and acquisitions is the most common example. A corporation can easily accelerate its sales growth by buying other companies and adding their sales to its own. Creating genuine value for shareholders through acquisitions is more difficult, although unwary investors sometimes fail to recognize the distinction.

In the fictitious example in Exhibit 3.5, Big Time Corp.'s sales increase by 5% between Year 1 and Year 2. Small Change, a smaller, privately owned company in the same industry, also achieves 5% year-over-year sales growth. Suppose now that at the end of Year 1, Big Time acquires Small Change with shares of its own stock. The Big Time income statements under this assumption ("Acquisition Scenario") show a 10% sales increase between Year 1 and Year 2. (Note that Year 1 is shown as originally reported, with Small Change still an independent company, while in Year 2, the results of the acquired company, Small Change, are consolidated into the parent's financial reporting. Analysts might also examine a pro forma income statement showing the levels of sales, expenses, and earnings that Big Time would have achieved in Year 1, if the acquisition had occurred at the beginning of that year.)

On the face of it, a company growing at 10% a year is sexier than one growing at only 5% a year. Observe, however, that Big Time's profitability, measured by net income as a percentage of sales, does not improve as a result of the acquisition. Combining two companies with equivalent profit margins of 3% produces a larger company that also earns 3% on sales. Shareholders do not gain anything in the process, as the supplementary figures in Exhibit 3.5 demonstrate.

If Big Time decides not to acquire Small Change, its number of shares outstanding remains at 75.0 million. The earnings increase from $150.0 million in Year 1 to $157.5 million in Year 2 raises earnings-per-share from

EXHIBIT 3.5 Sales Growth Acceleration without Profitability Improvement Big Time Corporation and Small Change, Inc.—Illustration ($000 omitted)

	Nonacquisition Scenario				Acquisition Scenario	
	Big Time Corporation		Small Change Inc.		Big Time Corporation	
	Year 1	Year 2	Year 1	Year 2	Year 1	Year 2
Sales	$5,000.0	$5,250.0	$238.1	$250.0	$5,000.0	$5,500.1
Costs and expenses						
Cost of goods sold	3,422.7	3,591.4	160.6	171.1	3,422.7	3,762.5
Selling, general, and administrative expense	1,250.0	1,315.0	61.9	62.5	1,250.0	1,377.5
Interest expense	100.0	105.0	4.8	5.0	100.0	110.0
Total costs and expenses	4,772.7	5,011.4	227.3	238.6	4,772.7	5,250.0
Income before income taxes	227.3	238.6	10.8	11.4	227.3	250.0
Income taxes	77.3	81.1	3.7	3.9	77.3	85.0
Net income	$ 150.0	$ 157.5	$ 7.1	$ 7.5	$ 150.0	$ 165.0
Year-over-year sales increase	—	5%	—	5%	—	10%
Net income as a percentage of sales	3%	3%	3%	3%	3%	3%
Shares outstanding (million)	75	75			75	78.6
Earnings per share	$2.00	$2.10			$2.00	$2.10
Price-earnings multiple (times)	14	14			14	14
Price per share	$28.00	$29.40			$28.00	$29.40

$2.00 to $2.10. With the price-earnings multiple constant at 14 times, equivalent to the average of the company's industry peers, Big Time's stock price rises from $28.00 to $29.40 a share.

In the Acquisition Scenario, on the other hand, Big Time pays its industry-average earnings multiple of 14 times for Small Change, for a total acquisition price of $7.1 million × 14 = $99.4 million. At Big Time's Year 1 share price of $28.00, the purchase therefore requires the issuance of

$99.4 million ÷ $28.00 = 3.6 million shares. With the addition of Small Change's net income, Big Time earns $165.0 million in Year 2. Dividing that figure by the increased number of shares outstanding (78.6 million) produces earnings per share of $2.10. At a price-earnings multiple of 14 times, Big Time is worth $29.40 a share, precisely the price calculated in the Nonacquisition Scenario. The mere increase in annual sales growth from 5% to 10% has not benefited shareholders, whose shares increase in value by 5% whether Big Time acquires Small Change or not.

Analysts should note that this analysis is sensitive to the assumptions underlying the scenarios. Suppose, for instance, that Big Time finances the acquisition of Small Change with borrowed money, instead of issuing stock. Let us suppose that Big Time must pay interest at a rate of 8% on the $99.4 million of new borrowings. Interest expense in Year 2 of the Acquisition Scenario is now $118.0 million, rather than $100.0 million. Pretax income therefore falls from $250.0 million to $242.0 million, reducing net income from $165.0 million to $159.7 million at the company's effective tax rate of 34%. Only 75.0 million shares are outstanding at the conclusion of the transaction, however, rather than the 78.6 million observed in the acquisition-for-stock case. As a result, Big Time's earnings per share rise to $159.7 million ÷ 75.0 million = $2.13.

Assuming the market continues to assign a multiple of 14 times to Big Time's earnings, the stock is now worth $29.82, a bit more than in the Nonacquisition Scenario. In practice, the investors may reduce Big Time's price-earnings multiple slightly to reflect the heightened risk represented by its decreased interest coverage. (Following the formulas laid out in Chapter 13, income before interest and taxes declines from $360.0 million ÷ $110.0 million = 3.3 times in the stock-acquisition case to $360.0 million ÷ $118.0 million = 3.1 times in the debt-financed-acquisition case.) If the price-earnings multiple falls only from 14 to 13.8 times as a result of this decline in debt protection, Big Time's stock price in this variant again comes to $29.40, equivalent to the Year 2 price in the Nonacquisition Scenario. As in the case of Big Time paying with stock for the acquisition of Small Change, shareholders do not benefit if Big Time instead borrows the requisite funds, assuming investors are sensitive to the impact of the company's increased debt load on its credit quality.

Internal versus External Growth

More important than the fine-tuning of the calculations is the principle that a company cannot truly increase shareholders' wealth by accelerating its revenue growth without also improving profitability. This does not dissuade companies from attempting to mesmerize analysts with high rates of sales growth generated by grafting other companies' sales onto their own through acquisitions. Analysts may fall for the trick by failing to distinguish between **internal growth** and **external growth.**

Internal growth consists of sales increases generated from a company's existing operations, while the latter represents incremental sales brought in through acquisitions. An internal growth rate greater than the average recorded for the industry implies that the company is gaining market share from its competitors. As a precaution, the analyst must probe further to determine whether management has merely increased unit sales by accepting lower gross margins. If that is not the case, however, the company may in fact be improving its competitive position and, ultimately, increasing its value. On the other hand, if Company A generates external growth by acquiring Company B and neither Company A nor its new subsidiary increases its profitability, then the intrinsic value of the merged companies is no greater than the sum of the two companies' values.

External growth can increase shareholders' wealth, however, if the mergers and acquisitions lead to improvements in profitability. This effect is commonly referred to as **synergy.** It is a term much abused by companies that promise to achieve operating efficiencies, without offering many specific examples, through acquisitions that appear to offer few such opportunities. Nevertheless, even analysts who have grown cynical after years of seeing purported synergies remain unrealized will acknowledge the existence of several bona fide means of raising a company's profit margins through external growth.

For one thing, a company may be able to reduce its cost per unit by increasing the size of its purchases. Suppliers commonly offer volume discounts to their large customers, which they can service more efficiently than customers who order in small quantities. If the cost of materials, fuel, and transportation required to produce each widget goes down while the selling price of widgets remains unchanged in a stable competitive environment, the company's gross margin increases.

Another way to increase profitability through external growth involves **economies of scope.** In a simple illustration, a manufacturer of potato chips has a sales force calling on retail stores. Much of the associated expense represents the time and transportation costs incurred as the salespeople travel from store to store, as well as the salespeople's health insurance and other benefits. Now suppose that the potato chip manufacturer acquires a pretzel manufacturer. For the sake of explication, assume that the pretzel company formerly relied on food brokers, rather than an in-house sales force. The acquiring company terminates the contracts with the brokers and adds pretzels to its potato chip sales force's product line. Revenues and gross profits per sales call rise with the addition of the pretzel line. The number of sales calls per salesperson remains essentially constant, because taking orders for the additional product consumes little time. Accordingly, time and transportation costs per sales call do not rise materially, while the cost of health insurance and other benefits does not rise at all. Adding it all up, the profitability of selling both potato chips and pretzels through the same distribution channel is greater than the profitability of selling one snack food only.

Analysts should be forewarned that claims of potential economies of scope often prove, in retrospect, to be exaggerated. Over a period of several decades, for example, banks, brokerage houses, and insurance companies have frequently proclaimed the advent of the "financial supermarket," in which a single distribution channel will efficiently deliver all classes of financial services to consumers. A fair amount of integration between these businesses has certainly occurred, but cultural barriers between the businesses have turned out to be more formidable than corporate planners have foreseen. Considerable training is required to teach salespeople how to shift gears between the fast-paced business of dealing in stocks and the more painstaking process of selling insurance policies. In general, the less closely related the combining businesses are, the less certain it is that the hoped-for economies of scope will be realized. When disparate companies combine in pursuit of novel synergies, analysts should treat with extreme caution the margin increases shown in pro forma income statements produced by management.

Capturing Economies of Scale

Finally, and perhaps most famously, mergers can genuinely increase profitability and shareholder wealth through **economies of scale.** As illustrated in Exhibit 3.6, Central Widget is currently utilizing only 83.3% of its productive capacity. At the present production level, the company's **fixed costs** amount to $300 million ÷ 250 million = $1.20 per unit, or 12% of each sales dollar. These irreducible costs represent a major constraint on the company's net profit margin, just 2.0%, and in turn its return on equity (see Chapter 13), which is an unexciting 11.1%.

Central Widget spies an opportunity in the form of its smaller competitor, Excelsior Widget. Because the two companies operate in the same geographic region, it would be feasible to consolidate production in Central Widget's underutilized factories. Management proposes a merger premised on achieving economies of scale.

Excelsior's cost structure is similar to Central's, except that its general and administrative expense is higher as percentage of sales (6.7% versus

EXHIBIT 3.6   Economies of Scale (Illustration)

Selected Production and Financial Statement Data

	Central Widget	Excelsior Widget	Central Widget (Pro Forma)
Units of capacity (million)	300	36	300
Unit sales	250	30	280
Capacity utilization	83.3%	83.3%	93.3%
Unit sales (million)	250	30	280
Price per unit	$ 10.00	$ 10.00	$ 10.00
Variable costs per unit			
Labor	$ 4.75	$ 4.75	$ 4.75
Materials	3.00	3.00	3.00
Variable sales costs	0.75	0.75	0.75
Total	$ 8.50	$ 8.50	$ 8.50
Total fixed costs ($million)			
Depreciation	$200.00	$ 24.00	$200.00*
Interest expense	25.00	3.00	28.00
General and administrative	75.00	20.00	85.00†
Total	$300.00	$ 47.00	$313.00
($000,000 omitted)			
Sales	$2,500.00	$300.00	$2,800.00
Variable costs	2,125.00	255.00	2,380.00
Fixed costs	300.00	47.00	313.00
Income before income taxes	75.00	2.00	107.00
Income tax	25.00	0.70	35.30
Net income	$50.00	$1.30	$ 71.70
Net income as a percentage of sales	2.0%	0.4%	2.6%
Shares outstanding (million)	20	3	22.2††
Earnings per share	$ 2.50	$ 0.43	$ 3.33
Price-earnings multiple (times)	13	N.M.	13
Price per share	$32.50	$18.00	$43.29

*Assumes closure of Excelsior Widget factory.
†Assumes elimination of 50% of Excelsior Widget's general and administrative expense through closure of company headquarters.
††Assumes acquisition price of $23.40 per Excelsior Widget share.

3.0%). The problem is that certain costs (such as the upkeep on a head-quarters building and salaries of senior executives) are nearly as great for Excelsior as for Central, but Excelsior has a smaller base of sales over which to spread them. As a result, Excelsior is running at a loss at current operating levels. Its board of directors therefore accepts the acquisition offer. Central pays $23.40 worth of its own stock (0.72 shares) for each share of Excelsior, a 30% premium to Excelsior's prevailing market price.

Unlike the acquisition of Small Change by Big Time depicted in Exhibit 3.5, this transaction not only increases the acquiring company's sales, but also improves its profitability. Following the acquisition, on a pro forma basis, Central Widget's fixed cost per unit is $313.0 million ÷ 280 million = $1.12, down from $1.20. The net margin is up from 2.0% to 2.6%, while earnings per share have jumped from $2.50 to $3.33, pro forma. If the market continues to assign a multiple of 13 times to Central's earnings, the stock should theoretically trade at $43.29, up from $32.50 before the transaction. Realistically, that increase probably overstates the actual rise that Central Widget shareholders can expect. Aside from severance costs not shown in the pro forma income statement, investors may reduce the price-earnings multiple to reflect the myriad uncertainties faced in any merger, such as potential loss of key personnel and the predictable traumas of melding distinct corporate cultures. After all the dust has settled, however, Central Widget's shareholders will assuredly benefit from the economies of scale achieved through the acquisition of Excelsior Widget.

Scale economies become available for a variety of reasons. Technological advances can make a sizable portion of existing capacity redundant. For example, computerization has increased the productivity of financial services workers engaged in clearing transactions. Consolidation in the banking and brokerage industries has been hastened by cost savings achievable through handling two companies' combined volume of transactions with fewer back office workers than the companies previously employed in aggregate.

Economies of scale also arise through consolidation of a "mom-and-pop" business, that is, an industry characterized by many small companies operating within small market areas. For example, waste hauling has evolved from a highly localized business to an industry with companies operating on a national scale. Among the associated efficiencies is the ability to reduce garbage trucks' idle time by employing them in several adjacent municipalities.

Behind the Numbers: Fixed versus Variable Costs

As synergies go, projections of economies of scale in combinations of companies within the same business tend to be more plausible than economies of scope purportedly available to companies in tangentially connected businesses. The existence of chronically underutilized capacity is apparent to operations analysts within corporations and to outside management consultants. Word inevitably spreads from there until the possibility of achieving sizable efficiencies through consolidation becomes common knowledge among investors. Companies' published financial statements typically provide too little detail to quantify directly the potential for realizing economies of scale.

Companies do not generally break out their fixed and variable costs in the manner shown in Exhibit 3.6. Instead, they include a combination of variable and fixed costs in cost of goods sold. Somewhat helpfully, the essentially fixed costs of depreciation and interest appear as separate lines. On the whole, however, a company's published income statement provides only limited insight into its **operating leverage,** or the rate at which net income escalates once sales volume rises above the **breakeven rate.** This is unfortunate, because a breakout of fixed and variable costs would be immensely helpful in quantifying the economies of scale potentially achievable through a merger. More generally, such information would greatly facilitate the task of forecasting a company's earnings as a function of projected sales volume.

Exhibit 3.7 uses data from the Central Widget example to plot the relationship between sales volume and pretax income (income before income taxes). The company breaks even at a sales volume of 200 million units, the level at which the $1.50 per unit contribution (margin of revenue over variable cost) exactly offsets the $300 million of fixed costs. Once fixed costs are covered, the contribution on each incremental unit sold flows directly to the pretax income line. At full capacity, 300 million units, Central Widget earns $150 million before taxes. (Note that analysts can alternatively remove interest expense from the calculation and base a breakeven analysis on operating income.)

In theory, an analyst can back out the fixed and variable components of a company's costs from reported sales and income data. The object is to produce a graph along the lines of the one shown in Exhibit 3.7, while also estimating the contribution per unit. At that point, the analyst can create a table like that shown in the exhibit and establish the sensitivity of profits to the portion of capacity being utilized.

Exhibit 3.8 presents the fictitious case of West Coast Whatsit. The top graph plots the company's reported unit sales volume versus pretax income for each of the past 10 years. (West Coast is debt-free and has no other non-operating income or expenses, so the company's operating income is equivalent to its pretax income.) Observe that the plotted points are concentrated in the upper right-hand corner of the graph, reflecting that annual sales

EXHIBIT 3.7 Operating Leverage—Illustration Central Widget

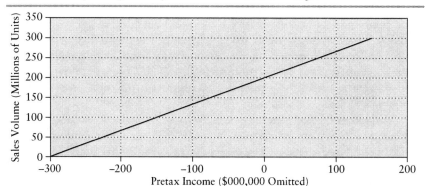

Pretax Income ($000,000 Omitted)

Units	*	Contribution per Unit	=	Contribution	−	Fixed Costs	=	Pretax Income
300		$1.50		$450		$300		$150
250		1.50		375		300		75
200		1.50		300		300		0
150		1.50		225		300		(75)
100		1.50		150		300		(150)
50		1.50		75		300		(225)
0		1.50		0		300		(300)

(Units in millions. Contribution, fixed costs, and pretax income in millions of dollars.)

*Price per unit − Variable cost per unit = Contribution per unit.
　$10.00　　−　　　8.50　　　=　　　$1.50

volume never declined to less than 380 million units (63% of capacity) during the period. At that low ebb, pretax income fell below zero.

The next step is to fit a diagonal line through the points, as shown in the upper graph. (For a precise technique of fitting a line, see the discussion of the least-squares method in Chapter 14.) According to the line derived from the empirical observations, the company's breakeven sales volume is 400 million units, that is, the point on the diagonal line that corresponds to zero on the horizontal scale (pretax income). Although West Coast Whatsit has not utilized 100% of its capacity in any of the past 10 years, the graph indicates that at that level (600 million on the vertical scale), pretax income would amount to $400 million.

To complete the analysis, the analyst must also plot the reported unit sales volume versus dollar sales for the past 10 years, as shown in the lower graph. The remaining task is to back into the data required to fill in the

EXHIBIT 3.8 Backing out Fixed and Variable Costs—Illustration West Coast Whatsit

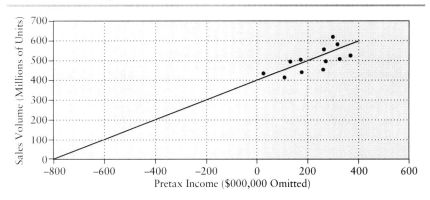

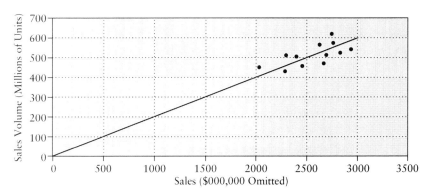

Sales/ Units	=	Unit Price	−	Variable Cost per Unit	=	Contribution per Unit	×	Units	=	Contribution	−	Fixed Costs	=	Pretax Income
0	0	5		3		2		0		0		800		−800
500	100	5		3		2		100		200		800		−600
1000	200	5		3		2		200		400		800		−400
1500	300	5		3		2		300		600		800		−200
2000	400	5		3		2		400		800		800		0
2500	500	5		3		2		500		1000		800		200
3000	600	5		3		2		600		1200		800		400

table at the bottom of Exhibit 3.8. At the outset, the analyst knows only the figures shown in boldface, which can be derived directly from the two graphs. For example, the fitted line shows that at full capacity (600 million units), sales would total $3.0 billion.

According to the known data, the increase in pretax income between the breakeven volume (400 million units) and a volume of 500 million units is $200 million. That dollar figure must represent the contribution on 100 million units. Dividing $200 million by 100 million yields the contribution per unit of $2.00, enabling the analyst to fill in that whole column. Dividing any figure in the sales column by its corresponding number of units (e.g., $2.5 billion and 500 million) provides the unit price of $5.00, which goes on every line in that column. Cost per unit, by subtraction, is $3.00.

At the breakeven level (pretax income = $0), contribution totals 400 million units times $2.00 = $800 million. The analyst can put that number on every line in the entire Fixed Costs column. All that remains is to fill in the Contribution column by multiplying each remaining line's number of units by the $2.00 contribution per unit figure.

Regrettably, the elegant procedure just described tends to be highly hypothetical, even though it is useful to go through the thought process. To begin with, companies engaged in a wide range of products do not disclose the explicit unit volume figures that the analysis requires. Relating their sales volumes to prices and costs is more complicated than in the case of a producer of a basic metal or a single type of paper. The Management Discussion and Analysis section of a multiproduct company's financial report may disclose period-to-period *changes* in unit volume, but not absolute figures, by way of explaining fluctuations in revenues. A rise or drop in revenue, however, may also reflect changes in the sales price per unit, which may in turn be sensitive to industrywide variance in capacity utilization. In addition, revenue may vary with product mix. When a recession causes consumers to turn cautious about spending on major appliances, for example, they may trade down to lower-priced models that provide smaller contributions to the manufacturers. Finally, multiproduct companies' product lines typically change significantly over periods as long as the 10 years assumed in Exhibit 3.8.

For all these reasons, analysts generally cannot back out fixed and variable costs in practice. When projecting a company's income statement for the coming year, they instead work their way down to the operating income line by making assumptions about cost of goods sold (COGS) and selling, general, and administrative expenses (SG&A) as percentages of sales (see Chapter 12). They try in some sense to take into account the impact of fixed and variable costs, but they cannot be certain that their forecasts are internally consistent.

In Exhibit 3.8, total pretax costs are equivalent to the sum of COGS and SG&A. (Remember that West Coast Whatsit has no interest expense or other nonoperating items.) An analyst who projects that the two together will represent 92% of sales is making a forecast consistent with sales volume of 500 million units, or 83% of capacity. At that unit volume, variable costs total 500 million × $3.00 = $1.5 billion, which when added to fixed costs of $800 million, produces total costs of $2.3 billion, or 92% of sales measuring $2.5 billion. The assumption of a total pretax cost 92% ratio would be too pessimistic if the analyst actually expected West Coast to operate in line with the whatsit industry as a whole at 90% of capacity. That would imply unit sales of 540 million, resulting in variable costs of $1.62 billion and total costs of $2.42 billion. The ratio of operating expenses to sales of $2.7 billion (540 million units @ $5.00) would be only 90%. Observe that not only operating income, but also the operating margin rises as sales volume increases.

Estimating COGS and SG&A as percentages of sales is an imperfect, albeit necessary, substitute for an analysis of fixed and variable costs. Conscientious analysts must strive to mitigate the distortions introduced by the shortcut method. They should avoid the trap of uncritically adopting the projected COGS and SG&A percentages kindly provided by companies' investor relations departments. Analysts who do so risk sacrificing their independent judgment. After all, the preceding paragraph demonstrates that a forecast of the operating margin must reflect an implicit assumption about sales volume. Accordingly, a company's "guidance" regarding COGS and SG&A percentages necessarily incorporates management's assumption about the coming year's sales volume. At the risk of stating the obvious, management's embedded sales projection will often be more optimistic than the analyst's independently generated forecast.

Readers should not infer from the absence of disclosure about fixed and variable costs that the information is unimportant to understanding companies' financial performance. On the contrary, a company's fixed-variable mix can be a dominant factor in analyzing both its credit quality and its equity value (see Chapters 13 and 14, respectively). A company with relatively large fixed costs has a high breakeven level. Even a modest economic downturn will reduce its capacity utilization below the rate required to keep the company profitable. A cost structure of this sort poses a substantial risk of earnings falling below the level needed to cover the company's interest expense. On the other hand, if the same company has low variable costs, its earnings will rise dramatically following a recession. Each incremental unit of sales will contribute prodigiously to operating income. Two real-life examples demonstrate the analytical value of understanding the fixed-versus-variable nature of a company's cost structure, even though it may not be feasible to document the mix precisely from the financial statements.

As an amusement park operator, Six Flags exemplifies the high-fixed-cost company. Attendance (and therefore revenue), shows wide seasonal variations, but the company's costs are concentrated in categories that do not vary with attendance. Examples include occupancy, depreciation on rides, insurance, and wages of employees who must be on site whether the parks are full or nearly empty.

A time series of the company's cost of sales as a percentage of sales (Exhibit 3.9) shows wide quarterly fluctuations, largely reflecting extreme seasonality in the company's business. In 2000, for example, the warm-weather second and third calendar quarters accounted for more than 90% of the parks' attendance. During those two quarters, which perennially contribute the vast majority of annual revenues, cost of sales runs less than 50% of revenues. In the cold-weather quarters ending December 31 and March 31, by contrast, the ratio soars to over 100%. Year-over-year variances in profit margins, also arising from wide fluctuations in attendance, are substantial as well. Cost of sales soared to 272% of sales in the quarter ending December 31, 1996, but measured only 109% in the corresponding quarter of 1999.

Washington Group International, known as Morrison Knudsen during most of the period shown in Exhibit 3.10, represents the opposite extreme in

EXHIBIT 3.9   Six Flags, Inc. Cost of Sales as a Percentage of Sales. Quarterly 1996–2000.

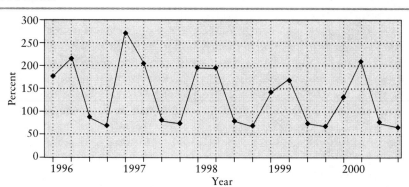

Source: Compustat.

EXHIBIT 3.10 Washington Group International, Inc. Cost of Sales as a Percentage of Sales. Quarterly 1996–2000.

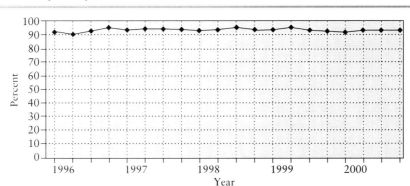

Source: Compustat.

cost structures. The engineering and construction concern incurs variable labor and material costs with each contract it obtains. Once Washington Group completes the project, the associated costs cease. If the volume of available work declines from one year to the next, the company's total costs decline nearly in proportion, as fixed costs are too low to have a large impact.

Consistent with this qualitative description of Washington Group's mix of fixed and variable costs, the company's cost of sales as a percentage of sales scarcely budges from period to period. The ratio consistently ran between 90% and 95% from 1996 through 2000. In the quarter ending December 31, 1997, the percentage was identical to the preceding quarter's, at 94.0%. Similar quarter-to-quarter stability, at the 93.9% level, was observed in the successive quarters ending December 31, 1998 and March 31, 1999.

Credit analysts ordinarily perceive substantial risk in the sort of high-fixed-cost pattern revealed by the Six Flags graph in Exhibit 3.9. Even a comparatively modest drop in revenue and, by extension, contribution can drive operating income below the level required to cover interest expense. By contrast, a highly variable cost structure like Washington Group's inherently provides a great deal of financial flexibility. With few other fixed costs to meet in the event of a revenue decline, an engineering and construction company ought to be able to stay current on its interest expense, provided it keeps its debt burden at a prudent level.

Surprisingly, however, Washington Group defaulted on its debt and filed for bankruptcy in May 2001. The action followed a severe liquidity squeeze arising from unprofitable contracts that the company took over in connection with its April 2000 acquisition of Raytheon Engineers & Constructors (RE&C). In response to the credit crisis, Washington Group halted certain work on two major projects related to the acquisition and sued the seller of RE&C, Raytheon Company, alleging fraud and breach of contract.

Washington Group's sudden descent into bankruptcy did not negate the general rule that a predominantly variable cost structure aids financial flexibility. Rather, the lesson for students of financial statements was the possibility of discontinuities in any company's earnings record. Ordinarily, the sort of consistency in profit margins depicted in Exhibit 3.10 is reassuring to credit analysts, but they must never feel reassured to the point of complacency.

Playing with Price-Earnings Multiples

Vigilance, as exemplified by the need to watch for earnings discontinuities, has been a recurring theme throughout this exploration of the ins and outs of income statements. Other pitfalls to watch out for include unrealizable synergies and company-furnished projections of cost ratios that incorporate management's assumptions regarding sales volume. Before moving on, vigilant analysts should familiarize themselves with a device that companies have developed to get around the general proposition that mergers do not increase value unless they increase profitability.

Turning back to the fictitious acquisition case presented in Exhibit 3.5, let us change one assumption (see Exhibit 3.11). As a comparatively small company within its industry, Small Change probably will not command as high a price-earnings multiple as its larger industry peers. Therefore, we shall assume that Big Time is able to acquire the company for only 12 times earnings, rather than 14 times, as indicated in Exhibit 3.5.

Our revised assumption does not alter the income statements in either year under either the Acquisition or Nonacquisition Scenario. The acquisition price, however, falls from $99.4 million to $7.1 million x 12 = $85.2 million. Big Time issues only $85.2 million ÷ $28.00 = 3.0 million shares to pay for the acquisition, rather than 3.6 million under the previous assumption. Consequently, Big Time has 78.0 million shares outstanding at the end of Year 2 under the Acquisition Scenario, instead of 78.6 million. Earnings per share come to $165.0 million ÷ 78.0 million = $2.12. At a price-earnings multiple of 14 times, Big Time's stock is valued at $29.68 a share following the Small Change acquisition, slightly higher than the $29.40 figure shown in the Nonacquisition Scenario. Big Time could vault its share price to a considerably loftier level by making a series of acquisitions on a similar basis.

In contrast to the outcome depicted in Exhibit 3.5, Big Time increases the value of its stock through the acquisition of Small Change. The company

EXHIBIT 3.11   Exploiting a Difference in Price-Earnings Multiples Big Time Corporation and Small Change, Inc.—Illustration ($000 omitted)

	Nonacquisition Scenario				Acquisition Scenario	
	Big Time Corporation		Small Change, Inc.		Big Time Corporation	
	Year 1	Year 2	Year 1	Year 2	Year 1	Year 2
Sales	$5,000.0	$5,250.0	$238.1	$250.0	$5,000.0	$5,500.0
Cost and Expenses						
Cost of goods sold	3,422.7	3,591.4	160.6	171.1	3,422.7	3,762.5
Selling, general, and administrative expenses	1,250.0	1,315.0	61.9	62.5	1,250.0	1,377.5
Interest expense	100.0	105.0	4.8	5.0	100.0	110.0
Total costs and expenses	4,772.7	5,011.4	227.3	238.6	4,772.7	5,250.0
Income before income expenses	227.3	238.6	10.8	11.4	227.3	250.0
Income taxes	77.3	81.1	3.7	3.9	77.3	85.0
Net income	$ 150.0	$ 157.5	$ 7.1	$ 7.5	$ 150.0	$ 165.0
Year-over-year sales increase	—	5%	—	5%	—	10%
Net income as a percentage of sales	3%	3%	3%	3%	3%	3%
Shares outstanding (million)	75.0	75.0			75.0	78.0
Earnings per share	$2.00	$2.10			$2.00	$2.12
Price-earnings multiple (times)	14	14			14	14
Price per share	$28.00	$29.40			$28.00	$29.68

achieves this effect without realizing operating efficiencies through the combination. Following the transaction, Big Time's ratio of net income to sales is 3%, unchanged from its preacquisition level.

The rational explanation of this apparent alchemy lies in Big Time's ability to exchange its stock for shares of privately owned Small Change on highly favorable terms. By acquiring the smaller company at a price of 12 times earnings with stock valued at a multiple of 14 times, Big Time spreads Small Change's earnings across fewer shares than would be the case if the market valued the two companies at the same multiple. The effect, achieved purely through financial engineering, is a parody of the economies of scale realized in mergers premised instead of improvements in operations.

In fairness to the many real-world companies that have exploited disparities in price-earnings multiples over the years, Big Time's share-price-enhancing acquisition rests squarely within the bounds of fair play. Companies legitimately take advantage of favorable currency exchange rates when deciding whether to purchase materials and equipment domestically or overseas. If the dollar is high relative to the Euro, companies based in the United States can source goods more economically in Europe than at home. In principle, it is no less appropriate or beneficial to shareholders to buy earnings with a highly valued "acquisition currency," that is, its own stock.

Furthermore, as shareholders of a private company, Small Change's owners do not have to be coerced to sell out to Big Time. The disparity in price-earnings multiples is justified by the private company's owners' opportunity to exchange an illiquid investment for public stock, for which a deep and active trading market exists. If anything, the difference between Big Time's multiple of 14 times and Small Change's 12 times understates the valuation gap between the public and private shares. Lacking a secondary market that would reward higher reported income with a higher share price, private owner-managers commonly extract compensation through perquisites that their companies can lawfully account for as business expenses. The result is lower net income than comparably successful public companies would report, but with the value of the "perks" delivered on a pretax basis. Instead of buying cars with dividends distributed from aftertax income, the owner-managers can drive fancier, more expensive company-provided cars purchased with pretax dollars. After adjusting Small Change's reported income for expenses that would not be incurred at a public company such as Big Time, the $85.2 million acquisition price might represent a multiple of only 10 or 11 times, rather than 12 times.

In short, there is nothing inherently unsavory about paying for low-multiple companies with high-multiple stock. Why, then, does the technique warrant special focus in a chapter covering the broad subject of income statements? The answer is that like many other legitimate financial practices, exploiting disparities in price-earnings multiples is prone to abuse. Capitalizing on disparities in price-earnings multiples can lead to trouble in several ways.

To begin with, suppose a high-multiple company acquires a low-multiple company during a period of exceptionally wide dispersion in valuations. In a shift from normal conditions to a "two-tiered" market, the respective multiples might go, for sake of example, from 15 and 12 to 25 and 10. Selling stockholders of the low-multiple company would likely consider it a fair exchange to accept payment in shares of the high-multiple company at the prevailing market price. Their feelings would probably change dramatically, however, if the two-tiered market abruptly ended with the purchaser's stock receding from 25 times earnings to a more ordinary 15 times. Sellers who retained the acquiring company's shares would discover that their value received had suddenly fallen by 40%. (It is reasonable to assume that many shareholders would have held on to the shares, because doing so would ordinarily delay the incurrence of capital gains taxes on the sale. Unlike cash-for-stock transactions, stock-for-stock acquisitions generally qualify as tax-free exchanges.)

Readers might accuse the selling shareholders of being crybabies. After all, they knew when they accepted the acquiring company's shares as payment that they would be exposed to stock market fluctuations, much as they were prior to the deal. The difference, however, is that if they had held onto their low-multiple stock, their loss would not have been 40%, but only 17%, that is, from 12 times to 10 times earnings. (A complete comparison must also take into account any premium over the previously prevailing stock price received by the selling shareholders.)

Financial statement analysis would not have warned the selling shareholders of the impending marketwide drop in price-earnings multiples. Careful scrutiny of the acquiring company's income statement might very well have determined, however, that its shares were susceptible to a sharp decline. Over the years, many voracious acquirers have temporarily achieved stratospheric multiples on their acquisition currency through financial reporting gimmicks that hard-nosed analysts were able to detect before the share prices fell back to earth.

In some instances, the basis for an exaggerated P/E multiple is rapid earnings per share growth achieved through financial engineering, rather than bona fide synergies. Starting with a modest multiple on its stock, a company can make a few small acquisitions of low-multiple companies to get the earnings acceleration started. Each transaction may be too small to be deemed material in itself. That would eliminate any obligation on the company's part to divulge details that would make it easy for analysts to quantify the impact of the company's exploitation of disparities in P/E multiples. As quarter-to-quarter percentage increases in EPS escalate, the company's equity begins to be perceived as a high-growth glamour stock. Obliging investors award the stock a higher multiple, which increases the company's ability to buy earnings on favorable terms. Management may succeed in pumping up the P/E multiple even further by asserting that it can achieve economies of scope through acquiring enterprises outside, yet in some previously unrecognized way, complementary to the company's core business.

The conglomerate craze of the 1960s relied heavily on these techniques, and with variations, they have been reused in more recent times. Massive declines in the share prices of the insatiable acquirers' stock prices have frequently resulted. Contributing to the downslides have been the practical problems of integrating the operations of diverse companies. Deals that work on paper have often foundered on incompatible information systems, disparate distribution channels, clashes of personality among senior executives, and contrasting corporate cultures. In addition, the process of boosting earnings per share through acquisition of lower-multiple companies may prove unsustainable. For example, if competition heats up among corporations seeking to grow through acquisition, the P/E gap between acquirers and target companies may narrow. That could get in the way of the continuous stream of acquisitions needed to maintain EPS growth in the absence of profit improvements. Inevitably, too, the voracious acquirer will suffer a normal cyclical decline in the earnings of its existing operations. The company's price-earnings multiple may then decline relative to the multiples of its potential targets, interrupting the necessary flow of acquisitions.

It is no small task to dissect the income statement of a corporation that makes frequent acquisitions and discloses as few details as possible. Nevertheless, an energetic analyst can go a long way toward segregating ongoing operations from purchased earnings growth. Acquisitions of public companies leave an information trail in the form of regulatory filings. Conscientious searching of the media, including the industry-specialized periodicals and local newspapers, may yield useful tidbits on acquisitions of private companies. Such investigations will frequently turn up the phrase, "terms of the acquisition were not disclosed," but reliable sources may provide informed speculation about the prices paid. Finally, the acquirers may furnish general information regarding the range of earnings multiples paid in recent deals. If an analysis of the available data indicates that management is expanding its empire without creating additional value through genuine economies of scale or scope, the prudent action is to sell before the bottom falls out.

Is Fraud Detectable?

As a final point on the reality underlying the numbers, readers should note that although the tactics detailed in the preceding discussion may not win awards for candor in financial reporting, neither will most of them land corporate managers in the penitentiary. Analysts must be mindful that there are many ways for companies to pull the wool over investors' eyes without fear of legal retribution. Sometimes, however, corporate executives step over the line into illegality.

Outright misrepresentation falls into a category entirely separate from the mere exploitation of financial reporting loopholes. Moreover, the gravity of such misconduct is not solely a matter of temporal law. In 1992, the Roman Catholic Church officially classified fraudulent accounting as a sin. A catechism unveiled in that year listed book-cooking in a series of "new" transgressions, that is, offenses not known in 1566, the time of the last previous overhaul of church teachings.

Neither fear of prosecution nor concern for spiritual well-being, however, entirely deters dishonest presenters of financial information. Audits, even when conducted in good faith, sometimes fail to uncover dangerous fictions. Financial analysts must therefore strive to protect themselves from the consequences of fraud.

No method is guaranteed to uncover malfeasance in financial reporting, but neither are analysts obliged to accept a clean auditor's opinion as final. Even without the resources that are available to a major accounting firm, it is feasible to find valuable clues about the integrity of financial statements.

Messod Daniel Beneish, Professor of Accounting and Information Systems at the Kelley School of Business at Indiana University, has developed a model for identifying companies that are likely to manipulate their earnings, based on numbers reported in their financial statements.[17] (Beneish defines manipulation to include both actual fraud and the management of earnings or disclosure within GAAP. In either case, his definition specifies that the company subsequently must have been required to restate results; write off assets; or change its accounting estimates or policies at the behest of its auditors, an internal investigation, or a Securities and Exchange Commission probe.) Beneish finds, by statistical analysis, that the presence of any of the following five factors increases the probability of earnings manipulation:

1. Increasing days sales in receivables.
2. Deteriorating gross margins.
3. Decreasing rates of depreciation.
4. Decreasing asset quality (defined as the ratio of noncurrent assets other than property, plant, and equipment to total assets).
5. Growing sales.

Note that Beneish does not characterize these indicators as irrefutable evidence of accounting malfeasance. Indeed, it would be disheartening if every company registering high sales growth were shown to be achieving its results artificially. Nevertheless, Beneish's data suggest a strong association between the phenomena he lists and earnings manipulation.

CONCLUSION

At several points in this chapter, analysis of the income statement has posed questions that could be answered only by looking outside the statement. Mere study of reported financial figures never leads to a fully informed judgment about the issuer. Financial statements cannot capture certain non-quantitative factors that may be essential to an evaluation. These include industry conditions, corporate culture, and management's ability to anticipate and respond effectively to change.

In a few applications of income statement analysis, the limitations of looking only at the reported numbers pose no difficulty. For example, an investment organization may be permitted to buy the bonds only of companies that meet a quantitative financial test such as a minimum ratio of earnings to interest expense. If the analyst's task is narrowly defined as calculating the ratio to see whether it meets the guideline, then there is no need to go beyond the income statement itself. In most instances, however, the object of the analysis is to assess the company's future financial performance. For analysts engaged in forward-looking tasks, poring over the income statement is merely the jumping-off point. Armed with an understanding of what happened in past periods, the analyst can approach the issuer and other sources to find out why.

QUESTIONS

1. According to Professor Beneish's statistical studies, what are some of the indicators whose presence increases the probability of earnings manipulation?
2. Are "extraordinary items" reported above or below the line of income (or loss) from continuing operations?
3. Based on the language used by the Accounting Principles Board in setting the tests for an item to be considered "extraordinary," how often would you expect to find such items in a firm's income statement? What statistics can you provide to support your conclusion?
4. How can a company increase the wealth of its shareholders by accelerating its revenue growth?
5. How can a low P/E multiple company accelerate its earnings growth and thus become perceived as a high-growth stock?

6. How can an analyst detect artificial expansion of revenues on a retrospective basis? On a current basis?

7. How can an analyst segregate ongoing operations from purchased growth?

8. How can an analyst use the common form income statement to tell the difference between strategy and superior (or inferior) management skills?

9. How can you tell if the earnings of Boston Beer are sensitive to fluctuations in interest rates?

10. How can you tell which of the two companies (Boston Beer and Anheuser-Busch) is more efficient?

11. How can you use the Common Form Income Statement to evaluate a company's competitive standing?

12. How can careful study of financial statements help raise warning flags regarding risk in merger-and-acquisitions driven stock-for-stock transactions?

13. How can the techniques of corporate finance be used to boost revenues?

14. How do credit analysts use the concepts of fixed and variable cost to assess risk?

15. How do the assumptions underlying the analysis of the Big Time acquisition of Small Change affect the conclusions?

16. How do economies of scope increase profitability? Does it always work?

17. How do you construct the "common form income statement"?

18. How does the existence of a secondary market influence price-earnings multiples?

19. How does the use of Common Form Income Statements for a peer group allow the analyst to uncover capitalization abuses?

20. How is taking advantage of favorable currency exchange rates similar to mergers and acquisitions?

21. How is the Central Widget acquisition of Excelsior Widget different from the Big Time acquisition of Small Change?

22. Is making adjustments to reported earnings inherently misleading?

23. Under what circumstances does the analyst need to look no further than the income statement?

24. Under what circumstances is poring over the financial statements the jumping-off point?

25. What "envelope-pushing" action did Amazon undertake that required a disclaimer?

26. What alternative explanations are available to account for a change in selling, general, and administrative expenses?

27. What are some analogies between business and athletics?

28. What are some examples of the need to watch for earnings discontinuities?

29. What are some of the challenges you encounter when attempting to calculate the breakeven level of sales?
30. What are some of the conditions that give rise to economies of scale?
31. What are some of the nonquantitative factors essential for an evaluation that are not found in financial statements?
32. What are some of the useful, albeit limited observations you can make from observing an Income Statement in its raw form?
33. What are the preferred sources of views on trends observed in the Common Form Income Statement?
34. What can derail deals that appear to work on paper?
35. What does it mean to "make the numbers talk?"
36. What does the analysis of cost of goods sold tells the analyst about the differences between the operating strategies of Boston Beer and Anheuser-Busch?
37. What does the term *core net earnings* have to do with *pro-forma*? Why does it matter?
38. What happens when a company's earnings and cash flow diverge to an extent that becomes unsustainable?
39. What happens when the measure of achievement becomes more important than the accuracy of the measure itself?
40. What is synergy? Does it exist?
41. What is a *restructuring*, and what is the dangerous trap that users of financial statements must avoid?
42. What is a *two-tiered market* and how does a shift from normal conditions and back influence the results of mergers?
43. What is an alternative to estimating fixed and variable costs? What are its shortcomings?
44. What is documented in the section "How Accurate Are the Numbers"?
45. What is one way gross profit margins can increase?
46. What is the difference between operating income and operating earnings? Why does it matter?
47. What is an example (in the text) of a high fixed-cost company? And the opposite extreme?
48. What is the goal of analyzing an Income Statement?
49. What is the lesson for students of financial statements of Washington Group's bankruptcy?
50. What is the rational explanation of the apparent alchemy in the Big Time acquisition of Small Change?
51. What is the relationship between operating leverage and breakeven level of sales?
52. What must a conscientious analyst do?

53. What particular form of characterizing the extraordinary as standard did Coca-Cola use, and what were the implications and results?
54. What recent FASB ruling eliminated the most contentious expense typically added back in pro-forma earnings calculations?
55. What standing do the terms *nonrecurring* and *unusual* have under GAAP? How and why do firms use them?
56. What profitability measure is known as EBITDAM?
57. What type of analysis does the Common Form Income Statement facilitate?
58. When examining a company's financial statements, are you interested in the past or the future? Explain.
59. Which use (reporting above or below the line of income, or loss, from continuing operations) is limited by accounting rules? Why?
60. Why is it imperative for the analyst to consider the underlying trend in any of the major items in the Common Form Income Statement?
61. Would a careful reading of the Notes to Financial Statements disclose whether a company is exaggerating revenues?

CHAPTER 4

The Statement of Cash Flows

The present version of the statement that traces the flow of funds in and out of the firm, the statement of cash flows, became mandatory, under SFAS 95, for issuers with fiscal years ending after July 15, 1988. Exhibit 4.1, the fiscal 2000 cash flow statement of battery producer Rayovac, illustrates the statement's division into cash flows from operations, investments in the business, and financing. The predecessor of the statement of cash flows, the statement of changes in financial position, was first required under APB 19, in 1971.

Prior to that time, going as far back as the introduction of **double-entry bookkeeping** in Italy during the fifteenth century, financial analysts had muddled through with only the balance sheet and the income statement. Anyone with a sense of history will surely conclude that the introduction of the cash flow statement must have been premised by expectations of great new analytical insights. Such an inference is in fact well founded. The advantages of a cash flow statement correspond to the shortcomings of the income statement, and more specifically, the concept of profit. Over time, profit has proven so malleable a quantity, so easily enlarged or reduced to suit management's needs, as to make it useless, in many instances, as the basis of a fair comparison among companies.

An example of the erroneous comparisons that can arise involves the contrasting objectives that public and private companies have in preparing their income statements.

For financial-reporting (as opposed to tax-accounting) purposes, a publicly owned company generally seeks to maximize its reported net income, which investors use as a basis for valuing its shares. Therefore, its incentive in any situation where the accounting rules permit discretion is to minimize expenses. The firm will capitalize whatever expenditures it can and depreciate its fixed assets over as long a period as possible. All that restrains the

EXHIBIT 4.1   Rayovac Corporation

Consolidated Statements of Cash Flows
(in thousands, except per share amounts)
Year Ended September 30, 2000

Cash flows from operating activities	
Net income	$ 38,350
Adjustments to reconcile net income to net cash provided (used) by operating activities:	
Amortization	6,309
Depreciation	16,024
Deferred income taxes	2,905
(Gain) loss on disposal of fixed assets acquired	(1,297)
Accounts receivable	(15,697)
Inventories	(20,344)
Prepaid expenses and other assets	(5,416)
Accounts payable and accrued liabilities	22,126
Accrued recapitalization and other special charges	(5,147)
Net cash (used) provided by operating activities	37,813
Cash flows from investing activities	
Purchases of property, plant, and equipment	(18,996)
Proceeds from sale of property, plant, and equipment	1,051
Net cash used by investing activities	(17,945)
Cash flows from financing activities	
Reduction of debt	(215,394)
Proceeds from debt financing	203,189
Cash overdraft	(4,971)
Proceeds from (advances for) notes receivable from officers/shareholders	(2,300)
Acquisition of treasury stock	(886)
Exercise of stock options	621
Payments on capital lease obligation	(1,233)
Net cash provided (used) by financing activities	(20,974)
Effect of exchange rate changes on cash and cash equivalents	(202)
Net increase (decrease) in cash and cash equivalents	(1,308)
Cash and cash equivalents, beginning of year	11,065
Cash and cash equivalents, end of year	$ 9,757
Supplemental disclosure of cash flow information:	
Cash paid for interest	27,691
Cash paid for income taxes	14,318

Source: Rayovac Corporation Form 10-K December 19, 2000.

public company in this respect (other than conscience) is the wish to avoid being perceived as employing liberal accounting practices, which may lead to a lower market valuation of its reported earnings. Using depreciation schedules much longer than those of other companies in the same industry could give rise to such a perception.

In contrast, a privately held company has no public shareholders to impress. Unlike a public company, which shows one set of statements to the public and another to the Internal Revenue Service, a private company typically prepares one set of statements, with the tax authorities foremost in its thinking. Its incentive is not to maximize, but to minimize, the income it reports, thereby minimizing its tax bill as well. If an analyst examines its income statement and tries to compare it with those of public companies in the same industry, the result will be an undeservedly poor showing by the private company.

THE CASH FLOW STATEMENT AND THE LBO

Net income becomes even less relevant when one analyzes the statements of a company that has been acquired in a **leveraged buyout,** or LBO (Exhibit 4.2). In a classic LBO, a group of investors acquires a business by putting up a small amount of equity and borrowing the balance (90% in this example) of the purchase price. As a result of this highly leveraged capital structure, interest expense is so large that the formerly quite profitable company reports a loss in its first year as an LBO (2002). Hardly an attractive investment, on the face of it, and one might also question the wisdom of lenders who provide funds to an enterprise that is assured of losing money.

A closer study, however, shows that the equity investors are no fools. In 2002, the company's sales are expected to bring in $1,500 million in cash. Cash outlays include cost of sales ($840 million), selling, general, and administrative expense ($300 million), and interest expense ($265 million), for a total of $1,405 million. Adding in depreciation of $105 million produces total expenses of $1,510 million, which when subtracted from sales results in a $10-million pretax loss. The amount attributable to depreciation, however, does not represent an outlay of cash in the current year. Rather, it is a bookkeeping entry intended to represent the gradual reduction in value, through use, of physical assets. Therefore, the funds generated by the leveraged buyout firm equal sales less the cash expenses only. (Note that the credit for income taxes is a reduction of cash outlays.)

EXHIBIT 4.2   Leveraged Buyout Forecast—Base Case ($000 omitted)

Capitalization
December 31, 2001

Senior debt	$1,375	55%
Subordinated debt	875	35
Total debt	2,250	90%
Common Equity	250	10
Total capital	$2,500	100%

Projected Income Statement

	2001	2002	2003	2004	2005	2006
Sales	$1,429	$1,500	$1,575	$1,654	$1,737	$1,824
Cost of sales	800	840	882	926	973	1021
Depreciation	100	105	110	116	122	128
Selling, general, and administrative expense	286	300	315	331	347	365
Operating income	243	255	268	281	295	310
Interest expense	70	265	265	263	251	257
Income before income taxes	173	(10)	3	18	44	53
Provision (credit) for income taxes	61	(3)	1	6	12	18
Net income	$ 112	$ (7)	$ 2	$ 12	$ 22	$ 35

Projected Cash Flow

	2002	2003	2004	2005	2006
Net income	$ (7)	$ 2	$ 12	$ 22	$ 35
Depreciation	105	110	116	122	128
Cash from operations	98	112	128	144	163
Less: Property and equipment additions	95	100	105	110	116
Cash available for debt reduction	$ 3	$ 12	$ 23	$ 34	$ 47

Projected Capitalization

	2001	2002	2003	2004	2005	2006
Senior debt	$1,375	$1,372	$1,360	$1,337	$1,303	$1,256
Subordinated debt	875	875	875	875	875	875
Total debt	2,250	2,247	2,235	2,212	2,178	2,131
Common equity	250	243	245	257	279	314
Total capital	$2,500	$2,490	$2,480	$2,469	$2,457	$2,445

	Sales	$1,500 million
Less:	Cash expenses	
	Cost of sales	840
	Selling, general, and administrative expense	300
	Interest expense	265
	Provision (credit) for income taxes	(3)
Equals:	Cash generated	$ 98 million

The same figure can be derived by simply adding back depreciation to income.[1]

	Net income	$ (7) million
Plus:	Depreciaton	105
Equals:	Cash generated	$ 98 million

Viewed in terms of cash inflows and outflows, rather than earnings, the leveraged buyout begins to look like a sound venture. Projected net income remains negative, but as shown under "Projected Cash Flow," cash generation should slightly exceed cash use in 2002. (Note that the equity investors take no dividends but instead dedicate any surplus cash generated to reduction of debt.)

The story improves even more during subsequent years. As sales grow at a 5% annual rate, the Projected Income Statement shows a steady increase in operating income. In addition, a gradual paydown of debt causes interest expense to decline a bit, so net income increases over time. With depreciation rising as well, funds from operations in this example keep modestly ahead of the growing capital expenditure requirements.

If the projections prove accurate, the equity investors will, by the end of 2006, own a company with $1.8 billion in sales and $310 million of operating income, up from $1.4 billion and $243 million, respectively, in 2001. They will have captured that growth without having injected any additional cash beyond their original $250 million investment.

Suppose the investors then decide to monetize the increase in firm value represented by the growth in earnings. Assuming they can sell the company for the same multiple of EBITDA (earnings before interest, taxes, depreciation, and amortization)[2] that they paid for it, they will realize net proceeds of $685 million, derived as follows ($000 omitted):

1. Calculate the multiple of EBITDA paid in 2001.

$$= \frac{\text{Purchase price} \left(\text{Equity} + \text{borrowed funds}\right)}{\begin{array}{c}\text{Net income} + \text{Income taxes} + \text{Interest expense} \\ + \text{Depreciation} + \text{Amoritization}\end{array}}$$

$$= \frac{\$2,500}{\$112 + \$61 + \$70 + \$100}$$

$$= 7.3$$

2. Multiply this factor by 2006 EBITDA to determine sale price in that year.

$$(7.3) \times (\$35,000 + \$18,000 + \$257,000 + \$128,000) = \$3,197,400$$

3. From this figure subtract remaining debt to determine pretax proceeds.

$$\$3,197,400 - \$2,131,000 = \$1,066,400$$

4. Subtract taxes on the gain over original equity investment to determine net proceeds.

$1,066,400	Pretax proceeds
− 250,000	Original equity investment
$ 816,400	Capital gain
× .34	Capital gains tax rate
$ 277,576	Tax on capital gain
$1,066,400	Pretax proceeds
− 277,576	Tax on capital gain
$ 788,824	Net proceeds

The increase in the equity holders' investment from $250 million to $789 million over five years represents a compounded annual return of 25.8% after tax. Interestingly, the annual return on equity (based on reported net income and the book value of equity) averages only 4% during the period of the projection. Analysts evaluating the investment merits of the LBO proposal would miss the point if they focused on earnings rather than cash flow.

The same emphasis on cash flow, rather than reported earnings, is equally important in analyzing the downside in a leveraged buyout.

As one might expect, the equity investors do not reap such spectacular gains without incurring significant risk. There is a danger that everything will not go according to plan and that they will lose their entire investment. Specifically, there is a risk that sales and operating earnings will fall short of expectations, perhaps as a result of a recession or because the investors' expectations were unrealistically high at the outset. With a less debt-heavy capital structure, a shortfall in operating earnings might not be worrisome. In a leveraged buyout, however, the high interest expense can quickly turn disappointing operating income into a sizable net loss (Exhibit 4.3). The loss may be so large that even after depreciation is added back, the company's funds generated from operations may decline to zero or to a negative figure. (Note that the shortfall shown here resulted from deviations of just 8% each in the projections for sales, cost of sales, and selling, general and administrative expense, shown in Exhibit 4.2.)

Now the future does not look so rosy for the equity investors. If they cannot reduce operating expenses sufficiently to halt the cash drain, they will lack the cash required for the heavy interest expenses they have incurred, much less the scheduled principal payments. Most of the choices available if they cannot cut costs sufficiently are unappealing. One option is for the investors to inject more equity into the company. This will cause any

EXHIBIT 4.3   Leveraged Buyout Forecast—Pessimistic Case ($000 omitted)

Projected Income Statement	2002
Sales	$1,380
Cost of sales	907
Depreciation	105
Selling, general, and administrative expense	324
Operating income	44
Interest expense	265
Income before income taxes	(221)
Provision (credit) for income taxes	(75)
Net income	$ (146)

Net income	$(146) million
Plus: Depreciation	105
Equals: Cash generated	$ (41) million

profits they ultimately realize to represent a smaller percentage return on the equity invested, besides possibly straining the investors' finances. Alternatively, the existing equity holders can sell equity to a new group of investors. The disadvantage of this strategy is that anyone putting in new capital at a time when the venture is perceived to be in trouble is likely to exact terms that will severely dilute the original investors' interest and, possibly, control. Comparably harsh terms may be expected from lenders who are willing (if any are) to let the company try to borrow its way out of its problems. A distressed exchange offer, in which bondholders accept reduced interest or a postponement of principal repayment, may be more attractive for the equity holders but is likely to meet stiff resistance.

If all these options prove unpalatable or unfeasible, the leveraged company will default on its debt. At that point, the lenders may force the firm into bankruptcy, which could result in a total loss for the equity investors. Alternatively, the lenders may agree to reduce the interest rates on their loans and postpone mandatory principal repayments, but they will ordinarily agree to such concessions only in exchange for a larger influence on the company's management. In short, once cash flow turns negative, the potential outcomes generally look bleak to the equity investors.

The key point here is that the cash flow statement, rather than the income statement, provides the best information about a highly leveraged firm's financial health. Given the overriding importance of generating (and retaining) cash to retire debt, and because the equity investors have no desire for dividends, there is no advantage in showing an accounting profit, the main consequence of which is incurrence of taxes, resulting in turn in reduced cash flow. Neither are there public shareholders clamoring for increases in earnings per share. The cash flow statement is the most useful tool for analyzing highly leveraged companies because it reflects the true motivation of the firm's owners—to generate cash, rather than to maximize reported income.

ANALYTICAL APPLICATIONS

Although privately held and highly leveraged companies illustrate most vividly the advantages of the cash flow statement, the statement also has considerable utility in analyzing publicly owned and more conventionally capitalized firms. One important application lies in determining where a company is in its life cycle, that is, whether it is "taking off," growing rapidly, maturing, or declining. Different types of risk characterize these various stages of the life cycle. Therefore, knowing which stage a company is in can focus the analyst's efforts on the key analytical factors. A second use of the cash flow statement is to assess a company's financial flexibility. This term refers to a company's capacity, in the event of a business downturn, to continue making expenditures that, over the long term, minimize its cost of capital and enhance its competitive position. Finally, the cash flow statement is the key statement to examine when analyzing a troubled company. When a company is verging on bankruptcy, its balance sheet may overstate its asset value, as a result of write-offs having lagged the deterioration in profitability of the company's operations. On the other hand, the balance sheet may fail to reflect the full value of certain assets recorded at historical cost, which the company might sell to raise cash. The income statement is not especially relevant in the context of pending bankruptcy. For the moment, the company's key objective is not to maintain an impeccable earnings record, but to survive. The cash flow statement provides the most useful information for answering the critical question: Will the company succeed in keeping its creditors at bay?

CASH FLOW AND THE COMPANY LIFE CYCLE

Business enterprises typically go through phases of development that are in many respects analogous to a human being's stages of life. Just as children are susceptible to illnesses different from those that afflict the elderly, the risks of investing in young companies are different from the risks inherent in mature companies. Accordingly, it is helpful to understand which portion of the life cycle a company is in and which financial pitfalls it is therefore most likely to face.

Exhibit 4.4 depicts the business life cycle in terms of sales and earnings growth over time. Revenues build gradually during the start-up phase, during which time the company is just organizing itself and launching its products. Growth and profits accelerate rapidly during the emerging growth phase, as the company's products begin to penetrate the market and the production reaches a profitable scale. During the established growth period, growth in sales and earnings decelerates as the market nears saturation. In the mature industry phase, sales opportunities are limited to the replacement of products previously sold, plus new sales derived from growth in the population. Price competition often intensifies at this stage, as companies seek sales growth through increased market share (a larger piece of a pie that is growing at a slower rate). The declining industry stage does not automatically follow maturity, but over long periods some industries do get swept away by technological change. Sharply declining sales and earnings, ultimately resulting in corporate bankruptcies, characterize industries in decline.

EXHIBIT 4.4   The Business Life Cycle

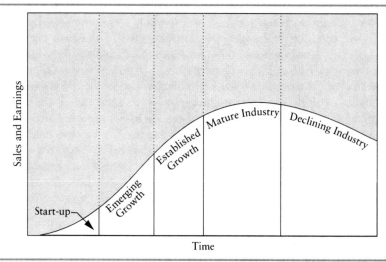

The characteristic growth patterns of firms at various stages in the company life cycle correspond to typical patterns of cash generation and usage. For example, outright *start-up companies* are typically voracious cash users. They require funds to pay the salaries of the employees who plan the initial attempts to gear up production and launch marketing efforts. With no revenues yet coming in, the risk is high that the organization will fail to gel. Such companies offer little basis for conventional financial statement analysis. Before offering their securities in the public market and subjecting their financial results to scrutiny by general investors, they operate as privately owned companies under the auspices of venture capitalists. "VCs" are professional investors with special expertise in evaluating infant companies. They assess the new ventures' prospects for generating sufficient revenues to go public.[3]

Emerging growth companies are start-ups that survive long enough to reach the stage of entering the public market. Focal Communications (Exhibit 4.5) illustrates the cash flow pattern of an emerging growth company. As a competitive local exchange carrier (CLEC), Focal offers long-distance voice and data telecommunications services to large business customers. Its market is characterized by rapid growth, but Focal is not yet at the point of being able to harvest profits on its large capital investments.

EXHIBIT 4.5   Focal Communications Corporation

Consolidated Statements of Cash Flows
for the Three Years Ended December 31, 2000
(Dollars in thousands, except share amounts)

	2000	1999	1998
CASH FLOWS FROM OPERATING ACTIVITIES:			
Net loss	$(105,857)	$ (22,386)	$ (7,969)
Adjustments to reconcile net loss to net cash provided by operating activities—			
Depreciation and amortization	56,985	23,763	6,671
Amortization of obligation under capital lease	2,275	1,077	—
Noncash compensation expense	6,360	7,186	3,070
Amortization of discount on senior discount notes	23,487	20,713	16,080
Loss on disposal of fixed assets	—	609	—
Gain on sale of investment affiliate	(199)	—	—
Provision for losses on accounts receivable	6,987	7,090	720
Changes in operating assets and liabilities—			
Accounts receivable	(26,563)	(24,545)	(8,157)
Other current assets	(16,526)	(3,699)	(718)
Accounts payable and accrued liabilities	105,755	8,522	12,491
Other noncurrent assets and liabilities, net	(508)	219	319
Net cash provided by operating activities	52,196	18,549	22,507
CASH FLOWS FROM INVESTING ACTIVITIES:			
Capital expenditures	(309,617)	(128,550)	(64,229)
Change in short-term investments	(320)	(2,040)	(7,960)
Net cash used in investing activities	(309,937)	(130,590)	(72,189)
CASH FLOWS FROM FINANCING ACTIVITIES:			
Deferred debt issuance cost	(14,549)	—	—
Proceeds from issuance of long-term debt	273,020	31,768	163,103
Payments on long-term debt	(9,254)	(5,985)	(3,537)
Net proceeds from the issuance of common stock	1,799	138,359	13,900
Net cash provided by financing activities	251,016	164,142	173,466
NET INCREASE (DECREASE) IN CASH AND CASH EQUIVALENTS	(6,725)	52,101	123,784
CASH AND CASH EQUIVALENTS Beginning of period	178,142	126,041	2,257
CASH AND CASH EQUIVALENTS End of period	$ 171,417	$178,142	$126,041

Source: Focal Communications Corporation Form 10K March 30, 2001.

Over the past three years shown in the exhibit, Focal has recorded mounting losses on operations. Noncash expenses, principally depreciation and amortization of fixed assets and amortization of debt discount,[4] represent much of the reported losses. With increases in accounts payable and accrued liabilities as additional sources, operations have been cash-flow-positive. Focal's capital budget is several times as great as its depreciation charges, which conceptually represent the requirement to replace existing plant and equipment as a consequence of wear and tear. This large ongoing construction has required outside financing, consisting of both long-term debt and stock issuance.

Heavy reliance on external financing creates substantial vulnerability in periods of limited access to capital. Late in 2000, emerging growth telecommunications companies lost the ability to raise funds in the public equity and high yield bond markets. By the summer of 2001, Focal indicated that it would run out of cash by the first quarter of 2002 unless it could raise new funds, either in the private market or as a result of the public markets reopening to telecom issuers. The company's stock price and bond ratings declined in reaction to the funding squeeze.

Established growth companies are in a less precarious state in terms of cash flow than their emerging growth counterparts. Solectron (Exhibit 4.6), a provider of electronics manufacturing and supply-chain management services, has reached the stage of profitability. Still in its high-growth phase, the company has chalked up increases of approximately 40% in each of the past two years. Capital expenditures exceed depreciation, although not by as large a margin as observed in emerging growth companies. In 2000, Solectron substantially increased its inventories and acquired $1.1 billion of manufacturing locations and assets. The company funded this expansion primarily with debt issuance.

Mature industry companies such as American Greetings, the second-largest greeting card manufacturer in the United States (Exhibit 4.7), are past the cash strain faced by growth companies that must fund large construction programs. Cash flow from depreciation and amortization more than covers American Greetings's capital budget. Consequently, the company has consistently generated positive cash flow from operations, although working capital accounts represented a net use of cash in two of the past three years. Even in fiscal 2001, when the company suffered a net loss, operations generated $110 million of cash. The external funding requirement arose from $180 million of acquisitions, which included the purchase of Gibson Greetings, the third-largest company in its business. Consolidation is a typical feature of mature industries, where companies seek to bolster their diminishing profit margins by capturing **economies of scale.**

EXHIBIT 4.6 Solectron Corporation Supplemental Consolidated Statements of Cash Flows (in millions)

	Years Ended August 31		
	2000	1999	1998
Cash flows from operating activities:			
Net income	$ 497.20	$ 350.30	$ 251.30
Adjustments to reconcile net income to net cash provided by (used in) operating activities:			
Depreciation and amortization	251.4	200.4	134.6
Noncash interest expense	52.5	18.5	—
Tax benefit associated with the exercise of stock options	60.1	35.4	11.5
Adjustment to conform fiscal year ends of pooled acquisitions	(11.8)	—	—
Cumulative effect of change in accounting principle for start-up costs	3.5	—	—
Gain on disposal of fixed assets	(8.7)	(4.6)	(2.3)
Other	20.9	5.5	(0.6)
Changes in operating assets and liabilities:			
Accounts receivable	(934.1)	(505.2)	(271.2)
Inventories	(2,096.00)	(329.7)	(165.2)
Prepaid expenses and other current assets	(102.9)	16.2	(38.7)
Accounts payable	1,710.70	294.8	248.8
Accrued expenses and other current liabilities	214.5	15	44.1
Net cash (used in) provided by operating activities	(342.7)	96.6	212.3
Cash flows from investing activities:			
Purchases and sales of short-term investments	982	(598)	(244.9)
Purchases and sales and maturities of short-term investments	(1,498.60)	327.8	358.1
Acquisition of manufacturing locations and assets	(1,097.90)	(164.2)	(204)
Capital expenditures	(506)	(449.4)	(279.1)
Proceeds from sales of fixed assets	88.9	41.7	60.4
Other	(35.1)	(32)	(15.6)
Net cash used in investing activities	(2,066.70)	(874.1)	(325.1)

(continued)

EXHIBIT 4.6   *(Continued)*

	Years Ended August 31		
	2000	1999	1998
Cash flows from financing activities:			
Net proceeds from bank lines of credit	16.9	22.1	22.8
Proceeds from issuance of long-term debt	2,296.30	729.4	(0.9)
Repayment of long-term debt	(0.8)	—	—
Repurchase of common stock	—	(7.1)	(9.2)
Proceeds from exercise of stock options	121.9	81.5	54.3
Net proceeds from issuance of common stock	11.2	1,069.90	15.7
Dividends paid	(1.4)	(1.4)	(0.4)
Other	29.9	(0.4)	(2.2)
Net cash provided by financing activities	2,474.00	1,894.00	80.1
Effect of exchange rate changes on cash and cash equivalents	(6.5)	5.2	1.7
Net increase (decrease) in cash and cash equivalents	58.1	1,121.70	(31)
Cash and cash equivalents at beginning of year (1)	1,417.40	306.4	337.4
Cash and cash equivalents at end of year	$ 1,475.50	$ 1,428.10	$ 306.40
Cash paid:			
Interest	$ 17.60	$ 27.70	$ 25.70
Income taxes	$ 135.70	$ 114.50	$ 93.70
Noncash investing and financing activities:			
Issuance of common stock upon conversion of long-term debt, net	$ —	$ 225.40	$ —
Issuance of common stock for business combination, net of cash acquired	$ 6.40	$ 14.70	$ —

Source: Solectron Corporation Form 10-K November 13, 2000.

Declining industry companies struggle to generate sufficient cash as a consequence of meager earnings. Polaroid (Exhibit 4.8) earned no cumulative profit over the period 1998–2000. For the three years, net cash provided by operating activities of $228.6 million fell considerably short of additions to property, plant, and equipment of $490.8 million. The camera manufacturer nearly made up the difference with $243.7 million of proceeds from sales of property, plant, and equipment. In 2000, however, the cash squeeze became more acute as a result of a rising need to finance inventories.

EXHIBIT 4.7 American Greetings Corporation

Consolidated Statement of Cash Flows
Years Ended February 28 or 29, 2001, 2000, and 1999
(Dollars in thousands)

	2001	2000	1999
OPERATING ACTIVITIES:			
Net (loss) income	$(113,814)	$ 89,999	$180,222
Adjustments to reconcile to net cash provided by operating activities:			
Cumulative effect of accounting change, net of tax	21,141	—	—
Write-down of equity investment	32,554	—	—
Nonrecurring items	—	30,704	5,544
Depreciation and amortization	98,057	76,600	74,783
Deferred income taxes	61,227	54,248	(8,940)
Changes in operating assets and liabilities, net of effects of acquisitions:			
Decrease (increase) in trade accounts receivable	29,201	(35,883)	(10,450)
(Increase) decrease in inventories	(46,587)	11,655	17,809
Increase in other current assets	(67,292)	(57,261)	(3,271)
Decrease (increase) in deferred costs—net	4,110	(5,640)	(65,588)
Increase (decrease) in accounts payable and other liabilities	87,256	(689)	24,211
Other—net	3,947	4,786	(3,052)
Cash provided by operating activities	109,800	168,519	211,268
INVESTING ACTIVITIES:			
Business acquisitions	(179,993)	(65,947)	(52,957)
Property, plant, and equipment additions	(74,382)	(50,753)	(60,950)
Proceeds from sale of fixed assets	22,294	1,490	2,522
Investment in corporate-owned life insurance	181	2,746	18,413
Other	33,944	(25,183)	8,040
Cash used by investing activities	(197,956)	(137,647)	(84,932)
FINANCING ACTIVITIES:			
Increase in long-term debt	—	1,076	317,096
Reduction of long-term debt	(80,431)	(16,397)	(22,669)
Increase (decrease) in short-term debt	257,541	81,097	(158,657)
Sale of stock under benefit plans	—	1,171	18,981
Purchase of treasury shares	(45,530)	(130,151)	(131,745)
Dividends to shareholders	(52,743)	(51,213)	(52,410)
Cash provided (used) by financing activities	78,837	(114,417)	(29,404)
(DECREASE) INCREASE IN CASH AND EQUIVALENTS	(9,319)	(83,545)	96,932
Cash and equivalents at beginning of year	61,010	144,555	47,623
Cash and equivalents at end of year	$ 51,691	$ 61,010	$144,555

Source: American Greetings Corporation Form 10-K405 May 3, 2001.

EXHIBIT 4.8   Polaroid Corporation and Subsidiary Companies

Consolidated Statement of Cash Flows
(Dollars in millions)

	Year Ended December 31		
	2000	1999	1998
CASH FLOWS FROM OPERATING ACTIVITIES			
Net earnings/(loss)	$ 37.7	$ 8.70	$ (51.00)
Depreciation of property, plant, and equipment	113.9	105.9	90.7
Gain on the sale of real estate	(21.8)	(11.7)	(68.2)
Other noncash items	22.9	73.8	62.2
Decrease/(increase) in receivables	41.8	(52.7)	79
Decrease/(increase) in inventories	(100.6)	88	(28.4)
Decrease in prepaids and other assets	32.9	62.4	39
Increase/(decrease) in payables and accruals	9.2	(16.5)	25.3
Decrease in compensation and benefits	(105)	(72.5)	(21)
Decrease in federal, state and foreign income taxes payable	(31.5)	(54)	(29.9)
Net cash provided/(used) by operating activities	(0.5)	131.4	97.7
CASH FLOWS FROM INVESTING ACTIVITIES			
Decrease/(increase) in other assets	4.5	16.5	(25.4)
Additions to property, plant, and equipment	(129.2)	(170.5)	(191.1)
Proceeds from the sale of property, plant, and equipment	56.6	36.6	150.5
Acquisitions, net of cash acquired	—	—	(18.8)
Net cash used by investing activities	(68.1)	(117.4)	(84.8)
CASH FLOWS FROM FINANCING ACTIVITIES			
Net increase/(decrease) in short-term debt (maturities 90 days or less)	108.2	(86.2)	131.2
Short-term debt (maturities of more than 90 days)			
Proceeds	—	41.8	73
Payments	—	(24.9)	(117.2)
Proceeds from issuance of long-term debt	—	268.2	—
Repayment of long-term debt	—	(200)	—
Cash dividends paid	(27)	(26.6)	(26.5)
Purchase of treasury stock	—	—	(45.5)
Proceeds from issuance of shares in connection with stock incentive plan	0.1	0.3	6
Net cash provided/(used) by financing activities	81.3	(27.4)	21
Effect of exchange rate changes on cash	(7.5)	0.4	3.1
Net increase/(decrease) in cash and cash equivalents	5.2	(13)	37
Cash and cash equivalents at beginning of year	92	105	68
Cash and cash equivalents at end of year	$ 97.20	$ 92.00	$105.00

Source: Polaroid Corporation Form 10-K April 2, 2001.

Polaroid's underlying problem was deterioration in its core business. The company introduced instant photography with the Land Camera in 1947, following up that success with an instant color photography system in 1971. Consumer interest waned, however, with the advent of one-hour photo developing stores and digital cameras. New products failed to revive Polaroid's fortunes, while costs became bloated through sales force expansion far in excess of sales growth.[5] The company compounded its problems in 1988 by aggressively repurchasing stock in an effort to fend off an attempted **hostile takeover**, sharply increasing its **financial leverage** as a consequence. Polaroid had an opportunity to reduce its debt load in 1991, when it received $925 million from a settlement of a patent violation suit against Eastman Kodak. Instead, the company used the proceeds to retire more shares and purchase resource-planning software in an attempt to boost efficiency.[6]

By the summer of 2001, Polaroid was failing to meet its scheduled bond coupons. As a cost-saving measure, the company slashed health care benefits for employees and required retirees to shoulder an increased portion of their health care costs. After attempts to sell all or part of the company bore no fruit, Polaroid filed for bankruptcy on October 12, 2001.

THE CONCEPT OF FINANCIAL FLEXIBILITY

Besides reflecting a company's stage of development, and therefore the categories of risk it is most likely to face, the cash flow statement provides essential information about a firm's financial flexibility. By studying the statement, an analyst can make informed judgments on such questions as:

- How safe (likely to continue being paid) is the company's dividend?
- Could the company fund its needs internally if external sources of capital suddenly become scarce or prohibitively expensive?
- Would the company be able to continue meeting its obligations if its business turned down sharply?

Exhibit 4.9 provides a condensed format that can help answer these questions. At the top is basic cash flow, defined as net income (excluding noncash components), depreciation, and deferred income taxes. The various uses of cash are deducted in order, from least to most discretionary.

In difficult times, when a company must cut back on various expenditures to conserve cash, management faces many difficult choices. A key objective is to avoid damage to the company's long-term health. Financial

EXHIBIT 4.9 Wal-Mart Stores Inc.

Analysis of Financial Flexibility
Fiscal Years Ended January 31, 2001
(000 omitted)

Basic cash flow (1)	$9,749
Increase in adjusted working (2)	(145)
Operating cash flow	9,604
Capital expenditures	(8,042)
Discretionary cash flow	1,562
Dividends	(1,070)
Investing activities	(672)
Cash flow before financing	(180)
Net increase in long-term debt (3)	2,086
Net decrease in short-term debt	(2,022)
Net issuance of common stock	388
Other	(74)
Increase in cash and cash equivalents	$ 198

(1) Includes net income, depreciation and amortization, deferred income taxes, and other.
(2) Excludes cash and notes payable.
(3) Includes capital lease obligations.

Source: Wal-Mart Stores Inc. Form 10-K/A April 17, 2001.

flexibility, as captured by the presentation in Exhibit 4.9, is critical to meeting this objective.

Wal-Mart, the United States' largest retailer, exhibited exceptional financial flexibility in the fiscal year ended January 31, 2001. Cash generated by operations, at a robust $9.6 billion, precluded any need to borrow or issue stock to pay for the company's ambitious $8.0 billion capital spending program. Wal-Mart floated $2.1 billion of long-term debt (net of retirements), but that issuance merely refunded a similar amount of outstanding short-term debt. Proceeds of the company's $388 million of net stock issuance essentially made up the small amount ($180 million) by which investing activities (primarily investment in international operations) exceeded internally generated cash after dividends.

Wal-Mart's ability to self-finance most of its expansion is a great advantage. At times, new financing becomes painfully expensive, as a function of high interest rates or depressed stock prices. During the "credit crunches" that occasionally befall the business world, external financing is unavailable at any price.

Underlying Wal-Mart's lack of dependence on external funds is a highly profitable discount store business. If this engine were to slow down for a time, as a result of an economic contraction or increased competitive pressures, the company would have two choices. It could reduce its rate of store additions and profit-enhancing investments in technology or it could become more dependent on external financing. The former approach could further impair profitability, while the latter option would earmark a greater portion of Wal-Mart's EBITDA for interest and dividends. Loss of financial flexibility, in short, leads to further loss of financial flexibility.

If the corporation's financial strain becomes acute, the board of directors may take the comparatively extreme step of cutting or eliminating the dividend. (About the only measures more extreme than elimination of the dividend are severe retrenchment, entailing a sell-off of core assets to generate cash, and cessation of interest payments, or default.) Reducing the dividend is a step that corporations try very hard to avoid, for fear of losing favor with investors and consequently suffering an increase in **cost of capital**. Boards sometimes go so far as to borrow to maintain a dividend at its existing rate. This tactic cannot continue over an extended period, lest interest costs rise while internal cash generation stagnates, ultimately leading to insolvency.

Notwithstanding the lengths to which corporations sometimes go to preserve them, dividends must be viewed as a potential source of financial flexibility in a period of depressed earnings. After all, the term "discretionary," applied to the cash flow that remains available after operating expenses and capital expenditures, emphasizes that dividends are not contractual payments, but disbursed at the board's discretion. When preservation of the dividend jeopardizes a company's financial wellbeing, shareholders may actually urge the board to *cut* the payout as a means of enhancing the stock value over the longer term.

To gauge the safety of the dividend, analysts can observe the margin by which discretionary cash flow covers it. In Wal-Mart's case, the ratio is a comfortable $1.562 billion ÷ $1.070 billion = 1.46x. By the same token, that ratio would fall below 1.0x if Wal-Mart's net income (a component of basic cash flow) declined by $1.562 billion − $1.070 billion = $492 million. That would represent a drop of only 8% in Wal-Mart's earnings. (Net income, which is not shown in Exhibit 4.9, was $6.295 million in the fiscal year.)

Wal-Mart, however, has an additional cushion in the form of potential cutbacks in its capital budget. Management could not only reduce the pace of store additions, but also defer planned refurbishment of existing stores.

The latter measure, though, could cut into future competitiveness. Retailers find that their sales drop off if their stores start to look tired. Similarly, industrial companies can lose their competitive edge if they drop back to "maintenance level capital spending" for any extended period. This is the amount required just to keep existing plant and equipment in good working order, with no expenditures for adding to capacity or upgrading of facilities to enhance productivity. Analysts, by the way, should seek independent confirmation of the figure that management cites as the maintenance level, possibly from an engineer familiar with the business. Companies may exaggerate the extent to which they can cut capital spending to conserve cash in the event of a downturn.

A final factor in assessing financial flexibility is the change in adjusted working capital. Unlike conventional working capital (current assets minus current liabilities), this figure excludes notes payable, as well as cash and short-term investments. In Exhibit 4.9, the former is part of the net change in short-term debt, while the period's increase or decrease in cash is treated as a residual in the analysis of financial flexibility.

For Wal-Mart, adjusted working capital represented a minor ($145 million) use of funds during the fiscal year. In general, inventories and receivables expand as sales grow over time. A company with a strong balance sheet can fund much of that cash need by increasing its trade payables (credit extended by vendors). External financing may be needed, however, if accumulation of unsold goods causes inventories to rise disproportionately to sales. Similarly, if customers begin paying more slowly than formerly, receivables can widen the gap between working capital requirements and trade credit availability. The resulting deterioration in credit quality measures (see Chapter 13), in turn, may cause vendors to reduce the amount of credit they are willing to provide. Once again, loss of financial flexibility can feed on itself.

IN DEFENSE OF SLACK

Conditions are tough enough when credit is scarce, either because of general conditions in the financial markets or as a result of deterioration in a company's debt quality measures. Sometimes the situation is much worse, as a company finds itself actually prohibited from borrowing. Bank credit agreements typically impose restrictive covenants, which may include limitations on total indebtedness (see "Projecting Financial Flexibility" in Chapter 12). Beyond a certain point, a firm bound by such covenants cannot continue borrowing to meet its obligations.

A typical consequence of violating debt covenants or striving to head off bankruptcy is that management reduces discretionary expenditures to avoid losing control. Many items that a company can cut without disrupting operations in the short run are essential to its long-term health. Advertising and research are obvious targets for cutbacks. Their benefits are visible only in future periods, while their costs are apparent in the current period. Over many years, a company that habitually scrimps on such expenditures can impair its competitiveness, thereby transforming a short-term problem into a long-term one.

Avoiding this pattern of decline is the primary benefit of financial flexibility. If during good times a company can generate positive cash flow before financing, it will not have to chop capital expenditures and other outlays that represent investments in its future. Nor, in all likelihood, will a company that maintains some **slack** be forced to eliminate its dividend under duress. The company will consequently avoid tarnishing its image in the capital markets and raising the cost of future financings.

Despite the blessings that financial flexibility confers, however, maintaining a funds cushion is not universally regarded as a wise corporate policy. The opposing view is based on a definition of free cash flow as "cash flow in excess of that required to fund all of a firm's projects that have positive net present values when discounted at the relevant cost of capital."[7] According to this argument, management should dividend all excess cash flow to shareholders. The only alternative is to invest it in low-return projects (or possibly even lower-return marketable securities), thereby preventing shareholders from earning fair returns on a portion of their capital. Left to their own devices, argue the proponents of this view, managers will trap cash in low-return investments because their compensation tends to be positively related to the growth of assets under their control. Therefore, management should be encouraged to remit all excess cash to shareholders. If encouragement fails to do the trick, the threat of hostile takeover should be employed, say those who minimize the value of financial flexibility.

The argument against retaining excess cash flow certainly sounds logical. It is supported, moreover, by numerous studies[8] indicating the tendency of companies to continue investing even after they have exhausted their good opportunities. Growing as it does out of economic theory, though, the argument must be applied judiciously in practice. Overinvestment has unquestionably led, in many industries, to prolonged periods of excess capacity, producing in turn chronically poor profitability. In retrospect, the firms involved would have served their shareholders better if they had increased their dividend payouts or repurchased stock, instead of constructing new plants. That judgment, however, benefits from hindsight. Managers may have overinvested because they believed forecasts of economic growth that ultimately proved too optimistic. Had demand grown at the expected rate, a firm that had declined to expand capacity might have been unable to maintain its market share. In the long run, failing to keep up with the scale economies achieved by more expansion-minded competitors could have harmed shareholders more than a few years of excess capacity. The financial analyst's job includes making judgments about a firm's reinvestment policies—without the benefit of hindsight—and does not consist of passively accepting the prevailing wisdom that low returns in the near term prove that an industry has no future opportunities worth exploiting.

A subtler point not easily captured by theorists is that financial flexibility can translate directly into operating flexibility. Keeping cash "trapped" in marketable securities can enable a firm to gain an edge over "lean-and-mean" competitors when tight credit conditions make it difficult to finance working capital needs. Another less obvious risk of eschewing financial flexibility is the danger of permanently losing experienced skilled workers through temporary layoffs occasioned by recessions. Productivity suffers during the subsequent recovery as a consequence of laid-off skilled employees finding permanent jobs elsewhere. It may therefore be economical to continue to run plants, thereby deliberately building up inventory, to keep valued workers on the payroll. This strategy is difficult to implement without some capability of adjusting to a sudden increase in working capital financing requirements.

CONCLUSIONS

Over the past three decades, the statement of cash flow has become a valuable complement to the other statements. It is invaluable in many situations where the balance sheet and income statement provide only limited insight. For example, the income statement is a dubious measure of the success of a highly leveraged company that is being managed to minimize, rather than maximize, reported profits. Similarly, it is largely irrelevant whether the balance sheet of a company with an already substantially depleted net worth shows 10% lower equity in the current quarter than in the previous one. The primary concern of the investor or creditor at such times is whether the company can buy enough time to solve its operating problems by continuing its near-term obligations.

The cash flow statement does more than enrich the analysis of companies encountering risks and opportunities that the income statement and balance sheet are not designed to portray. It also helps to identify the life-cycle categories into which companies fit. At all stages of development, and whatever challenges a company faces, financial flexibility is essential to meeting those challenges. The cash flow statement is the best tool for measuring flexibility, which, contrary to a widely held view, is not merely a security blanket for squeamish investors. In the hands of an aggressive but prudent management, a cash flow cushion can enable a company to sustain essential long-term investment spending when competitors are forced to cut back.

QUESTIONS

1. Describe the growth of sales and earnings over time in terms of life-cycle stages of the firm.
2. Does Wal-Mart have any additional cushion?
3. Explain how financial flexibility is essential to meeting challenges no matter what the stage of development.
4. Explain why it is that Wal-Mart exhibited exceptional financial flexibility in the fiscal year that ended January 31, 2001.
5. Given that expectations about future cash flows are not realized and investors find themselves lacking the cash required to meet interest expense and the scheduled principal payments, briefly explain the consequences of each of the options available to the investors.
6. How can analysts gauge the safety of dividends?
7. How can financial flexibility translate into operating flexibility?
8. How did Polaroid compound its cash flow problems?
9. How do the cash flow characteristics of an emerging growth company and the conditions prevailing in the capital markets combine to influence the ability of the company to fund its growth?
10. How is the gap between cash outflows and cash inflows covered in most startups?
11. How is the incentive of a private company to report income different from a public company?
12. In general, what is the principal cash flow characteristic of startup companies?
13. In which way does depreciation influence the cash flows of the firm?
14. In what way does the advantage of the Statement of Cash Flows correspond to the shortcomings of the Income Statement?
15. Is depreciation a cash flow?
16. Is it unethical (or illegal) for a company to keep two sets of books?
17. Is maintaining a funds cushion universally regarded as a wise corporate policy?

18. Under what circumstances does a formerly profitable company report a loss in its first year as an LBO?
19. Under what circumstances is the cash flow statement invaluable?
20. What are the cash flow characteristics of mature industry companies, and what drives their sources and uses of funds?
21. What are the cash-flows characteristics of an established growth company? What is the role of depreciation?
22. What is a key objective of management as it faces various choices in difficult times?
23. What is a typical consequence of violating debt covenants?
24. What is adjusted working capital and what role does it play in assessing financial flexibility?
25. What is happening when a company is said to be experiencing "net negative reinvestment" in its business?
26. What is Polaroid's underlying problem?
27. What is the argument against retaining excess cash flow?
28. What is the best tool for measuring financial flexibility?
29. What is the force underlying Wal-Mart's lack of dependence on external funds?
30. What is the primary benefit of financial flexibility?
31. What is the risk of heavy reliance on external financing for rapid growth?
32. What must be emphasized when evaluating the downside of an LBO?
33. What questions regarding financial flexibility can an analyst answer after a careful study of the cash flow statement?
34. What term is applied to the cash flow that remains available after operating expenses and capital expenditures?
35. What would analysts evaluating the LBO miss if they focused on earnings instead of cash flows?
36. When did SFAS 95 (the FASB statement that requires firms to report the statement of cash flows) become mandatory?
37. Why is an established growth company less vulnerable to disruptions in the capital markets than its startup counterpart?
38. Why is it that the Income Statement is not especially relevant in the context of pending bankruptcy?
39. Why is the Statement of Cash Flows the most useful tool for analyzing highly leveraged companies?
40. Why is Wal-Mart's ability to self-finance growth a great advantage?
41. Why must emerging growth companies aggressively expand their productive facilities, and what is the implication of this strategy for their cash flow needs?

three

A Closer Look at Profits

5

What Is Profit?

Profits hold an exalted place in the business world and in economic theory. The necessity of producing profits imposes order and discipline on business organizations. It fosters cost-reducing innovations, which in turn promote the efficient use of scarce resources. The profit motive also encourages savings and risk-taking, two indispensable elements of economic development. Finally, profitability is a yardstick by which businesspeople can measure their achievements and justify their claims to compensation.

In view of all these essential economic functions, one might suppose that users of financial statements would have long since devised a universally agreed-on definition of profit. This is the case, however, only at the following, extremely rudimentary level:

$$Profit = Revenue - Costs$$

Defining profit in such a manner merely stirs up questions, however: What is revenue? Which costs count? Or, more precisely, which costs count now and which count later? Because these questions can be answered in many different ways, countless definitions of profit are in common use. For analysts of financial statements, the most important distinction to understand is between bona fide profits and accounting profits.

BONA FIDE PROFITS VERSUS ACCOUNTING PROFITS

In defining bona fide profits, the simple formula, revenue minus costs, represents a useful starting point. When calculating this kind of profit, the analyst must take care to consider only genuine revenues and deduct all relevant costs. A nonexhaustive list of costs includes labor, materials, occupancy, services purchased, depreciation of equipment, and taxes. No matter how meticulously the analyst carries out these computations, however, no calculation of profit can be satisfactory unless it passes a litmus test:

> *After a company earns a bona fide profit, its owners are wealthier than they were beforehand.*

To underscore the point, there can be no bona fide profit without an increase in wealth. Bona fide profits are the only kind of profits that truly matter in financial analysis.

As for accounting profits, Generally Accepted Accounting Principles define voluminous rules for calculating them with extraordinary precision. For financial analysts, however, the practical definition of an accounting profit is simple:

> *An accounting profit is whatever the accounting rules say it is.*

If, during a stated interval, a business adds nothing to its owners' wealth, but the accounting rules state that it has earned a profit, that is good enough. An accounting profit that reflects no genuine increase in wealth is certainly sufficient for many stock market investors. They cheerfully assign a price-earnings multiple to any number that a reputable accounting firm waves its magic wand over and declares to be a profit.

WHAT IS REVENUE?

Suppose, for example, that an entrepreneur launches a restaurant franchising business. The fictitious Salsa Meister International does not operate any Salsa Meister restaurants. It merely sells franchises to other entrepreneurs and collects franchise fees.

The franchised restaurants, sad to say, consistently lose money. That fact has no bearing on Salsa Meister International's accounting profit, however. The restaurants' operations are not part of Salsa Meister International, their revenues are not its revenues, and their costs are not its costs. Salsa Meister International's income consists entirely of franchise fees, which it earns by rendering the franchisees such services as developing menus, providing accounting systems, training restaurant employees, and creating advertising campaigns.

An astute analyst will ask how money-losing franchisees come up with cash to pay fees. The diagram in Exhibit 5.1 answers this riddle. Salsa Meister International sells stock to the public, then lends the proceeds to the

EXHIBIT 5.1 Turning Stock Market Proceeds into Revenue

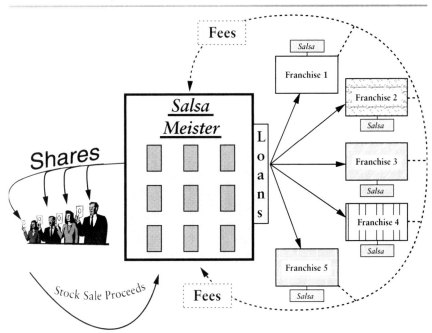

franchisees. The franchisees send the cash right back to Salsa Meister International under the rubric of fees. Salsa Meister International gratefully accepts the fees, which exceed the modest costs of running a corporate headquarters, and renames them revenue.

According to generally accepted accounting principles, Salsa Meister International has earned a profit. Investors apply a price-earnings multiple to the accounting profit. On the strength of that valuation, the company goes forward with its next public stock offering. Once again, the proceeds finance the payment of fees by franchisees, whose numbers have meanwhile increased in connection with the Salsa Meister chain's expansion into new regions. Accounting profits rise and the cycle of relabeling stock market proceeds first as fees and finally as earnings starts all over again.

The astute analyst is troubled, however. Cutting through the form of the transactions to the substance, it is clear that Salsa Meister International's wealth has not increased. Cash has simply traveled from the shareholders to the company, to the franchisees, and then back to the company, undergoing a few name changes along the way.

Merely circulating funds does not increase wealth. If Jack hands Jill a dollar, which she promptly hands right back to him, neither party is better off after the "transaction" than before it. By definition, neither Jack nor Jill has earned a bona fide profit. Salsa Meister International has not earned a bona fide profit, either, regardless of what GAAP may say about accounting profits.

Sooner or later, investors will come to this realization. When that happens, the company will lose its ability to manufacture accounting profits by raising new funds in the stock market. Salsa Meister's stock price will then fall to its intrinsic value—zero. Investors will suffer heavy losses that they could have avoided by asking whether the company's reported profits truly reflected increases in wealth. Moreover, the investors will continue making similar mistakes unless they begin to understand that bona fide profits sometimes differ radically from accounting profits.

WHICH COSTS COUNT?

The willingness to take accounting profits at something other than face value is an essential element of genuinely useful financial statement analysis. It is likewise imperative that analysts exercise care in deciding what to substitute for a GAAP definition of profit. Once they leave the GAAP world of agreed-on rules, analysts enter a free market of ideas, where numerous parties hawk competing versions of earnings.

Many of the variations hang on the question of which costs to deduct in deriving the most analytically informative definition of earnings. Although some of the popular variants offer insight into knotty problems of financial statement analysis, others have the opposite effect of obscuring the facts. Many issuers of financial statements attempt to exploit dissatisfaction with GAAP by encouraging analysts to adopt earnings measures that make their own profits appear higher than either their accounting profits or their bona fide profits.

The archetype for most of today's alternative earnings measures is a version that adds back depreciation. As far back as 1930, an investment expert urged investors to ignore accounting-based earnings in the following words:

Textbooks will advise the investor to look for earnings figures which give effect to depreciation charges. But depreciation, after all, is a purely accounting item, and can be adjusted, within limits, to show such net earnings as are desired. Therefore it would seem preferable for the investor to obtain, if possible, earnings before depreciation, and to make his own estimate of depreciation in arriving at approximate net earnings.[1]

Observe that the author does not dispute the relevance of depreciation to the calculation of earnings. Rather, he objects that they are too malleable.[2] The issuer of the statements can raise or lower its reported earnings simply by using its latitude to assume shorter or longer average lives for its depreciable assets.

It is fair to assume, in the case of financial statements that companies present to potential investors, that "such net earnings as are desired" are higher than the company's bona fide profits. Therefore, the necessary adjustment is to *increase* depreciation and thereby *reduce* earnings. The author agrees with today's boosters of alternative earnings measures that proper analysis requires adjustments to reported income, but he is very far from urging analysts to ignore depreciation altogether.

Promoters of many companies with negligible reported earnings, on the other hand, are not bashful about urging investors to disregard depreciation. This audacious assault on the very foundations of accrual accounting draws its inspiration from the world of privately owned real estate, where the logic of managing a public company is turned upside-down. Instead of exploiting every bit of latitude in the accounting rules to maximize reported earnings, private owners of real estate strive to minimize reported income, and by extension, income taxes. Accordingly, when a private investor acquires a building (a depreciable asset) and the land that it sits on (which is not depreciable), she typically attributes as large a portion of the purchase price as possible to the building. That treatment maximizes the depreciation expense and minimizes the owner's taxes.

Let us suppose that annual rental revenue on the building offsets the landlord's out-of-pocket expenses, such as maintenance, repairs, property taxes, and interest on the property's mortgage. The owner, in other words, is breaking even, before taking into account the noncash expense of depreciation. Including depreciation, the property shows an annual loss, which reduces the owner's income tax bill. Let us also assume that after a few years, the owner sells the land and building. After paying off the mortgage balance, she walks away with more cash than she originally invested, thanks to the tendency of real estate values to rise over time.

Recapping the real estate investor's experience, she has sold the property for more than she paid. Her gain has not been reduced along the way by net cash outlays on operations. On the contrary, the tax savings produced by the noncash depreciation expense have contributed to the rise in her wealth. The key point is that the investor is wealthier than she was before she bought the building. According to our definition, she has realized a bona fide profit, despite reporting losses every single year. Adding to the paradox is the investor's success in selling the property for a gain. Economic theory states that an investment has value only because it produces profits. By extension, the value can increase only if the profits increase. In this instance, however, the property's value rose despite an uninterrupted flow of red ink. (The result calls to mind the observation of two officials of the Soviet Union in the 1939 film *Ninotchka:* "Capitalistic methods . . . They accumulate millions by taking loss after loss."[3])

Naturally, these curious events have a rational explanation. The rate at which the tax code allows owners to write off property overstates actual wear-and-tear. Over the typically very long life of a building, it may get depreciated several times over for tax purposes. The disparity between economic depreciation and tax-based depreciation may be viewed as a subsidy for socially productive investment. Alternatively, it can be seen as a testament to the real estate operators' influence over the legislators who write the United States Tax Code.

Either way, a conventional income statement provides a cockeyed view of the profitability of buying and selling buildings. A closer approximation of reality ignores the depreciation expense altogether and focuses on **cash-on-cash profit.** In the simplest terms, the owner lays out a sum at the beginning of the investment and takes out a bigger sum at the end, while also generating cash—through tax savings—during the period in which she owns the building.

HOW FAR CAN THE CONCEPT BE STRETCHED?

To a limited extent, a profitability analysis that ignores depreciation is applicable outside the world of real estate. In the broadcasting business, companies typically record depreciation and amortization expense that far exceeds physical wear-and-tear on assets. For example, when a company buys a radio or television station, the price reflects a comparatively small component of plant and equipment. The larger portion of the station's value derives from its exclusive right to utilize part of the broadcasting spectrum, a scarce resource that tends to become more valuable over time. Much as in the real estate illustration, the broadcaster may show perennial losses after depreciation, yet realize a handsome profit when it finally sells the station. Instead of analyzing broadcasters on the basis of conventional net income, it is appropriate for analysts to focus on broadcast cash flow, usually defined as:

operating income + depreciation and amortization + corporate overhead

(A more meticulous calculation of broadcast cash flow deducts cash outlays for acquisition of new programming while deducting the amortization of the cost of previously acquired programming, both of which can be found on the statement of cash flows.)

The deliberate neglect of depreciation is an analytical option that should be used with discretion. In many industries, fixed assets consist mainly of machines or vehicles that really do diminish in value through use. The major risk of analytical error does not arise from the possibility that reported depreciation expense will substantially exceed economic depreciation, but the reverse.

Through a false analogy with real estate and broadcasting, any marginally unprofitable company in a capital-intensive business can declare itself to be in the black. The trick is simply to proclaim that analysts should no longer consider depreciation. Supposed earnings generated in such fashion, however, qualify as neither accounting profits nor bona fide profits.

CONCLUSION

Despite the critical importance of measuring profit, businesspeople cannot produce a definition that is satisfactory in every situation. Even the simple formula of revenue minus costs founders on the malleability of accounting-based revenues and costs. As Chapters 6 and 7 demonstrate, these basic measures of corporate performance are far too subject to manipulation and distortion to be taken at face value. Also, our brief discussions of real estate and leveraged buyouts show that net earnings can be calculated in perfect accordance with GAAP, yet bear little relation to an investor's rate of return.

In light of such observations, financial analysts must walk a fine line. On the one hand, they must not lose touch with economic reality by hewing to accounting orthodoxy. On the other hand, they must not accept the version of reality that seekers of cheap capital would like to foist on them. Analysts should be skeptical of claims that a business's alleged "costs" are mere accounting conventions and that anyone who believes otherwise is a fuddy-duddy.

QUESTIONS

1. For analysis of financial statements, what is the most important distinction to understand?
2. For financial analysts, what is the practical definition of an accounting profit?

3. How can Salsa Meister International show a profit when the franchised restaurants consistently lose money?
4. How can the riddle of a franchiser's profits and franchisee's losses be resolved?
5. How does the major risk of analytical error in the reporting of depreciation expense arise?
6. In what way are real estate and the broadcasting business similar?
7. Under what conditions is "red ink" (showing losses) not a sign that the firm is in trouble?
8. Under what conditions is there a universally agreed-upon definition of profit?
9. Under what conditions is the physical wear-and-tear of plant and equipment not considered an expense in the calculation of profits?
10. What are some of the real-life situations that would dampen the apparent profits in leveraged buyouts?
11. What are some of the reasons profits hold such an exalted place in the business world and economic theory?
12. What inspired the attack on the accrual accounting treatment of depreciation?
13. What is the essential idea of a leveraged buyout?
14. What is the fine line that financial analysts must walk?
15. What is the litmus test that a calculation of bona fide profits must pass?
16. What is the objection to the relevance of depreciation to the calculation of earnings?
17. What is the rational explanation of the phenomenon of an investment increasing in value while generating losses?
18. Why and how will Salsa Meister International's method of converting losses to profits end?
19. Why is conventional earnings analysis not well suited to measure the performance of a leverage buyout?
20. Why is it that the simple formula of revenues minus costs must not be taken at face value?
21. Why should the astute analyst be troubled by the way Salsa Meister International converts losses into profits?

Revenue Recognition

Experience teaches that it can be dangerous to accept reported revenues at face value, even if they have been audited. Many corporations employ highly aggressive recognition practices that comply with GAAP yet distort the underlying economic reality. Sometimes, executives hell-bent on "making their numbers" will cross the line into fraudulent revenue recognition. Often, outward signs of exceptional success indicate, in reality, a high probability of downward revisions of previously reported revenues. Under intense pressure to maintain their stock prices, companies characterized by extremely rapid sales growth seem particularly prone to take liberties. Informix vividly portrayed these hazards in 1997 by rescinding a substantial portion of its past revenues.

INFORMIX'S TROUBLES BEGIN

Informix was the best-performing United States software stock for the period 1990 through 1995.[1] By the beginning of 1997, the company was widely regarded as a serious challenger to Oracle's leadership in the business of creating large corporate databases. Informix even taunted its rival on a billboard alongside the interstate highway near Oracle's office towers, warning drivers that they were approaching a "dinosaur crossing."

At the same time that it was trash-talking the competition, however, management was taking a huge risk in its operating strategy. Hoping to boost its market share, Informix shifted its marketing resources to Universal Server, a new type of database intended to store different kinds of data, such as images and video. Informix's strategic initiative proved premature. Not only did the new product remain unperfected, but corporate customers were not yet indicating demand for multimedia database technology.

On top of the product-related woes, some analysts were questioning Informix's revenue recognition practices. They grew wary when Informix revealed that about $170 million of its 1996 sales to computer makers and other resellers represented software that had not yet been resold to final customers. Roughly $55 million of that total involved agreements by computer manufacturers to purchase software equivalent in value to the hardware that Informix bought from them.

The Fine Points of Software Revenues

Chairman and Chief Executive Officer Phillip E. White declared that his company's sales practices were properly disclosed and in compliance with the accounting rules. Several independent accounting experts backed up his statement. None of this meant, however, that Informix's revenue recognition policies were the only, or even the best, approach available under GAAP.

For software producers, shipping a product to a reseller does not necessarily represent a definitive sale. Just like "old-economy" manufacturers of basic industrial and consumer goods, software producers can expect run-of-the-mill returns of defective items. In addition, a reasonably predictable portion of customers will fail to pay their accounts in full. Deferring a portion of revenue for these contingencies is comparatively straightforward, but other recognition issues are more judgmental for a company such as Informix. Uncertainty lingers over a sale until the software has been installed at the end user and the end user's staff has been trained in its use. Furthermore, resellers often have latitude to return products they cannot sell. At the beginning of 1997, with the accounting profession still developing standards to address these complicating factors, software companies varied widely in their revenue recognition practices. Critics contended that Informix's approach was overly optimistic.

The Picture Worsens

As the year wore on, the company's troubles mounted. On April Fools' Day of 1997, Informix stunned investors by disclosing that its first-quarter sales had fallen short of analysts' expectations by $100 million, or 40%. Two days later, the company reported a $140.1 million loss for the quarter, down from a $15.9 million profit in the comparable 1996 period. Sales were 34% below year-earlier levels, at $133.7 million versus $204.1 million. Between March 31 and April 3, Informix's stock price plummeted by 41%.

Yet another shock arrived on May 1. Chief Financial Officer Alan Henricks resigned after just three months in the position. To seasoned investors, such an abrupt departure by a senior manager represented a telltale sign of trouble. They were not reassured when Henricks declined to explain his decision, even as former Informix executives reportedly said that he had pressed for more conservative accounting policies than CEO White favored.[2] White denied that policy differences caused his CFO to step down, instead citing unspecified personal considerations.

Before long, White himself was contributing to the front-office turmoil. In July, under pressure from the company's board of directors he resigned first as CEO and then as chairman. Meanwhile, Informix failed to meet the deadline for filing its second-quarter financials, another classic red flag for investors. When the quarterly filing belatedly arrived on August 7, it revealed a loss of $120.5 million, including a $62.1 million charge for restructuring costs. Informix's operating loss of $80.5 million before the special charge was larger than analysts had expected.

The charge for restructuring costs showed that the financial reporting controversy was heating up, rather than simmering down. To correct earlier instances of improper revenue recognition, Informix announced that it would reduce its previously reported 1996 revenue of $939.3 million by $70 million to $100 million. According to new chief executive officer Robert Finocchio, the company had booked some transactions in the wrong periods and others without proper documentation. He added that Informix would recognize some of the revenues in future quarters, but the rest would disappear.[3] The company's investigation of past accounting practices had uncovered forty incidents of improper recognition, primarily in Japan, the United Kingdom, Germany, and Central and Eastern Europe, with a few found in the United States.

Still, the parade of bad news continued. On September 22, Informix's already depressed share price tumbled 22% as the company announced that the downward restatement of 1997 revenues might be as great as $200 million, twice the previously announced high-end figure of $100 million. Moreover, management revealed that the improper recognition practices extended back to 1995, resulting in a possible revenue reduction of as much as $50 million for that year. In certain instances, said the company, sales representatives had made informal side agreements to provide resellers extra funds to finance sales.[4] Informix's 1997 10-K elaborated:

The unauthorized and undisclosed agreements with resellers introduced acceptance contingencies, permitted resellers to return unsold licenses for refunds, extended payment terms, or committed the Company to assist resellers in reselling the licenses to end-users. Accordingly, license revenue from these transactions that was recorded at the time product was delivered to resellers should have instead been recorded at the time all conditions on the sale lapsed.[5]

Lessons for Analysts

In the end, the company restated its revenues downward by a total of $244 million for the period 1994 through the second quarter of 1997. Informix acknowledged that it had overstated its revenue by 4.0% in 1994, 12.9% in 1995, and 29.1% in 1996. This year-by-year escalation followed a frequently observed pattern of falsification. Bonus-seeking managers may initially veer off the straight-and-narrow by "borrowing" a small amount from future revenue, intending to "pay it back" the following year, but they instead fall further and further behind. Eventually, the gap between reported revenues and economic reality grows too large to sustain. Outside analysts' skepticism mounts and closer auditing of the books unmasks the false reporting.

The Informix affair also teaches analysts not to construe auditor-certified compliance with GAAP as an assurance of integrity in financial reporting. If senior managers set the tone by pushing the rules to their limits, executives a step or two lower in hierarchy may feel emboldened to break the rules altogether. Liberal reporting differs from fraudulent reporting, in a legal sense, but a corporate culture that embraces the former can foster the latter.

In October 1997, the American Institute of Certified Public Accountants reduced the wiggle room for companies such as Informix. The accounting body's Statement of Position 97-2 (SOP 97-2), "Software Revenue Recognition," superseded SOP 91-1 and at long last addressed the industry-specific complexities of determining when a sale was truly a sale. SOP 97-2 required companies to recognize revenue from a software arrangement by allocating a fair value to each element, such as software products, enhancements, upgrades, installation, training, and post-contract customer support. Determination of each element's fair value was to be based on objective evidence specific to the software vendor. The AICPA subsequently deferred the effective date of SOP 97-2 until, with SOP 98-4 ("Modification of SOP 97-2, Software Revenue Recognition with Respect to Certain Transactions") in February 1998, the accounting body was able to specify what constituted "objective evidence."

As a consequence of adopting SOP 97-2 as of January 1998, Informix began deferring some license revenues that it formerly would have recognized on delivery of the software. That is to say, the company took considerable latitude in booking revenues until the accounting profession developed rules to deal with all the complexities of the software business. Investors should not have been lulled by the fact that Informix's pre-1998 financial reporting satisfied the minimum requirements of GAAP. Management's aggressiveness painted a rosier picture than it would have been allowed under standards better adapted to the intricacies of the software business.

Neither did the certification of Informix's statements by independent auditor Ernst & Young prevent investors from receiving revenue figures that proved too high, in retrospect. As the reliability of the company's past financial statements became increasingly suspect during 1997, Informix felt obliged to hire a second accounting firm to advise its directors. Meanwhile, both Informix and Ernst & Young became targets of a class action suit by shareholders. The plaintiffs alleged that the company's executives had overstated revenues by claiming to have sold software that was merely shipped to resellers temporarily and then returned. On the strength of these faked sales, the shareholders claimed, the officials had boosted Informix's share price to facilitate their personal sales of stock. In May 1999, Ernst & Young agreed to pay $34 million as its share of a $142 million settlement of the litigation. The auditor stated, as defendants often do under such circumstances, that it settled to avoid costly litigation.[6]

By the time Ernst & Young accepted the financial consequences of its role in the matter, Informix had replaced the firm with a new auditor. In dismissing Ernst & Young, Informix's board did not criticize the firm for signing off on 1994–1997 revenue figures that subsequently turned out to be overstated. The board did, however, mention a dispute over recognition of revenue from industrial manufacturers in the first quarter of 1998. The disagreement, in short, arose well after the earlier improper booking of sales came to light and new management controls were implemented. According to Informix, the company resolved the dispute to Ernst & Young's satisfaction, deferred approximately $6.2 million of revenue, and underwent yet another restatement of its financials. Ernst & Young responded that Informix's statement was incomplete. Shortly before its dismissal, said the auditing firm, it had informed the board's audit committee that a lack of necessary resources in Informix's financial reporting departments had created difficulty in accumulating the accurate information required for timely disclosure. This condition was a material weakness, in Ernst & Young's view.[7]

To an outside analyst, it appeared that Ernst & Young ran into conflict with Informix for enforcing strict standards in 1998 after being sued by shareholders for alleged laxity in earlier years. Dismissal of Informix's auditor was one more classic warning sign for analysts, on top of the senior management upheavals and delayed financial statement filing of 1997. Events throughout 1997 and 1998 reinforced an essential point about revenue recognition: Even when an independent accounting firm certifies that a company's financials have been prepared in accordance with generally accepted accounting principles, the analyst must stay alert for evidence that the numbers misrepresent the economic reality.

CALLING THE SIGNALS

Aspiring analysts should extract at least one invaluable lesson from the study of Informix's aggressive revenue recognition: Staying alert to evidence of flawed, or possibly fraudulent, reporting is essential, even when the auditors put their blessing on the numbers. Exactly what sort of evidence should one look for, however?

The specific answer is not the same in every case. As a rule, though, distorting one section of the financial statements throws the numbers out of whack in some other section. Assiduous tracking of financial ratios should raise serious questions about a company's reporting, at a minimum. To illustrate this point, let us consider another example from the computer software industry.

KnowledgeWare's chief executive officer was Pro Football Hall of Fame quarterback Fran Tarkenton. After retiring from the National Football League in 1978, the one-time record-holder in touchdowns and passing yards founded Tarkenton Software, which he merged with KnowledgeWare in 1986. Specializing in client-server development tools, a type of software used in creating programs for networked personal computers, the company came to be regarded as an emerging star in its industry. In the early 1990s, however, KnowledgeWare fell behind its competitors in adopting new technology[8] and overextended itself through a series of acquisitions.[9] As the company's new products failed to take off, KnowledgeWare began reporting losses and in July 1994 laid off a quarter of its workforce. With operations reporting negative cash flow, KnowledgeWare "appeared to be close to being out of money," according to an industry analyst.[10]

At that point, Tarkenton, who was renowned as a scrambler during his professional football days, managed to get KnowledgeWare out of an extremely tight spot. On August 1, 1994, the company announced an agreement to be acquired by Sterling Software. Sterling, a leader in electronic commerce and systems software, agreed to pay 0.2893 shares of its common stock for each KnowledgeWare share, producing a purchase price of approximately $143 million.

The rebound in KnowledgeWare's fortunes proved short-lived, however. Within a month of its pact with Sterling, the company announced a $19.0 million loss for the fiscal year ending June 30, 1994. In addition to recording

$15.4 million of red ink in the fourth quarter, KnowledgeWare restated its earnings for the first nine months. The previously reported $4.46 million profit turned into a $3.6 million loss and the company's stock price plunged by 45% in one day.

KnowledgeWare's new travails arose from a decision implemented during fiscal 1994. In an effort to boost revenues, the company began supplementing its own sales force's efforts with agreements to market its products through resellers. Almost immediately, the company started to encounter difficulties in collecting receivables generated by the resellers. In restating the results, management said that it had booked as revenues certain sales for which collections were not made.

The revelation of financial reporting problems initially threatened to scuttle the acquisition by Sterling Software.[11] In the end, though, Sterling agreed to go ahead on revised terms. Instead of paying 0.2893 of its own shares for each of KnowledgeWare's, Sterling slashed its offer to 0.1653 shares. Furthermore, Sterling announced that it would acquire only 80% of KnowledgeWare's stock for the time being. The other 20% of the purchase price would go into escrow as a contingency for possible lawsuits by KnowledgeWare shareholders.

Fran Tarkenton succeeded in obtaining approval of the reduced terms, but the shareholders' meeting was testy. Sterling's concerns about possible lawsuits had proven well founded, with the plaintiffs alleging that management had inflated KnowledgeWare's stock price by misrepresenting the company's financial condition. An attorney representing the disgruntled shareholders attempted to query Tarkenton about the merits of the Sterling offer, but the wily ex-quarterback refused to take questions.[12] His stiff-arm tactics worked. The favorable shareholder vote eliminated the final obstacle to the merger. By the terms of the agreement, Tarkenton gained a seat on Sterling's board and a three-year consulting agreement at $300,000 per annum.

Despite all his nimbleness, Tarkenton failed to emerge from the affair entirely unscathed. In 1999, the Securities and Exchange Commission charged him with directing a plan to overstate KnowledgeWare's revenues and profits during 1993 and 1994. According to the allegations, the company recorded sales in instances in which distributors were told that they did not have to pay for software unless they succeeded in reselling it. The SEC claimed that the objective was to convince investors that KnowledgeWare was making a comeback from its fiscal 1992 operating loss.[13]

Tarkenton settled the SEC charges by paying a $100,000 civil penalty and disgorging an amount equivalent to the bonus he received as a consequence of the overstated profits—$54,187, plus interest. His attorney hastened to say that his client had neither admitted nor denied the charges and was "pleased to have this matter behind him." Continuing in a vein familiar to aficionados of financial reporting scandals, the lawyer added, "The events in question took place about five or six years ago during Mr. Tarkenton's tenure at KnowledgeWare, and he has long since moved on with his life and to other business ventures."[14]

To be fair, KnowledgeWare amended its financial reporting practices once the receivables problem came to light. The company altered its method of recognizing revenue to bring reported results into line with the collection experience in its reseller program. Under the new, more conservative policy, KnowledgeWare recognized software license revenue from resellers only on receipt of payment. Reasonably enough, the company continued to book sales on shipment when it sent the goods directly to end users, as long as specific credit information was available to form a reasonable basis for estimating the collectibility of the receivables.

Fixing the accounting problem after the fact, however, did not help investors who valued KnowledgeWare on the basis of its originally reported profits. Analysts had to rely on their own devices to identify the potential for an earnings restatement before the disclosure devastated Knowledge-Ware's stock price. At least a few analysts, it appears, did just that. Around the time that the Sterling Software deal was announced, some analysts were reportedly worried that liberal revenue recognition would lead to a write-off.[15] They could have drawn that inference by careful scrutiny of standard financial ratios.

Exhibit 6.1 shows that revenues and receivables began moving out of sync from the moment KnowledgeWare launched its reseller program. In the first quarter of fiscal 1994 (ending September 30, 1993), revenues dropped by 15.5% from the preceding quarter, yet receivables rose by

EXHIBIT 6.1   Revenues and Accounts Receivable
KnowledgeWare, Inc. ($000 omitted)

	Quarter Ending			
	1993		1994	
	June 30	September 30	December 31	March 31
Revenues	$40,426	$34,144	$38,178	$38,928
Accounts receivable	36,894	37,084	41,506	50,252
Days sales outstanding*	83	98	100	117

*As reported by company.

Source: KnowledgeWare Forms 10Q and 10K.

0.5%. Management's discussion and analysis in the Form 10-Q for the period noted that in terms of days sales outstanding, receivables leaped from 83 to 98 days. The adverse trend continued, with DSO growing to 100 days in the second fiscal quarter, then soaring to 117 in the third, when receivables increased by 21.1% on nearly flat revenues. By the end of the third fiscal quarter (March 31, 1994), accounts receivable stood roughly one-third higher than at the preceding fiscal year-end, even though revenues had fallen slightly.

To seasoned financial analysts, the diverging trends of revenues and receivables looked worrisome even in fiscal 1994's first quarter. Management's discussion of the matter, however, was as brief as its analysis was thin. The "Liquidity and Capital Resources" section of the MD&A for September 30, 1993, elaborated on the data only to offer the encouraging news that the percentage of gross trade accounts receivable subject to payment terms beyond 90 days had fallen from 25.0% to 21.7% during the quarter. The change implied that KnowledgeWare would be able to convert assets to cash more swiftly than formerly, thereby bolstering its liquidity. On the face of it, the quality of KnowledgeWare's receivables was improving, possibly offsetting concerns about their increasing quantity. In the quarter ending December 31, 1993, management proudly reported a further drop in the portion of receivables dated beyond ninety days, to 10.4%.

During the quarter ending March 31, 1994, according to KnowledgeWare's Form 10-Q, the percentage declined once again, to 9.4%. Curiously, though, the company now indicated that the beyond-90-days ratio on June 30, 1993 had been 17.8%, rather than 25.0%, as previously reported. Management did not explain the discrepancy or even draw attention to it. Analysts had to discover the restated number by comparing the latest 10-Q with its predecessors.

The March 31, 1994, report also contained several entirely new disclosures:

- On top of the 9.4% of receivables subject to payment terms beyond 90 days, another 16% were subject to government funding provisions and would likely take more than 90 days to collect. Federal and state government agencies, which are generally slow to pay, represented a growing portion of KnowledgeWare's business.
- Notwithstanding the relative decline in receivables dated beyond 90 days, the number of transactions with "extended payment terms" (not specifically defined) was growing.
- Resellers in the nongovernment market accounted for approximately 6.2% of revenues for the three months ending March 31, 1994. Many of the resellers, said KnowledgeWare, were not well capitalized and

therefore represented greater credit risk than the company's typical end-user customers. KnowledgeWare compounded the inherent credit risk of dealing with resellers by offering them payment terms in excess of 90 days. Management hoped that the generous terms would induce resellers to initiate, increase, or accelerate revenues.

■ On March 31, 1994, KnowledgeWare had $3.1 million of accounts receivable (6.1% of the net total) that were past their due date by 90 days or more.

In summary, the receivables-related bombshell that KnowledgeWare dropped on August 30, 1994 was telegraphed by a simple comparison of revenues and receivables in KnowledgeWare's 10Q for the first fiscal quarter, received by the SEC way back on November 2, 1993. The company blunted the impact of that danger signal by stressing the declining ratio of receivables subject to payment terms beyond 90 days. Days sales outstanding continued to escalate over the following two quarters, however. In the fiscal third-quarter report, KnowledgeWare suddenly began disclosing additional, less upbeat, details about its receivables. Battle-scarred analysts of financial statements would have guessed that management's increased candor was the product of external prodding. To those alert enough to notice the unexplained change in the previously reported receivables-beyond-90-days ratio for the end of fiscal 1993, the sense of impending disaster should have become inescapable. By the middle of May 1994, more than three months before KnowledgeWare's restatement, the company's reported revenues were highly suspect. Not even the great Fran Tarkenton, in his glory days in the National Football League, benefited from so many tip-offs of his opponents' moves.

An Income versus Cash Disparity

The financial statements of a computer manufacturer likewise telegraphed future problems in the area of revenue recognition. Shortly before Kendall Square Research's October 1993 revision of its previously reported earnings, a research service known as *Financial Statement Alert* warned that the company was recognizing revenues too early.

Kendall Square reported $45.4 million in revenue in the first six quarters after it went public in March 1992. Loren Kellogg, copublisher of *Financial Statement Alert,* compared this income statement information with a figure from the company's statement of cash flows. Over the same 18-month period, Kendall Square's "cash received from customers" was just $25.7 million. Kellogg viewed the $19.7 million disparity between the two numbers as evidence that a large proportion of sales being booked by Kendall were dubious.

The warning proved prescient. Less than a month after Kellogg's analysis was reported in *The Wall Street Journal,* Kendall Square disclosed that its third-quarter 1993 revenues would be "substantially below" securities analysts' expectations. In lieu of earnings per share of 11 cents (the consensus forecast according to the forecast-tracking firm of Zacks Investment Research), the company said that it would report a loss. Additionally, Kendall Square delayed the release of its third-quarter earnings and announced the resignation of its senior vice president/treasurer, who had joined the company only a month earlier. All these developments, by the way, were classic indications of serious corporate problems.

Revenue recognition controversies were central to Kendall Square's difficulties. The company indicated that although third-quarter shipments were "generally in line with expectations," there was some question about the proper amount of revenue to recognize from the shipments. Jeffry Canin, an analyst at Salomon Brothers, speculated about a possible area of disagreement within the company. Some officials, he suggested, may have objected to counting as revenue rebates that might have been given to customers who agreed to upgrade to Kendall's next generation of computers. Smith Barney Shearson analyst Barry Bosak proposed the possibility that Kendall Square had been hurt by its reliance on sales to universities. A number of these institutions, which were in turn dependent on diminishing government funding, proved unable to pay. Indeed, some critics insinuated that Kendall Square had made research grants to educational institutions as quid pro quos for orders, a charge that management denied.

At any rate, Kendall Square's troubles continued, as auditor Price Waterhouse withdrew its clean opinion from the company's 1992 financial statements. Management revealed that the year's sales figure, originally reported as $20.5 million, included $4.2 million of "improperly recognized" revenue. Unaudited numbers for the first half of 1993 would also require restatement, the company added.

In the wake of these announcements, Kendall Square demoted and then fired its president, its chief financial officer, and the head of its technical products group. The company's acting chief executive officer announced that henceforth, Kendall Square would concentrate on building computers to order, instead of creating inventories in anticipation of orders. That reform was likely to reduce problems associated with revenue recognition, but by the time it was introduced, the damage to users of financial statements was substantial. At 7½, the company's stock price was down by about 70% from its peak three months earlier.[16]

ASTRAY ON LAYAWAY

On August 9, 2000, Wal-Mart Stores reported a 28% year-over-year increase in net income for its fiscal second quarter ending July 31. At $0.36, earnings per share (diluted) were up by 29%. Sales rose by a healthy 20%, climbing 5% at Wal-Mart units open for more than one year.

In light of these results, which one analyst characterized as "a very good quarter," the discount chain's share price might have been expected to rise. At the very least, investors would have expected the stock to hold steady, given that the EPS increase was in line with Wall Street analysts' consensus forecast, as reported by First Call/Thomson Financial. As it turned out, however, Wal-Mart's shares fell by $4.375 to $53.125. That represented an 8% decline on a day on which the Dow Jones Industrial Average changed only modestly (down 0.6%).

Both the *Wall Street Journal*[17] and the *Bloomberg* newswire[18] linked the paradoxical drop in Wal-Mart's stock to an accounting change that was expected to reduce the following (third) quarter's earnings. The retailer's management advised analysts to lower their earnings per share estimates for the August-to-October period by one-and-a-half to two cents, to reflect a shift in the company's method of accounting for layaway sales. In such transactions, customers reserve goods with down payments, then make additional payments over a specified period, receiving their merchandise when they have paid in full. Prior to the change in accounting practice, which FAS 101 made mandatory, Wal-Mart booked layaway sales as soon as it placed the merchandise on layaway. Under the new and more conservative method, the company began to recognize the sales only when customers completed the required payments and took possession of the goods.

According to one analyst, Wal-Mart's 8% stock price decline represented "somewhat of an overreaction." In reality, the price drop was an overreaction in its entirety. Changing the accounting method altered neither the amount of cash ultimately received by the retailer nor the timing of its receipt. The planned change in Wal-Mart's revenue recognition process therefore entailed no loss in time value of money. Lest anyone mistakenly continue to attribute economic significance to the timing of the revenue recognition, Wal-Mart explained that the small reduction in reported earnings in the third fiscal quarter would be made up in the fourth. On top of everything else, management had already announced the accounting change prior to its August 9 conference call.

An institutional portfolio manager spoke truly when he called the market's reaction to the supposed news "more confusion than anything else." If taken at face value, the press reports indicate that investors bid the shares down on "news" that was both dated and irrelevant. Alternatively, investors may have had other reasons for driving down the shares. For one thing, store traffic declined in the three months ended July 31 from the preceding quarter's level. Additionally, German operations posted a larger loss than management had forecast. If these events were the true causes of Wal-Mart's slide, then the *Wall Street Journal* and the *Bloomberg* newswire erred in attributing the sell-off to an accounting change with no real economic impact. Either way, confusion reigned; the only question is whether it was the investors or the journalists who were confused.

RECOGNIZING MEMBERSHIP FEES

Bally Total Fitness provided another case in which questions about revenue recognition contributed to an unfavorable stock market reaction to seemingly upbeat earnings news. On July 30, 1998, the health club chain reported diluted earnings per share of $0.08, up from a year-earlier loss of $0.59. According to the *Wall Street Journal*,[19] the improved profits were "unexpectedly encouraging." They suggested that the success of the company's newer, more upscale clubs was bolstering overall performance. In the month following the earnings report, however, Bally's shares declined by 44%. The Dow Jones Industrial Average fell by a less severe 16% over the same period. In the wake of Bally's report, moreover, short sales (representing bets that the price would fall) accounted for 15% of all outstanding shares. During the first quarter of 1998, the company's **short interest ratio** fluctuated in a range of 3% to 5%.

Investors were unwilling to accept Bally's earnings increase at face value because of the company's growing reliance on memberships that it financed, as opposed to selling for cash. Bally's financed customers' initial membership fees, which ranged from $600 to $1,400, for up to 36 months, charging annual interest rates of 16% to 18%.[20] (Ongoing dues represented just 27.9% of net revenues, with approximately 90% of members paying an average of only about seven dollars a month in 1998.) On the whole, the company's reported profit margins benefited from the increase in financed memberships as a percentage of total revenues. The reported earnings, however, rested on assumptions regarding the percentage of customers who would ultimately fail to make all of the scheduled installments.

Even under the best of circumstances, a considerable portion of any health club's new members let their memberships lapse, despite paying an initial fee. As New York University accounting professor Paul Brown notes, "People have little to lose from walking away from a health-club membership.

It's not a health-care plan we're talking about, or even a car, which they might need for transportation."[21]

To be sure, Bally set aside reserves for uncollectible amounts, consistent with good accounting practice. The size of the reserves, however, required judgment about the credit quality of the new members. Because financed memberships were not entirely new to Bally, management had some experience on which to base its assumptions. In addition, the company had succeeded in increasing the use of an electronic funds transfer payment option in recent years. Collection rates were higher for members whose credit cards or bank accounts were automatically charged for fees than for those billed through monthly statements. There were risks, though, in stepping up reliance on customers who needed to borrow in order to join. As in any sales situation, aggressive pursuit of new business could result in acceptance of more marginally qualified customers. On average, the newer members might prove to be less financially capable or less committed to physical fitness than the previous purchasers of financed memberships. If more members failed on their payments than management assumed, Bally would prove in hindsight to have been too aggressive in recognizing revenue and would have to rescind previously reported income.

By taking the second-quarter 1998 earnings with a grain of salt, users of financial statements were not necessarily casting aspersions on Bally's management. Rather, they were understandably applying caution in evaluating a company in a service industry historically identified with questionable revenue recognition practices. Some analysts sprang to Bally's defense following the *Wall Street Journal*'s critical article by highlighting the company's adoption of a conservative practice at the Securities and Exchange Commission staff's behest in July 1997. Previously, Bally had fully recognized initial membership fees at the time that the memberships were sold. A health club operator could abuse this approach by using high-pressure tactics to book financed memberships for individuals who were highly unlikely to keep up their payments. Outsiders relying on the financial statements would perceive a growth in revenues that must, in time, prove unsustainable. Under the new accounting treatment, Bally spread the revenues from the initial fees over the expected membership lives—36 months for sales made for cash on the barrelhead and 22 months for financed sales.

The SEC's urging of Bally's to spread out its recognition of membership fees was part of a broader effort extending beyond the health club industry. There was no change in the accounting principle, namely, the matching concept. In the case of a health club, members' up-front fees represent payments for services received over the terms of their membership. Club operators should therefore recognize the revenue over the period in which they render the service. During the late 1990s, the underlying theory underwent no change, but the SEC intensified its focus on membership fees after determining that some companies were interpreting the rules too liberally. Among the industries that came under increased scrutiny were the membership club retailers. In this type of operation, consumers pay up-front fees for the privilege of shopping at stores that sell discounted merchandise.

On October 19, 1998, BJ's Wholesale Club switched from immediate recognition of its annual membership fee (typically $35 for two family members) to incremental recognition of the fee over the full membership term, generally 12 months. In conjunction with the change in accounting policy, BJ's restated its net income for the fiscal first half ending August 1 to $10.4 million. That was down 64% from the previously reported $28.6 million. The restatement reflected a one-time charge for the accounting change's cumulative effect on preceding years, as well as a $1.1 million aftertax charge arising from a change to more conservative accounting for new-store preopening expenses.

Just a month-and-a-half before these events, BJ's had issued a press release asserting that its practice of immediately recognizing annual membership fees was consistent with GAAP.[22] Management had also argued that no deferral was required, on the grounds that BJ's offered its members the right to cancel and receive refunds for only 90 days after enrollment. A mere 0.5% of members actually requested refunds. In contrast to the situation at Bally Total Fitness, moreover, membership fees represented a minor portion of BJ's revenues, 98% of which derived from merchandise sales.

Under GAAP, however, the general requirement was to spread membership fees over the full membership period. If a company offered refunds, it could not book *any* of the revenue until the refund period expired, unless there was a sufficiently long history to enable management to estimate future experience with reasonable confidence. At most, BJ's refund record might have entitled the company to begin booking the fees on the date that members enrolled. Spreading the revenue recognition over the membership period would have been mandatory in any case.[23]

In December 1999, the SEC staff clarified the point by issuing "Staff Accounting Bulletin No. 101—Revenue Recognition in Financial Statements" (SAB 101). The staff stated its preference that companies not book membership fees until refund privileges expired. MemberWorks, a provider of membership programs offering services and discounts in a wide range of fields including health care, personal finance, and travel, altered its accounting in response to SAB 101, effective July 1, 2000. A one-time noncash charge of $25.7 million resulted, reflecting the deferral of previously recognized membership fees.[24]

A POTPOURRI OF LIBERAL
REVENUE RECOGNITION TECHNIQUES

By intensifying its enforcement of established revenue recognition rules in SAB 101, the SEC put a stop to techniques that the staff considered overly aggressive. Professional Detailing, a recruiter and manager of sales staff for pharmaceutical companies, had to stop including in revenues the reimbursements that it received from clients for placing help wanted ads. Within a month, the company's share price fell by 31%. Physician & Hospital Systems & Services, a unit of National Data Corporation, abandoned its long-standing policy of booking revenues for its back-offices services not merely before it completed the work, but before it mailed out bills. National Data ended the practice and took a $13.8 million one-time charge to correct the previous pumping up of revenues. First American Financial took a cumulative $55.6 million charge when it embraced the matching principle by beginning to book revenues for loan services over the loan's duration, rather than immediately.[25]

Percentage-of-Completion Method

Under certain circumstances, a company engaged in long-term contract work can book revenue before billing its customer. This result arises from GAAP's solution to a mismatch commonly observed at construction firms. A variety of service companies, defense contractors, and capital goods manufacturers come up against the same accounting issue.

Typically, the company agrees to bill its customers in several installments over the life of the contract. The billing may lag behind the company's incurring of expenses to fulfill its obligations. Without some means of correcting this mismatch, reported profit will be inappropriately high in the contract's early stages and inappropriately low in the late stages.

GAAP addresses the problem through the percentage-of-completion method, which permits the company to recognize revenue in proportion to the amount of work completed, rather than in line with its billing. The percentage-of-completion method can rectify the mismatch, but may also entail considerable subjectivity. This is particularly so when the company specializes in finding creative solutions to particular companies' unique problems, a sort of work that cannot be readily measured by engineering standards. Management can speed up revenue recognition on such contracts by making assumptions that are liberal, yet difficult for the auditors to reject on objective grounds. As is generally the case with artificial acceleration, taking liberties with the percentage of completion borrows future revenues, making a surprise shortfall inevitable at some point.

Crossing the Line

In the foregoing cases, the regulators merely complained that the companies' existing revenue recognition policies painted too rosy a picture, but in other instances the management has been accused of misrepresentation. For example, in 1996, the SEC claimed that computer manufacturer Sequoia Systems and four former executives engaged in a "fraudulent scheme" aimed at inflating the company's revenue and income. According to the complaint filed in U.S. District Court in Washington, the ex-chairman and three other officials booked letters of intent as revenue, backdated some purchase orders, and granted customers special terms that Sequoia never disclosed. Furthermore, charged the SEC, the executives profited from the scheme by selling stock before a true picture of the company's financial condition emerged. The company and its former officials settled the SEC's civil charges without admitting or denying guilt.[26]

Loading the Distribution Channels

A classic technique that manufacturing companies use to exaggerate revenues over the short run is to "load" their distribution channels. Loading consists of inducing distributors or retailers to accept larger shipments of goods than their near-term sales expectations warrant. This produces a temporary bulge in the commercial customers' inventories, which they must work off by reducing purchases in later periods. By loading the distribution channels, the manufacturer reports higher current-period revenue than it would have otherwise. The apparent gain is necessarily offset, however, by lower reported revenue down the road. Loading does not boost physical sales volume, but merely shifts the timing of its recognition as reported revenues.

As a further distortion of economic reality, the distributors will probably agree to accept higher-than-necessary inventories only if the manufacturer offsets the resulting increase in their inventory-financing costs by granting price concessions. In so doing, the manufacturer reduces its bona fide profits to make earnings *seem* higher in the near term. Loading therefore creates the appearance of higher company value (based on the implied trajectory of profits) but the reality of lower value.

Worse still, the manufacturer may try to bolster revenues indefinitely by loading the distribution channels year after year. Inevitably, the underlying trend of final sales to consumers slows down, at least temporarily. At that point, the manufacturer's growth in reported revenue will maintain its trend only if its distributors take on even bigger inventories, relative to their sales. If the distributors balk, the loading scheme will unravel, forcing a sizable write-off of previously recorded profits.

Through a Lens Darkly

At a special December 13, 1993, meeting, according to a *Business Week* report,[27] Bausch & Lomb (B&L) informed its 32 independent contact lens distributors of a new policy. Going forward, the company would make fewer direct shipments to eye doctors and do a larger portion of its business through the distributors. On the face of it, the distributors appeared to be big winners under B&L's revised strategy. Lens division head Harold O. Johnson then revealed a substantial quid pro quo. To meet the increased demand, he said, the distributors would have to expand their lens inventories.

B&L's sales representatives promptly presented distributors with lists of the products they were expected to buy. The distributors were dismayed to learn that they would have to pay carrying costs on inventories equivalent to as much as two years' sales. Furthermore, they discovered that B&L's prices were 50% or more above the levels of just three months earlier. To top it off, Johnson told the distributors that they would have to purchases the lenses by December 24, when the company closed its books for the year. Any firm that refused to accept its quota, he added, would lose its distributorship. By January 1994, B&L had terminated the two distributors that rejected the new arrangement.

Bausch & Lomb's aggressive stance in December 1993 may not have generated much Christmas cheer among its contact lens distributors, but the near-term impact on reported earnings was like a gift from Santa. The company loaded $25 million into the distribution channels in the last few days of the year, raising 1993 lens sales by 20%, to $145 million. Half of the division's $15 million of earnings for the year were attributable to the enforced buildup of distributors' inventories.

To outside analysts, it was not clear that the fourth-quarter sales rise resulted from channel-loading, rather than increased consumer demand for B&L lenses. Presumably, the distributors' inventory-to-sales ratios rose as they reluctantly stocked up on lenses, a classic clue that something was out of kilter. Those private companies' financial statements were not generally available to analysts, however. As a consequence, investors were caught off guard in June 1994, when the company announced that its results for the year would suffer as a result of "high distributor inventories" in both contact lenses and sunglasses. Between May 31, 1994, just prior to the disclosure of the inventory problem, and the end of the year, the company's stock plunged by 31.2%, a far worse performance than the 2.0% rise in the Dow Jones Industrial Average over the same interval.

The ostensible rationale for Bausch & Lomb's stepped-up inventory requirement, a shift toward greater reliance on distributors, was somewhat undercut by the company's continued direct sales to high–volume eye doctors and optical retailing chains. An executive of one small chain reported that early in 1994, he was able to buy a particular type of lens directly from B&L at 75% of the price that the distributors were charged. Many distributors saw their sales rise in response to the company's new strategy, but by only modest amounts.

As for B&L's insistence that the distributors place new orders by December 24, 1993, even though they said their inventories were already high as a result of an earlier promotion in September, one distributor's contact lens marketing manager commented, "It was just a blatant attempt to make their numbers." For lens chief Johnson, it appears, achieving sales targets was an outcome much to be desired. According to the company's proxy statement, he received a 64% bonus on top of his 1993 salary of $275, 000 for performance "substantially in excess" of corporate goals. (B&L later declined to discuss Johnson's compensation, but claimed that the year-end sales surge accounted for just "a small fraction" of the bonuses received by contact lens executives.)

Business Week contended that in addition to presenting an overly rosy impression of consumer demand for its contact lenses, Bausch & Lomb improperly recognized the revenue generated by its channel-loading. Generally accepted accounting principles forbid the recognition of a sale until the risk of owning the goods has passed from buyer to seller. According to *Business Week*, however, the loading up of the distribution channels prior to year-end 1993 did not meet that standard:

> *In interviews with more than a dozen of B&L's distributors, most tell a remarkably similar tale: Company executives promised that the distributors wouldn't have to pay for the lenses until they were sold and said that a final payment would be renegotiated if the program flopped.*[28]

B&L executives admitted telling distributors that during the first six months of the new arrangement, they would have to pay only for the merchandise they sold. The company officials insisted, however, that final payment was unequivocally due in June 1994. Nevertheless, in October 1994 the company agreed to take back approximately three-quarters of the December 1993 shipments and discount the remainder. By then, Harold O. Johnson had stepped down as head of the lens division and shareholders had filed a class action accusing B&L of falsely overstating its sales and profits.

The Bausch & Lomb affair teaches the valuable lesson that analysts who uncover solid evidence of inaccurate financial reporting should stick to their guns, even in the face of indignant and vehement denials by corporate management. Franklin T. Jepson, B&L's vice president of communications and investor relations immediately decried *Business Week*'s December 1994 report as an "unwarranted assault on the reputation and ethics of Bausch & Lomb" and "the product of poor editorial and journalistic judgment."[29] His comment appeared in a B&L press release that claimed *Business Week*'s article "falsely allege[d] the company may have improperly accounted for sales related to" its December 1993 marketing program. The press release further stated:

- Company officials had not represented that lenses sold in the special program were returnable if unsold.
- The distributors understood that the sales were final and irrevocable.
- B&L's financial and accounting staff, as well as its independent accountants, continued to believe that questions about revenue recognition were unmerited.

A month after issuing its strongly worded press release, Bausch & Lomb conceded that a reexamination by Price Waterhouse and a second independent accounting firm "identified certain items which were inappropriately recorded as sales."[30] According to the newest comment, the company continued to believe that the improperly recognized revenue was immaterial to 1993 full-year results and that the accounting for the contact lens division's special marketing initiative was appropriate. At the same time, B&L noted, the Securities and Exchange Commission staff had begun an inquiry "apparently prompted" by the program.

In October 1995, the company's board named four independent directors to a committee to review the 1994 internal review that produced an essentially clean bill of health. Three months later, B&L restated 1993 results for its contact lens and sunglass businesses. The downward revisions, which B&L had said a year earlier it believed would be immaterial, totaled $42.1 million in sales and $17.6 million in earnings. Those numbers were hardly inconsequential, compared with originally reported fourth-quarter 1993 revenues of $479.1 million and a loss of $62.9 million. The company added that its 1994 results would rise by corresponding amounts.[31]

By the time B&L disclosed the restatement, Chairman and Chief Executive Officer Daniel Gill had announced that he would step down from his posts at the age of 59, an action attributed by some observers to the company's lackluster earnings.[32] Outside analysts could not know all of the internal machinations that led to the 1993 special marketing program, but the subsequent resignations of both the contact lens division's head and the CEO made it plausible to suppose that senior management was indeed under pressure to make the numbers.

After six months of internal investigation, though, B&L's committee of outside directors concluded that the company's top executives were not to blame for the accounting improprieties. Without issuing a written report, the committee characterized the January 1996 restatement of contact lens and sunglass earnings as "appropriate" and said that control procedures had been strengthened. Committee chairman William Balderston III added that no future meetings were planned.[33]

The committee had added credibility to its findings by hiring Gary Lynch, former director of enforcement for the SEC, to assist in the investigation. Some seasoned observers of such inquiries, however, said that it was impossible to assess the quality of an internal investigation without information on the methods employed and the basis for its conclusions. "An investor can't find comfort in just the reputation of the investigator," shareholder advocate Ralph Whitworth asserted. Commented attorney Edwin H. Stier, "A lot of what is called an independent investigation is really advocacy."[34]

In any case, Bausch & Lomb's step-by-step retreat in the months following the December 1994 *Business Week* article is instructive. The company began by saying that the magazine "flagrantly disregarded facts presented to the magazine's reporter."[35] A month later, the company fell back to the position that immaterial amounts of revenue had been recorded improperly. Eventually, management conceded that the incorrect accounting was material enough to warrant a $42.1 million restatement. In light of this sequence, which has countless parallels in the annals of financial reporting controversies, users of financial statements should not be intimidated by corporate press releases that denounce allegedly irresponsible securities analysts and journalists.

Making the Numbers . . . Up, if Necessary

An executive on the receiving end of Bausch & Lomb's 1993 channel-loading escapade cited a desire to "make the numbers" as a motive for the lens division's pumping up of its reported revenues. In the achievement-oriented world of business, gung-ho salespeople sometimes go so far as to make the numbers *up*. A desire for bragging rights, rather than revenue figures, appear to have caused General Motors' Cadillac division to exaggerate its 1998 performance.

In December of that year, GM's luxury car unit was trailing its archrival, Ford's Lincoln division, in the annual competition to make the most final sales of vehicles to motorists. Cadillac's six-decade reign as the top American luxury car brand was in jeopardy. This danger was regarded as nothing short of apocalyptic, reflecting a strong view among auto industry executives that capturing the number-one position in a product category conferred a valuable marketing advantage.[36]

When Cadillac announced December results in January 1999, however, it appeared that the hard-charging sales force had achieved a come-from-behind victory straight out of *Chariots of Fire,* the cinematic epic of the Olympiad. According to the division's report, sales surged from 13,698 in November to a remarkable 23,861 in December. Even more astonishingly, and implausibly, in the view of many observers, sales of Cadillac's Escalade sport-utility vehicle skyrocketed from 960 to 3,642 in the space of a month.

After Escalade volume mysteriously receded to just 225 in January 1999, Lincoln's executives quietly began circulating data from the consumer marketing company R. L. Polk. The figures showed a sizable discrepancy between the number of cars that Cadillac claimed to have sold and the number registered by consumers during December. Cadillac officials responded by vehemently denying that its reported sales reflected any improper manipulation.

In May 1999, however, General Motors abruptly changed its story. Management confessed that Cadillac had inflated its December sales by 4,773 vehicles. The revelation followed an internal audit that resulted in vaguely described "appropriate disciplinary action." A spokesman blamed the false sales report on "a combination of an internal control breakdown and overzealousness on the part of some folks."

Interestingly, the automaker added that the revision of December vehicle sales would not necessitate a restatement of its 1998 financials. GM's accounting practice was to recognize a sale when a vehicle left the factory and became the dealer's property. The vehicles involved in the overcount had left the factory, but had not yet been sold to consumers.

Evidently, Cadillac officials manipulated the numbers solely to beat out Lincoln, rather than to puff up revenues or earnings. Strictly speaking, the affair lay outside the realm of financial statement analysis. Still, the overstatement of Cadillac's competitive position may have caused investors to place slightly too high a value on General Motors stock. After all, a stock's value is a function of expected future earnings (see Chapter 14), which partly depend on the popularity of the company's products vis-à-vis those of its competitors.

For analysts of financial statements, Cadillac's fib reinforces the message that when an issuer's numbers look too good to be true, they probably are. Generally, the initial response of corporate executives caught in a lie is to dig themselves a deeper hole, but gratifyingly often, the truth ultimately emerges. An equally valuable object lesson is Lincoln's detection of the mischief through checking Cadillac's figures against an independent source,

R. L. Polk. Analysts who strive to go beyond routine number-crunching can profit by seeking independent verification of corporate disclosure, even when the auditors have already placed their stamp of approval on it.

Managing Earnings with "Rainy Day" Reserves

Overstating near-term reported earnings by recognizing sales prematurely is the revenue-related abuse that creates the greatest notoriety. Analysts must also watch out for the opposite sort of finagle, however. Sometimes, management *delays* revenue recognition to *understate* short-run profits. The motive for this paradoxical behavior is a desire to report the sort of smooth year-to-year earnings growth that equity investors reward with high price-earnings multiples (see Chapter 14).

Steady earnings growth rarely occurs naturally. A company can produce it artificially, however, by creating a "rainy day" reserve. When net profit happens to be running above expectations, management stows part of it in a "rainy day" reserve. Later on, when the income is needed to boost results to targeted levels, management pulls the earnings out of storage. Smoothing the bottom line is not uncommon, but companies are touchy about the subject.

Chemical producer W. R. Grace reacted with indignation when it was accused of managing its earnings through improper reserves. On December 22, 1998, the Securities and Exchange Commission charged the company and six of its former executives with falsely reporting earnings over the preceding five years by improperly shifting revenue. Grace followed the standard script, declaring that it would "vigorously contest"[37] the charges, stating its belief that its financial reporting was proper, and pointing out that its outside auditors had raised no objections to the accounting. An attorney for former Grace chief executive officer J. P. Bolduc, who was among the accused executives, said that his client would fight the charges and expected to be vindicated. The SEC, complained the lawyer, was trying to punish Bolduc for carrying out his duties exactly as he should have.

The SEC specifically alleged that Grace had declined to report $10 million to $20 million of revenue that its kidney dialysis services subsidiary, National Medical Care (NMC), received in the early 1990s as the result of a change in Medicare reimbursement rules. According to the commission's enforcement division, the Grace executives reckoned that with earnings already meeting Wall Street analysts' forecasts, the windfall would not help the company's stock price. Such an inference would have been consistent with investors' customary downplaying of profits and losses that they perceive to be generated by one-time events (see Chapter 3). In fact, it was possible that the unexpected revenue would actually hurt the stock price down the road by causing NMC's profits to increase by 30 %, an above-target and unsustainable level.

To solve the perceived problem of excessively high profits at NMC, Grace's management allegedly placed the extra revenue in another account, which it later drew on to increase the health care group's reported revenues between 1993 and 1995. As an example, claimed the SEC, senior managers of Grace asked NMC's managers to report an extra $1.5 million of income in the fourth quarter of 1994, when corporate earnings needed a boost.

Brian J. Smith, who was Grace's chief financial officer until July 1995, testified in a deposition that because the kidney dialysis unit could not maintain its pace of earnings increases, "We believed that it was prudent to reduce the growth rates."[38] His attorney denied, however, that the goal was to please Wall Street analysts by keeping reported earnings smooth, as former Grace and NMC employees asserted. Smith had bona fide liabilities in mind, claimed the attorney.

A senior partner at Grace's auditing firm, Price Waterhouse, did not agree that the additions to reserves were appropriate. Eugene Gaughan testified that in 1991, he pointed out the accounting rules clearly stated that profits could be set aside only for foreseeable and quantifiable liabilities. GAAP did not give companies discretion to create rainy day funds.

In its year-end audit, Price Waterhouse proposed reversing the reserves, but management refused. According to the auditing firm's records, the Grace executives said that they wanted a "cushion for *unforeseen* future events.[39] (Italics added.) Eventually, Price Waterhouse allowed the additions to reserves to stand. The auditors' decision reflected a finding that the amount placed in the reserve was not material from Grace's corporatewide standpoint, although it would be if NMC were a stand-alone company. (At the time, auditors generally judged an item material if it affected earnings by 5% or 10%. The Securities and Exchange Commission later established the criterion that an event was material if it would affect an investor's decision.)

According to Gaughan, Price Waterhouse objected again around the end of 1992, after seeing a memo that described Grace's use of reserves to influence reported growth in profits, while gearing NMC executives' incentive compensation to "actual results." Another Price Waterhouse partner, Thomas Scanlon, said that he told Grace CEO Bolduc that stockpiling reserves was wrong and would have to stop. By that time, the contents of the "rainy day" reserve had grown to about $55 million.

It appears, in short, that Grace's 1998 statement that its auditors had raised no objections to its accounting for the Medicare reimbursement windfall was true only in the technical sense that Price Waterhouse issued clean financials, based on materiality considerations. As a spokeswoman for the auditing firm pointed out, such an opinion does not imply agreement with everything in the statements. As late as April 1999, however, Grace was still insisting that Price Waterhouse had approved its accounting "without reservation."[40]

On June 30, 1999, Grace settled the case without admitting or denying the SEC's charges. The company agreed to cease and desist from further securities law violations and also to set up a $1 million education fund to promote awareness of and education about financial statements and generally accepted accounting principles. Adhering again to the standard script, the corporation explained that it settled the case "because we think it is in the best interests of our employees and shareholders to put this matter behind us and move forward."[41]

The Grace affair serves as a reminder that almost invariably, an allegation of irregularities in corporate financial reporting is followed by a vehement, formulaic denial. No matter how offended the company purports to be about having its integrity questioned, analysts should take the protests of innocence with a grain of salt. The record does not suggest that the companies that bray loudest in defending their accounting practices are sure to be vindicated in the end.

Fudging the Numbers: A Systematic Problem

As the preceding examples demonstrate, manipulation of reported revenue is distressingly common. Readers may nevertheless wonder whether this discussion presents too bleak a picture of human nature. Are not most people basically honest, after all? To a novice analyst who has never been blindsided by revisions of previously reported sales figures that proved misleading or fraudulent, it may seem paranoid to view every company's income statement with suspicion.

Harvard Business School Professor Emeritus Michael C. Jensen observes, however, that misrepresenting revenues is the inevitable consequence of using budget targets in employee compensation formulas.[42] "Tell a manager that he will get a bonus when targets are realized and two things will happen," writes Jensen. "First, managers will attempt to set easy targets, and, second, once these are set, they will do their best to see that they are met even if it damages the company." He cites real-life examples of managers who "did their best" through such stratagems as:

- Shipping fruit baskets that weighed exactly the same amount as their product and booking them as sales.

- Announcing a price increase, effective January 2, to induce customers to order before year-end and thereby help managers achieve their sales targets. The price hike put the company out of line with the competition.
- Shipping unfinished heavy equipment from a plant in England (resulting in revenue recognition in the desired quarter) to the Netherlands. At considerable cost and inconvenience, the manufacturer then completed the assembly in a warehouse located near its customer.

Compounding the problem of managers who play games with their revenues is the willingness of some corporate customers to play along. "All too often, companies wouldn't be able to accomplish the frauds without the assistance of their customers," observes Helane L. Morrison, a district administrator for the Securities and Exchange Commission.[43] For example, one-third of wireless communications provider Hybrid Networks's revenue in the fourth quarter of 1997 consisted of a sale made on the final day of the reporting period to a distributor, Ikon Office Solutions. Ikon agreed to purchase $1.5 million worth of modems from Hybrid, despite knowing that it had no customers for the equipment. Hybrid closed the sale by providing a side letter essentially permitting Ikon to return the modems without paying for them. Ikon exercised that option in 1998, yet Ronald Davies, the Ikon executive who handled the purchase, sent an e-mail to Hybrid denying any knowledge of the side letter. Unfortunately, Hybrid later gave a copy of the side letter to its auditors. The SEC then sued Hybrid, which was forced to restate its revenues to eliminate the nonfinal sale of modems to Ikon. Furthermore, Davies received a cease-and-desist order to refrain from further violations of the securities laws. In certain other recent enforcement actions alleging improper recognition of sales, as well, the SEC has charged executives of corporate customers with collusion.

How widespread are revenue recognition gambits that enrich managers but impair bona fide profits? According to Ikon executive Davies, "It's very common for a manufacturer to call you up and say, 'I need to hit my quarterly number, would you mind giving me a purchase order for $100,000?' "[44] In the litigation surrounding W. R. Grace's alleged delay of revenue recognition to smooth earnings, the chief financial officer's attorney defended his client's action by arguing, "Any CFO anywhere has managed earnings in a way the SEC is now jumping up and down and calling fraud."[45] Michael Jensen chimes in, "Almost every company uses a budget system that rewards employees for lying and punishes them for telling the truth." He proposes reforming the system by severing the link between budget targets and compensation. Realistically, however, radical reforms are not likely to occur any time soon.

Analysts therefore need to scrutinize carefully the revenues of every company they examine. Even in the case of the bluest of the blue chips, watching for rising levels of accounts receivable or inventory, relative to sales, should be standard operating procedure. Regardless of management's programmed reassurances, conspicuous surges in unbilled receivables and deferred income are telltale danger signals. It is imperative that analysts raise a red flag when a membership-based company's registrations deviate from their customary relationship with reported sales. "Budget-gaming is rife," says Jensen, and "in most corporate cultures, much of this is expected, even praised." Let the analyst beware.

Restatements of revenues and earnings arise in a wide range of circumstances. Many well-publicized cases involve young companies in comparatively new industries. Until the potential abuses have been demonstrated, managements may be able to take greater liberties than the auditors will countenance at a later point. On the other hand, major, long-established corporations are sometimes overzealous in booking sales. Mature companies may pump up revenues out of a desire to meet high expectations created by earlier, rapid growth.

After the fact, companies variously attribute excesses in reporting to misjudgment, bookkeeping errors, deliberate misrepresentation by "rogue managers," or some combination of the three. Seasoned analysts, having been burned on many occasions by revenue revisions, tend to doubt that overstatements are ever innocent mistakes. To gain some of the veterans' perspective, if not necessarily their jaundiced view of human nature, it is worthwhile to review a few case histories of adjustments to previously recorded revenues.

In November 1991, Citicorp restated $23 million in revenues associated with its credit card processing division. The bank holding company dismissed the unit's head and several other officials, saying they had been misreporting data for nearly two years. Financial executives were among those involved in the scam, which helped to explain why it had gone undetected for so long. Deadpanned the *Wall Street Journal,* "[Citicorp] officials didn't specify why the employees had been inflating revenue, although their bonuses were tied directly to the unit's performance."[46]

Cincinnati Milacron credited an anonymous tip for its uncovering of a $2.3 million overstatement of sales in the first half of 1993. The "isolated" incident, said the company, involved a failure by the Sano plastic machinery unit to observe the "sales cutoff" rule. Contrary to Cincinnati Milacron's policy, Sano had counted in sales units that had not been shipped. The obligatory firing centered on a senior manager, while others escaped with reprimands.[47]

First Financial Management blamed accounting errors, rather than policy violations, for its restatement of revenues for the first nine months of 1991. (Some of the employees at fault were fired, all the same.) The problem arose in the Basis Information Technologies subsidiary, a unit that First Financial had formed by consolidating 19 separate companies. Basis Information Technologies reportedly lost track of certain accruals of revenue, which should have been reduced as contracts expired. While uncovering the mess, First Financial also found that certain acquisition-related expenses had been amortized improperly.[48]

In July 1993, T2 Medical placed in *Fortune's* list of the 25 fastest growing companies. The following month, the manager of home infusion therapy centers acknowledged that accounting irregularities had contributed to its remarkable sales growth. T2 (pronounced "T squared") had evidently recognized revenues on billings that neither patients nor insurers would cover. On the same day that T2's financial reporting came under a cloud, the Department of Health and Human Services announced it was investigating possible Medicare fraud at the company. T2's president resigned in the wake of the disclosures, and the company's stock price promptly fell 35% to $8.875. Only three months earlier, rumors of a management-led buyout of T2 had been rife, with one securities analyst speculating that the stock might run to $20 in such a scenario.[49]

CONCLUSION

Motivational speakers assure their audiences that if they visualize success, success will follow. Some of the corporate executives who live by the self-help creed take this advice a bit too literally. Seeing conditional sales and dubious memberships, they visualize GAAP revenues, believing that reality will follow. They transfer their own mirage to the financial statements, pumping up their companies' perceived market value and credit quality. When the revenues derived from wishful thinking fail to materialize, the managers may resort to fraud to maintain the illusion. The positive mental attitude that overstates revenues in the early stage is no less damaging, however, than the fraud responsible at a later point. When evidence of overly aggressive revenue recognition appears, analysts must act swiftly and decisively, lest they become infected by the managers' dangerous optimism.

QUESTIONS

1. What hazards for the financial analyst did Informix portray in 1997?
2. Does shipping a product to a reseller represent a sale? Explain why or why not.
3. What announcements by Informix and consequent events stunned investors?
4. What classic red flag for investors did Informix raise in July?
5. When should the agreements with resellers have been booked as sales? Why?
6. What pattern of falsification, frequently observed, does the Informix affair show?
7. What does the Informix affair teach analysts?
8. When and how did the software industry address the industry-specific issues of determining when a sale is truly a sale?
9. How did the fact that independent auditors certified Informix's statements affect the accuracy of the information received by investors?
10. What did its auditors consider a material weakness in the statements of Informix?
11. What is a classic warning sign for analysts that the case of Informix illustrates?
12. What is one invaluable lesson that aspiring analysts should extract from the study of Informix's aggressive revenue recognition?
13. What should assiduous tracking of a variety of financial ratios do?
14. What led the SEC to claim that KnowledgeWare's objective was to convince investors that the firm was making a comeback from its fiscal 1992 operating losses?
15. Was it possible for analysts to discern KnowledgeWare's problems by careful scrutiny of standard financial ratios? Why? Why not?
16. How could analysts have discovered the restated number of the portion of KnowledgeWare receivables beyond 90 days did not indicate that the quality of its receivables was improving?
17. How was the receivables-related bombshell that KnowledgeWare dropped on August 30, 1994, telegraphed?
18. To whom was the sense of impending disaster for KnowledgeWare inescapable?
19. What was central to Kendall Square's difficulties?
20. What reform, introduced by the acting CEO of Kendall Square, was likely to reduce the problems associated with revenue recognition?
21. Explain why a drop in the stock price accompanied the apparent good news of increasing revenues at Wal-Mart.

22. What role, if any, did the treatment of layaway sales at Wal-Mart have on the paradoxical drop in stock prices after an announcement of a sales increase?
23. Why were investors unwilling to accept Bally's earnings increases at face value?
24. What were some of the risks associated with Bally's increased reliance on customers who had to borrow in order to join?
25. Explain the accounting principle of the matching concept in terms of Bally's revenue recognition practices.
26. How is the situation in Bally's different from the situation in BJ's Wholesale Club?
27. What is the treatment of membership refunds under GAAP?
28. Under what circumstances, if any, can companies book revenue before billing their customers?
29. Are the SEC regulators limited to complaining about a firm's existing revenue recognition policies? What else, if anything, can they do?
30. What is meant by "loading" the distribution channels? How does it work?
31. How did B&L revise its shipment policy?
32. What was the impact on the distributors of B&L of the firm's revised strategy?
33. Was the increase in fourth-quarter sales of B&L a result of channel loading, or increased consumer demand?
34. What does GAAP have to say about revenue recognition and the risk of owning the goods?
35. What invaluable lesson does the B&L affair teach analysts?
36. Why is it plausible to assume that the senior management of B&L was under pressure to make the numbers?
37. Describe the step-by-step retreat by B&L in the months following the 1994 *Business Week* article.
38. How is the B&L pumping of reported revenues different from the situation at the General Motors Cadillac division?
39. How does the General Motors Cadillac division affair fit within the realm of financial statement analysis?
40. What message is reinforced by the General Motors Cadillac division affair?
41. Under what circumstances does it make sense for management to delay revenue recognition?
42. Using an example from W. R. Grace, explain how increased earnings may not have an effect on the stock price of a firm.
43. What do accounting rules have to say about setting profits aside?

44. What does the Grace affair illustrate?
45. Why would it be seem paranoid to a novice analyst to consider every company's Income Statement with suspicion?
46. What two things must one expect after promising a manager a bonus if targets are realized?
47. What is the role of customers in facilitating revenue recognition fraud?
48. Corporate budget systems are designed to reward lies and punish truth. True or False? Explain.
49. What are telltale danger signals?
50. What are some after-the-fact explanations for excesses in income reporting?
51. What decision, taken in 1994, gave rise to problems for Knowledge-Ware later on?
52. What operating strategy risk was Informix taking in 1997?

CHAPTER 7

Expense Recognition

As Chapter 6 illustrated, companies can grossly distort their earnings through aggressive revenue recognition. Analysts who arm themselves with appropriate skepticism about financial statements are bound to wonder whether companies also pump up the bottom line by taking liberties in booking expenses. The answer is resoundingly affirmative. Corporate managers are just as creative in minimizing and slowing down the recognition of expenses as they are in maximizing and speeding up the recognition of revenues.

AOL'S SEARCH FOR WIGGLE ROOM

In 1994, the American Institute of Certified Public Accountants created an exception to the general rule that advertising expenditures must be expensed, rather than capitalized. The new rule permitted companies to capitalize outlays for direct mail, a form of advertising that makes an offer and solicits a direct response. To qualify for this special treatment, however, a direct mailer needed to demonstrate that it possessed historical evidence sufficient to predict response rates and, by extension, the revenue that the advertising would generate.

America Online (AOL), a leader in the then-young field of interactive media, quickly adopted the new accounting method. To attract subscribers, AOL mailed millions of solicitations and, through arrangements with computer manufacturers, gave away free trial subscriptions. The company did not recognize these costs as incurred. Instead, AOL capitalized the expenditures, then amortized them over periods of 12 to 18 months. By the end of its fiscal year ending June 30, 1994, AOL's balance sheet showed $37 million of subscriber capitalized acquisition costs. Thanks to the AICPA's exception for direct response advertising, AOL reported a $6.2 million net profit in fiscal 1994 instead of a loss of around $6 million.

AOL defended its accounting practice by arguing that its average subscriber remained on its system for 32 months, far longer than its maximum 18-month amortization period. The more conservative approach of expensing subscriber acquisition costs as incurred was the path chosen by AOL's largest competitor, however. CompuServe reasoned that its subscribers, like AOL's, could cancel at any time. Moreover, there was no way to predict how competition might heat up in an infant industry.

As early as October 1994, *Forbes* contributor Gary Samuels was voicing the skepticism of some security analysts toward AOL's reported earnings.[1] Investors lost none of their enthusiasm for the trendy Internet stock, however. Between the month in which Samuels's article appeared and April 1996, AOL shares rose by 624%.

Along the way, deferred subscriber acquisition costs on the company's balance sheet grew from $37 million in fiscal 1994 to $77 million in fiscal 1995. In fiscal 1996, the company squeezed out even bigger reported profits by extending the amortization period for its capitalized costs to 24 months. That change boosted net income by $48 million.

Pumping up earnings did not prevent the air from beginning to come out of AOL's stock, however. From its May 7, 1996, peak, the shares plunged by 67% through October 14, 1996. AOL precipitated the decline by cutting the price of its online service by 63%. The move represented a competitive response to rival providers' low rates, as well as to the migration of online services to the Internet, where most information and entertainment was offered to subscribers at no charge.

Investors did not buy AOL's story that reduced fees would generate enough new subscribers to offset the revenue loss.[2] A decision by International Business Machines and Sears, Roebuck & Co. to divest their jointly owned Prodigy Services venture underscored the lack of profitability in online services. AOL's accounting made its earnings look better than rival CompuServe's, but the industry's underlying economic reality was equally bad for all online providers.

By the end of fiscal 1996, AOL's capitalized subscriber acquisition costs had mushroomed to $314 million. On October 29, 1996, the company finally faced up to reality. The company announced that it would retroactively expense all of its capitalized subscriber acquisition costs and expense all future marketing outlays. Management linked the abandonment of its former practice to a new pricing policy.

Defending the integrity of the previous accounting approach, an AOL spokesman commented, "Look at the track record. For the past 16 quarters, this company delivered on expectations of revenues, profits, and subscribers."[3] This statement skated over the fact that all of the profits that the company had delivered, since inception, were wiped out by a $385 million one-time charge that accompanied the change in accounting policy.

More than three-and-a-half years later, AOL agreed to pay $3.5 million to settle SEC charges that it had exaggerated its earnings. The company also agreed to restate its fiscal 1995 and 1996 financials. In place of the one-time charge of $385 million, analysts would henceforth see the subscriber acquisition costs allocated to the periods in which they were incurred.

According to the SEC, AOL had never qualified for the exemption to the general rule that advertising costs must be expensed. Amortization was permitted "only when persuasive historical evidence exists that allows the entity to reliably predict future net revenues that will be obtained as a result of the advertising."[4] The environment in which AOL operated in the mid-1990s, said the commission, was not sufficiently stable to make its estimates of future revenue reliable. Repeating a recurrent theme in the annals of financial reporting controversies, AOL had initially managed to report net income, to which investors duly assigned a price-earnings multiple, by exploiting the not yet well defined accounting rules of a new industry.

As it happened, the wipeout of that income did not cause AOL to follow the path to extinction trod by countless other companies in similar circumstances. By the time the company settled the SEC's charges in 2000, its shares were trading at 38 times their low point following the accounting change. Building its subscriber base had been staggeringly expensive, but AOL had survived to become by far the largest provider of Internet access in the United States.

Analysts hoping to get a clear picture of the company's financial performance were not out of the woods, however. Partly to justify its earlier practice of capitalizing subscriber acquisition costs, AOL had traditionally disclosed its acquisition cost per customer and the number of canceled subscriptions. After switching to the more conservative approach of expensing its marketing expenditures, the company cut back to divulging only total market expenses and net subscriber growth. While disclosure of these details was not mandatory under the accounting rules, analysts complained that without the information they could not satisfactorily assess the value of AOL's customer base.[5] Once again, AOL was shown up by CompuServe, which continued to disclose the percentage of subscribers remaining on its system for 3, 6, 9, and 12 months. The company justified the reduced information flow by arguing that as a result of stepped-up emphasis on advertising revenues, subscriptions would play a smaller role in its success in the future.

Still, AOL could not seem to shake its image as an aggressive exploiter of wiggle room in the accounting rules. In 1998, the company raised some eyebrows by employing aggressive accounting while the controversy over its subscriber acquisition costs was still fresh in investors' minds. Through a clever gambit, management avoided booking as a one-time gain AOL's profit of approximately $380 million on the exchange of its ANS Communications network-services business for CompuServe's online unit.

As noted in Chapter 3, investors attach little significance to nonrecurring profits and losses in valuing stocks. Therefore, a public company has a strong incentive to aggregate cumulative losses into a one-time event and to break up a unique, nonrecurring gain into smaller pieces and recognize it over several years. AOL achieved the latter effect by structuring the swap of companies as a sale-leaseback, based on its agreement to use ANS's services for five years following the transaction.

Sale-leaseback accounting is more commonly used for individual assets, such as railcars and buildings. AOL's use of it for an entire operating company was nonetheless permissible. Several accountants commented, however, that it was unprecedented in their experience.[6]

IBM'S INNOVATIVE EXPENSE REDUCTION

One-time gains can be transformed in even more miraculous ways than turning them into operating income. International Business Machines has found a means of moving such items into its reported costs, where they surreptitiously reduce expenses. Instead of giving its bottom line a one-time boost, which investors will likely attribute little value to, IBM creates the illusion of a more sustained improvement in operating efficiency.

During 1999, Chairman Louis Gerstner hailed IBM's "strong expense management" as a key to its recent earnings improvement.[7] On the face of it, the numbers bore him out. For the full year, the world's largest computer manufacturer reported that selling, general, and administrative expense fell to $14.7 billion from $16.7 billion in 1998, even though total revenue increased to $87.5 billion from $81.7 billion. Taken at face value, IBM's numbers indicated that Gerstner's team had chopped SG&A spending from 20.4% to 16.8% of revenue. On closer examination, it turned out that IBM cut less fat than it appeared.

A portion of one sentence in the Management Discussion of IBM's 1999 annual report notes that the year-over-year decrease in SG&A expense "reflects the net pre-tax benefit associated with the sale of the Global Network." Analysts who doggedly followed the trail to the Notes to Consolidated Financial Statements discovered that the pretax gain on IBM's sale of its Global Network business to AT&T totaled $4.057 billion. That accounted two times over for the year's reduction in SG&A. Excluding the benefit of the unit's sale, one-time event, SG&A *rose* as a percentage of IBM's total revenues from 20.4% to 21.4% in 1998.

Diligent analysts could find all of this information in IBM's annual report. The company did not explain, however, why it categorized a gain on an asset sale as a reduction in expenses. Accounting expert Howard Schilit was perhaps too kind in calling the practice "pretty unusual."[8] An IBM spokesman, responding to a question raised about the treatment, said that the company had been putting one-time gains and charges into the "general" portion of selling, general, and administrative costs since about 1994.

The great advantage of this practice, from IBM's viewpoint, is that it boosts operating income. A $4 billion improvement at that level is likely to boost the stock price more than the aftertax equivalent amount highlighted as a once-only occurrence. It is precisely to prevent such repackaging of reality that GAAP requires material gains from asset sales to appear below the line as nonoperating income. A senior accounting fellow at the Securities and Exchange Commission opined that IBM's $4 billion gain on the Global Network "would seem to be material,"[9] implying that it ought to be booked as a nonoperating item. Taken together with the integration of pension plan investment returns into operating income in the same year (see Chapter 10), IBM's handling of the gain on the Global Network sale belied Chairman Gerstner's claims to have fortified profits through effective management—unless he meant earnings management.

SIMPLE ANALYSIS FOILS ELABORATE DECEPTION

Encouragingly, elementary techniques of financial statement analysis can often expose chicanery, as demonstrated by the case of Wickes PLC.

On June 25, 1996, the British building materials retailer's management disclosed that its 1995 profits and year-end shareholders' equity were overstated. Wickes shares promptly plummeted by 36.7%. Shares of Caradon PLC, another building materials company, traded down by as much as 5.3% on the day of the disclosure, merely because its finance director, Trefor Llewellyn, had held the comparable position at Wickes up until June 1995.[10]

Wickes's management explained that the accounting problem involved rebates offered by suppliers, conditioned on sales of their products reaching agreed-on levels. Llewellyn's successor as finance director, Stuart Stradling, said that the company had credited rebates (thereby reducing its cost of goods sold) before selling enough merchandise to qualify for the discounts. At the same time, Wickes assured investors that no fraud had occurred and that the company had no plans to bring in outsiders to conduct a probe to supplement its own internal investigation. Wickes added that there was little likelihood of chairman and chief executive officer Henry Sweetbaum being compelled to repay part of the bonus he had recently received, even though it was linked to both earnings and stock performance.[11]

Quickly reversing its earlier stance, Wickes hired both an accounting and a legal firm to examine its books and report on the company's financial position. Chairman Sweetbaum soon resigned, but the company said that there was no evidence that he was involved in the inaccurate accounting. It later emerged, however, that Wickes had given about £200,000 a year of business to Sweetbaum's privately owned travel firm, a fact never disclosed in the financial reports.[12]

Over the next two months, additional details of the financial reporting problem emerged. The prematurely booked items included not only volume-based discounts, but also payments in support of advertising and store openings. In some instances, new suppliers gave Wickes legitimate rebates as part of multiyear agreements. Instead of amortizing the amounts of the lives of the contracts, the company booked them entirely in the first year. Along with every formal contract, according to sources close to the company, there was a side letter containing the true terms of the deal.[13]

As the investigation continued, analysts' estimates of the potential overstatement of profits escalated from £15 million to £25 million. As it turned out, the overstatement totaled £26 million in 1995 alone, according to the report of the specially hired outside lawyers and accountants, which Wickes summarized for its shareholders in October 1996. Prematurely booked rebates had also inflated earnings by £14 million in 1994 and £11 million in earlier years, producing a grand total of £51 million.

In the wake of the report, former finance director Llewellyn paid back £485,000, or 92%, of his 1995 bonus, which was directly related to Wickes's share price. Chairman and Chief Executive Henry Sweetbaum, who had resigned shortly after the scandal broke in June, returned £720,000, representing about two-thirds of the payments he received under Wickes's long-term incentive plan, while denying any knowledge of the scheme to overstate profits. The company said that Sweetbaum was not directly responsible for the system, implemented within the purchasing department, to conceal the terms on which suppliers had made the rebates.[14] At the same time, Wickes declared that senior management had been aware of the accounting irregularities at least six months before the problems became public and "should have reacted more positively to [the] warning signals."[15]

As a further outgrowth of Wickes's October 1996 report, Britain's Serious Fraud Office (SFO) launched a formal investigation into the company's overstatement of profits. Two-and-a-half years later, the SFO charged ex-chairman Sweetbaum, former finance director Llewellyn, and three other executives with fraudulent trading and making false statements. By now, events had undercut Wickes's initial insistence that no fraud had occurred, its statement that there were no plans to engage outsiders to supplement management's own investigation, and its contention that Sweetbaum was unlikely to have to repay a portion of his bonus. Analysts should learn, from this example, to regard the statements of beleaguered companies with a high level of skepticism.

According to Stuart Stradling, Llewellyn's successor as finance director, the financial misrepresentations were "extremely well concealed and difficult to find."[16] He added that the deception would have remained undetected even longer if the company had not chanced on some previously unavailable documentation. The investigating accountants and lawyers interviewed more than 200 suppliers of Wickes to determine how many had paid rebates ahead of schedule. Outside analysts, working only with public statements, could not have pieced together all of the details of the scheme.

Interestingly, though, it was a simple income statement relationship that first aroused Stradling's suspicions. During the second quarter of 1996, sales improved, yet profits failed to rise in sympathy. Wickes had booked the upturn earnings earlier, through its premature recognition of rebates. Once Stradling joined the company in August 1995 and tightened up the company's audit procedures, the scam had ceased to be sustainable. Wickes's purchasing managers kept outside analysts in the dark, yet the affair underscores the analytical power of the elementary ratios described in Chapter 13. In other instances, such ratios, appearing in published financials, have signaled the breakdown of a similar ruse to borrow profits from future periods.

OXFORD'S PLANS GO ASTRAY

In contrast to the carefully controlled scheme by which employees of Wickes PLC artificially reduced the company's expenses, an utter lack of controls was the source of a massive understatement of costs at Oxford Health Plans. That difference mattered little to users of the companies' financial reports, who were misled in both instances. In both cases, moreover, an astute reader of the income statements determined through simple ratio analysis that something was amiss.

Stephen F. Wiggins started Oxford, a Connecticut-based health maintenance organization (HMO), in 1984 in a spare bedroom. By 1997, the company grew to 2.1 million members generating $4.1 billion of revenue.

Investors benefited richly from the Oxford's success. A $100 investment in the company's 1991 initial public offering rose to $4,000 at the stock's peak in July 1997.

Oxford's data handling systems failed to keep up with the company's explosive growth. The HMO had to track billing codes for hundreds of diagnoses, accounts for thousands of doctors, and personal data on members that numbered over one million by 1996. With claims beginning to back up, Oxford switched over to a new computer system created by its own people. Immediately, billing procedures began to misfire, data became corrupted through links between the old and new systems, and the claims-paying process broke down. The company temporarily ceased sending out monthly bills to many of its accounts, fearing that it might annoy them with incorrect statements. By the spring of 1997, uncollected premiums owed to Oxford had swollen to approximately 40 % of revenue, double the percentage of six months earlier.

These revenue problems and the resulting cash flow strains were compounded by a loss of control over costs. As many as 30,000 customers had their medical care paid by Oxford despite having withdrawn from its plans or having refused to pay their premiums after months of receiving no bills. In 1997, Oxford's health care cost per Medicare patient rose by 21%, about three times as much as the company had projected, while revenue per patient grew by only 4.3%. To make matters worse, the computer system breakdown prevented management from even becoming aware of the problem.[17]

Complaints by physicians, who were irate over Oxford's failure to pay its bills even as it was reporting robust profits, finally brought matters to a head. New York insurance regulators investigated the company's finances and determined that its reserves for future medical claims were inadequate. On October 28, 1997, the state's insurance commissioner told Oxford's board of directors that the company would either have to adopt the corrective measures that he prescribed or stop enrolling new members and possibly even put itself up for sale. Seeing that the regulators were about to lower the boom, the company announced on October 27 that it would post its first loss ever in its third-quarter report. That day, the HMO's stock plunged from $68¾ to $24¾. In the fourth quarter, Oxford reported a loss so large that it erased all profits reported since the company went public. On February 24, 1998, founder Stephen Wiggins resigned as chairman.

As in many other debacles involving expense recognition, rudimentary analysis of Oxford's financial statements provided more than a hint of the trouble that lay ahead. Consider the Form 10-Q report for the quarter ended June 30, 1997, the last filed by the company before the October bloodbath. The statement of cash flows (Exhibit 7.1) displayed the classic problem that first gave rise to cash flow analysis (see Chapter 4). Even

EXHIBIT 7.1   Oxford Health Plans, Inc.

Statement of Cash Flows
Six Months Ended June 30
($ in millions)

	June 1997	June 1996
INDIRECT OPERATING ACTIVITIES		
Income before extraordinary items	$ 71.6	$ 41.0
Depreciation and amortization	27.5	20.1
Deferred taxes	3.9	0.2
Equity in net loss (earnings)	1.0	2.0
Sale of property, plant, and equipment and sale of investments— loss (gain)	(7.5)	
Funds from operations—other	0.2	1.3
Receivables—decrease (increase)	(99.7)	(31.3)
Accounts payable and accrued liabilities—increase (decrease)	(71.9)	136.5
Income taxes—accrued—increase (decrease)	17.5	14.8
Other assets and liabilities—net change	(49.9)	(42.7)
Operating activities—net cash flow	(107.3)	141.8
INVESTING ACTIVITIES		
Investments—increase	20.6	6.3
Short-term investments—change	111.5	(282.6)
Capital expenditures	42.7	29.9
Investing activities—other	0.4	0.1
Investing activities—net cash flow	48.6	(318.7)
FINANCING ACTIVITIES		
Sale of common and preferred stock	10.3	226.8
Financing activities—net cash flow	10.3	226.8
Cash and equivalents—change	(48.4)	49.9
DIRECT OPERATING ACTIVITIES		
Income taxes paid	$ 35.0	$ 18.6

Source: Compustat.

though net earnings for 1997's first half rose by 74.6% over the comparable 1996 period, cash from operating activities deteriorated to −$107.3 million from $141.8 million. The bulk of that adverse swing resulted from medical costs payable turning from a large cash source to a major cash use. As the notes to financial statements disclosed, Oxford advanced cash to the

disgruntled physicians and hospitals while it tried to get its billing procedures back on track, deducting the amounts from the medical costs payable.

Readers should not imagine that analysts identified these signs of trouble only in hindsight. Christopher Teeters, an analyst at the Center for Financial Research & Analysis, highlighted the divergence between earnings
and cash flow in a report that he published ten days before Oxford's October 1997 bombshell. "We had no idea it was as bad as it was," Teeters acknowledged. "We just saw some indicators that looked kind of strange."[18]
As far back as 1994, Anne Anderson of Atlantis Investment Company noted
the haphazardness of Oxford's membership reports. They were prone to restatement and in some cases contained handwritten changes.

CONCLUSION

Just as companies have myriad ways of exaggerating revenues, they follow a
variety of approaches in downplaying expenses. Corporate managers make
liberal assumptions about costs that may be capitalized, dilute expenses
with one-time gains, and jump the gun in booking rebates from suppliers.
Sometimes they understate expenses through sheer sloppiness in their bookkeeping. Like corresponding techniques of aggressive revenue recognition,
misleading reporting of expenses can often be detected by careful scrutiny
of financial statements. To benefit from such insights, analysts must be dis-
ciplined enough to disbelieve the innocent explanations that companies routinely provide for ratios that in reality reveal trouble down the road.

QUESTIONS

1. Could a rudimentary analysis of the financial statements of Oxford
   Health Plans provide a hint of the trouble that lay ahead? Explain.
2. Could outside analysts, working only with public statements, piece together all of the details of the Wickes scheme? Explain.
3. Did analysts identify the troubles of Oxford Health Plans only in hindsight? Explain.
4. How could an analyst determine that IBM cut less fat than it appeared?
5. How did AOL incorporate into its financial statements the expenses associated with free trial subscriptions?
6. How did Oxford Health Plans scheme compare to Wickes's?
7. Is it common to take liberties with booking expenses?

8. What actions finally brought matters to a head in the Oxford Health Plans scheme?
9. What actions underscored the lack of profitability in online services?
10. What are some of the ways that companies downplay expenses?
11. What information did AOL withhold once it started expensing its marketing expenditures?
12. What is a sale-leaseback, how is it normally used, and how did AOL use it?
13. What is necessary to qualify for the special treatment that allows firms to capitalize some advertising expenditures?
14. What is the lesson for analysts in the Wickes example?
15. What must analysts do to benefit from the insights provided by the careful scrutiny of financial statements?
16. What punitive action, if any, did the SEC take against AOL regarding the charges of exaggerated revenues?
17. What recurring theme in the annals of reporting controversies had AOL managed?
18. What type of advertising was allowed to be capitalized starting in 1994?
19. What was AOL's rationale for treating expenses of acquiring customers more liberally than was the practice of its largest competitor?
20. Who was one of the first journalists who voiced skepticism regarding AOL accounting practices?
21. Why do companies have a strong incentive to aggregate cumulative losses into a one-time event?
22. Why does GAAP require material gains from asset sales to appear "below the line" as nonoperating income?

8

The Applications and Limitations of EBITDA

As noted in Chapter 3, corporations have attempted in recent years to break free from the focus on aftertax earnings that has traditionally dominated their valuation. The impetus for trying to redirect investors' focus to operating income or other variants has been the minimal net profits recorded by many "new economy" companies. Conventionally calculated price-earnings multiples of such companies, most inconveniently, make their stocks look expensive. "Old economy" companies generally have larger denominators (the E in P/E), so their multiples look extremely reasonable by comparison.

Long before the dot-com companies began seeking alternatives to net income, users of financial statements had discovered certain limitations in net income as a valuation tool. They observed that two companies in the same industry could report similar income, yet have substantially different total enterprise values. Similarly, credit analysts realized that in a given year, two companies could generate similar levels of income to cover similar levels of interest expense, yet represent highly dissimilar risks of defaulting on their debt in the future.

Net income was not, to the disappointment of analysts, a standard by which every company's value and risk could be compared. Had they thought deeply about the problem, they might have hypothesized that *no* single measure could capture financial performance comprehensively enough to fulfill such a role. Instead, they set off in quest of the "correct" single measure of corporate profitability, believing in its existence as resolutely as the conquistadors who went in search of El Dorado.

EBIT, EBITDA, AND TOTAL ENTERPRISE VALUE

The fictitious case of Deep Hock and Breathing Room (Exhibit 8.1) illus-trates the problems of relating net income to total enterprise value. Both companies compete within the thingmabob industry. Their net profits for the latest year are $28.6 million and $33.0 million, respectively.

When Breathing Room announces an agreement to be acquired by a multinational thingmabob producer for $666 million, Deep Hock's founder and controlling shareholder, Philip Atlee, realizes that his company is a hot item in the mergers-and-acquisitions market. Trusting his own skills as a ne-gotiator, he dispenses with M&A advisers and directly contacts an investor group that has previously approached him about buying Deep Hock. With thingmabob makers in strong demand, Atlee reasons, now is the time to sell.

Breathing Room's selling price represented a multiple of 20 times its $33.0 million net income, in line with levels paid in other recent thingmabob acquisitions. On that basis, Atlee sets his sights on a price of 20 times Deep Hock's $28.6 million of net income, or $572 million. He starts the negotia-tions at a higher level and, after some haggling, accepts a $572 million offer. After popping open the champagne, Atlee begins shopping for a yacht.

One month later, Atlee's quiet retirement is rudely disturbed by news that the investors who bought Deep Hock have quickly resold it to a large industrial corporation for $666 million. The ex-CEO realizes, to his dismay,

EXHIBIT 8.1   Comparative Financial Data ($000 omitted) Year Ended December 31, 2001

	Deep Hock Corporation	Breathing Room, Inc.
Total debt	$ 67.0	$ 0.0
Shareholders' equity	133.0	200.0
Sales	$500.0	$500.0
Cost of sales	415.0	415.0
Depreciation and amortization	25.0	25.0
Selling, general, and administrative expense	10.0	10.0
Operating income	50.0	50.0
Interest expense	6.7	0.0
Income before income taxes	43.3	50.0
Provision for income taxes	14.7	17.0
Net income	$ 28.6	$ 33.0

that he apparently left $94 million on the table. Dumbfounded by the turn of events, Atlee wonders why anyone would pay $666 million for Deep Hock. That is equivalent to the price paid for Breathing Room, a company with net income 15% higher. Surely, the investment group that paid $572 million for Deep Hock could not have boosted its profits materially in the space of a month. Neither have price-earnings ratios on thingmabob companies risen from 20 times in the interim.

Determined to solve the mystery, Atlee seeks an explanation from his niece, Alana, an intern at an investment management firm. Drawing on her experience in analyzing financial statements, she obliges by pointing out that Deep Hock's income from operations, at $50.0 million, is equivalent to Breathing Room's. The difference at the bottom line arises because Breathing Room, with a debt-free balance sheet, has no interest expense.

"If I had bought your company, Uncle Phil," Alana explains, "I would have immediately created pro forma financials showing what Deep Hock's net income would be if all of its debt were paid off. Without the $6.7 million of interest expense, its income before income taxes would be $50.0 million, just like Breathing Room's. At the company's effective tax rate of 34%, the tax bill would be higher ($17.0 million versus $14.7 million), but net income would rise from $28.6 million to $33.0 million, the same as at Breathing Room. Then I would put the company up for sale at 20 times earnings, or $666 million. That's probably what that group of investors did after they bought Deep Hock from you."

Pausing for effect, Alana adds a detail concerning the transaction. "In order to raise Deep Hock's earnings from $28.6 million to $33.0 million on an actual, as opposed to a pro forma basis, somebody has to retire the $67 million of debt. Assuming the investor group paid off the borrowings and sold the company debt-free, its net gain wasn't $94 million, as you assumed, but only $27 million. I mention that, just in case it's any consolation to you. An alternative way to structure the deal would have been to make the $67 million debt assumption part of the $666 million purchase price. Either way, the net cash proceeds to the seller come to $599 million, for a quick profit of $27 million."

Still unhappy about failing to get top-dollar, but intrigued by his niece's insights into financial statement analysis, Atlee asks a follow-up question. "I see now that applying a multiple to net income is not a good way to compare the total enterprise values of companies with dissimilar capital structures. This kind of situation must arise frequently. Is there a simple, direct valuation method that would have shown us what our company was truly worth, even if we weren't clever enough to think of increasing the earnings by eliminating the debt?"

"Yes," answers Alana. "Instead of calculating a multiple of net income on the comparable transaction, that is, the sale of Breathing Room, you should have calculated a multiple of EBIT. That stands for 'earnings before interest and taxes.' Add Breathing Room's net income, income taxes, and interest expense to get the denominator. The numerator is the sale price:

$$\frac{\text{Total Enterprise Value}}{\text{Net Income} + \text{Income Taxes} + \text{Interest Expense}} = \frac{\$666}{\$33.0 + 17.0 + 0.0} = 13.32X$$

"Let's apply that same EBIT multiple of 13.32 to the comparable data from Deep Hock's income statement," Alana continues.

$$\text{Net Income} + \text{Income Taxes} + \text{Interest Expense} = \$28.6 + 14.7 + 6.7$$
$$= \$50.0$$
$$\$50.0 \times 13.32 = \$666.0$$

"So that's how the pros ensure that valuation multiples will be consistent between companies with similar operating characteristics but different financial strategies?" asks the sadder but wiser ex-CEO of Deep Hock.

"Actually, Uncle Phil," Alana replies, "there's one more comparability issue that we need to address. As you know, the accounting standards leave companies considerable discretion regarding the depreciable lives they assign to their property, plant, and equipment. The same applies to amortization schedules for intangible assets. Now, let's imagine for a moment that Breathing Room's managers had been writing off its assets not at a rate of $25 million a year, but only $20 million a year. That means that they would have been depreciating assets more slowly than you were, since the two companies' rates of depreciation were identical. Here's Breathing Room's income statement, revised for this hypothetical change in depreciation rates (Exhibit 8.2).

"Let's calculate EBIT from this statement and apply the EBIT multiple that, according to our previous analysis, represents the value being assigned to thingmabob companies currently:

$$\text{Net Income} + \text{Income Taxes} + \text{Interest Expense} = \$36.3 + 18.7 + 0.0$$
$$= \$55.0$$
$$\$55.0 \times 13.32 = \$732.6 \text{ million}$$

"It appears that simply by stretching out the depreciable lives of its assets, Breathing Room has boosted its value from $666 million to $732.6 million.

EXHIBIT 8.2 Breathing Room, Inc.

Statement of Consolidated Income
Year Ended December 31, 2001
($000 omitted)

Sales	$500.0
Cost of sales	415.0
Depreciation and amortization	20.0
Selling, general, and administrative expense	10.0
Operating income	55.0
Interest expense	0.0
Income before income taxes	55.0
Provision for income taxes	18.7
Net Income	$ 36.3

But that can't be correct. Depreciation is an accrual, rather than a cash expense. Changing the depreciation rate for financial reporting purposes is therefore nothing but an alteration of a bookkeeping entry. It doesn't increase or decrease the number of dollars actually flowing into the company. If management had changed the depreciation rate for tax reporting purposes, then the actual tax payments would decline. In that case, more dollars *would* flow into Breathing Room. But that's another matter. What we're concerned about is that Breathing Room might fetch a higher price than Deep Hock, merely because of a difference in accounting policy that represents no difference in economic value.

"To prevent this sort of distortion, we calculate a multiple on a base that's even better than EBIT. It's called EBITDA. That stands for 'earnings before interest, taxes, depreciation, and amortization.' (Yes, I know that on the income statement, the correct order, moving from top to bottom, is EBDAIT. But the convention is to use the acronym EBITDA, pronounced "eebit-dah.") Breathing Room's EBITDA multiple is the same, whether it depreciates its assets at the rate of $25 million a year or $20 million a year:

EBITDA Multiple =

$$\frac{\text{Total Enterprise Value}}{\text{Net Income} + \text{Income Taxes} + \text{Interest Expense} + \text{Depreciation} + \text{Amortization}}$$

Original Depreciation Schedule:

$$\frac{\$666}{\$33 + 17.0 + 0.0 + 25.0} = \frac{\$666}{75} = 8.88X$$

Decelerated Depreciation Schedule:

$$\frac{\$666}{\$36.3 + 18.7 + 0.0 + 20.0} = \frac{\$666}{75} = 8.88X$$

"If we calculate Deep Hock's EBITDA and apply that same multiple of 8.88X, we get the correct total enterprise value of $666 million, meaning that we've achieved comparability with respect to both capital structure and depreciation policy:

$$\begin{aligned} \text{Net Income} + \text{Income Taxes} + \text{Interest Expense} \\ + \text{Depreciation} + \text{Amortization} \end{aligned} = \$28.6 + 14.7 + 6.7 + 25.0$$
$$= \$75.0$$
$$\$75.0 \times 8.88 = \$666.0$$

"In summary, Uncle Phil, it's much smarter to calculate total enterprise value as a multiple of EBITDA than to use net income. But the most important lesson is that if you decide to come out of retirement and start another company, be sure to hire me as your financial adviser."

Atlee grins. "I guess you're never too old to learn new and better approaches to financial statement analysis."

THE ROLE OF EBITDA IN CREDIT ANALYSIS

The dialogue between Phil Atlee and his niece shows that similar companies with similar net income can have substantially different total enterprise values. Much in the same way, companies with similar interest coverage can have substantially different default risk. In credit analysis, as in valuing businesses, EBITDA can discriminate among companies that look similar when judged in terms of EBIT. Consider the fictitious examples of Rock Solid Corporation and Hollowman, Inc. (Exhibit 8.3).

EXHIBIT 8.3 Comparative Financial Data ($000 omitted) Year Ended December 31, 2000

	Rock Solid Corporation	Hollowman, Inc.
Total debt	$ 950.0	$ 875.0
Shareholders' equity	750.0	675.0
Total capital	1,700.0	1,550.0
Sales	2,000.0	1,750.0
Cost of sales	1,600.0	1,400.0
Depreciation and amortization	75.0	30.0
Selling, general, and administrative expense	115.0	130.0
Operating income	210.0	190.0
Interest expense	100.0	90.0
Income before income taxes	110.0	100.0
Provision for income taxes	37.0	34.0
Net income	$ 73.0	$ 66.0

Measured by conventional fixed charge coverage (Chapter 13), the two companies look equally risky, with ratios of 2.10X and 2.11X, respectively:

Fixed Charge Coverage

Net Income + Income Taxes + Interest Expense

Interest Expense

$$\text{Rock Solid Corp.: } \frac{\$73.0 + 37.0 + 100.0}{\$100.0} = 2.10X$$

$$\text{Hollowman, Inc.: } \frac{\$66.0 + 34.0 + 90.0}{\$90.0} = 2.11X$$

(For convenience of exposition, we shall refer to this standard credit measure as the EBIT-based coverage ratio. Note that for some companies, the sum of net income, income taxes, and interest expense is not equivalent to

EBIT, reflecting the presence of such factors as extraordinary items and minority interest below the pretax income line.)

As it happens, Hollowman and Rock Solid are almost perfectly matched on financial leverage, another standard measure of credit risk. (For a discussion of calculating the total-debt-to-total-capital ratio in more complex cases, see Chapter 13.)

Total-Debt-to-Total-Capital Ratio

$$\frac{\text{Total Debt}}{\text{Total Debt} + \text{Equity}}$$

$$\text{Rock Solid Corp.:} \quad \frac{\$950.00}{\$950.0 + 750.0} = 55.9\%$$

$$\text{Hollowman, Inc.:} \quad \frac{\$875.0}{\$875.0 + 675.0} = 56.5\%$$

By these criteria, lending to Hollowman, Inc. is as safe a proposition as lending to Rock Solid Corp. Bringing EBITDA into the analysis, however, reveals that Rock Solid is better able to keep up its interest payments in the event of a business downturn.

In the current year, Rock Solid's gross profit—sales less cost of goods sold—is $400 million. Suppose that through a combination of reduced

EXHIBIT 8.4 Statements of Income ($000 omitted) Year Ended December 31, 2001

	Deep Hock Corporation	Breathing Room, Inc.
Sales	$1,800.0	$1,575.0
Cost of sales	1,560.0	1,365.0
Depreciation and amortization	75.0	30.0
Selling, general, and adminstrative expense	115.0	130.0
Operating income	50.0	50.0
Interest expense	100.0	90.0
Income (loss) before income taxes	(50.0)	(40.0)
Provision (credit) for income taxes	(17.0)	(14.0)
Net income (loss)	$ (33.0)	$ (26.0)

revenue and margin deterioration, the figure drops by 40% to $240 million, while other operating expenses remain constant (Exhibit 8.4). Operating income now totals only $50 million, just half of the $100 million interest expense. Fixed charge coverage falls to 0.50X from the previously calculated 2.10X.

Is Rock Solid truly unable to pay the interest on its debt? No, because the $75.0 million of depreciation and amortization charged against income is an accounting entry, rather than a current-year outlay of cash. Adding back these noncash charges shows that the company keeps its head above water, covering its interest by a margin of 1.25X:

EBITDA Coverage of Interest

$$\frac{\text{Net Income} + \text{Income Taxes} + \text{Interest Expense} + \text{Depreciation} + \text{Amortization}}{} = \text{Interest Expense}$$

$$\frac{(\$33.0) + (17.0) + 100.0 + 75.0}{100.0} = 1.25X$$

By contrast, if Hollowman's gross profit falls by 40%, as also shown in Exhibit 8.4, its interest coverage is below 1.0 times, even on an EBITDA basis:

$$\frac{(\$26.0) + (14.0) + 90.0 + 30.0}{90.0} = 0.89X$$

Rock Solid can sustain a larger decline in gross margin than Hollowman can before it will cease to generate sufficient cash to pay its interest in full. The reason is that noncash depreciation charges represent a larger portion of Rock Solid's total operating expenses—4.2% of $1.790 billion, versus 1.9% of $1.560 billion for Hollowman (Exhibit 8.3). This difference, in turn, indicates that Rock Solid's business is more capital-intensive than Hollowman's. Further examination of the companies' financial statements would probably show Rock Solid to have a larger percentage of total assets concentrated in property, plant, and equipment.

In summary, conventionally measured fixed charge coverage is nearly identical for the two companies, yet they differ significantly in their probability of defaulting on interest payments. Taking EBITDA into account enables analysts to discriminate between the two similar-looking credit risks. This is a second major reason for the ratio's popularity, along with its usefulness in ensuring comparability of companies with dissimilar depreciation policies, when estimating the total enterprise values.

ABUSING EBITDA

Like many other financial ratios, EBITDA can provide valuable insight when used properly. It is potentially misleading, however, when applied in the wrong context. A tip-off to the possibility of abuse is apparent from the preceding illustration. By adding depreciation to the numerator, management can emphasize (legitimately, in this case) that although Rock Solid's operating profits suffice to pay only 50% of its 2001 interest bill, the company is generating 125% as much cash as it needs for that purpose. Lenders derive a certain amount of comfort simply from focusing on a ratio that exceeds 1.0X, rather than one that falls below that threshold.

In their perennial quest for cheap capital, sponsors of leveraged buyouts have noted with interest the comfort that lenders derive from a coverage ratio greater than 1.0X, regardless of the means by which it is achieved. To exploit the effect as fully as possible, the sponsors endeavor to steer analysts' focus away from traditional fixed charge coverage and toward EBITDA coverage of interest. Shifting investors' attention was particularly beneficial during the 1980s, when some buyouts were so highly leveraged that projected EBIT would not cover pro forma interest expense even in a good year. The sponsors reassured nervous investors by ballyhooing EBITDA coverage ratios that exceeded the psychologically critical threshold of 1.0 times. Meanwhile, the sponsors' investment bankers insinuated that traditionalists who fixated on sub-1.0X EBIT coverage ratios were hopelessly antiquated and unreasonably conservative in their analysis.

In truth, a bit of caution is advisable in the matter of counting depreciation toward interest coverage. The argument for favoring the EBITDA-based over EBIT-based fixed charge coverage rests on a hidden assumption. Adding depreciation to the numerator is appropriate only for the period over which a company can put off a substantial portion of its capital spending without impairing its future competitiveness.

Over a full operating cycle, the capital expenditures reported in a company's statement of cash flows are ordinarily at least as great as the depreciation charges shown on its income statement. The company must repair the physical wear and tear on its equipment. Additional outlays are required for the replacement of obsolete equipment. If anything, capital spending is likely to exceed depreciation over time, as the company expands its productive capacity to accommodate rising demand. Another reason that capital spending may run higher than depreciation is that newly acquired equipment may be costlier than the old equipment being written off, as a function of inflation.

In view of the ongoing need to replace and add to productive capacity, the cash flow represented by depreciation is not truly available for paying interest, at least not on any permanent basis. Rather, the "D" in EBITDA is a safety valve that the corporate treasurer can use if EBIT falls below "I" for a short time. Under such conditions, the company can temporarily reduce its capital spending, freeing up some of its depreciation cash flow for interest payments. Delaying equipment purchases and repairs that are essential, but not urgent, should inflict no lasting damage on the company's operations, provided the profit slump lasts for only a few quarters. Most companies, however, would lose their competitive edge if they spent only the bare minimum on property, plant, and equipment, year after year. It was disingenuous for sponsors of the most highly leveraged buyouts of the 1980s to suggest that their companies could remain healthy while paying interest substantially greater than EBIT over extended periods.

Naturally, the sponsors were prepared with glib answers to this objection. Prior to the buyout, they claimed, management had been overspending on plant and equipment. The now-deposed chief executives allegedly had wasted billions on projects that were monuments to their egos, rather than economically sound corporate investments. In fact, the story went, investments in low-return projects were the cause of the stock becoming cheap enough to make the company vulnerable to takeover. Investors ought to be pleased, rather than alarmed, to see capital expenditures fall precipitously after the buyout. Naturally, this line of reasoning was less persuasive in cases where the sponsors teamed up with the incumbent CEO in a "management-led" buyout.

Investors in many of the 1980s transactions were advised to take comfort as well from the fact that a portion of the annual interest expense consisted of accretion on zero-coupon bonds, rather than conventional cash coupons (interest payments). By way of explanation, investors buy a zero-coupon issue in its initial distribution at a steep discount—say, 50%—to its face value. Instead of receiving periodic interest payments, the purchasers earn a return on their investment through a gradual rise in the bond's price. At the bond's maturity, the obligor must redeem the security at 100% of its face value.

By using zero-coupon financing along with conventional debt, LBO sponsors could generate financial projections that showed all interest being paid on schedule, while at the same time making capital expenditures large enough to keep the company competitive. Often, the projections optimistically assumed that the huge debt repayment obligations would be financed with the proceeds of asset sales. The sponsors declared that they would raise immense quantities of cash by unloading supposedly nonessential assets.

With the benefit of hindsight, the assumptions behind many of the LBOs' financial projections were extremely aggressive. Still, the sponsors' arguments were not entirely unfounded. At least some of the vast, diversified corporations that undertook leveraged buyouts during the 1980s had capital projects that deserved to be canceled. Some of the bloated conglomerates owned deadweight assets that were well worth shedding.

The subsequent wave of LBO-related bond defaults,[1] however, vindicated analysts who had voiced skepticism about the new-styled corporate finance. Depreciation was not, after all, available as a long-run source of cash for interest payments. This was a lesson applicable not only to the extremely leveraged deals of the 1980s, but also to the more conservatively capitalized transactions of later years.

A MORE COMPREHENSIVE CASH FLOW MEASURE

Despite its limitations as a tool for quantifying credit risk, EBITDA has become a fixture in securities analysis. Many practitioners now consider the ratio synonymous with cash flow, or more formally, operating cash flow (OCF). The interchangeability of EBITDA and OCF in analysts' minds is extremely significant in light of a long tradition of empirical research linking cash flow and bankruptcy risk.

In an influential 1966 study,[2] William H. Beaver tested various financial ratios as predictors of corporate bankruptcy. Among the ratios he tested was a definition of cash flow still widely used today:

Cash Flow (as defined by Beaver, 1966)

Net Income + Depreciation, Depletion, and Amortization

(Depletion, a noncash expense applied to natural resource assets, is ordinarily taken to be implicit in depreciation and amortization, hence the use of the acronym EBITDA, rather than EBITDDA.)

Beaver found that of all the ratios he tested, the best single predictor of bankruptcy was a declining trend in the ratio of cash flow to total debt. This relationship made intuitive sense. Practitioners reasoned that bankruptcy risk was likely to increase if net income declined or total debt increased, either of which event would reduce the cash-flow-to-total-debt ratio. The empirical evidence indicated that by adding depreciation to the numerator, analysts improved their ability to predict which companies would go bust, relative to comparing total debt with net income alone.

Note that Beaver's definition of cash flow was more stringent than EBITDA, since he did not add back either taxes or interest to net income. Even so, bond analysts have developed a tradition of telescoping default risk into the single ratio of cash flow (meaning EBITDA) as a percentage of total debt, all based ultimately on Beaver's 1966 finding.[3] In so doing, practitioners have institutionalized a method that Beaver never advocated and that subsequent experience has shown to be fatally flawed.

Beaver did not conclude that analysts should rely solely on the cash-flow-to-debt ratio, but merely that it was the single best bankruptcy predictor. As he noted in his study, other academic researchers were already attempting to build bankruptcy models with greater predictive power by combining ratios into a **multivariate** analysis. As of 1966, no one had yet succeeded, but just two years later, Edward I. Altman introduced a multivariate model composed of five ratios[4] (see Chapter 13). The development of Altman's Z-Score and other multivariate models has demonstrated that no single financial ratio predicts bankruptcy as accurately as a properly selected combination of ratios.

Since 1968, there has been no excuse for reducing bankruptcy risk to the sole measure of EBITDA-to-total-debt. Nevertheless, that procedure remains a common practice. Similarly unjustifiable, on the basis of empirical evidence, is the widely used one-variable approach of ranking a sample of corporate borrowers according to their EBITDA coverage of interest.

Bizarrely, investment managers sometimes ask bond analysts to provide rankings of companies by their "actual credit risk," as opposed to Moody's and Standard & Poor's ratings. Asked to elaborate on this request, the investment managers reply that "actual" risk *obviously* means EBITDA coverage. Apparently, they consider it self-evident that the single ratio of cash flow (as they define it) to fixed charges predicts bankruptcy better than all of the rating agencies' quantitative and qualitative considerations combined. Little do the investment managers realize that they are setting credit analysis back by more than 30 years!

Nearly as outmoded as exclusive reliance on a single EBITDA-based ratio is analysts' belief that they can derive a satisfactory measure of cash flow by simply selecting some version of earnings and adding back depreciation. It became apparent that neither EBITDA nor net-income-plus-depreciation was a valid proxy for cash flow at least as far back as 1975, when W. T. Grant filed for bankruptcy. The department store chain's collapse showed that reliance on an earnings-plus-depreciation measure could cause analysts to overlook weakness at a company with substantial working capital needs. Many subsequent failures in the retailing and apparel industries have corroborated that finding.

At the time of its bankruptcy filing, W. T. Grant was the largest retailer in the United States. Up until two years before it went belly-up, the company reported positive net income (see Exhibit 8.5). Moreover, the department store chain enjoyed positive and stable cash flow (as defined by Beaver, i.e., net income plus depreciation). Bankruptcy therefore seemed a remote prospect, even though the company's net income failed to grow between the late 1960s and early 1970s. In 1973, W. T. Grant's stock traded at 20 times earnings, indicating strong investor confidence in the company's future. The board of directors reinforced that confidence by continuing to authorize dividends up until mid-1974.

Investors would have been less sanguine if they had looked beyond the cash sources (earnings and depreciation) and uses (interest and dividends) shown on the income statement. It was imperative to investigate whether

EXHIBIT 8.5   W. T. Grant Alternative Cash Flow Measures 1967–1975

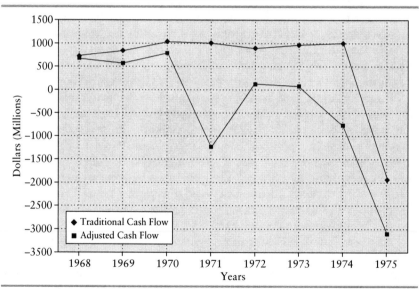

Sources: Clyde P. Stickney and Paul R. Brown, *Financial Reporting and Statement Analysis: A Strategic Perspective,* Fourth Edition, Orlando, Florida: The Dryden Press, a subsidiary of Harcourt Brace & Company, pp. 106–123. James Largay, "Cash Flows, Ratio Analysis and the W. T. Grant Company Bankruptcy," *Financial Analysts Journal,* July–August 1980, pp. 51–55.

two balance sheet items, inventories and accounts receivable, were tying up increasing amounts of cash. If so, it became vital to determine whether the company could generate an offsetting amount of cash by expanding its accounts payable. Recognizing the need for this added level of analysis, FASB eventually prescribed a more comprehensive definition of operating cash flow, as defined in SFAS 95, "Statement of Cash Flows":

Operating Cash Flow (as defined by FASB, 1987)

Net Income + Depreciation − Changes in Working Capital Requirements

Where:

$$\text{Working Capital Requirements} = \text{Accounts Receivable} + \text{Inventory} - \text{Accounts Payable}$$

Note that this definition focuses on the elements of working capital that ordinarily grow roughly in proportion with the scale of operations. FASB's formulation excludes cash and marketable securities, as well as short-term debt.

WORKING CAPITAL ADDS PUNCH TO CASH FLOW ANALYSIS

Adding working capital to cash flow analysis frequently reveals problems that may not be apparent from observing the trend of EBITDA or net-income-plus-depreciation. In fact, reported earnings often exceed true economic profits specifically as a function of gambits involving inventories or accounts receivable. Fortunately, such ploys leave telltale signs of earnings manipulation. Aside from seasonal variations, the amount of working capital needed to run a business represents a fairly constant percentage of a company's sales. Therefore, if inventories or receivables increase materially as a percentage of sales, analysts should strongly suspect that the earnings are overstated, even though management will invariably offer a more benign explanation.

Consider, for example, an apparel manufacturer that must produce its garments before knowing which new styles will catch the fancy of shoppers in the season ahead. Suppose that management guesses wrong about the fashion trend. The company now holds inventory that can be sold, if at all, only at knockdown prices. Instead of selling the unfashionable garments, which would force the manufacturer to recognize the loss in value, management may decide to retain the goods in its finished goods inventory. Accounting theory states that the company should nevertheless recognize the loss by writing down the merchandise. In practice, though, management may persuade its auditors that no loss of value has occurred. After all, judging what is fashionable is a subjective process. Moreover, management can always argue that the goods remain in its warehouse only because of a temporary slowdown in orders. If the auditors buy the story, it will not alter the fact that the company has suffered an economic loss. Analysts focusing exclusively on EBITDA will have no inkling that earnings are down or that the company' cash resources may be starting to strain.

In contrast, analysts will recognize that something is amiss if they monitor a cash flow measure that includes working capital as well as net income and depreciation. While the current season's goods remain in inventory, the company is producing clothing for the next season. Observe what happens to working capital requirements, bearing in mind the FASB 95 definition, as the new production enters inventory:

$$\frac{\text{Working Capital}}{\text{Requirements}} = \text{Accounts Receivable} + \text{Inventory} - \text{Accounts Payable}$$

Inventory increases, causing working capital requirements to increase. According to the FASB definition, a rise in working capital requirements reduces operating cash flow. Analysts receive a danger signal, even though net-income-plus-depreciation advances steadily.

A surge in accounts receivable, similarly, would reduce operating cash flow. The buildup in receivables could signal either of two types of underlying problems. On the one hand, management may be trying to prop up sales by liberalizing credit terms to its existing customers. Specifically, the company may be "carrying" financially strained businesses by giving them more time to pay up their accounts. If so, average accounts receivable will be higher than in the past. That will soak up more cash and force the company to absorb financing costs formerly borne by its customers. Alternatively, a buildup in receivables may result from extension of credit to new, less creditworthy customers that pay their bills comparatively slowly. To reflect the greater propensity of such customers to fail on their obligations, the company ought to increase its reserve for bad debts. Current-period reported income would then decline. Unfortunately, companies do not invariably do what they ought to do, according to good accounting practice. If they do not, a cash flow measure that includes working capital requirements will reveal a weakness not detected by net-income-plus-depreciation or EBITDA.

To be sure, management may attempt to mask problems related to inventory or receivables by pumping up the third component of working capital requirements, accounts payable. If the company takes longer to pay its own bills, the resulting rise in payables may offset the increase on the asset side. Fortunately for analysts, companies think twice before playing this card, because of potential repercussions on operations. The company's suppliers might view a slowdown in payments as a sign of financial weakness. Vital trade credit could dry up as a consequence.

In any case, analysts should use operating cash flow as one of many diagnostic tools. They should not rely on it exclusively, any more than they should limit their surveillance solely to tracking EBITDA. If a company resorts to stretching out its payables, other ratios detailed in Chapter 13 (receivables to sales and inventories to cost of goods sold) will nevertheless send out warning signals. Note, as well, that if the company does not finance the bulge in inventories and receivables by extending its payables or drawing down cash, it must add to its borrowings. Accordingly, a rising debt-to-capital ratio (see Chapter 13) can confirm an adverse credit trend revealed by operating cash flow.

CONCLUSION

Despite repeated demonstrations of the truism that no single measure encapsulates all of a company's pertinent financial traits, investors continue to search for the silver bullet. If a company's value is not a direct function of its net income, they tell themselves, the problem must be that net income is too greatly affected by incidental factors such as tax rates and financial leverage. The answer must be to move up the income statement to a measure that puts companies on a more even plane with one another. As Merrill Lynch investment strategist Richard Bernstein points out,[5] operating earnings tend to be more stable than reported earnings, EBIT tends to be more stable than operating earnings, and EBITDA tends to be more stable than EBIT. Companies welcome analytical migration toward less variable measures of performance, because investors reward stability with high price-earnings multiples. The trend of moving up the income statement reached its logical conclusion during the technology stock boom of the late 1990s. Investors latched onto the highest, most stable figure of all by valuing stocks on price-sales ratios. (To obscure what was going on, some companies actually resorted to discussing their earnings before expenses, or EBE.)

Strategist Bernstein found that by attempting to filter out the volatility inherent in companies' earnings, investors reduced the effectiveness of their stock selection. In a study spanning the period 1986 to July 2001, he compared the performance of portfolios of stocks based on low ratios of price to earnings with alternative portfolios of stocks priced at low multiples of EBITDA, cash flow, book value, and sales. The good old-fashioned low P/E criterion produced the highest average return (16.7%) of any of the strategies. Stocks chosen on the basis of low total enterprise value[6] to EBITDA produced the lowest average return, 12.3%. Adjusted for risk, as well, investors achieved far better results by relying on the bottom line, net income, instead of moving up the income statement to EBITDA. Bernstein's findings reinforced the message that instead of seeking an alternative to net income that summarizes corporate performance in its entirety, analysts of financial statements should examine a variety of measures to derive maximum insight.

QUESTIONS

1. According to Alana, what compatibility issues need to be addressed to value companies with similar operating characteristics but different financial strategies?
2. According to Alana, what is the smart way to calculate total enterprise value?
3. According to the Beaver study, what was the single best predictor of bankruptcy?
4. Can companies with similar interest coverage ratios have a substantially different default risk? Explain.
5. Can Rock Solid sustain a larger decline in gross margin than Hollowman before it is no longer able to pay its interest in full? Explain.
6. Did Beaver advocate the method that practitioners have institutionalized? Explain.
7. Explain why Atlee may have (or not) left a substantial amount of money on the table when he sold Deep Hock.
8. Explain why net income may be (or not) a standard by which every company's value and risk can be compared.
9. How can EBITDA help credit analysts discriminate between two similar-looking credit risks?
10. How did Breathing Room boost its value from $666 million to $732.6 million?
11. How does depreciation affect cash flows?
12. How is EBITDA dependent on the depreciable lives of assets?
13. How is the difference in the bottom line between Deep Hock and Breathing Room explained?

14. Does "actual credit risk" mean EBITDA coverage? Explain.
15. What did the failure of W.T. Grant bankruptcy show?
16. What is the added level of analysis (beyond sources and uses of cash) that prompted FASB to prescribe a more comprehensive definition of operating cash flows?
17. Aside from seasonal variations, what should analysts suspect when inventories or receivables increase materially as a percentage of sales?
18. Would a loss of value occur for an apparel manufacturer whose management guesses wrong about the fashion trend and is holding inventory that can be sold, if at all, only at knockdown prices?
19. What problems are signaled by a surge in accounts receivable?
20. How can management mask problems related to inventory or receivables?
21. How can a rising debt-to-capital ratio confirm an adverse credit trend revealed by operating cash flow?
22. Why do companies welcome the migration toward less variable measures of performance?
23. According to Bernstein's finding, how does filtering out volatility inherent in companies' earnings affect the performance of investors' portfolios?
24. What did Bernstein's findings reinforce?
25. Is EBITDA synonymous with operating cash flow?
26. Use an example to illustrate a misleading use of EBITDA.
27. What were the lessons learned from the wave of LBO-related bond defaults?
28. Were the lessons learned from the LBO-related defaults applicable only to the extremely leveraged deals of the 1980s?
29. What are some of the reasons that capital spending may exceed depreciation over time?
30. What are the differences, if any, between EBITDA and operating cash flow?
31. What are zero-coupon bonds, and what was their role in LBOs?
32. What did Altman's model demonstrate?
33. What did the group of investors who bought Deep Hock from Atlee probably do to achieve a higher valuation than the purchase price?
34. What did users of financial statements and credit analysts notice in regard to the reports of two companies in the same industry reporting similar income?
35. What does EBITDA stand for?
36. What happens to firms that spend the minimum on property, plant, and equipment, year after year?

37. What is the assumption that if not true weakens the argument for favoring the EBITDA-based over EBIT-based fixed charge coverage?
38. What is the incentive for "new economy" firms to break free from the focus of after-tax earnings as a basis for valuation?
39. What line of reasoning did Atlee follow to ask his niece about alternative valuation methods?
40. What was the rationale offered by sponsors of the 1980s leveraged buyouts who suggested that their companies could remain healthy while paying interest substantially greater than EBIT over extended periods?
41. Why was diverting analysts' focus away from traditional fixed charge coverage and toward EBITDA coverage of interest particularly beneficial during the 1980s?

CHAPTER 9

The Reliability of Disclosure and Audits

A naïve observer might consider it overkill to scrutinize a company's financial statements for signs that management is presenting anything less than a candid picture. After all, extensive regulations compel publicly traded corporations to disclose material events affecting the value of their securities. Even if a company's management is inclined to finagle, investors have a second line of defense in the form of mandatory annual certification of the financials by highly trained auditors.

These arguments accurately portray how the system is supposed to work for the benefit of the users of financial statements. As in so many other situations, however, the gap between theory and practice is substantial when it comes to relying on legal mechanisms to protect shareholders and lenders. Up to a point, it is true, fear of the consequences of breaking the law keeps corporate managers in line. *Bending* the law is another matter, though, in the minds of many executives. If their bonuses depend on presenting results in an unfairly favorable light, they can usually see their way clear to adopting that course.

"Getting the job done," in the corporate world's success-manual jargon, most definitely includes hard-nosed negotiating with auditors over the limits to which the accounting standards may be stretched. Technically, the board of directors appoints the auditing firm, but management is the point of contact in hashing out the details of presenting financial events for external consumption. A tension necessarily exists between standards of professional excellence (which, it must be acknowledged, matter a great deal to most accountants) and fear of the consequences of losing a client.

At some point, resigning the account becomes a moral imperative, but in the real world, accounting firms must be pushed rather far to reach that point. As a part of the seasoning process leading to a managerial role, accountants become reconciled to certain discontinuities between the bright, white lines drawn in college accounting courses and the fuzzy boundaries for applying the rules. Consequently, it is common for front-line auditors to balk at an aggressive accounting treatment proposed by a company's managers, only to be overruled by their senior colleagues.

Even if the auditors hold their ground against corporate managers who believe that everything in life is a negotiation, the outcome of the haggling will not necessarily be a fair picture of the company's financial performance. At the extreme, executives may falsify their results. Fraud is an unambiguous violation of accounting standards, but audits do not invariably catch it. Cost considerations preclude reviewing every transaction or examining every bin to see whether it actually contains the inventory attributed to it. Instead, auditors rely on sampling. If they happen to inspect the wrong items, falsified data will go undetected. Extremely clever scamsters may even succeed in undermining the auditors' efforts to select their samples at random, a procedure designed to foil concealment of fraud.

When challenged on inconsistencies in their numbers, companies sometimes blame error, rather than any intention to mislead the users of financial statements. On April 16, 2001, Computer Associates International preliminarily reported operating earnings of $0.40 a share for the fiscal year ended March 31. On May 4, the software producer put the figure at $0.16. The discrepancy, said management, resulted from a typographical error. According to the company, an employee transcribed a number incorrectly in preparing a news release.[1]

Investors might have been excused for reacting skeptically. Shortly before the May 4 announcement, Computer Associates's accounting practices had come under attack in the press. Besides, seasoned followers of the corporate scene realize that companies are not always as forthcoming as investors might reasonably expect. The following examples, drawn from the casino and consumer appliances businesses, illustrate the point.

AN ARTFUL DEAL

On October 25, 1999, Trump Hotels & Casino Resorts reported a year-over-year rise in its third-quarter earnings per share, from $0.24 to $0.63, excluding a one-time charge related to the closing of the Trump World's Fair Casino Hotel. The net exceeded analysts' consensus forecast of $0.54 a share,[2] resulting in a jump in the Trump's share price from $4 to $4⅝6. Also up on the day were the bonds of one of the company's casinos, Trump Atlantic City, which climbed about one point to 84¼.

"Our focus in 1999 was threefold," said president and chief executive officer Nicholas Ribis, in explaining the profit surge, which surprised industry analysts. "First, to increase our operating margins at each operating entity; second, to decrease our marketing costs; and third, to increase our cash sales from our non-casino operations. We have succeeded in achieving positive results in each of these three categories."[3]

The company's self-congratulatory press release contained no mention of another important contributor to the third-quarter surge in revenues, and by extension, net income. As the subsequently filed Quarterly Report on Form 10-Q finally acknowledged, $17.2 million of the period's revenue arose from bankrupt restaurant operator Planet Hollywood's abandonment of its lease on the All Star Café at Trump's Taj Mahal casino. With the termination of the lease, all improvements and alterations, along with certain other assets, became the property of Trump, which took over the restaurant's operation. An independent appraisal valued the assets received by Trump at $17.2 million. Without that boost, the company's revenues would have declined, year over year, and net income would have undershot, rather than exceeded, analysts' expectations.

The discrepancy between the October 25 disclosure and the fuller accounting in the 10-Q "became an embarrassment" to Trump Hotels & Casino Resorts, according to the *Wall Street Journal*.[4] Moreover, the timing was unfortunate. The incident occurred as management was making a round of investor presentations aimed at generating support for its plans to develop a new resort on the Atlantic City, New Jersey, site of the shuttered World's Fair casino.

Worse yet, from the company's standpoint, the fact that Trump had omitted some rather useful information was detectable. Bear, Stearns & Co. bond analyst Tom Shandell noticed that the company's press release reported mysteriously large revenues for the Trump Taj Mahal. The unit's revenues increased by $4.9 million over the comparable 1998 quarter, even though the New Jersey Casino Control Commission reported a $12.1 million decline in the Taj Mahal's *casino* revenues. Shandell was correct in suspecting that some other large, unspecified item was buried in the numbers; the difference between the purported $4.9 million increase and the Commission's reported decline of $12.1 million was essentially identical to the $17.2 million of All Star Café assets that later came to light. No such inference or backing-out of numbers would have been required if Trump's third-quarter 1999 press release had provided as much detail on the Taj Mahal's operations as the corresponding 1998 release. That was not the case, however, as Exhibit 9.1 demonstrates.

Was the drastic cutback in disclosure in Trump's third-quarter 1999 earnings release part of a deliberate attempt to conceal the fact that the year-over-year revenue gain was solely attributable to a nonrecurring event? Not to hear the company's president tell it. "It was never hidden," Ribis insisted.

EXHIBIT 9.1   Disclosure of Trump Taj Mahal Results in
Trump Hotels and Casino Resorts Earnings Release
Three Months Ended September 30, 1998 ($000 omitted)

Revenues		
Casino	$148,011	
Number of slots	4,137	
Win per slot/day	$ 277	
Slot win		$ 82,456
Number of tables	157	
Win per table/day	$ 4,160	
Table win	$ 60,087	
Table drop	$328,456	
Hold %		18.3%
Poker, keno, race win		$ 5,468
Rooms	$ 11,410	
Number of rooms sold	112,875	
Average room rates		$101.09
Occupancy %		98.2%
Food and beverage	$ 15,034	
Other	5,667	
Promotional allowances		(18,018)
Net revenues		$162,104
Costs and expenses		
Gaming	83,711	
Rooms		3,752
Food and beverage	4,844	
General and administrative	23,785	
Total expenses	116,092	
EBITDA*	$ 46,012	

*EBITDA reflects earnings before depreciation, interest,
taxes, Casino Reinvestment Development Authority write-
down, and nonoperating income.

Three Months Ended September 30, 1999		
($000 omitted)		
Revenues	$167.7	
Operating profit		41.4
EBITDA	51.0	
Margin	30.4%	

Sources: Trump Hotels and Casino Resorts Press Releases
dated October 7, 1998 and October 25, 1999.

"When there was a specific question about it, we broke it out."[5] The gain on the All Star Café simply got lost in the shuffle, he maintained, when the lawyers pressed him to put out third-quarter earnings before commencing the roadshow for the proposed new casino. "As soon as I learned of the accounting treatment we spoke with all of our investors and analysts," added Ribis.[6]

By apparently claiming that he discovered the true source of his company's year-over-year earnings increase only after the quarterly results had been released, Ribis did not burnish his reputation as a details man. That professed shortcoming may not explain why, seven months later, Trump Hotels & Casino Resorts decided not to renew Ribis's expiring contract as CEO. Perhaps it had more to do with the 56% drop in Trump's stock price in the 12 months ending May 2000. One thing is certain, however. Investors who relied solely on the company's disclosure were burned if they bought into the rally that followed the bullish-sounding press release. After analyst Shandell's inquiries uncovered the All Star Café's contribution to third-quarter results, the stock promptly sagged from $4⁵⁄₁₆ to $3⅞, while the Trump Atlantic City bonds slid from 84¼ to 80. On January 16, 2002, Trump Hotels and Casinos agreed to settle SEC charges that it "recklessly" misled investors in this incident, without admitting or denying the commission's findings.[7]

DEATH DUTIES

In roughly the same period in which the Trump Hotels & Casino Resorts controversy arose, the gambling industry provided another example of the hazards of relying on company disclosures. Arthur Goldberg, chief executive officer of Park Place Entertainment, entered the hospital in June 1999. The company attributed his confinement to a respiratory infection, but rumors began to circulate that he was gravely ill.[8] By the time Goldberg was released from the hospital on July 7, Park Place's stock had fallen by 6%. Over the same period, the 12 stocks constituting the Chicago Board Options Exchange Gaming Index rose by an average of 8%.

As late as September 2000, Park Place denied a report that Goldberg planned to step down as CEO the following year.[9] Asked about his health, the 58-year-old casino king tersely replied, "It's okay. Things wear out as you get older."[10] On October 19, 2000, Goldberg died of complications of bone marrow failure—decidedly not a condition that develops suddenly.

The stock market's reaction to Goldberg's death was surprising, in view of his reputation as "the driving force behind Park Place Entertainment, the man who in just ten years turned a failing casino company into a power-house that dominated the industry."[11] After dropping initially, the stock finished up a quarter-point on the day. Analysts credited the shares' resilience to Goldberg's success in assembling a strong management team. Be that as it may, investors who relied on the company's disclosures during Goldberg's 1999 hospitalization, while ignoring rumors of a potentially fatal illness, failed to capitalize on information that influenced the stock and ultimately proved to be correct.

Park Place Entertainment might be criticized for tardiness in divulging Goldberg's health problems, but at least its disclosure was more punctual than that of Sun City Industries under similar circumstances. On May 29, 1997, the food-service distributor announced with deepest regret the death of its president, Gustave Minkin. This initial disclosure of Minkin's passing came four days after the event. For investors who have noticed that senior-level personnel changes often affect the value of a stock, somewhat prompter reporting is desirable.

CHAINSAW AL

Plainly, corporate disclosure does not invariably satisfy investors' reasonable demands for information. What about the external auditors whom users of financial statements rely on to ensure that the information is presented in accordance with GAAP? Judging by certain details of the Sunbeam affair of the late 1990s, this second line of defense does not always prove dependable.

Few corporate managers in history have generated as wide a range of reactions as Albert Dunlap has. In June 1996, on the day after he signed on as chairman and chief executive officer of Sunbeam, a manufacturer of small appliances, the company's stock soared by nearly 50%. Dunlap's autobiography, *Mean Business,* became a best-seller, and he reportedly commanded fees of $100,000 per appearance[12] for lecturing on leadership. On the other hand, when Sunbeam's board dismissed him on June 13, 1998, there was open rejoicing by some of the 18,000 employees he had fired over the preceding four years. (That cost-cutting rampage had earned him the nickname "Chainsaw Al.") After hearing about the champion headcount-slasher's own firing on a news telecast, Dunlap's estranged son reported that he "laughed like hell," delighted at his father's failure. "He got exactly what he deserved," added Al Dunlap's sister.[13]

The hard-charging executive was determined to boost Sunbeam's reported profits, thereby replicating his earlier successes at American Can,

Lilly Tulip, Crown Zellerbach, and Scott Paper. In that pursuit, he pushed hard on the accounting principles to make them yield the numbers he coveted. Later on, however, a reexamination of the company's originally reported 1997 financial statements rejected huge chunks of earnings that the auditors had deemed consistent with GAAP.

One source of Sunbeam's supposedly robust 1997 profits, according to the accounting firm that the company's board hired for the review, was an excessively large restructuring charge in 1996. (The Securities and Exchange Commission subsequently alleged that the massive charge-off had created "cookie jar" reserves, which Dunlap's management team later reversed to inflate 1997 earnings.[14]) In addition, Sunbeam reduced its 1997 reported income by $29 million to undo the recognition of bill-and-hold sales. These were transactions in which the company booked sales while arranging to deliver merchandise to customers at a later date, rather than shipping it immediately. In one case, a distributor that (according to Sunbeam's revenue account) bought $4 million of electric blankets was paid a one-percent-a-month fee to hold the items in storage.[15] Sunbeam shipped another $10 million of blankets to a warehouse that it rented near its Hattiesburg, Mississippi, distribution center, booking a sale to Wal-Mart despite keeping the goods in the warehouse for weeks.[16] A further $36 million of retroactive reductions in income resulted from invalidating sales made under such liberal return policies that they could be considered consignments, rather than bona fide sales under GAAP.

Although such practices were not previously unheard of in the corporate world, the Dunlap regime refined them to new levels. Indeed, Chainsaw Al inspired one of the most lyrical descriptions of accounting practices we have ever encountered, in an article penned by Jonathan Laing of *Barron's* shortly before Dunlap got the boot:

> *Sunbeam's financials under Dunlap look like an exercise in high-energy physics, in which time and space seem to fuse and bend. They are a veritable cloud chamber. Income and costs move almost imperceptibly back and forth between the income statement and balance sheet like charged ions, whose vapor trail has long since dissipated by the end of any quarter, when results are reported.*[17]

Confronted with the overall conclusion of the board-mandated accounting review, which nullified 65% of the net income that the master of corporate turnarounds had claimed to produce in 1997, Dunlap dismissed the whole affair as a bunch of "technical accounting issues."[18] For investors, however, the fluff in the originally reported numbers had a substantial dollars-and-cents impact. On June 22, 1998, when the *Wall Street Journal* reported that the SEC was probing Sunbeam's accounting practices, the company's stock plummeted by 22% to close at $8^{13}/$_{16}$. That was on top of an earlier plunge from $53 on March 4, as Sunbeam, unable to maintain the earnings momentum produced by artificial means in 1997, reported a first-quarter loss. Still worse news was to come, as the company filed for bankruptcy in February 2001.

The restatements of 1997 earnings came long after the fact, but the problems were apparent to some observers much earlier. In March 1998, three months before the board of directors ordered a reexamination of the results that the external auditors had certified for the preceding year, a 26-year-old Sunbeam internal auditor raised a red flag about the Dunlap team's financial reporting practices. Deidra DenDanto, formerly of the accounting firm of Arthur Andersen, stated in a memo (which never reached the board) that booking the bill-and-hold transactions as sales was "clearly in violation of GAAP."[19]

Even without the benefit of an inside look at the numbers, other practitioners of basic financial statement analysis voiced skepticism that ultimately proved well founded. A year before the board authorized its review, Laing of *Barron's* argued[20] that the large reserves taken in 1996 for litigation and bad debts might be drawn on to boost future earnings. He further pointed out that the $90 million inventory write-down could boost 1997 earnings as the goods in question were sold. Additionally, Laing observed that after making much bigger allowances for bad debts than in the immediately preceding years, Sunbeam could potentially juice its 1997–1998 earnings by cutting back on bad-debt provisions. The *Barron's* contributor also pointed out that in light of the company's sizable write-down of property, plant, and equipment and trademarks, one would expect depreciation and amortization charges to decline in 1997, yet they were on the rise. This raised the possibility that Sunbeam was capitalizing certain advertising and product-development costs previously expensed, which would be allowed under GAAP but considered aggressive. Finally, Laing reported that a 13% surge in sales during 1997's first quarter had prompted the press to speculate about possible "inventory stuffing" (see "Loading the Distribution Channels," in Chapter 6).

With the financial statements raising eyebrows both inside and outside the company, why did the auditors fail to curb the Dunlap regime's aggressive reporting practices? Insight into this question is provided by the tale of the spare parts. Briefly, Sunbeam stored spare parts for the repair of its appliances in the warehouse of a company known as EPI Printers. Near the end of 1997, Dunlap's colleagues hatched a scheme to sell the parts to EPI for $11 million and book a profit of $8 million. When EPI balked, saying that it believed the parts to be worth only $2 million, Sunbeam induced the company to sign an "agreement to agree" to pay $11 million, with a clause allowing EPI to opt out of the deal after year-end. With that contract in hand, Sunbeam booked an $8-million profit. When the accounting firm partner in charge of the Sunbeam audit objected that GAAP did not permit such treatment, Dunlap's minions commenced a negotiation. They agreed to knock $2 million off the recorded profit, leaving an amount that the partner deemed immaterial. In the end, the auditors provided a clean opinion on Sunbeam's 1997 statements, despite a number of such messy little items.[21]

Floyd Norris, the journalist who brought the spare parts tale to widespread attention, filed an even more remarkable story following Sunbeam's bankruptcy filing in 2001.[22] The *New York Times* columnist found that in August 1976, Al Dunlap was fired as president of Nitec, a paper mill operator in Niagara Falls, New York. Dunlap's abrasive management style was reportedly the cause. A short while later, Nitec's auditors concluded that far from earning a profit of nearly $5 million in the fiscal year ended September 30, 1976, as had been expected, the company had suffered a $5.5 million loss.

When Nitec canceled an agreement to repurchase Dunlap's stock in the company, he sued and was promptly countersued by Nitec, which alleged that a fraud had occurred. According to Norris, whose employer obtained the relevant court records from the National Archives, the auditors found evidence of nonexistent sales, overstated inventory and cash figures, and unrecorded expenses. Albert J. Edwards, Nitec's former financial vice-president and the principal witness against Dunlap, testified that Dunlap had ordered him to falsify the financial reports to meet profit targets.

Chainsaw Al called Edwards's testimony "outrageously false." Indeed, the witness had denied, in an earlier deposition, that he had played any part in cooking the books. Dunlap also suggested that Nitec's principal owner was trying to drive down earnings to reduce the amount he would have to pay him under a stock repurchase agreement.

Whatever the truth of the matter was, Dunlap omitted any mention of his Nitec stint from his self-celebratory book. The executive search firm that Sunbeam retained in connection with hiring Chainsaw Al failed to uncover the gap in his résumé, a classic red flag, even though Norris turned up mentions of Dunlap's tenure at Nitec, using electronic retrieval services. More diligent checking might have given Sunbeam's board second thoughts about hiring a chief executive whose commitment to accurate financial reporting had been questioned.

STUMBLING DOWN THE AUDIT TRAIL

The Sunbeam affair will probably make readers wonder how confident they can be in the quality of audits in general. They are right to be concerned. Abundant evidence has emerged over the years of corporate managers leaning on auditors to paint as rosy a picture as possible. The following examples convey the magnitude of the problem:

- Following a downward restatement of results for the second through fourth quarters of 1993, Woolworth launched an internal investigation by a special committee of its outside directors. The committee's report quoted the company's auditor as saying that the retailer's management had repeatedly pushed for reporting "another good quarter." Several employees told the committee that it was a company "tradition" to record a profit, however small, in every period. The former controller of Woolworth Canada said that in pursuit of that objective, he was instructed to send corporate headquarters first-half 1993 numbers that bore no resemblance to the actual results. He added that he was told to keep track of the discrepancy and offset it in the second half of the year by underreporting that period's performance.[23] The committee concluded that "senior management failed to create an environment in which it was clear to employees at all levels that inaccurate financial reporting would not be tolerated."[24] On the contrary, the committee found, otherwise capable and conscientious financial staff people evidently concluded that such behavior was acceptable.
- In 1997, National Auto Credit's auditors warned the board of directors that the company's internal accounting controls were inadequate. Supposedly, the finance company, which had previously been obliged to restate downward by $9 million the profit on the sale of its rental car business, corrected the shortcomings. A short time later, however, the auditors received information from some current or former employees of the company that cast doubt on the validity of the financial statements. Concluding that management was untrustworthy, the auditors resigned. A committee of three of National Auto Credit's outside directors investigated and found "substantial competent evidence"[25] that the auditors' mistrust of management was well grounded. The committee advised the full board to suspend the company's top management and recommended that chairman and majority shareholder Sam J. Frankino place his stock in a voting trust. Frankino responded by appointing two new directors, who voted with him and the company's president to reject the special committee's report. The outside directors resigned following their defeat.

In 1989, the auditor of California Micro Devices's cited "material internal control weaknesses" and urged the manufacturer of computer chips to replace Chief Financial Officer Steven J. Henke. The company responded by switching Henke to the treasurer's slot. He later testified at a criminal trial that contrary to what his résumé stated, he had not majored in accounting, but had taken only one course in the subject and received a D. A new auditing firm took over in 1990 and found that contrary to the preferred practice of having outside directors serve on the board's audit committee, in Cal Micro's case the panel included Chairman Chan Desaigoudar, who owned 45.7% of the company's stock. On August 4, 1994, Cal Micro's stock plunged by 40% after the company wrote off nearly half of its accounts receivable. The following month, Cal Micro's financials received a clean opinion, but it soon became apparent that the auditors had missed a massive accounting fraud. An internal investigation disclosed that one-third of fiscal 1994 revenue was spurious. According to Wade Meyercord, an outside director who helped to uncover the fraud and took over as chairman, the fakery included fictitious sales of nonexistent goods to imaginary companies. A Cal Micro staffer testified that the outside auditor assigned inexperienced employees "fresh out of college" to the job. One of the novices asked a bookkeeping question so elementary that it gave rise to a running joke among Cal Micro accounting officials. Imitating cartoon character Elmer Fudd, they asked one another, "What's wevenue?"[26]

In theory, the audit committee of the board of directors serves as an additional line of defense in the struggle for candid financial reporting. This added protection does not invariably guarantee the integrity of the financial statements, however. In a study of financial frauds that came to light between 1987 and 1997, the Securities and Exchange Commission found that the audit committees of many of the companies involved met only once a year or so. Some had no audit committees. In one of the few encouraging notes of recent years, the SEC has imposed a "financial literacy" requirement on audit committee members. This might seem too obvious a criterion to necessitate a specific regulation, but readers should bear in mind that O. J. Simpson once served on the audit committee of Infinity Broadcasting Corporation.[27]

CONCLUSION

If the horror stories recounted in this chapter were isolated incidents, it might be valid to argue that in most cases, the combined impact of corporate disclosure requirements and external audits ensures a high level of reliability in financial statements. Intense analysis of the statements by the users would then seem superfluous. Many companies, however, are either stingy with information or slippery about the way they present it. Rather than laying down the law (or GAAP), the auditors typically wind up negotiating with management to arrive at a point where they can convince themselves that the bare minimum requirements of good practice have been satisfied. Taking a harder line may not produce fuller disclosure for investors, but merely mean sacrificing the auditing contract to another firm with a more accommodating policy. Given the observed gap between theory and practice in financial reporting, users of financial statements must provide themselves an additional layer of protection through tough scrutiny of the numbers.

QUESTIONS

1. Elaborate on the conditions that result in the wide gap between theory and practice when it comes to why the system is supposed to work for the benefit of the users of financial statements.
2. How large a percentage of net income would it require for Dunlap to consider the change not "technical accounting issues?"
3. How surprising was the stock market reaction to Park Place CEO Arthur Goldberg's death? Explain.
4. Is it common for senior managers of accounting firms to overrule the frontline auditors? Explain.
5. Was Ribis's (Trump Hotels & Casino Resorts president) reputation as a details man damaged by his assertion that he discovered the discrepancy in the October 1999 earnings report only after its release? Elaborate on the subsequent events.
6. Was the information omitted from the Trump Hotels & Casino Resorts October 1999 report detectable? Explain.
7. Were all the skeptics in the Sunbeam example privy to inside looks at the numbers? Explain.
8. Were the practices implemented by "Chainsaw Al" common practice? What were his "contributions"?
9. What are some of the reasons that the financial statements will not reflect a fair picture of the company's financial performance?
10. What is illustrated in the California Micro Devices example?
11. What is illustrated in the National Auto Credit example?
12. What is illustrated in the Woolworth example?

13. What is the difference between the theory and practice of the role of the audit committee of the board of directors?
14. What is the tension that exists for the auditing firm?
15. What was Dunlap's explanation of the controversy involving Nitec's earnings reports?
16. What was one of the sources of Sunbeam's supposedly robust 1997 profits?
17. What was the classic red flag raised by Floyd Norris in the Dunlap affair?
18. What was the substance of Floyd Norris's story following Sunbeam's bankruptcy filing in 2001?
19. What were the reasons given by Trump Hotels & Casino Resorts for its reported year-over-year rise in third-quarter earnings per share in October 1999? Was that the whole picture?
20. What would make intense analysis of financial statements superfluous?
21. Why did the auditors fail to curb the Dunlap regime's aggressive reporting practices?
22. Why might investors have been excused for reacting skeptically to the reasons given for Computer Associates earnings report discrepancies?
23. Why should users of financial statements provide themselves with an additional layer of protection through tough scrutiny of the numbers?
24. Why would a naïve observer consider it overkill to scrutinize a company's financial statements for signs that management is presenting anything less than a candid picture?

10

Mergers-and-Acquisitions Accounting

Choosing a method of accounting for a merger or acquisition does not affect the combined companies' subsequent competitive strength or ability to generate cash. The discretionary accounting choices can have a substantial impact, however, on reported earnings. As a consequence, seemingly esoteric debates over mergers and acquisitions (M&A) have turned into high-level political issues.

In September 2000, Democratic vice presidential nominee Joseph Lieberman took a position on the long-standing debate over pooling-of-interests accounting (see following section). Along with 12 other United States senators, he urged the Financial Accounting Standards Board to postpone a decision until all of the alternatives had been fully considered.[1]

On March 14 of the same year, Cisco Systems chairman John Chambers donated $100,000 to the Republican House of Representatives and Senate campaign committees. The next day, Virginia congressman Tom Davis, head of the Republicans' House campaign, and the House Commerce Committee chairman, Republican Thomas Bliley of Virginia, wrote to FASB chairman Edmund Jenkins urging a delay of the proposal to ban pooling. Chambers, whose company had been an active user of the pooling method,[2] insisted that the timing of the contribution and letter was coincidental. "I had no knowledge of a letter being written," he said.[3] Indeed, Chambers indicated that he had written the check a few weeks before it was reported, while Davis said that he had been pursuing the pooling issue on his own constituents' behalf before the letter went to FASB's Jenkins.

THE TWILIGHT OF
POOLING-OF-INTERESTS ACCOUNTING

Political contributions may or may not have been what induced leaders of both major parties to become energetic lobbyists on pooling-of-interests accounting. Unquestionably, however, the seemingly esoteric issue attracted attention in high places. Exhibit 10.1 helps to explain why, by detailing the alternative accounting treatments for Company A's acquisition of Company B.

Under purchase accounting, the combined companies' balance sheet includes the acquiring company's assets at book value (historical cost less accumulated depreciation) plus the acquired company's assets at fair market value. In Company B's case, fair market value exceeds book value by $198,750, representing the difference between the price paid by Company A (5,000 shares @ $88 per share = $440,000) and Company B's shareholders' equity ($250,000), plus $8,750 (35% of $25,000) of deferred income tax liability. Of the $198,750, the auditors allocate $25,000 to ordinary depreciable (tangible) assets, which rise from $250,000 to $275,000. The remainder, $173,750, becomes an intangible asset called goodwill, which must be amortized over a period no longer than 40 years.

In this example, we assume that the combined companies amortize the newly created goodwill over the maximum allowable period, resulting in an annual expense of $4,344. Amortization of goodwill entails no cash outlay. Neither does it generate cash through tax savings, because it is not a tax-deductible expense. The amortization does reduce reported income, however, along with the $5,000 annual depreciation (over five years) of the $25,000 write-up of Company B's tangible assets. All told, the combined companies' initial-post-merger-year pretax income of $740,000 ($600,000 from Company A + $90,000 from Company B + $50,000 of efficiencies gained through combining operations) is reduced by $5,000 (pretax) of new depreciation and $4,344 (after tax) of goodwill amortization.

Under pooling-of-interests accounting, by contrast, the combined balance sheet includes the assets of both Company A and Company B at book value. There is no excess over Company B's book value to allocate to tangible assets or goodwill, so no new depreciation or amortization arises. Taxes alone reduce the combined companies' pretax income of $740,000. Net income, at $481,000, exceeds the $473,406 figure reported under the purchase method.

From a cash flow standpoint, investors are actually better off under the purchase method, in this example. Assuming that changes in working capital accounts will be identical under the two scenarios we shall use net income + depreciation + amortization as a proxy for cash flow. (Depreciation of net property, plant, and equipment is calculated at 20% per annum.)

EXHIBIT 10.1   Alternative Accounting Treatments for Company A's Acquisition of
Company B

	Historical Costs		B Shown at Current Market Values	Companies A and B Consolidated at Date of Acquisition	
	A	B		Purchase	Pooling of Interests
Balance Sheet					
Assets					
Current assets	$1,500,000	$450,000	$450,000	$1,950,000	$1,950,000
Property, plant, and equipment, net of accumulated depreciation	1,700,000	250,000	275,000	1,975,000	1,950,000
Goodwill			173,750	173,750	
Total assets	$3,200,000	$700,000	$898,750	$4,098,750	$3,900,000
Liabilities					
Current liabilities	$1,300,000	$450,000	$450,000	$1,750,000	$1,750,000
Deferred income tax liability			8,750	8,750	
Shareholders' equity	1,900,000	250,000	440,000	2,340,000	2,150,000
Total liabilities and shareholders' equity	$3,200,000	$700,000	$898,750	$4,098,750	$3,900,000
Income Statement					
Precombination income before income taxes	$600,000	$90,000	$690,000	$690,000	
From combination cost savings				50,000	50,000
Total income after cost savings				740,000	740,000
Extra depreciation expense				5,000	
Base for income tax expense	$600,000	$90,000	$735,000	$740,000	
Income tax expense	210,000	31,500	257,250	259,000	
Goodwill amortization	4,344				
Net income	$390,000	$58,500	$473,406	$481,000	
Number of common shares outstanding	100,000	20,000	105,000	105,000	
Earnings per share	$3.90	$2.93	$4.51	$4.58	
Market price per share	$88.00	$22.00	A issues 5,000 shares of its stock to B stockholders		
Tax rate 35%					
Depreciation: Straight line					
Accounting asset life	5 yrs				
Goodwill life	40 yrs				
Price earnings ratio	23	8			

Adapted from Clyde P. Stickney, *Financial Reporting and Statement Analysis: A Strategic Perspective*, Third Edition, The Dryden Press, a subsidiary of Harcourt Brace & Company, (1996) p. 371.

Under purchase accounting, the total comes to $473,406 + $390,000 + $5,000 + $4,344 = $872,750. Cash generated under pooling of interests, on the other hand, totals just $481,000 + $390,000 = $871,000. The difference represents the tax savings on the extra depreciation expense under the purchase method: $5,000 × 35% = $1,750.

Before FASB abolished pooling of interests in 2001, companies typically structured mergers and acquisitions to qualify for pooling-of-interests treatment, even though the cash flow impact of using the purchase method was either favorable or neutral. (The latter would be the case if none of the excess of purchase price over shareholders' equity were allocated to tangible assets). Conceivably, managers believed that they could achieve the highest share price for stockholders by maximizing net income and, as indicated in Exhibit 10.1, earnings per share. Alternatively, they may have been trying to maximize their own performance bonuses, which at least in years past, tended to be tied to reported earnings, rather than performance of the company's stock.

The potential for abuse of pooling-of-interests accounting had been apparent for many years by the time Senator Lieberman and other politicians urged FASB to slow down its supposedly hasty effort to abolish the practice. In the layperson's mind, the pooling-of-interests method was reserved for transactions that represented a merger of equals. In practice, big fish routinely swallowed small fish in acquisitions that qualified as poolings under APB Accounting Opinion No. 16, "Business Combinations" (1970). As discussed later in this chapter, certain acquisitions made by Navigant Consulting qualified for pooling-of-interests accounting while also being small enough, relative to Navigant, to be deemed immaterial for financial reporting purposes.

On January 24, 2001, the protracted wrangling ended in a compromise. The Financial Accounting Standards Board officially marked the pooling method for extinction. As a quid pro quo, FASB eliminated the requirement to amortize the goodwill created in mergers consummated after June 30, 2001. Neither did companies have to continue amortizing existing goodwill in fiscal years beginning after December 15, 2001.

Gone was the mandatory annual reduction of earnings, which had been the issuers' primary objection to the purchase method all along. Cisco Systems controller Dennis Powell, for example, found the resolution highly satisfactory. "Clearly," commented Powell, "the FASB listened and responded to extensive comments from the public and the financial community to make the purchase method of accounting more effective and realistic."[4]

To be sure, the new rules required companies to test annually for possible impairment of the goodwill on their books. Any loss of value would have to be recognized through a partial or complete write-down. Inevitably, however, there would be a sizable judgmental component to the determination that impairment had occurred.

Remarkably, Wall Street securities analysts recommended certain stocks that they contended would benefit from FASB's decision. Reported earnings, the analysts noted, would rise as a consequence of the elimination of goodwill amortization. This argument made no sense, given that the change in financial reporting practice could not improve the companies' economic profits one iota. The analysts nevertheless insisted that the stocks would rise, asserting that investors were too unsophisticated to understand that goodwill was a noncash expense.

One member of the analysts' own ranks, Morgan Stanley managing director Trevor J. Harris, conspicuously rejected the notion that the change in financial reporting practices would vault shares higher. "It makes no economic sense," said Harris, who doubled as a professor of accounting at Columbia Business School. "There should be no long-term price effect." [5]

Pepperdine University Professor of Accounting Michael Davis added that there were approximately 10 academic studies of the issue, covering periods from the 1960s to the 1990s. The studies consistently found that the higher reported earnings generated by pooling did not cause the stocks of the acquiring companies to outperform the stocks of companies employing the purchase method.[6] This empirical evidence did not necessarily guide the practices of analysts, however. Assistant Professor of Accounting Patrick E. Hopkins of the Kelley School of Business at Indiana University conducted an experiment in which he showed three versions of a company's financial statements to 113 analysts employed by money management organizations. The statements differed only in that one version used pooling-of-interests accounting for mergers, whereas the other two did not. Based only on the cosmetic difference in accounting treatment, the analysts awarded higher valuations to the company's stock when pooling was not used.[7]

MAXIMIZING POSTACQUISITION REPORTED EARNINGS

Among technology companies, a popular way to boost earnings in the pooling-of-interests era involved write-offs of in-process research and development of acquired companies. By getting rid of that component of the acquisition price at the outset, the acquirer could avoid a drag on future earnings through goodwill amortization. The Securities and Exchange Commission cracked down on the practice, forcing some companies to restate their earnings and limiting the practice in future years. Closing down that scheme did not exhaust corporate managers' bag of M&A-related tricks.

The conglomerate Tyco International devised an ingenious means of dressing up postacquisition performance in its 1998 acquisition of United States Surgical. Shortly before closing its deal with Tyco, the acquiree took a

$190 million write-off, reducing future depreciation charges and thereby boosting future earnings. United States Surgical filed no further financial statements after taking the write-off, however. The reduction in asset values was consequently never reported to investors. After the renowned short-seller James Chanos drew journalist Floyd Norris's attention to the issue, Tyco's chief financial officer provided more details than the *New York Times* columnist had managed to back out of the Tyco's SEC filings. Norris commented that the unreported write-off was significant for the light that it shed on Tyco's reputation for improving the operations of companies that it acquired.[8]

MANAGING ACQUISITION DATES AND AVOIDING RESTATEMENTS

Although the pooling-of-interests method has been abolished, M&A accounting remains an area in which analysts must be on their toes. Companies have developed increasingly subtle strategies for exploiting the discretion afforded by the rules. Maximizing reported earnings in the postacquisition period remains a key objective.

For example, one M&A-related gambit entails the GAAP-sanctioned use, for financial reporting purposes, of an acquisition date other than the actual date on which a transaction is consummated. Typically, companies use this discretion to simplify the closing of their books at month- or quarter-end. For example, if an acquisition agreement is completed on May 27, the acquirer may begin reporting the acquired company's results in its own figures as of May 31.

In 1999, Navigant Consulting (formerly known as Metzler Group and unrelated to the travel-management company Navigant International) exploited the acquisition-date leeway in an unusually aggressive fashion. The utilities consulting company acquired Penta Advisory Services in mid-September, but designated July 1 as the acquisition date. Following standard practice under purchase accounting rules, Navigant included Penta's revenues in its own totals from the acquisition date forward. Navigant's revenue therefore received a boost for the entire third quarter, even though Penta entered the corporate fold only at the tail end of the period.

To be sure, the numbers involved were small. Penta's trailing-12-months revenues were in the range of $5 million to $6 million, while Navigant's 1998 sales were $348 million. Nevertheless, Merrill Lynch analyst Thatcher Thompson took management to task for shifting the acquisition date by 2½ months. It was a more aggressive approach, he wrote, than he had ever previously observed under comparable circumstances.[9]

Thompson was not the only commentator with qualms about Navigant's merger accounting, notwithstanding its number-three ranking, at the time, on the *Forbes* list of the Best Small Companies in America. Other critics focused on management's exploitation of the standards, which were later tightened up, governing the classification of acquisitions as material to overall financial results. Under Securities and Exchange Commission rules, companies do not have to restate previous statements to reflect the revenues and earnings of acquired businesses deemed immaterial in size. Navigant grew rapidly after going public in 1996 by making many moderate-size acquisitions. Individually, the acquired consulting businesses were immaterial under GAAP, but collectively, they had a large impact on the company's results.

Barron's columnist Barry Henderson estimated revenues for Navigant's 1998 acquisitions for the final three quarters of 1998 by tracing the increase in shares outstanding, quarter by quarter.[10] He deducted the number of shares representing exercise of management stock options to estimate how many shares were issued to pay for acquisitions. Multiplying this figure by the share price gave the estimated dollar amount paid for acquisitions during the quarter. (To be conservative, the journalist used the minimum stock price for the period.) Next, Henderson divided the estimated aggregate acquisition price by 2.2, the multiple of trailing-12-months revenue that Navigant said it usually paid for consulting businesses. The answer represented a reasonable estimate of the revenues produced by the "immaterial" companies acquired during the second through fourth quarters of 1998. If Navigant had been required to restate its 1998 first-quarter results for these transactions, Henderson concluded, revenue would have been $83 million to $84 million, instead of the $79 million reported. That would have reduced first-quarter 1999 year-over-year revenue growth to around 16% from the sexier 22% commonly cited by securities analysts.

As it turned out, investors were wise to react to the red flag raised by Navigant's liberal accounting for acquisitions. On November 22, chairman and chief executive officer Robert P. Maher resigned under pressure, touching off a 48% plunge in Navigant's stock. The company's directors had uncovered evidence that Maher and two other senior officials were involved in "inappropriate" stock purchases.

In brief, Maher borrowed $10 million from the company in August 1999, saying it was for a real estate investment.[11] Navigant's board subsequently came to believe that he in fact advanced the funds to Stephen Denari, the company's vice president of corporate development. Denari had borrowed a like amount to purchase Navigant shares at $28.39[12] from the former owner of a company that Navigant had acquired for stock. A short while later, the shares soared to $54.25 when Navigant hired a financial adviser to explore strategic options, including a possible sale of the company.[13]

Besides leading to the CEO's resignation, these machinations affected the accounting for four acquisitions that Navigant had treated as pooling-of-interests transactions in the first quarter of 1999. To qualify as a pooling under APB 16, a business combination must entail no planned transactions that would benefit some shareholders. For example, there can be no guarantee of loans secured by stock issued in the combination, which would effectively negate the transfer of risk implicit in a bona fide exchange of securities. Reacquisitions of stock and special distributions are likewise prohibited. After a review by a special committee of the board of directors, Navigant's auditors reclassified the earlier pooling transactions as purchases. The retroactive change necessitated a 34% downward restatement of the company's operating income for the first three quarters of 1999, reflecting the goodwill amortization required under purchase accounting.

CONCLUSION

With the abolition of pooling-of-interests accounting, companies will undoubtedly turn to new methods of disguising the true impact of their mergers and acquisitions. Navigant Consulting's aggressiveness in determining the transaction date is but one illustration of financial executives' boundless ingenuity in playing with numbers. Regulators may tighten up rules that can be abused, such as the standards for materiality, but corporate managers usually manage to stay one step ahead. Analysts who hope to understand the thought process of the field's most notorious innovators would do well to study the classic gambits employed in the M&A area.

QUESTIONS

1. Are investors better off, from a cash standpoint, under a purchase method, or pooling of interests?
2. Before FASB abolished pooling of interests in 2001, how did companies typically structure mergers and acquisitions?
3. Does the empirical evidence of the academic studies regarding choice of method reflect the practice of analysts? Explain.
4. How does the method of accounting for a merger or acquisition affect the combined companies subsequent competitive strength, ability to generate cash, or reported earnings?

5. How does the Navigant example demonstrate the flaw with the current SEC rules regarding restatement of previous statements after an acquisition?
6. Now that the pooling-of-interests method has been abolished, analysts can relax in their assessment of M&A accounting. True or false? Explain.
7. Under what grounds did Trevor Harris reject the notion that the change in financial reporting practices would vault shares higher?
8. What did the academic studies of the issue of the choice of accounting method for mergers and acquisitions show?
9. What happens to the difference between fair market value and book value under purchase accounting?
10. What happens to the difference between fair market value and book value under pooling-of-interests accounting?
11. What is the role of political contributions in the pooling versus purchase controversy?
12. What was the commonsense interpretation of pooling of interests? What, if any, were the differences in practice?
13. What was the practice common among technology companies in the pooling-of-interests era? What was accomplished?
14. What was the primary objection by the issuers of financial statements to the purchase method?
15. What was the rationale offered by some Wall Street securities analysts in recommending certain stocks that would benefit from FASB's decision to eliminate the pooling method for accounting for mergers and acquisitions?
16. What was Tyco International's ingenious means of dressing up post-acquisition performance of its 1998 acquisition of United States Surgical?
17. What were some of management motivations behind the choice of method of accounting for mergers and acquisitions?

CHAPTER 11

Profits in Pensions

In 1999, International Business Machines (IBM) reported operating income of $11,927 billion. Of that amount, $799 million, or 6.7%, had nothing directly to do with the sale of computers. Instead, it represented investment returns on the computer manufacturer's pension plans.

Under SFAS No. 87, "Accounting for Pensions," the investment returns on a corporate pension plan's investment portfolio flow into the sponsoring company's operating income. Management can elect to capitalize all or a portion of the year's net pension benefit (cost) as part of inventory and then run it through cost of goods sold. Alternatively, the company can recognize the pension-related income by reducing its selling, general, and administrative expenses.

As Exhibit 11.1 shows, IBM's income statement for 1999 does not break out this component of earnings. The statement highlights several Notes to Financial Statements (indicated by the letters K, P, Q, S, and T), but not Note W ("Retirement Plans"). Neither does IBM mention the impact of pension-related income in the 1999 Management Discussion. To ascertain the pension plans' $799 million contribution to the bottom line, analysts must be diligent in plucking from Note W the net periodic pension benefit of $638 million for U.S. plans and $161 million for non-U.S. plans.

By contrast, the Management Discussion in General Electric's 1999 annual report explicitly refers to pension-related income, which represented a smaller portion (4.1%) of GE's operating income than IBM's.[1]

Principally because of the funding status of the GE Pension Plan (described in Note 5) and other benefit plans (described in Note 6), principal U.S. postemployment benefit plans contributed cost reductions of $1,062 million and $703 million in 1999 and 1998, respectively.[2]

There is a good reason why General Electric does, and analysts should, take careful note of pension-related income, even though IBM makes no effort to draw attention to it. During any given year, net pension cost or benefit depends importantly on the short-run return that the pension plan

EXHIBIT 11.1   Statement of Earnings

**International Business Machines Corporation
and Subsidiary Companies
($000 omitted)**

	Notes	Year Ended December 31 1999	Year Ended December 31 1998
Revenue			
Hardware		$37,041	$35,419
Global services		32,172	28,916
Software		12,662	11,863
Global financing		3,137	2,877
Enterprise investments/other		2,536	2,592
Total revenue		87,548	81,667
Cost			
Hardware		27,071	24,214
Global		23,304	21,125
Software		2,240	2,260
Global financing		1,446	1,494
Enterprise investments/other		1,558	1,702
Total cost		55,619	50,795
Gross profit		31,929	30,872
Operating Expenses			
Selling, general and administrative	Q	14,729	16,662
Research, development and engineering	S	5,273	5,046
Total operating expenses		20,002	21,708
Operating income		11,927	9,164
Other income, principally interest		557	589
Interest expense	K	727	713
Income before Income Taxes		11,757	9,040
Provision for income taxes	P	4,045	2,712
Net income		$ 7,712	$ 6,328
Earnings per share of common stocks			
Assuming dilution	T	$4.12	$3.29*
Basic	T	$4.26	$3.38*

The indicated notes appear on pages 69 through 92 of the IBM document.
*Adjusted to reflect a two-for-one stock split effective May 10, 1999.

Source: IBM 1999 Annual Report.

earns on its assets. As explained in Exhibit 11.2, the plan's expected return increases if the market-related value of plan assets increases.

The 1996–1999 period was a bull market for stocks. Not surprisingly, a growing portion of IBM's reported earnings reflected the rising value of the pension plan's investment portfolio, as opposed to management's effectiveness in producing and marketing competitive products. From 1.8% of operating income in 1996, net pension benefit grew to 6.7%, as already noted, in 1999. When projecting IBM's future earnings, it is important to segregate genuinely business-related income from profits on retirement plans. Otherwise, the analysis will give management undeserved credit for a general rise in stock prices.

Accounting specialists within investment bank Bear Stearns's research department used the IBM example to underscore further the importance of scrutinizing pension plan disclosures in the Notes to Financial Statements. They stripped IBM's 1999 operating income of all pension and retiree health effects except service cost, which represents the present value of future benefits earned by employees in the current year. This purer measure of earnings from operations grew at a **compound annual growth rate** (CAGR) of 38%, far below the 97% CAGR for the version of operating income that IBM reported.[3] No other company in the Standard & Poor's 500 index had as wide a disparity in CAGR, calculated in terms of reported and adjusted operating income for the period. Considering the key role that compound annual growth rates play in stock valuations (see Chapter 14), it behooves analysts to scrutinize the impact of net pension cost (benefit) on operating income, even if the reporting company does not remind them to explore that subtlety.

Analysts should also note that the accounting rules for pension income allow management, within certain bounds, to divert earnings from the non-operating to the operating category. Such a transfer involves form more than substance. Nevertheless, it may raise the company's stock price because investors value operating income more highly than the non-operating variety.

To illustrate, suppose that a company accumulates more cash than its business requires. If management leaves the cash in the current assets section of its balance sheet and invests it, the dividends and interest thereby generated must be recorded as other income. By using the cash to step up the funding of the pension plan, however, management can produce operating income under SFAS No. 87, as explained previously. Fortunately for unwary investors, the exploitation of this quirk is limited by Internal Revenue Service rules that discourage excessive funding of pension plans.

Another matter meriting close attention involves the multiple opportunities for earnings management that pension accounting provides. To begin

EXHIBIT 11.2 Components of Net Pension Cost (Benefit)

Service cost

Present value of retirement benefits earned by employees working during the current year.

Interest cost on the benefit obligation

Interest cost arising from deferred payment of previously earned retirement benefits. (The benefit obligation consists of all earned and unpaid service cost.)

Amortization of net deferred gains and losses

Deferred recognition of actual earnings on the pension portfolio above or below the expected return and changes in the benefit obligation that arise from changes in the assumptions (including such items as the discount rate, employee turnover, and mortality) used to estimate it.

Amortization of prior service cost

Recognition over several periods of an increase or decrease in the benefit obligation that results from the employer deciding to increase or reduce the amount that it expects to pay retired employees for services already performed.

Amortization of the transition amount

Amortization of the difference (either positive or negative) between the benefit obligation and the fair value of the assets in the fund at the time the company adopted FAS No. 87 (sometime between January 1, 1985 and January 1, 1987).

Gain or loss recorded due to a settlement or curtailment

Current recognition of some or all previously deferred gains and losses and prior service costs. A settlement occurs when an employer takes an irrevocable action to relieve itself of primary responsibility for the benefit obligation. A curtailment occurs when an employer significantly reduces the expected years of service of existing employees or eliminates the accrual of defined benefits for some or all of existing employees' future service.

Expected return on plan assets

A deduction from the other components of pension cost that is a surrogate for the annual return on the fund's assets. Defined as the product of an expected long-term rate of return and a market-related value of plan assets. Expected return is used in lieu of actual return to minimize annual fluctuations in net pension cost (benefit) resulting from volatility in stock and bond prices.

Adapted from Pat McConnell, Janet Pegg, and David Zion, "Retirement Benefits Impact Operating Income," *Bear Stearns*, September 17, 1999, pp. 21–22.

with, GAAP specifies no period for amortizing the deferred amounts by which the plan's actual earnings exceed or fall short of expected earnings. Five-to-seven-year amortization is typical, but management may abruptly alter the period to boost or restrain reported earnings as desired.

Furthermore, SFAS No. 87 provides little guidance on determining the expected rate. In principle, one would expect a company to base its assumption on the long-run rates of return observed in stocks, bonds, and other types of investments. Once in a great while, the plan might overhaul its long-range investment strategy. The plan's trustees might deemphasize bonds in favor of a heavier concentration in common stocks, which entail greater risk but have historically provided higher returns. On still rarer occasions, the pension plan's actuaries might conclude that a profound structural change in the financial markets warranted a revision of the expected return. Under no reasonable scenario, however, would the plan's expected return rise or fall with each annual report. Implicit in the long-run expectation is an assumption that returns will fluctuate from one year to the next.

In light of this reasoning, some companies' expectations for long-run return change with remarkable frequency. Two of the corporations in Exhibit 11.3 (IMC Global and E.W. Scripps) revised their expected returns seven years in succession. Boeing displayed extraordinary confidence in fine-tuning its forecast of investment performance, raising its expected return by 0.33% in 1997 and nudging it up another 0.42% the following year. Note, too, that the companies did not simply grow steadily more optimistic or pessimistic over the period shown. Instead, they lowered

EXHIBIT 11.3   Expected Return on Plan Assets (Percent)—Selected Companies

Company Name	1991	1992	1993	1994	1995	1996	1997	1998
Boeing	8.5	8.5	8.5	8.0	8.0	8.0	8.33	8.75
Caterpillar	9.6	9.9	9.9	9.4	9.4	9.4	9.5	9.6
Del Laboratories	9.5	9.5	9.5	9.5	8.0	8.0	8.0	9.0
IMC Global	9.6	9.7	9.2	7.9	7.8	7.0	9.6	9.9
Laclede Steel	11.0	11.0	11.7	9.9	9.8	9.8	9.9	10.0
Moog	9.0	9.0	9.0	8.9	8.2	8.6	8.5	9.0
Northeast Utilities	9.7	9.0	8.5	8.5	8.5	8.75	9.25	9.5
Scripps (E.W.)	9.5	9.0	8.0	9.5	8.0	8.5	7.5	8.5
Sysco	12.0	12.0	12.0	10.0	9.0	9.0	9.0	10.5
UST	12.0	12.0	9.5	9.0	9.0	8.0	8.0	9.0

Source: Standard & Poor's Compustat.

their expected returns during the mid-1990s, by and large, then raised them again toward the end of the decade. Skeptical analysts are bound to suspect corporate managers of ratcheting expected returns up and down to smooth reported operating earnings, rather than to reflect profound, long-lasting changes in the financial markets.

A final point to keep in mind regarding pension plans is that management cannot invariably modulate their impact on reported earnings as desired. Among the effects described in Exhibit 11.2 is the gain or loss that may arise from settlement of a pension liability. Such events may be large enough to spoil attempts to fine-tune the bottom line.

Westinghouse Electric's 1994 performance represented a case in point. Management cut 1,200 jobs as part of a corporate restructuring. As a result, the company was obliged to distribute pension benefits in lump sums to the employees eliminated in the program. Under SFAS No. 88 ("Employers' Accounting for Settlements and Curtailments of Defined Benefit Pension Plans and for Termination of Benefits"), management had no choice but to recognize a $308 million loss. This was a highly material item, considering that pretax income from continuing operations, before minority interest, came to only $157 million in 1994.

AN ADMONITION FROM THE SEC

Corporate reticence regarding dependence on pension-related earnings has not gone unnoticed by journalists and investors. Reacting to the amount of sleuthing required to nail down IBM's pension-related income, shareholder-employees of the company urged management to provide better information on the matter. IBM's senior counsel responded with a letter to the Securities and Exchange Commission emphasizing that the company's disclosure of pension income was consistent with the accounting rules.

The SEC, for its part, came down clearly on the side of more explicit disclosure. In an October 13, 2000, letter to accountants, SEC accounting chief Lynn Turner focused on the impact on pension costs of large swings in the market value of pension assets. He also noted that companies might reduce their pension costs by converting from traditional **defined benefit** plans to **cash balance** plans. Like any other event materially affecting current or future operations and cash flows, wrote Turner, these pension-related events ought to be addressed in the management discussion and analysis section of the financial statements. The chief accountant added that the SEC would order companies to redo their annual reports if they failed to provide adequate information. For good measure, Turner reminded companies to use the "best estimate" for any assumption underlying their estimates of pension liabilities. This comment was taken to reflect analysts' concerns that companies were overly optimistic about future rates of return on their pension portfolios.[4]

CONCLUSION

A corporation's pension plan is not an obvious place to look for artificially inflated profits. In principle, the company does not derive benefits from the plan, which is administered by the trustees for the sole benefit of the employees. Rather, the corporation's chief role in the pension fund is to contribute money to it. By rights, the main reason that users of financial statements should be concerned about the pension accounting is that if the plan is inadequately funded, the required contributions may strain the corporation's finances. In the event of a bankruptcy, creditors might find themselves waiting in line behind a huge claim on the company's assets, in the form of unfunded liabilities.

That, at least, is how things ought to work. Clever corporate managers, however, have transformed pension plans into devices for smoothing earnings and shifting income from the nonoperating to the operating category. Analysts must be on the lookout for potential abuses, notwithstanding the arcane calculations that underlie the pension plans' stated assets, liabilities, and investment returns.

QUESTIONS

1. Can earnings, within the bounds of accounting rules for pension income, be diverted from nonoperating to operating? Explain.
2. How can the diligent analyst ascertain the pension plan's contribution to IBM's bottom line? Is this contribution significant?
3. How often do companies change the long-run rate of return expectations on pension assets?
4. What did accounting specialists within investment bank Bear Stearns's research department do, using IBM as an example?
5. What does SFAS No. 87 say about the investment returns on a corporate pension plan?
6. What does the Westinghouse example illustrate?
7. What guidance does SFAS No. 87 provide on determining the expected rate of return on pension fund assets?

8. What is the difference, if any, between the GE annual report references to pension-related income and IBM's annual report?

9. What is the position of the SEC accounting chief Lynn Turner? Elaborate.

10. What period does GAAP specify for amortizing the deferred amounts by which the plan's actual earnings exceed or fall short of expected earnings?

11. What role do Internal Revenue Service rules play in the ability of companies to overfund their pension funds?

12. Why does it behoove analysts to scrutinize the impact of net pension cost (benefit) on operating income?

four

Forecasts and Security Analysis

12

Forecasting Financial Statements

Analysis of a company's current financial statements, as described in the Chapters 2 through 4, is enlightening, but not as enlightening as the analysis of *its future* financial statements. After all, it is future earnings and dividends that determine the value of a company's stock (see Chapter 14) and the relative likelihood of future timely payments of debt service that determines credit quality (see Chapter 13). To be sure, investors rely to some extent on the past as an indication of the future. Because already-reported financials are available to everyone, however, studying them is unlikely to provide any significant advantage over competing investors. To capture fundamental value that is not already reflected in securities prices, the analyst must act on the earnings and credit quality measures that will appear on future statements.

Naturally, the analyst cannot know with certainty what a company's future financial statements will look like. Neither are financial projections mere guesswork, however. The process is an extension of historical patterns and relationships, based on assumptions about future economic conditions, market behavior, and managerial actions.

Financial projections will correspond to actual future results only to the extent that the assumptions prove accurate. Analysts should therefore energetically gather information beyond the statements themselves. They must constantly seek to improve the quality of their assumptions by expanding their contacts among customers, suppliers, and competitors of the companies they analyze.

A TYPICAL ONE-YEAR PROJECTION

The following one-year projection works through the effects of the analyst's assumptions on all three basic financial statements. There is probably no better way than following the numbers in this manner to appreciate the

EXHIBIT 12.1 Financial Statements of Colossal Chemical Corporation Year Ended December 31, 2001 ($000 omitted)

Income Statement

Sales	$1,991
Cost of goods sold	1,334
Selling, general, and administrative expense	299
Depreciation	119
Research and development	80
Total costs and expenses	1,832
Operating Income	159
Interest expense	36
Interest (income)	(6)
Earnings before income taxes	129
Provision for income taxes	44
Net income	$ 85

Statement of Cash Flows

Sources	
Net income	$ 85
Depreciation	119
Deferred income taxes	20
Working capital changes, excluding cash and borrowings	(8)
Funds provided by operations	216
Uses	
Additions to property, plant, and equipment	125
Dividends	28
Reduction of long-term debt	60
Funds used by operations	213
Net increase in funds	$ 3

Balance Sheet

Cash and marketable securities	$ 69
Accounts receivable	439
Inventories	351
Total current assets	859
Property, plant, and equipment	895
	$1,754
Notes payable	$ 21
Accounts payable	263
Current portion of long-term debt	32
Total current liabilities	316
Long-term debt	379
Deferred income taxes	70
Shareholders' equity	989
	$1,754

interrelatedness of the income statement, the cash flow statement, and the balance sheet.

Exhibit 12.1 displays the current financial statements of a fictitious company, Colossal Chemical Corporation. The historical statements constitute a starting point for the projection by affirming the reasonableness of assumptions about future financial performance. It will be assumed throughout the commentary on the Colossal Chemical projection that the analyst has studied the company's results over not only the preceding year but also over the past several years.

Projected Income Statement

The financial projection begins with an earnings forecast (Exhibit 12.2). Two key figures from the projected income statement, net income and depreciation, will later be incorporated into a projected statement of cash flows. The cash flow statement, in turn, will supply data for constructing a projected balance sheet. At each succeeding stage, the analyst will have to make additional assumptions. The logical flow, however, begins with a forecast of earnings, which will significantly shape the appearance of all three statements.

EXHIBIT 12.2   Earnings Forecast

Colossal Chemical Corporation Projected Income Statement
($000 omitted)

	2002
Sales	$2,110
Cost of goods sold	1,393
Selling, general, and administrative expense	317
Depreciation	121
Research and development	84
Total costs and expenses	1,915
Operating Income	195
Interest expense	34
Interest (income)	(5)
Earnings before income taxes	166
Provision for income taxes	56
Net income	$ 110

Immediately following is a discussion of the assumptions underlying each line in the income statement, presented in order from top (sales) to bottom (net income).

Sales   The projected $2.110 billion for 2002 represents an assumed rise of 6% over the actual figure for 2001 shown in Exhibit 12.1. Of this increase, higher shipments will account for 2% and higher prices for 4%.

To arrive at these figures, the analyst builds a forecast "from the ground up," using the historical segment data shown in Exhibit 12.3. Sales projections for the company's business, basic chemicals, plastics, and industrial chemicals, can be developed with the help of such sources as trade publications, trade associations, and firms that sell econometric forecasting models.

EXHIBIT 12.3   Sales Forecast

Colossal Chemical Corporation Results by Industry Segment ($000 omitted)					
	2001	2002	2003	2004	2005
Sales					
Basic chemicals	$ 975	$ 921	$ 878	$ 807	$ 786
Plastics	433	422	399	370	373
Industrial chemicals	583	546	531	475	461
Total	$1,991	$1,889	$1,808	$1,652	$1,620
Operating Income					
Basic chemicals	$ 94	$ 82	$ 65	$ 52	$ 59
Plastics	24	16	25	41	26
Industrial chemicals	41	35	28	31	28
Total	$ 159	$ 133	$ 118	$ 124	$ 113
Depreciation					
Basic chemicals	$ 55	$ 51	$ 50	$ 46	$ 46
Plastics	27	25	22	20	19
Industrial chemicals	37	36	35	31	31
Total	$ 119	$ 112	$ 107	$ 97	$ 96
Identifiable Assets					
Basic chemicals	$ 813	$ 772	$ 741	$ 676	$ 674
Plastics	390	369	352	314	309
Industrial chemicals	551	530	510	457	456
Total	$1,754	$1,671	$1,603	$1,447	$1,439

Certain assumptions about economic growth (increase in gross domestic product) in the coming year underlie all such forecasts. The analyst must be careful to ascertain the forecaster's underlying assumptions and judge whether they seem realistic.

If the analyst is expected to produce an earnings projection that is consistent with an in-house economic forecast, then it will be critical to establish a historical relationship between key indicators and the shipments of the company's various business segments. For example, a particular segment's shipments may have historically grown at 1.5 times the rate of industrial production or have fluctuated in essentially direct proportion to housing starts. Similarly, price increases should be linked to the expected inflation level. Depending on the product, this will be represented by either the Consumer Price Index or the Producer Price Index.

Basic industries such as chemicals, paper, and capital goods tend to lend themselves best to the macroeconomic-based approach described here. In technology-driven industries and "hits-driven" businesses such as motion pictures and toys, the connection between sales and the general economic trend will tend to be looser. Forecasting in such circumstances depends largely on developing contacts within the industry being studied. The objective is to make intelligent guesses about the probable success of a company's new products.

A history of sales by geographic area (Exhibit 12.4) provides another input into the sales projection. An analyst can modify the figures derived

EXHIBIT 12.4 Colossal Chemical Corporation Results by Geographic Area ($000 omitted)

	2001	2002	2003	2004	2005
Sales					
North America	$1,077	$1,019	$ 968	$ 896	$ 873
Europe	649	622	601	551	526
Latin America	102	87	90	99	103
Far East	163	161	149	106	118
	$1,991	$1,889	$1,808	$1,652	$1,620
Operating Income					
North America	$ 43	$ 36	$ 29	$ 32	$ 25
Europe	77	62	61	47	52
Latin America	26	16	17	24	17
Far East	13	19	11	21	19
	$ 159	$ 133	$ 118	$ 124	$ 113

from industry segment forecasts to reflect expectations of unusually strong or unusually weak economic performance in a particular region of the globe. Likewise, a company may be experiencing an unusual problem in a certain region, such as a dispute with a foreign government. The geographic sales breakdown can furnish some insight into the magnitude of the expected impact of such occurrences.

Cost of Goods Sold   The $1,393-billion cost-of-goods-sold figure in Exhibit 12.2 represents 66% of projected sales. That corresponds to a gross margin of 34%, a slight improvement over the preceding year's 33%. The projected gross margin for a company in turn reflects expectations about changes in costs of labor and material. Also influencing the gross margin forecast is the expected intensity of industry competition, which affects a company's ability to pass cost increases on to customers or to retain cost decreases.

In a capital-intensive business such as basic chemicals, the projected capacity utilization percentage (for both the company and the industry) is a key variable. At full capacity, fixed costs are spread out over the largest possible volume, so unit costs are minimized. Furthermore, if demand exceeds capacity so that all producers are running flat out, none will have an incentive to increase volume by cutting prices. When such conditions prevail, cost increases will be fully (or more than fully) passed on and gross margins will widen. That will be the result, at least, until new industry capacity is built, bringing supply and demand back into balance. Conversely, if demand were expected to fall rather than rise in 2002, leading to a decline in capacity utilization, Exhibit 12.2's projected gross margin would probably be lower than in 2001, rather than higher. (For further discussion of the interaction of fixed and variable costs, see Chapter 3.)

As with sales, the analyst can project cost of goods sold from the bottom up, segment by segment. Since the segment information in Exhibit 12.3 shows only operating income, and not gross margin, the analyst must add segment depreciation to operating income, then make assumptions about the allocation of selling, general, and administrative expense and research and development expense by segment. For example, operating income by segment for 2001 works out as shown in Exhibit 12.5, if SG&A and R&D expenses are allocated in proportion to segment sales.

By compiling the requisite data for a period of several years, the analyst can devise models for forecasting gross margin percentage on a segment-by-segment basis.

Selling, General, and Administrative Expense   The forecast in Exhibit 12.2 assumes continuation of a stable relationship in which SG&A expense has historically approximated 15% of sales. The analyst would vary this percentage

EXHIBIT 12.5   Colossal Chemical Corporation Operating Income by Segment

	Basic Chemicals	Plastics	Industrial Chemicals	Total
Operating income	$ 94	$ 24	$ 41	$ 159
Plus: Depreciation	55	27	37	119
Plus: SG&A	146	65	88	299
Plus: R&D	39	17	24	80
Equals: Gross margin	$334	$133	$190	$ 657
Sales	$975	$433	$583	$1,991
Gross margin percentage	34.3%	30.7%	32.6%	33.0%
Memo: Segment sales as percentage of total	49.0%	21.7%	29.3%	100.0%

for forecasting purposes if, for example, recent quarterly income statements or comments by reliable industry sources indicated a trend to a higher or lower level.

Depreciation   Depreciation expense is essentially a function of the amount of a company's fixed assets and the average number of years over which it writes them off. If on average, all classes of the company's property, plant, and equipment (PP&E) are depreciated over eight years, then on a straight-line basis the company will write off one-eighth (12.5%) each year. From year to year, the base of depreciable assets will grow to the extent that additions to PP&E exceed depreciation charges.

Exhibit 12.2 forecasts depreciation expenses equivalent to 13.5% of PP&E as of the preceding year-end, based on a stable ratio between the two items over an extended period. Naturally, a projection should incorporate any foreseeable variances from historical patterns. For example, a company may lengthen or shorten its average write-off period, either because it becomes more liberal or more conservative in its accounting practices, or because such adjustments are warranted by changes in the rate of obsolescence of equipment. Also, a company's mix of assets may change. The average write-off period should gradually decline as comparatively short-lived assets, such as data-processing equipment, increase as a percentage of capital expenditures and long-lived assets, such as "bricks and mortar," decline.

Research and Development   R&D, along with advertising, is an expense that is typically budgeted on a percentage-of-sales basis. The R&D percentage may change if, for example, the company makes a sizable acquisition in an industry that is either significantly more, or significantly less, research-intensive than its existing operations. In addition, changing incentives for research, such as extended or reduced patent protection periods, may alter the percentage of sales a company believes it must spend on research to remain competitive. Barring developments of this sort, however, the analyst can feel fairly confident in expecting that the coming year's R&D expense will represent about the same percentage of sales as it did last year. Such an assumption (at 4% of sales) is built into Exhibit 12.2.

Operating Income The four projected expense lines are summed to derive total costs and expenses. The total ($1,915 million) is subtracted from projected sales to calculate projected operating income of $195 million.

EXHIBIT 12.6   Details of Long-Term Debt, Short-Term Debt, and Interest Expense

Colossal Chemical Corporation ($000 omitted)		
Long-Term Debt (Excluding Current Maturities)	**2001**	**2000**
10.0% notes payable 2003	$ 52	$ 78
8.1% notes payable 2007	77	111
9.5% debentures due 2010	75	75
8.875% debentures due 2014	125	125
6.5% industrial development bonds due 2017	50	50
	$379	$439

Long-Term Debt	2001
Average interest rate for year	8.50%
Average annual amount outstanding	$29

Annual maturities of long-term debt for the next five years are as follows:

2002	$27 million
2003	$13 million
2004	$22 million
2005	$18 million
2006	$31 million

Interest Expense	**2001**
Interest incurred	41
Capitalized interest	5
Interest expense	36

Interest Expense   Exhibit 12.6 displays information found in the Notes to Financial Statements that can be used to estimate the coming year's interest expense. (Not every annual report provides the amount of detail shown here. Greater reliance on assumptions is required when the information is sketchier.)

The key to the forecasting method employed here is to estimate Colossal Chemical's embedded cost of debt, that is, the weighted average interest rate on the company's existing long-term debt. Using the details of individual long-term issues shown in Exhibit 12.5, the calculation goes as follows:

($000 omitted)

(2000 Amount + 2001 Amount) ÷ 2 =		Average Amount Outstanding	@Rate	=	Estimated Interest Charges on Long-Term Debt
(78 + 52)	÷ 2 =	65	@ 10.0% =		$ 6,500
(111 + 77)	÷ 2 =	94	@ 8.1% =		7,614
(75 + 75)	÷ 2 =	75	@ 9.5% =		7,125
(125 + 125)	÷ 2 =	125	@ 8.875% =		11,094
(50 + 50)	÷ 2 =	50	@ 6.5% =		3,250

Interest Charges on Long-Term Debt	Average Amount of Total Long-Term Debt Outstanding	Embedded Cost of Long-Term Debt
$35.58	÷ ([$439 + $379]/2) =	8.70%

($000 omitted)

Interest charges on long-term debt	$35.80
Interest charges on short-term debt ($32 @ 9%)	2.9
Total interest charges	$38.70
Interest incurred	$39
Capitalized interest	5
Interest expense	$34

Applying the embedded cost of 8.7% to Colossal's 2001 year-end long-term debt (*including* current maturities, which are assumed to carry the same average interest rate) produces projected interest charges of $35.8 million. As shown in Exhibit 12.6, the 2002 cash flow projection suggests no substantial reduction in debt outstanding during 2002. Accordingly, the method employed here should not prove far off the mark, even though it is merely an approximation.

To the $35.8-million figure, the forecaster must add interest charges related to the short-term debt. These projections assume an average outstanding balance of $32 million, 10% higher than in 2001. The assumed average interest rate is 9%, based on an expectation of slightly higher rates in 2002:

($000 omitted)	
Interest charges on long-term debt	$35.8
Interest charges on short-term debt ($32 at 9%)	2.9
Total interest charges	$38.7

The $38.7-million figure represents total interest that Colossal is expected to incur in 2002. From this amount, the forecaster must subtract an assumed level of capitalized interest to obtain projected interest expense. Exhibit 12.2 simply projects capitalized interest at the same level in 2002 as in 2001:

($000 omitted)	
Interest expense	
Interest incurred	$39
Capitalized interest	5
	$34

Readers should bear in mind that the method described here for projecting interest expense involves a certain amount of simplification. Applied retroactively, it will not necessarily produce the precise interest expense shown in the historical financial statements. For one thing, paydowns of long-term debt will not come uniformly at midyear, as implicitly assumed by the estimation procedure for average amounts of long-term debt outstanding. Certainly, analysts should recognize and adjust for major, foreseeable changes in interest costs, such as refinancing of high-coupon bonds with cheaper borrowings. By the same token, forecasters should not go overboard in seeking precision on this particular item. For conservatively capitalized industrial corporations, interest expense typically runs in the range of 1% to 2% of sales, so a 10% error in estimating the item will have little impact on the net earnings forecast. Analysts should reserve their energy in projecting interest expense for more highly leveraged companies. Their financial viability may depend on the size of the interest expense "nut" they must cover each quarter.

Interest Income   Exhibit 12.2 incorporates a forecast of an unchanged cash balance for 1995. Based on expectations of an average money market rate of return of 7.0% on corporate cash, the average balance of $69 million will generate (in round figures) $5 million of interest income.

Provision for Income Taxes   Following the deduction of interest expense and the addition of interest income, earnings before income taxes stand at $166 million. The forecast reduces this figure by the statutory tax rate of 34%, based on Colossal's effective rate having historically approximated the statutory rate. For other companies, effective rates could vary widely as a result of tax loss carryforwards and investment tax credits, among other items. Management will ordinarily be able to provide some guidance regarding major changes in the effective rate, while changes in the statutory rate are widely publicized by media coverage of federal tax legislation.

Projected Statement of Cash Flows

The completed income statement projection supplies the first two lines of the projected statement of cash flows (Exhibit 12.7). Net income of $110 million and depreciation of $121 million come directly from Exhibit 12.2 and largely determine the total sources (funds provided by operations) figure. The other two items have only a small impact on the projections.

Deferred Income Taxes   This figure can vary somewhat unpredictably from year to year, based on changes in the gap between tax and book depreciation and miscellaneous factors such as leases, installment receivables, and unremitted earnings of foreign subsidiaries. Input from company management may help in the forecasting of this figure. The $25-million figure shown in Exhibit 12.7 is a trend-line projection.

Working Capital Changes (Excluding Cash and Borrowings)   Details of the derivation of the $43-million projection appear at the bottom of Exhibit 12.7. The forecast assumes that each working capital item remains at the same percentage of sales shown in the historical statements in Exhibit 12.1. Accounts receivable, for example, at 22% of sales, rises from $439 million to $464 million (an increase of $25 million) as sales grow from $1,991 million in 2001 to a projected $2,110 million in 2002. Before assuming a constant-percentage relationship, the analyst must verify that the most recent year's ratios are representative of experience over several years. Potential future deviations from historical norms must likewise be considered. For example, a sharp drop in sales may produce involuntary inventory accumulation or a

EXHIBIT 12.7   Projected Statement of Cash Flows, 2002

<table>
<tr><td colspan="2" align="center">Colossal Chemical Corporation
($000 omitted)</td></tr>
<tr><td>**Sources**</td><td></td></tr>
<tr><td>Net income</td><td>$110</td></tr>
<tr><td>Depreciation</td><td>121</td></tr>
<tr><td>Deferred income taxes</td><td>25</td></tr>
<tr><td>Working capital changes, excluding
   cash and borrowings</td><td>(43)</td></tr>
<tr><td>Cash provided by operations</td><td>213</td></tr>
<tr><td>**Uses**</td><td></td></tr>
<tr><td>Additions to property, plant,
   and equipment</td><td>165</td></tr>
<tr><td>Dividends</td><td>37</td></tr>
<tr><td>Repayment of current maturities
   of long-term debt</td><td>32</td></tr>
<tr><td>Cash used by operations</td><td>234</td></tr>
<tr><td>Net cash provided (used) by operations</td><td>(21)</td></tr>
<tr><td>Increase in notes payable</td><td>$ 21</td></tr>
</table>

Changes in Working Capital	
Decrease (increase) in accounts receivable	$ (25)
Decrease (increase) in inventories	(29)
Increase (decrease) in accounts payable	11
	$ (43)

rise in accounts receivable as the company attempts to stimulate its sales by offering easier credit terms.

Additions to Property, Plant, and Equipment   The first and largest of the uses on this cash flow projection is capital expenditures. A company may provide a specific capital spending projection in its annual report, then, as the year progresses, update its estimate in its quarterly statements or 10-Q reports and in press releases. Even if the company does not publish a specific number, its investor-relations officer will ordinarily respond to questions about the range, or at least the direction (up, down, or flat) for the coming year.

Dividends   The $37-million figure shown assumes that Colossal will continue its stated policy of paying out in dividends approximately one-third of its sustainable earnings (excluding extraordinary gains and losses). Typically, this sort of guideline is interpreted as an average payout over time, so that the dividend rate does not fluctuate over a normal business cycle to the same extent that earnings do. A company may even avoid cutting its dividend through a year or more of losses, borrowing to maintain the payout if necessary. This practice often invites criticism and may stir debate within the board of directors, where the authority to declare dividends resides.

Until the board officially announces its decision, an analyst attempting to project future dividends can make only an educated guess. In a difficult earnings environment, moreover, a decision to maintain the dividend in one quarter is no assurance that the board will decide the same way three months later.

Repayment of Current Maturities of Long-Term Debt The $32-million figure shown comes directly from the current liabilities section of the balance sheet in Exhibit 12.1.

Increase in Notes Payable Subtracting $234 million of cash used in operations from the $213 million provided by operations produces a net use of $21 million. This projection assumes that any net cash generated will be applied to debt retirement. A net cash use, on the other hand, will be made up through drawing down short-term bank lines. Underlying these assumptions about the company's actions are management's stated objectives and some knowledge of how faithfully management has stuck to its plans in the past. Other assumptions might be more appropriate in other circumstances. For example, a net provision or use of cash might be offset by a reduction or increase in cash and marketable securities. A sizable net cash provision might be presumed to be directed toward share repurchase, reducing shareholders' equity, if management has indicated a desire to buy in stock and is authorized to do so by its board of directors. Instead of making up a large cash shortfall with short-term debt, a company might instead fund the borrowings as quickly as possible (add to its long-term debt). Alternatively, a company may have a practice of financing any large cash need with a combination of long-term debt and equity, using the proportions of each that are required to keep its ratio of debt to equity at some constant level.

Projected Balance Sheet

Constructing the projected balance sheet (Exhibit 12.8) requires no additional assumptions beyond those made in projecting the income statement and statement of cash flows. The analyst simply updates the historical balance sheet in Exhibit 12.1 on the basis of information drawn from the other statements.

EXHIBIT 12.8 Colossal Chemical Corporation Projected Balance Sheet December 31, 2002 ($000 omitted)

Cash and marketable securities	$ 69	Notes payable	$ 42
Accounts receivable	464	Accounts payable	274
		Current portion of	
Inventories	380	long-term debt	27
Total current assets	913	Total current liabilities	343
		Long-term debt	352
		Deferred income taxes	95
Property, plant and equipment	939	Shareholders' equity	1,062
	$1,852		$1,852

Most of the required information appears in the projected statement of cash flows (Exhibit 12.7). Accounts receivable, inventories, and accounts payable, for example, reflect the projected changes in working capital. The cash flow projection would likewise show any increase or decrease in cash and marketable securities, an item that in this case remains flat. Property, plant, and equipment rises from the prior year's level of $895 million by $165 million of additions, less $121 million of depreciation. The projected cash flow statement also furnishes the increases in notes payable and deferred income taxes, as well as the change in shareholders' equity (net income less dividends).

The details of long-term debt in the historical balance sheet (Exhibit 12.6) provide the figures needed to complete the projection of long-term debt. With the 2001 current maturities of long-term debt ($32 million) having been paid off, the 2002 current maturities ($27 million) take their place on the balance sheet. The $27-million figure is also deducted from 2001's (noncurrent) long-term debt of $379 million to produce the new figure of $352 million. (Any further adjustments to long-term debt, of which there are none in these projections, would appear in the projected statement of cash flows.)

SENSITIVITY ANALYSIS WITH PROJECTED FINANCIAL STATEMENTS

Preparing a set of projected financial statements provides a glimpse at a company's future financial condition, given certain assumptions. The analyst can study the projected statements using the same techniques discussed in Chapters 2 through 4 for the historical statements and also use them to calculate the ratios employed in credit analysis (Chapter 13) and equity analysis (Chapter 14). Based on the historical and projected data in Exhibits 12.1 through 12.8, Colossal Chemical's credit quality measures will improve in 2002 (Exhibit 12.9). Total debt will decline, not only in absolute terms, but also as a percentage of total capital—from 29.0% to 26.7%. Similiarly, total debt as a multiple of cash provided by operations will fall from 1.93x to 1.64x. As explained in Chapter 13, both of these trends indicate reduced financial risk. These projected ratios are only as reliable as the assumptions underlying the projected statements that generated them. Logical though they may seem, the assumptions rest heavily on macroeconomic forecasting, which is far from an exact science, to put it charitably. Typically, the analyst must modify the underlying economic assumptions, and therefore the projections, several times during the year as business activity diverges from forecasted levels.

Knowing that conditions can, and in all likelihood will, change, wise investors and lenders will not base their decisions entirely on a single set of

EXHIBIT 12.9   Trend of Credit Quality Measures—Base Case

	Colossal Chemical Corporation ($000 omitted)	
	2002 (Projected)*	2001 (Actual)[†]
Total Debt		
Notes payable	$ 42	$ 21
Current portion of long-term debt	27	32
Long-term debt	352	379
	421	432
Deferred income taxes	95	70
Shareholders' equity	1,062	989
Total capital	$1,578	$1,491
Total debt as a percentage of total capital	26.7%	29.0%
Cash provided by operations (before working capital charges)	256	224
Total debt	421	432
Total debt as a multiple of cash provided	1.64x	1.93x

*From Exhibit 12.8.
[†] From Exhibit 12.1.

EXHIBIT 12.10 Sensitivity Analysis Projected Financial Statements

Colossal Chemical Corporation
Year Ended December 31, 2001
($000 omitted)
Base Case (Exhibit 12.2) Sales Growth Assumption Reduced from 6% to 3%
(No improvement in gross margin over preceding year)

Income Statement		Statement of Cash Flow	
Sales	$2,051	Sources	
Cost of goods sold	1,374	Net income	$ 90
Selling, general, and		Depreciation	121
administrative expense	308	Deferred income taxes	25
Depreciation	121	Working capital changes, exclud-	
Research and development	82	ing cash and borrowings	(26)
Total costs and expenses	1,885	Cash provided by operations	$ 210
Operating Income	166	Uses	
Interest expense	34	Additions to property, plant,	
Interest (income)	(5)	and equipment	165
Earnings before income taxes	137	Dividends	30
Provision for income taxes	47	Repayment of current	
		maturities of long-term debt	32
Net income	$ 90	Cash provided by operations	227
		Net cash provided (used) by	
		operations	(17)
		Increase in long-term debt	17
		Net change in cash	$ 0

Balance Sheet

Cash and marketable		Notes payable	$ 21
securities	$ 69	Accounts payable	267
Accounts receivable	451	Current portion of long-term debt	27
Inventories	369	Total current liabilities	$ 315
Total current assets	889	Long-term debt	369
Property, plant, and		Deferred income taxes	95
equipment	939	Shareholders' equity	1,049
	$1,828		$1,828

projections, or "point forecast." Instead, they will assess the risks and potential rewards in light of a range of possible outcomes.

Exhibit 12.10 illustrates how the analyst can modify the underlying assumptions and then observe the extent to which projected ratios will be altered. This process is known as sensitivity analysis. In the example, the analyst projects a sales increase over the preceding year of just 3%. That is one-half the growth rate assumed in the base case (the most probable scenario) represented by Exhibit 12.2. The less optimistic sales forecast implies a less robust economy than assumed in the base case. For example, the analyst may assume no real growth and a 3% inflation rate. In the revised scenario, the analyst assumes that chemical producers will have no opportunity to increase their gross margins over the preceding year. Keeping the other assumptions intact, the revised projections show smaller increases, relative to the base case, in net income, shareholders' equity, and funds provided by operations. Long-term debt declines more slowly under the new assumptions.

Using Exhibit 12.10's revised statements, the analyst can recalculate Exhibit 12.9's credit quality measures as shown in Exhibit 12.11. Under the

EXHIBIT 12.11   Trend of Credit Quality Comparison

Colossal Chemical Corporation
Year Ended December 31, 2002 (Projected)
($000 omitted)

	Pessimistic Case*	Base Case†
Total debt		
Notes payable	$ 21	$ 42
Current portion of long-term debt	27	27
Long-term debt	369	352
	417	421
Deferred income taxes	95	95
Shareholders' equity	1,049	1,062
Total capital	$1,541	$1,578
Total debt as a percentage of total capital	26.7%	26.7%
Funds provided by operations (before working capital changes)	236	256
Total debt	417	421
Cash provided as a percentage of total debt	56.6%	60.8%

*From Exhibit 12.10.
† From Exhibit 12.9.

new, more pessimistic sales growth and gross margin assumptions, projected funds provided by operations represent 56.6% of total debt. The implied improvement over 2001 is smaller than indicated by the 60.8% ratio projected in the base case. Interestingly, though, total debt as a percentage of total capital is unaffected by the changed assumptions, measuring 26.7% in both the base and the pessimistic cases. Although the addition to retained earnings (and hence growth in shareholders' equity) is smaller in the pessimistic case, so is the need for new working capital to support increased sales. The borrowing need is therefore reduced, offsetting the slower growth in equity.

To complete the analysis, an investor or lender will also want to project financial statements on an optimistic, or best-case, scenario. Sample assumptions for a three-scenario sensitivity analysis might be:

	Assumed Sales Growth	Assumed Gross Margin
Optimistic case (best realistic scenario)	8%	36%
Base case (most likely scenario)	6%	34%
Pessimistic case (worst realistic scenario)	3%	33%

Note that the assumptions need not be symmetrical. The optimistic case in this instance assumes sales only two percentage points higher than the base case, whereas the pessimistic case reduces base case sales by three percentage points. The analyst simply believes that the most likely scenario embodies more downside than upside.

Other assumptions can be modified as well, recognizing the interaction among the various accounts. Colossal Chemical may have considerable room to cut its capital spending in the short run if it suffers a decline in funds provided by operations. A projection that ignored this financial flexibility could prove overly pessimistic. Conversely, the assumption that a company will apply any surplus funds generated to debt reduction may produce an unrealistic projected capital structure. Particularly in a multiyear projection for a strong cash generator, the ratio of debt to capital may fall in the later years to a level that the company would consider excessively conservative. In such cases, it may be appropriate to alter the assumption from debt retirement to maintenance of a specified leverage ratio. Surplus cash will thus be applied to stock repurchase to the extent that not doing so would cause the debt component of capital to fall below a specified percentage.

In addition to creating a range of scenarios, sensitivity analysis can also enable the analyst to gauge the relative impact of changing the various assumptions in a projection. Contrast, for example, the impact of a 1%

change in gross margins with the impact of a 1% change in the tax rate on Colossal Chemical's income statement. Exhibit 12.12 shows the effects of these two changes in assumptions on the projected income statement in Exhibit 12.2, holding all other assumptions constant. The sensitivity of net income to a 1% change in gross margins is $14 million ($110 million minus $96 million), all other things being equal. A 1% change in the tax rate, on the other hand, affects net income by just $2 million, all other things again being equal.

This type of analysis is popular among investors. They may, for example, estimate the impact on a mining company's earnings, and hence on its stock price, of a 10-cent rise in the price of a pound of copper. Another application is to identify which companies will respond most dramatically to some expected economic development such as a drop in interest rates. A rate decline will have limited impact on a company for which interest costs represent a small percentage of expenses. The impact will be greater on a company with a large interest cost component and with much of its debt at floating rates. (This assumes the return on the company's assets is not similarly rate-sensitive.)

EXHIBIT 12.12   Sensitivity Analysis: Impact of Changes in Selected Assumptions on Projected Income Statement

Colossal Chemical Corporation
Year Ended December 31, 2002
($000 omitted)

	Base Case	1% Decline in Gross Margin	1% Rise in Tax Rate
Sales	$2,110	$2,110	$2,110
Cost of goods sold	1,393	1,414	1,393
Selling, general, and administrative expense	317	317	317
Depreciation	121	121	121
Research and development	84	84	84
Total costs and expenses	1,915	1,936	1,915
Operating Income	195	174	195
Interest expense	34	34	34
Interest (income)	(5)	(5)	(5)
Earnings before income taxes	166	145	166
Provision for income taxes	56	49	58
Net income	$ 110	$ 96	$ 108

Alluring though it may be, sensitivity analysis is a technique that must be used with caution. As suggested, it generally isolates a single assumption and proceeds on the basis that all other things remain equal. In the real world, this is rarely the case. When sales fall, typically, so do gross margins. The reason is that declining capacity utilization puts downward pressure on prices. Similarly, rising interest rates do not affect only interest expense and interest income. Higher rates depress the level of investment in the economy, which can eventually depress the company's sales.

HOW ACCURATE ARE PROJECTIONS IN PRACTICE?

The Colossal Chemical example explains how to build a financial forecast from the bottom up, but because it is fictitious, readers cannot test the projections against the company's actual, subsequent performance. Exhibit 12.13, however, provides a real-life illustration of the potential and limitations of financial forecasting. The middle column is an actual forecast for Jostens, a provider of class rings, yearbooks, school photography, and graduation products, as well as employee achievement and sports awards, for the second quarter of 2001. It was created by George Chalhoub, a Merrill Lynch high-yield bond analyst specializing in consumer goods. Actual figures for the corresponding 2000 period appear in the left-hand column, while the right-hand column shows the actual outcome for 2001's second quarter. In Jostens's highly seasonal business, the second quarter is the biggest in terms of sales and earnings.

Even though sales were lower in the first quarter of 2001 than in the corresponding period of 2000, Chalhoub expected strong orders for yearbooks and jewelry, along with improved profit margins, in the second quarter. He projected net sales of $350 million, up slightly from $344.7 million in the year-earlier period, and a rise in gross profit to $196 million from $189.9 million. (Observe that analysts are generally not arrogant enough to try to forecast the figures accurately to the first decimal place, that is, to the hundred-thousands for a company with revenues in the hundreds of millions.)

Evidently, the analyst had a good handle on how business was going in yearbooks and class rings. Actual sales came in at $351.0 million, just 0.3% above the projection. The accuracy of the forecast was likewise highly respectable at the EBITDA line, where the actual number, $100.2 million, was just 1.2% higher than the forecast.

As usually happens, changed circumstances caused the outcome to deviate somewhat from the analyst's forecast. In the course of the second quarter, Jostens decided to postpone certain equipment upgrades until

EXHIBIT 12.13 Jostens (JOSEA) ($000 omitted)

Operating Data	Second Quarter 6/30/00	Second Quarter 6/30/01(P)	Second Quarter 6/30/01
Net Sales	344.7	350	351.0
Cost of sales	154.8	154	155.3
Gross Profit	189.9	196	195.7
Selling, general, and administrative	104.3	104	102.8
Special one-time charge	45.7	0	0.6
Operating Income	39.9	92	92.3
Depreciation and amortization	6.6	7	7.4
Nonrecurring expenses	46.0	0	0.6
EBITDA	92.5	99	100.2
Total interest	20.5	20	19.6
Cash interest	20.5	20	19.6
Capital expenditures	4.4	10	4.7
Margin Data			
Sales growth	NA	1.5%	1.8%
EBITDA growth	NA	7.0%	8.4%
Gross margin	55.1%	56.0%	55.8%
Selling, general, and administrative/sales	30.3%	29.7%	29.3%
Operating margin	11.6%	26.3%	26.3%
EBITDA margin	26.8%	28.3%	28.6%
Capitalization			
Revolver	0	0	0
Term loans	495.0	474	470.0
$12\frac{3}{4}$% Sr. Sub. notes due 2010	225.0	225	225.0
Other long-term debt	0	0	0
Total Debt	720.0	699	695.0
Book equity	(556.4)	(556.4)	(564.1)
Total capitalization	163.6	142.6	130.9
Interest coverage and leverage			
EBITDA/cash interest	4.5	5.0	5.1
EBITDA-C*/cash interest	4.3	4.5	4.9
EBITDA/Total Interest	4.5	5.0	5.1
EBITDA-C/total interest	4.3	4.5	4.9
Total Debt/EBITDA	NA	NA	NA
Net debt/EBITDA	NA	NA	NA
Liquidity			
Cash	35.9	30	43.1
Availability ($150 MM)	150	144	144
Debt maturities	2003	2004	2004
As of Dec. 30, 2000	27.8	32.3	32.3

(P) = Projected.

*EBITDA-C is EBITDA less Capital Expenditures.

Source: Merrill Lynch & Co.

2002. That caused Chalhoub's $10 million capital spending projection to overshoot the actual figure by $5.3 million. The lower-than-projected capital spending, in turn, helped to produce a higher end-of-period cash balance ($43.1 million) than the forecasted $30 million. Also contributing to the variance was higher-than-expected cash generation from reductions in working capital.

Although the variances in capital spending and ending cash balance were substantial in percentage terms, they did not cause key financial ratios to vary greatly from their forecasted levels. The ratios, rather than the absolute amounts shown on individual lines of the financial statements, form the basis of credit analysis, as explained in Chapter 13. As a practical matter, fixed income portfolio managers were no less disposed to invest in the Jostens bonds on the basis of Chalhoub's projected 5.0x EBITDA coverage of total interest than they would have been if he had nailed it exactly by forecasting 5.1x.

Naturally, the variance was greater in the case of total interest coverage EBITDA minus capital expenditures (an actual 4.9x versus a projected 4.5x), reflecting Jostens's lower-than-projected capital spending. On another fine point, Chalhoub's quarterly projection shows "NA" (not applicable) for the standard ratio of total debt to EBITDA. As explained in the "Combination Ratios" section of Chapter 13, it is generally inappropriate to compare a quarterly income statement item (EBITDA) with a balance sheet figure, especially in the case of a highly seasonal company such as Jostens. Analysts can, however, calculate a meaningful ratio of total debt to EBITDA for the second quarter by using a denominator consisting of combined EBITDA for the second half of 2000 and the first half of 2001.

PROJECTING FINANCIAL FLEXIBILITY

Just as projected statements can reveal a company's probable future financial profile, they can also indicate the likely direction of its financial flexibility, a concept discussed in Chapter 4. For example, the projected statement of cash flows shows by how comfortable a margin the company will be able to cover its dividend with internally generated funds. Likewise, the amount by which debt is projected to rise determines the extent to which nondiscretionary costs (in the form of interest charges) will increase in future income statements.

There is one important aspect of financial flexibility, continuing compliance with loan covenants, for which projections are indispensable. As Exhibit 12.14 illustrates, debt covenants may require the borrower to maintain a specified level of financial strength. Compliance may be measured

EXHIBIT 12.14   Sample Debt Restriction Disclosures

"The credit agreement contains various financial and operating covenants, which, among other things, require the maintenance of certain financial ratios, place limitations on distributions to stockholders and restrict the Company's ability to borrow funds from other sources. In July 1999, the Company obtained a waiver which, among other things, raised the existing limitations on stockholder distributions."

(World Wrestling Federation Entertainment, Inc. 2000 Annual Report)

"Each bank's obligation to make loans under the Credit Facility is subject to, among other things, compliance by the Corporation with various representations, warranties, and covenants, including, but not limited to, covenants limiting the ability of the Corporation and certain of its subsidiaries to encumber their assets and a covenant not to exceed a maximum leverage ratio. . . . Certain of the Corporation's other financing agreements contain restrictive covenants relating to debt, limitations on encumbrances and sale and leaseback transactions, and provisions which relate to certain changes in control."

(Lockheed Martin Corporation 2000 Annual Report)

"The covenant restrictions for the Syndicated Facility and Credit Facility include, among others, interest coverage and debt capitalization ratios, limitations on dividends, additional indebtedness and liens. . . . Under the terms of the Syndicated Facility and the Credit Facility, the Company is obligated to repay the borrowings under the facilities with the cash proceeds from the strategic plan divestitures. The Company was required to use all of the first $1,500 million of net proceeds from the divestitures to repay indebtedness, which it has done. Additionally, the Company is required to use 50% of the additional cash proceeds greater than $1,500 million and up to $2,500 million from divestitures to repay the indebtedness under the Syndicated and Credit Facilities."

(Waste Management, Inc. 2000 Annual Report)

"The May 15, 2000 refinancing agreements require the Company to maintain a minimum EBITDA on a quarterly basis, a minimum fixed charge coverage amount on a quarterly basis, and a positive quarterly EBITDA (beginning with the quarter ending September 30, 2000) at the Cleveland SBQ facility. In addition, quarterly dividend and all other restricted payments, as defined, are limited to the lesser of $750,000 or 50% of income from continuing operations."

(Birmingham Steel Corporation, 2000 Annual Report)

either by absolute dollar amounts of certain items or by ratios.[1] Sanctions against an issuer that commits a technical default (violation of a covenant, as opposed to the failure to pay interest or principal on schedule) can be severe. The issuer may be barred from paying further dividends or compelled to repay a huge loan at a time when refinancing may be difficult.

Curing the default may necessitate unpleasant actions such as a dilution of shareholders' interests by the sale of new equity at less than book value. Alternatively, the borrower can request that its lenders waive their right to accelerate payment of the debt. The lenders, however, are likely to demand some quid pro quo along the lines of reducing management's freedom to act without consulting them.

Analysts can anticipate this sort of loss of financial flexibility by applying covenanted tests of net worth, leverage, and fixed charge coverage to projected balance sheets and income statements. General descriptions of the tests can be found in the Notes to Financial Statements. These descriptions may omit some subtleties involving definitions of terms, but since the projections are by their nature also prone to imprecision, the objective is not in any case absolute certainty regarding a possible breach of covenants. Rather, the discovery that a company is likely to be bumping up against covenanted limits a year or two into the future means it is time to ask management how it plans to preserve its financial flexibility. If the answers prove unsatisfactory, the effort of having made the projections and run the tests may be rewarded by a warning, well in advance, of serious trouble ahead.

PRO FORMA FINANCIAL STATEMENTS

Another way that the analyst can look forward with financial statements is to construct pro forma statements that reflect significant developments, prior to reflection of those developments in subsequent published statements. It is unwise to base an investment decision on historical statements that antedate a major financial change such as a stock repurchase, write-off, acquisition, or divestment. By the same token, it can be important to determine quickly whether news that flashes across the screen will have a material effect on a company's financial condition. For example, will a just-announced repurchase of 3.5 million shares materially increase financial leverage? To answer the question, the analyst must adjust the latest balance sheet available, reducing shareholders' equity by the product of 3.5 million and an assumed purchase price per share, then reduce cash or increase debt as the accounting offset.

Pro Forma Statements for Divestments

Exhibit 12.15 presents a pro forma income statement dealing with a more complex set of circumstances. As detailed in Exhibit 12.16, on September 13, 2000, specialty chemical producer Cabot Corporation spun off its

EXHIBIT 12.15   Cabot Corporation

Unaudited Pro Forma Consolidated Statement of Income
for the Year Ended September 30, 1999
(in millions, except per Share Data)
(Unaudited)

	Historical	Pro Forma Adjustments			
	Cabot Corporation	LNG (A)	CMC (A)	Other	Cabot Corporation
Revenues:					
Net sales and other operating revenues	$1,695	$(265)	$(96)	$20(B)	$1,354
Interest and dividend income	4	—	—	—	4
Total revenues	1,699	(265)	(96)	20	1,358
Costs and expenses:					
Cost of sales	1,213	(248)	(45)	20(B)	940
Selling and administrative expenses	208	(13)	(16)	7(C)	186
Research and technical service	73	—	(15)	—	58
Interest expense	46	—	—	(7)(D)	39
Special items(1)	26	—	—	—	26
Gain on sale of equity securities	(10)	—	—	—	(10)
Other (income) expense, net	7	—	(1)	—	6
Total costs and expenses	1,563	(261)	(77)	20	1,245
Income before income taxes	136	(4)	(19)	—	113
Provision for income taxes	(49)	1	7	—	(41)
Equity in net income of affiliated companies	13	—	—	—	13
Minority interest	(3)	—	—	—	(3)
Income from continuing operations	97	(3)	(12)	—	82
Income from operations of discontinued businesses, net of income tax	—	3	12	—	15
Net income	$ 97	$ —	$ —	$—	$ 97
Weighted average common shares outstanding:					
Basic	64				64
Diluted	73				73
Income per common share:					
Basic:					
Continuing operations	1.47				1.24
Discontinued operations	—				0.23
Net income	$1.47				$1.47
Diluted					
Continuing operations	1.31				1.11
Discontinued operations	—				0.2
Net income	$1.31				$1.31

Source: 8-K October 3, 2000.

EXHIBIT 12.16   Cabot Corporation Details of Divestments

Sale of Liquefied Natural Gas Business

On September 19, 2000, Cabot Corporation ("Cabot" or "registrant"), through a subsidiary, sold all of the outstanding shares of Cabot LNG Business Trust ("Cabot LNG") to Tractebel, Inc. ("Tractebel"). The agreement of sale was previously reported in Note C to the Consolidated Financial Statements and in the Management's Discussion and Analysis of Financial Condition and Results of Operations in Cabot's Form 10-Q for the quarter ended June 30, 2000. Cabot LNG is engaged in the liquefied natural gas ("LNG") business. The assets of Cabot LNG included the LNG terminal in Everett, Massachusetts, the LNG tanker "Matthew," Cabot's equity interest in the Atlantic LNG liquefaction plant in Trinidad, and all related properties and equipment. The purchase price was $688 million in cash. The price was determined through a bidding process. There is no material relationship between Tractebel and Cabot or any of its affiliates, directors and officers or any associate of any such director or officer. A copy of the registrant's press release dated September 19, 2000 relating to this sale is filed herewith as Exhibit 99.1. A copy of the Stock Purchase and Sale Agreement, dated as of July 13, 2000, by and among Cabot Business Trust, Cabot Corporation, Tractebel, Inc. and Tractebel, S.A. is filed herewith as Exhibit 2 and is made a part hereof. Registrant agrees to furnish supplementally a copy of any omitted schedule to the Commission upon request.

Spin-Off of Cabot Microelectronics Corporation Stock

As previously reported in registrant's Form 8-K dated September 14, 2000, on June 25, 2000 a committee of the Board of Directors of Cabot voted to spin-off its remaining 80.5% equity interest in Cabot Microelectronics Corporation ("CMC") by distributing a special dividend of its equity interest in CMC to Cabot's shareholders of record as of 5:00 P.M., Eastern time, on September 13, 2000. Cabot owned 18,989,744 shares of common stock of CMC on the September 13, 2000 record date. The tax-free distribution took place on September 29, 2000. The basis for the distribution to Cabot's shareholders was approximately 0.280473721 shares of CMC common stock for each share of Cabot common stock owned. Fractional shares were not distributed, but were to be sold and the net proceeds distributed to Cabot shareholders on a pro rata basis. A copy of the registrant's press release dated October 2, 2000 relating to this spin-off is filed herewith as Exhibit 99.2.

remaining 80.5% equity interest in Cabot Microelectronics (CMC), a producer of compounds used to polish semiconductors. Cabot implemented the spin-off by distributing its equity interest as a special dividend to its shareholders. Separately, on September 19, 2000, Cabot sold all outstanding shares of its liquefied natural gas (LNG) business to Tractebel, Inc. for $688 million in cash. By making pro forma adjustments to its fiscal 1999 income statement, Cabot gives analysts a basis from which they can project the performance of the businesses that constitute the ongoing company.

In principle, the pro forma adjustments are straightforward. If Cabot had not owned LNG and CMC during fiscal 1999, its sales would have been lower by $265 million + $96 million = $361 million, less $20 million of intercompany sales,[2] for a net reduction of $341 million. Similar adjustments isolate the costs and expenses attributable to continuing operations from those being shed by Cabot. The pro forma statement enables analysts to make several useful observations. For example, they can infer that the stripped-down Cabot will have a higher gross margin and operating margin than its more widely diversified forerunner, as shown in the following calculations. (Note that in accordance with the formulas presented in Chapter 13, the calculations are based on net sales, rather than total revenues, which include interest and dividend income.)

Margin Comparison
($000 omitted)

Historical	Pro Forma
Gross margin:	
$(1,695 - 1,213) \div 1,695 = 28.4\%$	$(1,354 - 940) \div 1,354 = 30.6\%$
Operating margin:	
$(1,695 - [1,213 + 208]) \div 1,695 = 16.2\%$	$(1,354 - [940 + 186]) \div 1,354 = 16.8\%$

Chucking low-margin operations is often the motivation for a corporation's disposal of a business. In the case of a spin-off, however, the goal may be to increase shareholders' wealth by unlocking the value in a rapidly growing subsidiary that would receive a high price-earnings multiple as a stand-alone public company. Theoretically, a corporation consisting of two subsidiaries, one with high and one with low earnings growth, may be priced at a multiple that represents a blend of the multiples that the two subsidiaries would garner if they traded as separate companies. Many market participants, however, believe that the whole represents less than the sum of the parts in such situations. They therefore advocate the maneuver that Cabot used with its microelectronics business—establishing a multiple by selling a minority interest of the high-growth subsidiary in an initial public offering, then distributing the remainder to shareholders as a special dividend.

In Cabot's case, the subsequent stock performance vindicated the decision to spin off CMC. Shortly before the transaction, Cabot had a market capitalization of around $2 billion. Six months later, the combined market capitalization of Cabot and Cabot Microelectronics was $4 billion.

To be sure, several factors affected both companies' valuations following the spin-off. The essential point for analysts, though, is that a pro forma income statement for a single year provides no information about the historical growth in sales and earnings of the subsidiary that is being spun off. To gauge the spin-off's potential impact on aggregate market capitalization, it is important to examine as well the prospectus for the subsidiary's initial public offering.

A pro forma income statement for one year likewise gives no information about year-to-year variability in the earnings of the operations being sold or spun off. Although the business that is being discarded may have dragged down margins in the past few years, it also may have been more stable during recessions than the rest of the company's operations. The new, trimmer corporation may therefore experience wider cyclical profit swings than in the past.

Finally, pro forma adjustments for a divestment do not capture the potential benefits of increased management focus on the company's core operations. The entity being disposed of may be the remnant of a long-abandoned plan to expand aggressively in a particular region or a line of business tangential to the corporation's primary activity. By eliminating the distraction, the senior executives may be able to boost profits more substantially than the pro forma statements suggest. The pro forma adjustments simply attribute to the discarded unit a share of corporate overhead proportional to its size.

Pro Forma Statements for Acquisitions

Just as pro forma statements provide a useful basis for forecasting a company's results following a major divestment, subject to certain caveats, they are helpful in the context of acquisitions when used judiciously. If anything, though, analysts must exercise greater care in extrapolating from an acquisition-related pro forma income statement. The effects of shedding a business are highly predictable compared with the uncertainties inherent in combining companies. Mergers of companies in the same industry often work out poorly due to clashes of corporate culture. When a corporation acquires a business in the belief that it will be complementary to its existing operations, it runs the risk of inappropriately applying its own management style to an industry with very different requirements. Moreover, the acquired company's owners may be shrewdly selling out at top dollar, anticipating a deceleration in earnings growth that is foreseeable by industry insiders, but not to the acquiring corporation's management. For all of these reasons, the earnings shown in a merger-related pro forma income statement may be higher than the company can sustain. On the other hand, GAAP does not allow management to make pro forma statements reflect all of the cost savings that *might* be achievable in a merger. In some instances, projections that merely extrapolate from the pro forma income statement will prove too conservative.

Exhibits 12.17 and 12.18 are, respectively, semiconductor manufacturer Broadcom's balance sheet for June 30, 2000, and income statement for the six months ended June 30, 2000, with pro forma adjustments for three acquisitions completed during September-October 2000. The adjustments are explained in accompanying notes *a* through *h*.

As a result of using a combination of its own shares and stock options to acquire three companies with aggregate shareholders' equity of $77.5 million, the shareholders' equity on Broadcom's balance sheet swells by $1,8378.9 million to $2,681.7 million. At the same time, the company's long-term debt (including current portion) rises only slightly, from $2.1 million to $14.6 million. Seemingly, a company can reduce its credit risk, measured by the ratio of long-term debt to the sum of long-term debt and shareholders' equity, by acquiring other companies for stock (see Chapter 13). According to this logic, Broadcom's credit quality would have improved even more if instead of shelling out $2,941.2 million worth of shares and options for Altima, Newport, and Silicon Spice (this figure appears in the pro forma adjustments column of Exhibit 12.17), the company had paid $4 billion. Seemingly, a company can strengthen its balance sheet by drastically overpaying for acquisitions.

The resolution of this paradox lies in the $1,891.6 million of goodwill added to Broadcom's balance sheet through the transactions. As discussed in Chapter 2, credit analysts take a skeptical view of the debt protection afforded by intangible assets such as goodwill. Increasing the size of the intangibles by paying more than fair value in an acquisition does not, in practice, raise a company's perceived credit quality.

In fact, one aspect of the pro forma income statement (Exhibit 12.18) suggests that Broadcom has become a *worse* credit risk as a result of the three acquisitions. On a historical basis, the company had $110.1 million of operating income during the first half of 2000. The pro forma adjustments produce an operating loss of $200.9 million. Again, the effect of goodwill

EXHIBIT 12.17 Broadcom Corporation

Unaudited Pro Forma Condensed Combined Balance Sheet
June 30, 2000
(in thousands)

	Historical			Silicon Spice	Pro Forma Adjustments (Restated)	Pro Forma Combined (Restated)
	Broadcom	Altima	Newport			
Assets						
Current assets:						
Cash and cash equivalents	$280,880	$ 5,045	$18,120	$49,716	$ —	$ 353,761
Short-term investments	98,982	—	—	3,145	—	102,127
Accounts receivable, net	117,075	5,753	54	—	—	122,882
Inventory	38,617	2,413	—	—	—	41,030
Deferred taxes	8,380	520	—	—	—	8,900
Prepaid expenses and other current assets	26,317	190	205	1,037	—	27,749
Total current assets	570,251	13,921	18,379	53,898	—	656,449
Property and equipment, net	62,786	939	3,696	9,368	—	76,789
Deferred taxes	293,160	—	—	—	(116,460)[a]	176,700
Goodwill and purchased intangibles, net	—	940	—	—	1,890,646[a]	1,891,586
Other assets	15,309	74	2	585	—	15,970
Total assets	$941,506	$15,874	$22,077	$63,851	$1,774,186	$2,817,494

Liabilities and Shareholders' Equity

Current liabilities:

Trade accounts payable	$ 62,400	$ 3,159	$ 699	$ 2,864	$—	$ 69,122
Wages and related benefits	11,025	—	—	449	—	11,474
Accrued liabilities	22,139	4,324	401	—	13,770 [b]	40,634
Current portion of long-term debt	1,167	939	889	4,636	—	7,631
Total current liabilities	96,731	8,422	1,989	7,949	13,770	128,861
Long-term debt, less current portion	966	—	2,451	3,518	—	6,935
Shareholders' equity						
Common stock	681,092	23,907	29,050	96,802	(149,759) [c] 2,941,151 [d]	3,622,243
Notes receivable from employees	(1,426)	—	—	(1,025)	—	(2,451)
Deferred stock-based compensation	(10,414)	(12,610)	—	—	(680,717) [a] 12,610 [c]	(691,131)
Retained earnings (accumulated deficit)	174,557	(3,845)	(11,413)	(43,393)	(421,520) [e] 58,651 [c]	(246,963)
Total shareholders' equity	843,809	7,452	17,637	52,384	1,760,416	2,681,698
Total liabilities and shareholders' equity	$941,506	$15,874	$22,077	$63,851	$1,774,186	$2,817,494

(a) To record the preliminary allocation of the purchase price to goodwill and purchased intangibles, deferred tax liabilities and deferred stock-based compensation.

(b) To accrue estimated transaction costs.

(c) To eliminate the Acquired Companies' common stock and retained earnings accounts.

(d) To record the acquisitions of the Acquired Companies' equity securities by the issuance of the Company's common stock, restricted common stock and the assumption of employee stock options.

(e) To record the allocation of purchase price to in-process research and development.

Source: 8-K/A March 30, 2001.

EXHIBIT 12.18 Broadcom Corporation

Unaudited Pro Forma Condensed Combined Statement of Operations
for the Six Months Ended June 30, 2000
(in thousands, except per share data)

| | Historical | | | | Pro Forma Adjustments (Restated) | Pro Forma Combined (Restated) |
	Broadcom	Altima	Newport	Silicon Spice		
Revenue	$436,768	$14,722	$ 507	$ —	$ —	$ 451,997
Cost of revenue	181,597	6,627	—	—	—	188,224
Gross profit	255,171	8,095	507	—	—	263,773
Operating expense:						
Research and development	97,558	3,846	4,548	11,562	—	117,514
Selling, general and administrative	42,761	3,456	1,883	3,858	—	51,958
Stock-based compensation expense	—	—	—	—	98,380 (a)	98,380
Amortization of goodwill and purchased intangibles	—	—	—	—	192,059 (b)	192,059
Merger-related costs	4,745	—	—	—	—	4,745
Income (loss) from operations	110,107	793	(5,924)	(15,420)	(290,439)	(200,883)
Interest and other income, net	8,050	130	333	1,265	—	9,778
Income (loss) before income taxes	118,157	923	(5,591)	(14,155)	(290,439)	(191,105)
Provision (benefit) for income taxes	23,631	140	1	—	(28,810) (c)	(5,038)
Net income (loss)	$ 94,526	$ 783	$(5,592)	$(14,155)	$(261,629)	$(186,067)

Basic earnings (loss) per share	$0.44	$(0.84)
Diluted earnings (loss) per share	$0.37	$(0.84)
Weighted average shares (basic)	212,911	222,199
Weighted average shares (diluted)	253,261	222,199

(a) To record amortization expense for goodwill and purchased intangibles over an expected estimated period of benefit ranging from two to five years.

(b) To record stock-based compensation expense generally over a three- to four-year period.

(c) Reflects the estimated tax effects of the pro forma adjustments. The pro forma adjustments for the amortization of goodwill and purchased intangibles, in-process research and development, and certain stock-based compensation are excluded from such computations, as the Company does not expect to realize any benefit from these items.

Source: 8-K/A March 30, 2001.

creation modifies the analytical conclusion. Roughly two-thirds ($192.1 million) of the pro forma adjustment to reported earnings is amortization of goodwill, a noncash expense that credit analysts will downplay.

The remaining pro forma adjustment to operating income (a $98.4 million reduction) reflects the recording of stock-based compensation over three to four years. Note that the recognition of the cost of employee stock options has been a contentious issue in the determination of financial reporting principles. Corporations have lobbied hard and, so far, successfully, to avoid showing the cost of employee stock options on the income statement, even though it reduces income available to shareholders just as ordinary wages and salaries do. Understandably, corporations would prefer to report higher net income by disclosing the impact of stock options only in the Notes to Financial Statements. In October 2001, Representative Michael Oxley, chairman of the House Committee on Financial Services, advocated that approach to the likes of Securities and Exchange Commission Chairman Harvey Pitt and Paul Volcker, chairman of the board of trustees of the International Accounting Standards Board.[3]

Notwithstanding a general reluctance to display the cost of employee stock options on its income statement, Broadcom had no choice about it. In acquiring Altima, Newport, and Silicon Spice, Broadcom assumed the companies' obligations under employee stock option plans. The accounting rules required Broadcom to begin recognizing the expense.

Incidentally, the acquisitions of Altima and Silicon Spice involved one additional stock-related instrument. Broadcom assumed the two companies' obligations under arrangements whereby customers earned warrants to buy stock, generally for $0.01 a share, on fulfillment of requirements for minimum purchases of goods. Initially, Broadcom recorded the assumed agreements as purchased intangible assets and goodwill, which set in motion annual amortization charges. After reevaluating the accounting with its outside auditor, the company switched to a method of recording no assets on its balance sheet and recognizing the warrants as reductions of revenue as they are earned by customers.

MULTIYEAR PROJECTIONS

So far, this chapter has focused on one-year projections and pro forma adjustments to current financial statements. Such exercises, however, represent nothing more than the foundation of a complete projection. A fixed-income investor buying a 30-year bond is certainly interested in the issuer's financial prospects beyond a 12-month horizon. Similarly, a substantial percentage of the present value of future dividends represented by a stock's price lies in years beyond the coming one. Even if particular investors plan to hold the securities for one year or less, they have an interest in estimating longer-term projections. Their ability, 6 or 12 months hence, to sell at attractive prices will depend on other investors' views at the time of the issuer's prospects.

The inherent volatility of economic conditions makes long-term projections a perilous undertaking. In the late 1970s, prognosticators generally expected then-prevailing tightness in energy supplies to persist and to worsen, resulting in continued escalation of oil prices. The implications of this scenario included large profits for oil producers and boom conditions for manufacturers of oil exploration supplies, energy-conservation products, and alternative-energy equipment. By the early 1980s, the energy picture had changed from scarcity to glut, and many companies that had expected prosperity instead suffered bankruptcy. In subsequent years, numerous other discontinuities have forced companies to revise their long-range plans. They have included:

- A wave of sovereign debt defaults by less developed countries in Latin America.
- A stock market crash on October 19, 1987.
- A huge wave of leveraged buyout bankruptcies.
- A war in the Persian Gulf.
- A boom-and-bust in Internet stocks.
- A financial crisis in Asia.
- The September 11, 2001, terrorist attacks on the Pentagon and World Trade Center.

The frequency of such shocks makes it difficult to have high confidence in projections covering periods even as short as five years.

Notwithstanding their potential for badly missing the mark, multiyear projections are essential to financial analysis in some situations. For example, certain capital-intensive companies such as paper manufacturers have long construction cycles. They add to their capacity not in steady, annual increments but through large, individual plants that take several years to build. While a plant is in construction, the company must pay interest on the huge sums borrowed to finance it. This increased expense depresses earnings until the point, several years out, when the new plant comes onstream and begins to generate revenues. To obtain a true picture of the company's long-range financial condition, the analyst must somehow factor in the income statements for the fourth and fifth years of the construction project. These are far more difficult to forecast than first- or second-year results, which reflect cyclical peak borrowings and interest costs.

Radical financial restructurings also necessitate multiyear projections. Examples include leveraged buyouts, megamergers, and massive stock buybacks. The short-term impact of these transactions is to increase financial risk sharply. Often, leverage rises to a level investors are comfortable with only if they believe the company will be able to reduce debt to more customary levels within a few years. Sources of debt repayment may include both cash flow and proceeds of planned asset sales. Analysts must make projections to determine whether the plan for debt retirement rests on realistic assumptions. A lender cannot prudently enter into a highly leveraged transaction without making some attempt to project results over several years, notwithstanding the uncertainties inherent in such long-range forecasts.

Fortunately for analysts, electronic spreadsheets make it feasible to run numerous scenarios for proposed transactions. Analysts can vary the underlying economic assumptions and deal terms as they change from day to day. Once the company's financial structure becomes definitive, the analyst can input the final numbers into the spreadsheet. From that point, the critical task is to monitor the restructured company's quarter-by-quarter progress, comparing actual results with projections.

Electronic spreadsheets are helpful in analyzing conventionally capitalized companies, as well as highly leveraged transactions. In projecting the financials of companies with already-strong balance sheets, however, analysts should not assume that all excess cash flow will be directed toward debt retirement. Conservatively capitalized companies generally do not seek to reduce their financial leverage below some specified level. Instead, they use surplus funds to repurchase stock or make acquisitions.

Essentially, multiyear projections involve the same sorts of assumptions described in the one-year Colossal Chemical projection (Exhibits 12.1 through 12.12). When looking forward by as much as five years, though, the analyst must be especially cognizant of the impact of the business cycle. Many companies' projected financial statements look fine as long as sales grow "like a hockey stick" (sloping uninterruptedly upward). Their financial strength dissipates quickly, however, when sales turn downward for a year or two.

Notwithstanding the many uncertainties that confront the financial forecaster, carefully constructed projections can prove fairly accurate. The results can be satisfying even when the numbers are strongly influenced by hard-to-predict economic variables. The two detailed projections reproduced as Exhibits 12.19 through 12.31 were generated by Merrill Lynch high-yield health care analyst Susannah Gray. These exhibits show how the bottoms-up approach illustrated in the fictitious Colossal Chemical example can be applied in real life to companies outside the basic industry sphere.

Select Medical

Select Medical operates specialty acute care hospitals for long-term stay patients with serious medical conditions such as cancer and cardiac disorders. The company also operates outpatient rehabilitation clinics that provide physical, speech, and occupational therapy.

Historical financials (Exhibits 12.19–12.22) provide a reality check for projections. Helpfully, the company provides an inpatient versus outpatient breakdown of revenues (Exhibit 12.20). The challenge of forecasting Select Medical's financial results is underscored by the variability of its historical performance. On a quarterly basis, the company's EBITDA margin (EBITDA ÷ Total Net Revenue) ranged between 7.5% and 12.6% between the beginning of 1999 and the middle of 2001 and was only 2.4% during the full year 1998 (Exhibit 12.21).

Gray's forecast through the end of 2002 (Exhibits 12.23 and 12.24) show EBITDA margin stabilizing in a range of 11.3% to 11.8%. The analyst projects a rise in EBITDA coverage of total interest expense, from 3.0× in the third quarter of 2001 to 3.6× for the full year 2002. She also foresees a favorable trend in financial leverage, with the ratio of total debt to EBITDA declining from 2.7× on December 31, 2001 to 4.6× one year later.

Exhibit 12.24 goes a level deeper to show the expected margins that produce the projected income statement. Underlying those percentages, in turn, are the forecasted operating statistics of Exhibit 12.25. A key determinant of Select Medical's revenue and earnings growth is the number of long-term acute care (LTAC) hospitals that it operates. Gray projects an increase from 58 in the second quarter of 2001, the last historical quarter preceding her forecast, to 76 in the fourth quarter of 2002. Revenues are also sensitive to the occupancy rate, which is influenced in turn by admissions and length of stay. Similarly, revenue at the outpatient rehabilitation clinics is sensitive to the number of clinics owned and operated, as well as the number of visits. Exhibits 12.26 through 12.28 indicate the fixed and working capital requirements implied by the growth projections and the resulting impact on outstanding debt and interest expense.

EXHIBIT 12.19 Select Medical: Quarterly Income Statement

Income Statement data:	FY 98 12/31/98	1Q 99 3/31/99	2Q 99 6/30/99	3Q 99 9/30/99	4Q 99 12/31/99	FY 99 12/31/99	1Q 00 3/31/00	2Q 00 6/30/00	6 Mos 6/30/00	3Q 00 9/30/00	4Q 00 12/31/00	FY 00 12/31/00	1Q 01 3/31/01	12 Mos 3/31/01	2Q 01 6/30/01
Revenues															
(Specialty hospitals) inpatient net revenue	62.7	70.3	78.0	77.1	82.1	307.5	87.4	91.0	178.3	95.5	105.1	378.9	113.2	404.7	119.0
Outpatient net revenue	83.1	27.7	28.6	26.5	58.9	141.7	106.9	107.2	214.1	99.1	103.6	416.8	108.7	418.6	112.0
Other revenue	3.3	1.6	1.9	1.7	1.6	6.8	2.5	2.5	5.0	2.3	2.9	10.2	3.3	11.0	3.2
Total net revenue	149.0	99.5	108.5	105.2	142.7	456.0	196.7	200.7	397.4	196.9	211.6	805.9	225.1	834.3	234.2
YOY % change						205.9%	97.6%	85.0%	277.6%	87.1%	48.3%	76.7%	14.4%	16.7%	
Cost of service	128.9	84.7	90.0	87.0	121.8	383.5	167.1	167.9	335.1	169.6	181.1	685.8	189.6	708.3	197.0
General and administrative	12.5	4.3	5.0	5.9	6.3	21.4	7.3	7.4	14.8	6.8	6.9	28.4	8.4	29.5	8.6
Bad debt expense	4.0	1.3	1.7	1.9	3.9	8.9									
Depreciation and amortization	4.9	3.5	3.3	3.6	6.3	16.7	7.0	7.1	14.1	7.3	9.0	30.4	7.8	31.2	7.9
Operating income	(1.3)	5.7	8.4	7.0	4.4	25.5	15.2	18.3	33.5	13.2	14.6	61.3	19.2	65.3	20.8
Interest income	(0.4)	(0.1)	(0.1)	(0.1)	(0.0)	(0.4)									
Interest expense	5.4	4.1	4.8	5.2	7.5	21.5	8.8	9.3	18.1	8.9	8.2	35.2	7.8	30.7	7.5
Net interest expense (income)	5.0	4.0	4.7	5.0	7.4	21.1	8.8	9.3	18.1	8.9	8.2	35.2	7.8	30.7	7.5
Other income/(charges)	(10.2)	—	—	—	(5.2)	(5.2)									
Income before minority literest	(16.5)	1.8	3.7	2.0	(8.3)	(0.8)	6.5	9.0	15.4	4.3	6.4	26.1	11.4	34.5	13.3
Minority interest	1.7	1.1	1.1	0.8	0.8	3.7	1.1	1.1	2.2	0.8	1.1	4.1	1.4	4.4	0.9
Pretax income	(18.2)	0.7	2.7	1.2	(9.0)	(4.5)	5.3	7.9	13.3	3.4	5.3	21.9	10.0	30.1	12.5
Taxes	(0.2)	0.0	3.4	1.5	(2.1)	2.8	2.5	3.7	6.2	2.4	1.4	10.0	3.9	13.2	4.9
Net Income, before extraordinary items	(18.0)	0.7	(0.7)	(0.3)	(7.0)	(7.3)	2.8	4.2	7.0	1.0	3.9	12.0	6.1	16.9	7.6
Extraordinary item	—	—	—	—	5.8	5.8				6.2		6.2			8.7
Net income	(18.0)	0.7	(0.7)	(0.3)	(12.8)	(13.1)	2.8	4.2	7.0	(5.2)	3.9	5.7	6.1	16.9	(1.1)
Less: Preferred dividends	—	1.1	1.1	1.1	2.0	5.2	2.1	2.2	4.3	2.2	2.3	8.8	2.3	—	
Net available to common	(18.0)	(0.4)	(1.8)	(1.3)	(14.8)	(18.3)	0.7	2.0	2.8	(7.4)	1.6	(3.1)	3.8	16.9	(1.1)
Net available to common, excluding extra items	(18.0)	(0.4)	(1.8)	(1.3)	(9.0)	(12.5)	0.7	2.0	2.8	(1.1)	1.6	3.2	3.8	16.9	7.6
W'td. average shares outstanding															
Basic	21.73	24.50	24.49	24.47	24.77	24.6	25.49	25.45	25.48	25.45	25.48	25.5	35.00	44.79	47.21
Diluted	21.73	24.50	24.49	24.47	24.77	24.6	25.50	25.51	25.48	26.11	26.86	25.9	36.08	46.11	47.21
Earnings per share:															
Basic	$(0.83)	$(0.02)	$(0.07)	$(0.05)	$(0.36)	$(0.51)	$0.03	$0.08	$0.11	$(0.04)	$0.06	$0.12	$0.11	$0.38	$0.16
Diluted, excluding one-time items	$(0.83)	$(0.02)	$(0.07)	$(0.05)	$(0.36)	$(0.51)	$0.03	$0.08	$0.11	$(0.04)	$0.06	$0.12	$0.11	$0.37	$0.16
Diluted, as reported	$(0.83)	$(0.02)	$(0.07)	$(0.05)	$(0.60)	$(0.74)	$0.03	$0.08	$0.11	$(0.28)	$0.06	$(0.12)	$0.11	$0.37	$(0.03)

Source: Merrill Lynch & Co.

EXHIBIT 12.20 Select Medical: Balance Sheet Data

	FY 98 12/31/98	1Q 99 3/31/99	2Q 99 6/30/99	3Q 99 9/30/99	4Q 99 12/31/99	FY 99 12/31/99	1Q 00 3/31/00	2Q 00 6/30/00	6 Mos 6/30/00	3Q 00 9/30/00	4Q 00 12/31/00	FY 00 12/31/00	1Q 01 3/31/01	12 Mos 3/31/01	2Q 01 6/30/01
Cash	13.0				4.1	4.1					3.2	3.2	2.2	3.4	14.1
Total debt	156.1				340.8	340.8					302.8	302.8	289.4	272.5	294.2
Shareholders' equity	60.5				49.4	49.4					48.8	48.8	52.3	201.2	204.7
Credit statistics:															
EBITDA/total interest expense	(0.3)x	1.4x	1.8x	1.4x	0.6x	1.2x	1.7x	2.0x	1.9x	1.5x	1.8x	1.7x	2.5x	2.1x	2.8x
EBITDA-capital expenditures/ total interest expense	(1.4)x	1.4x	1.8x	1.4x	0.6x	0.7x	1.1x	2.0x	1.9x	1.5x	1.8x	1.1x	1.8x	1.4x	2.8x
Total debt/EBITDA	(115.7)x	0.0x	0.0x	0.0x		13.4x								2.8x	
Total adjusted debt/EBITDAR															
Revenue mix:															
Inpatient revenues	42.1%	70.6%	71.9%	73.2%	57.6%	67.4%	44.4%	45.3%	44.9%	48.5%	49.7%	47.0%	50.3%	48.5%	50.8%
Outpatient revenues	55.8%	27.8%	26.4%	25.2%	41.3%	31.1%	54.3%	53.4%	53.9%	50.3%	49.0%	51.7%	48.3%	50.2%	47.8%
Other	2.2%	1.6%	1.7%	1.6%	1.1%	1.5%	1.3%	1.2%	1.3%	1.2%	1.4%	1.3%	1.5%	1.3%	1.4%
Total	100.0%	100.0%	100.0%	100.0%	100.0%	100.0%	100.0%	100.0%	100.0%	100.0%	100.0%	100.0%	100.0%	100.0%	100.0%
EBITDA mix:															
Inpatient EBITDA	3.1					35.9	9.9	11.0	20.9			44.6	13.4	48.0	13.6
Outpatient EBITDA	12.6					22.7	17.2	19.3	36.4			65.4	19.1	67.3	20.6
Other EBITDA	(12.2)					(16.4)	(4.8)	(4.9)	(9.8)			(18.3)	(5.4)	(18.9)	(5.5)
	3.6					42.2	22.3	25.4	47.6			91.7	27.0	96.5	28.7
Inpatient margin	5.0%					11.7%	11.3%	12.1%	11.7%			11.8%	11.8%	11.9%	11.4%
Outpatient margin	15.2%					16.0%	16.1%	18.0%	17.0%			15.7%	17.5%	16.1%	18.4%
Total margin	2.4%					9.3%	11.3%	12.6%	12.0%			11.4%	12.0%	11.6%	12.2%
YOY% change															
Inpatient						1041.7%						24.0%	35.2%		23.3%
Outpatient						80.2%						188.2%	11.0%		7.0%
Other						34.8%						11.7%	12.1%		12.3%
Total						1075.7%						117.0%	21.5%		13.0%

Source: Merrill Lynch & Co.

EXHIBIT 12.21 Select Medical: Cash Flow Data

	FY 98 12/31/98	1Q 99 3/31/99	2Q 99 6/30/99	3Q 99 9/30/99	4Q 99 12/31/99	FY 99 12/31/99	1Q 00 3/31/00	2Q 00 6/30/00	6 Mos 6/30/00	3Q 00 9/30/00	4Q 00 12/31/00	FY 00 12/31/00	1Q 01 3/31/01	12 Mos 3/31/01	2Q 01 6/30/01
Operating income	(1.3)	5.7	8.4	7.0	4.4	25.5	15.2	18.3	33.5	13.2	14.6	61.3	19.2	65.3	20.8
Depreciation and amortization	4.9	3.5	3.3	3.6	6.3	16.7	7.0	7.1	14.1	7.3	9.0	30.4	7.8	31.2	7.9
EBITDA	3.6	9.2	11.7	10.6	10.7	42.2	22.3	25.4	47.6	20.5	23.6	91.7	27.0	96.5	28.7
EBITDA margin	2.4%	9.3%	10.8%	10.0%	7.5%	9.3%	11.3%	12.6%	12.0%	10.4%	11.1%	11.4%	12.0%	11.6%	12.2%
YOY % change						1075.7%	141.2%	116.2%	350.8%	94.1%	119.7%	117.0%	21.5%		13.0%
Estimated rent	11.1	9.0	9.0	9.0	9.0	35.9	17.2	17.2	34.4	17.2	17.2	68.7	17.18	68.7	17.2
EBITDAR	14.7	18.2	20.7	19.5	19.7	78.2	39.4	42.5	82.0	37.7	40.8	160.4	44.2	165.2	45.8
EBITDAR margin	9.9%	18.3%	19.1%	18.6%	13.8%	17.1%	20.0%	21.2%	20.6%	19.1%	19.3%	19.9%	19.6%	19.8%	19.6%
Capital expenditures	6.4					10.9	5.9					22.4	(13.4)	21.8	
Source (use) working capital													5.3		
Total interest expense	5.4	4.1	4.8	5.2	7.5	21.5	8.8	9.3	18.1	8.9	8.2	35.2	7.8	30.7	7.5
Amortization requirements															

Source: Merrill Lynch & Co.

EXHIBIT 12.22 Select Medical: Operating Margins

	FY 98 12/31/98	1Q 99 3/31/99	2Q 99 6/30/99	3Q 99 9/30/99	4Q 99 12/31/99	FY 99 12/31/99	1Q 00 3/31/00	2Q 00 6/30/00	6 Mos 6/30/00	3Q 00 9/30/00	4Q 00 12/31/00	FY 00 12/31/00	1Q 01 3/31/01	12 Mos 3/31/01	2Q 01 6/30/01
Cost of service	86.5%	85.1%	83.0%	82.6%	85.3%	84.1%	85.0%	80.3%	81.1%	86.1%	85.6%	85.1%	84.2%	84.9%	80.6%
General and administrative	8.4	4.3	4.6	5.6	4.4	4.7	3.7	3.7	3.7	3.5	3.2	3.5	3.7	3.5	3.7
Bad debt expense (included in COS)	2.7	1.3	1.6	1.8	2.7	1.9	0.0	3.4	3.2	0.0	0.0	0.0	0.0	0.0	3.5
Depreciation and amortization	3.3	3.5	3.1	3.4	4.4	3.7	3.6	3.5	3.5	3.7	4.2	3.8	3.5	3.7	3.4
EBITDA	2.4	9.3	10.8	10.0	7.5	9.3	11.3	12.6	12.0	10.4	11.1	11.4	12.0	11.6	12.2
Operating income	(0.9)	5.8	7.7	6.6	3.1	5.6	7.7	9.1	8.4	6.7	6.9	7.6	8.5	7.8	8.9
Minority interest	1.2	1.1	1.0	0.7	0.5	0.8	0.6	0.5	0.5	0.4	0.5	0.5	0.6	0.5	0.4
Tax rate	1.0	5.0	127.6	121.6	23.0	(62.7)	47.0	47.0	47.0	69.2	26.3	45.5	39.0	43.9	39.0

Source: Merrill Lynch & Co.

EXHIBIT 12.23 Select Medical: Income Statement Data

	3Q 01E 9/30/01	4Q 01E 12/31/01	FY 01E 12/31/01	Q1 02E 3/31/02	Q2 02E 6/30/02	Q3 02E 9/30/02	Q4 02E 12/31/02	FY 02 12/31/02
Revenues								
(Specialty hospitals) inpatient net revenue	112.9	119.0	464.1	138.5	129.9	135.4	143.9	547.7
Outpatient net revenue	103.1	103.9	427.6	108.2	109.1	105.4	106.1	428.8
Other revenue	3.5	4.5	14.5	5.0	5.0	5.0	5.0	20.0
Total net revenue	219.5	227.4	906.2	251.7	244.0	245.8	255.0	996.6
YOY % Change								
Cost of service	186.6	192.7	765.9	213.0	206.7	208.2	215.7	843.6
General and administrative	8.2	8.5	33.8	9.1	9.0	9.1	9.2	36.4
Bad debt expense	—	—	—	—	—	—	—	—
Depreciation and amortization	7.7	8.0	31.3	8.6	8.3	8.1	8.4	33.4
Operating income	17.0	18.2	75.2	21.1	20.0	20.4	21.7	83.2
Interest income	—	—	—	—	—	—	—	—
Interest expense	8.3	8.2	31.7	8.1	8.1	8.0	7.9	32.0
Net interest expense (income)	8.3	8.2	32.5	8.1	8.1	8.0	7.9	32.0
Other income/(charges)	—	—	—	—	—	—	—	—
Income before minority interest	8.8	10.0	40.5	13.0	12.0	12.4	13.8	51.2

Minority interest	0.2	0.3	2.9	1.0	1.0	1.0	1.0	4.0
Pretax income	8.5	9.6	38.2	12.0	11.0	11.4	12.8	47.2
Taxes	3.3	3.8	15.8	4.7	4.3	4.5	5.0	18.4
Net Income, before extraordinary items	5.2	5.9	23.3	7.3	6.7	7.0	7.8	28.8
Extraordinary item	—	—	8.7	—	—	—	—	—
Net income	5.2	5.9	23.3	7.3	6.7	7.0	7.8	28.8
Less: Preferred dividends	—	—	2.3	—	—	—	—	—
Net available to common	5.2	5.9	21.0	7.3	6.7	7.0	7.8	21.5
Net available to common, excluding extra items	5.2	5.9	21.0	7.3	6.7	7.0	7.8	28.8
Wtd. average shares outstanding								
Basic	47.00	47.00	41.20	47.20	47.20	47.20	47.20	47.2
Diluted	46.40	46.40	43.82					
Earnings per share:								
Basic	$0.11	$0.13	$0.51	$0.16	$0.14	$0.15	$0.17	$0.61
Diluted, excluding one-time items	$0.11	$0.13	$0.48					
Diluted, as reported	$0.11	$0.13	$0.48					

(continued)

273

EXHIBIT 12.23 *Continued*

Cash Flow Data:								
Operating income	17.0	18.2	75.2	21.1	20.0	20.4	21.7	83.2
Depreciation and amortization	7.7	8.0	31.3	8.6	8.3	8.1	8.4	33.4
EBITDA	24.7	26.2	106.5	29.7	28.3	28.5	30.1	116.6
EBITDA margin	11.3%	11.5%	11.8%	11.8%	11.6%	11.6%	11.8%	11.7%
YOY % change								
Estimated rent	17.9	18.3	71.0	18.7	19.1	19.5	19.9	77.3
EBITDAR	42.6	44.5	177.5	48.4	47.4	48.0	50.0	193.9
EBITDAR margin	19.4%	19.6%	19.6%	19.2%	19.4%	19.5%	19.6%	19.5%
Capital expenditures	(5.1)	(5.1)	(21.9)	(5.75)	(5.75)	(5.75)	(5.75)	(23.0)
Source (use) working capital	(10.7)	(8.5)	(40.1)	(9.0)	(9.3)	(11.4)	(11.7)	(41.4)
Total interest expense	(8.3)	(8.2)	(32.6)	(8.1)	(8.1)	(8.0)	(7.9)	(32.0)
Amortization requirements	(3.7)	(3.7)	(11.0)	(5.4)	(5.4)	(5.4)	(5.4)	(21.7)
	(3.0)	0.8	1.0	1.3	(0.2)	(2.0)	(0.6)	(1.6)
Balance sheet data:								
Cash	11.1	11.9	9.5	10.8	10.6	8.6	7.9	7.9
Total debt	291.3	287.7	287.7	282.2	276.8	271.4	266.0	266.0
Shareholders' equity	209.8	215.7	215.7	223.0	229.7	236.7	244.5	244.5
Credit statistics:								
EBITDA/total interest expense	3.0x	3.2x	3.4x	3.6x	3.5x	3.6x	3.8x	3.6x
EBITDA-capital expenditures/ total interest expense	2.4x	2.6x	2.7x	2.9x	2.8x	2.9x	3.1x	2.9x
Total debt/EBITDA			2.7x					2.3x
Total adjusted debt/ EBITDAR	4.8x		4.8x					4.6x

Source: Merrill Lynch & Co.

EXHIBIT 12.24 Select Medical: Operating Margins

	3Q 01E 9/30/01	4Q 01E 12/31/01	FY 01E 12/31/01	Q1 02E 3/31/02	Q2 02E 6/30/02	Q3 02E 9/30/02	Q4 02E 12/31/02	FY 02 12/31/02
Operating margins:								
Cost of service	81.5%	81.3%	81.8%	81.1%	81.2%	81.2%	81.1%	81.1%
General and administrative	3.8%	3.8%	3.8%	3.6%	3.7%	3.7%	3.6%	3.6%
Bad debt expense (included in COS)	3.5%	3.5%	2.6%	3.5%	3.5%	3.5%	3.5%	3.5%
Depreciation and amortization	3.5%	3.5%	3.8%	3.4%	3.4%	3.3%	3.3%	3.3%
EBITDA	11.3%	11.5%	11.8%	11.8%	11.6%	11.6%	11.8%	11.7%
Operating income	7.8%	8.0%	8.3%	8.4%	8.2%	8.3%	8.5%	8.4%
Minority interest	0.1%	0.2%	0.3%	0.4%	0.4%	0.4%	0.4%	0.4%
Tax rate	39.0%	39.0%	39.0%	39.0%	39.0%	39.0%	39.0%	39.0%
Revenue mix:								
Inpatient revenues	51.4%	52.3%	51.2%	55.0%	53.2%	55.1%	56.4%	55.0%
Outpatient revenues	47.0%	45.7%	47.2%	43.0%	44.7%	42.9%	41.6%	43.0%
Other	1.6%	2.0%	1.6%	2.0%	2.0%	2.0%	2.0%	2.0%
Total	100.0%	100.0%	100.0%	100.0%	100.0%	100.0%	100.0%	100.0%
EBITDA mix:								
Inpatient EBITDA	13.1	15.9	55.49	18.6	17.4	18.1	19.3	73.4
Outpatient EBITDA	16.9	15.3	71.60	16.2	16.0	15.5	15.9	48.3
Other EBITDA	(5.3)	(5.1)	(21.67)	(5.1)	(5.1)	(5.1)	(5.1)	(5.1)
Total	24.7	26.2	106.5	29.7	28.3	28.5	30.1	116.6
Inpatient margin	11.6%	13.4%	12.0%	13.4%	13.4%	13.4%	13.4%	13.4%
Outpatient margin	16.4%	14.7%	16.7%	15.0%	14.7%	14.7%	15.0%	11.3%
Total margin	11.3%	11.5%	11.8%	11.8%	11.6%	11.6%	11.8%	11.7%

Source: Merrill Lynch & Co.

EXHIBIT 12.25 Select Medical: Revenue Projections

Days in Period	90 1Q 99 3/31/99	91 2Q 99 6/30/99	90 1Q 01 3/31/01	91 2Q01 6/30/01	92 Q3 01 9/30/01	92 Q4 01 12/31/01	90 Q1 02 3/31/02	91 Q2 02 6/30/02	92 Q3 02 9/30/02	92 Q4 02 12/31/02
Long-Term Acute Care										
Number of long-term acute cares	41	42	56	58	60	62	67	70	73	76
Total licensed beds	1,529	1,570	2,068	2,146	2,220	2,294	2,479	2,590	2,701	2,812
Average total licensed beds	1,479	1,550	2,025	2,107	2,183	2,257	2,424	2,535	2,646	2,757
Average beds/long-term acute care—PE	37	37	37	37	37	37	37	37	37	37
Admissions	3,054	2,952	4,191	4,086	4,096	4,293	5,016	4,915	4,964	5,244
Admissions/bed	2.1	1.9	2.1	1.9	1.9	1.9	2.1	1.9	1.9	1.9
Total length of stay	30.0	30.0	31.0	30.0	31.5	31.5	30.5	30.0	31.5	31.5
Inpatient days	85,206	89,151	123,740	125,587	129,017	135,242	152,980	147,451	156,351	165,172
Daily census	947	980	1,375	1,380	1,402	1,470	1,700	1,620	1,699	1,795
Occupancy rate	63.0%	0.63	68.0%	65.5%	64.2%	65.1%	70.1%	63.9%	64.2%	65.1%
Revenues per patient day	$825.06	$947.00	$914.42	$890.00	$875.00	$880.00	$905.27	$881.10	$866.25	$871.20
Total inpatient revenues	70.3	119.0	113.2	119.0	112.9	119.0	138.5	129.9	135.4	143.9
For projected periods										
Additional long-term acute cares opened			2	4	2	2	3	3	3	3
% P-o-P change in admissions/bed				0.5%	1.0%	2.0%	0.0%	0.0%	0.0%	0.0%
Change in length of stay (P-o-P)				0.0%	50.0%	50.0%	(50.0)%	0.0%	0.0%	0.0%
Change in revenue/patient day (P-o-P)				0.9%	(2.1)%	(4.4)%	(1.0)%	(1.0)%	(1.0)%	(1.0)%

Outpatient rehabilitation clinics
(excluding managed facilities)

Total number of clinics	42	43	43	538	548	558	568	578	588	598	608
Average number of clinics			43	544	543	553	563	573	583	593	603
Total visits				946,180	958,443	907,987	922,894	996,608	1,029,035	973,653	988,452
Average visits per average number of clinics				1,739	1,765	1,642	1,639	1,739	1,765	1,642	1,639
Average revenue per visit				$81.00	$79.30	$79.97	$79.53	$81.00	$79.30	$79.97	$79.53
Total clinic revenue	14.6	16.0		76.6	76.0	72.6	73.4	80.7	81.6	77.9	78.6
Managed clinic revenue	2.5	2.7		5.0	5.5	5.5	5.5	5.5	5.5	5.5	5.5
Other outpatient revenue	10.6	9.9		27.0	25.0	25.0	25.0	22.0	22.0	22.0	22.0
Total outpatient revenue	27.7	28.6		108.6	106.5	103.1	103.9	108.2	109.1	105.4	106.1
For projected periods											
Additional clinics opened				(12)	10	10	10	10	10	10	10
% P-o-P change in average visits					0.5%	0.5%	0.5%	(2.0)%	(2.0)%	(2.0)%	(2.0)%
Change in average revenue per visit					2.0%	1.5%	2.5%	0.0%	0.0%	0.0%	0.0%

Source: Merrill Lynch & Co.

EXHIBIT 12.26 Select Medical: Debt Service Projection Pro Forma as of March 31, 2001

	3/31/01	6/30/01	9/30/01	12/31/01	3/31/02	6/30/02	9/30/02	12/31/02
Revolver	—	—	3.0	(1.0)				
Term loan	100.0	100.0	100.0	100.0	96.0	92.0	88.0	84.0
9.5% Sr. Sub. notes '09	175.0	175.0	175.0	175.0	175.0	175.0	175.0	175.0
Seller notes	21.4	17.7	14.0	10.4	8.9	7.5	6.1	4.7
Other	2.3	2.3	2.3	2.3	2.3	2.3	2.3	2.3
Total debt	298.7	295.0	291.3	287.7	282.2	276.8	271.4	266.0
Amortization Requirements								
Term loan					4.0	4.0	4.0	4.0
Seller notes		3.7	3.7	3.7	1.4	1.4	1.4	1.4
LIBOR = 4								
Interest rates								
Revolver L + 2.75		6.8%	6.8%	6.8%	6.8%	6.8%	6.8%	6.8%
Term loan L + 3		7.0%	7.0%	7.0%	7.0%	7.0%	7.0%	7.0%
Sr. Sub. notes		9.5%	9.5%	9.5%	9.5%	9.5%	9.5%	9.5%
Seller notes		6.0%	6.0%	6.0%	6.0%	6.0%	6.0%	6.0%
Other		7.0%	7.0%	7.0%	7.0%	7.0%	7.0%	7.0%
Interest expense								
Revolver interperiod		1.5	1.5	1.5	1.5	1.5	1.5	1.5
Revolver L + 2.75								
Term Loan L + 3		1.8	1.8	1.8	1.7	1.6	1.6	1.5
Sr. Sub. notes		4.2	4.2	4.2	4.2	4.2	4.2	4.2
Seller notes		0.3	0.2	0.2	0.1	0.1	0.1	0.1
Other		0.6	0.6	0.6	0.6	0.6	0.6	0.6
Total interest expense		8.3	8.3	8.2	8.1	8.1	8.0	7.9

Source: Merrill Lynch & Co.

EXHIBIT 12.27 Select Medical: Capital Spending Projection Cash Flow Items

	6/30/01	9/30/01	12/31/01	3/31/02	6/30/02	9/30/02	12/31/02
Capital expenditures							
Maintenance	3.0	3.0	3.0	3.0	3.0	3.0	3.0
Development	3.5	2.1	2.1	2.8	2.8	2.8	2.8
	6.5	5.1	5.1	5.8	5.8	5.8	5.8
Working capital source (use)							
Amortization requirements	3.7	3.7	3.7	5.4	5.4	5.4	5.4
Development capital expenditures							
Number of long-term acute cares added	4.0	2.0	2.0	3.0	3.0	3.0	3.0
Capex/long-term acute care	0.7	0.7	0.7	0.7	0.7	0.7	0.7
Total long-term acute care development capital expenditures	2.8	1.4	1.4	2.1	2.1	2.1	2.1
Working capital per long-term acute care	2.0	2.0	2.0	2.0	2.0	2.0	2.0
Water fall (assuming 2 Q buildup)							
Q2 01	4.0	4.0					
Q3 01		2.0	2.0				
Q4 01			2.0	2.0			
Q1 02				3.0	3.0		
Q2 02					3.0	3.0	
Q3 02						3.0	3.0
Q4 02							3.0
Total long-term acute care working capital	4.0	6.0	4.0	5.0	6.0	6.0	6.0
Number of rehabilitation clinics added	10.0	10.0	10.0	10.0	10.0	10.0	10.0
Capital expenditures/clinic	0.1	0.1	0.1	0.1	0.1	0.1	0.1
Total rehabilitation development capital expenditures	0.7	0.7	0.7	0.7	0.7	0.7	0.7
Working capital per clinic	0.07	0.07	0.07	0.07	0.07	0.07	0.07
Total working capital	0.7	0.7	0.7	0.7	0.7	0.7	0.7

Source: Merrill Lynch & Co.

279

EXHIBIT 12.28 Select Medical: Working Capital Projection

	12/31/00	3/31/01	6/30/01	9/30/01	12/31/01	3/31/02	6/30/02	9/30/02	12/31/02
Working capital accounts									
Receivables	196.5	201.6	209.1	214.5	219.8	224.8	228.6	235.0	241.7
Payables	38.8	28.9	33.0	33.7	34.5	35.5	36.0	36.9	38.0
Receivables as % of long-term management revenue	24.4%	24.2%	24.3%	24.3%	24.3%	24.3%	24.3%	24.3%	24.3%
Payables as % of long-term management cost of service	5.7%	4.1%	4.5%	4.5%	4.5%	4.5%	4.5%	4.5%	4.5%
Source (use) cash									
Receivables		(5.1)	(7.5)	(5.5)	(5.2)	(5.1)	(3.8)	(6.4)	(6.7)
Payables		(9.9)	4.0	0.8	0.7	1.1	0.4	1.0	1.0
New build working capital			(4.0)	(6.0)	(4.0)	(5.0)	(6.0)	(6.0)	(6.0)
Total working capital			(7.4)	(10.7)	(8.5)	(9.0)	(9.3)	(11.4)	(11.7)

Source: Merrill Lynch & Co.

EXHIBIT 12.29 AdvancePCS: Historical and Projected Financial Data

	Q3 01 12/31/00	Q4 01 3/31/01	Q2 02E 9/30/01	Q3 02E 12/31/01	Q4 02E 3/31/02	Full Year 02E 3/31/02	Full Year 03E 3/31/03
Income statement data:							
Revenue	2,916.5	2,991.4	3,154.4	3,161.3	3,396.5	12,860.1	14,467.8
Cost of revenue	2,824.6	2,896.9	3,045.9	3,050.1	3,283.7	12,420.5	14,003.0
Selling, general, and administrative	55.1	52.2	47.0	48.0	50.0	190.4	200.0
Corporate restructuring			—	—	—		—
Nonrecurring charges	0.7	10.4				0.9	
Write-down of assets			—	—	—		—
Operating income	36.1	31.9	61.5	63.2	62.8	249.2	264.7
Interest income	1.6	—	0.8	0.8	0.8	3.0	3.0
Interest expense	22.1	19.9	18.0	18.0	18.0	73.3	62.1
Merger cost			—	—	—		—
Income before taxes	15.6	11.9	44.3	45.9	45.5	178.9	205.6
Provision for income taxes	8.6	8.5	17.5	18.1	18.0	70.7	81.2
Net income	6.978	3.405	26.8	27.8	27.5	108.2	124.4
EPS (basic)	$0.23	$0.09	$0.72	$0.75	$0.74	$2.93	$2.74
EPS (diluted)	$0.16	$0.08	$0.59	$0.61	$0.61	$2.38	
Average shares outstanding (basic)	29,913	36,490	37,000.0	37,000.0	37,000.0	37,000.0	45,400
Averages shares outstanding (diluted)	44,507	44,827	45,400	45,400	45,400	45,400	45,400

(continued)

EXHIBIT 12.29 *Continued*

	Q3 01 12/31/00	Q4 01 3/31/01	Q2 02E 9/30/01	Q3 02E 12/31/01	Q4 02E 3/31/02	Full Year 02E 3/31/02	Full Year 03E 3/31/03
Cash flow data:							
Operating income	36.8	42.3	61.5	63.2	62.8	249.2	264.7
Depreciation and amortization	21.8	19.4	9.5	9.5	10.2	38.3	43.4
EBITDA	58.6	61.7	71.0	72.7	73.0	287.5	308.1
EBITDA margin	2.1%	2.1%	2.3%	2.3%	2.1%	2.2%	2.1%
Capital expenditures	9.0	18.0	12.5	12.5	12.5	50.0	60
Working capital	—	—	—	—	—	—	—
Net interest expense	20.5	19.9	18.0	18.0	18.0	70.3	59.1
Debt amortization	—	—	6.6	6.6	6.6	26.3	34.0
Revolver payment	—	—	15.0	15.0	15.0	60.0	—
Cash taxes	—	—	8.7	9.1	9.0	35.3	40.6
Free cash flow	29.1	23.8	10.2	11.5	11.9	45.6	114.4
Balance sheet data:							
Cash	124.4	110.0	100.0	100.0	100.0	100.0	100.0
Total debt	810.0	845.0	818.3	805.0	791.5	791.5	757.5
Stockholders' equity	393.2	405.7	447.4	475.2	502.7	502.7	627.15
Credit statistics							
EBITDA/interest expense	2.6x	3.1x	3.9x	4.0x	4.1x	3.9x	5.0x
EBITDA-capital expense/interest expense	2.2x	2.2x	3.2x	3.3x	3.4x	3.2x	4.0x
Total debt/EBITDA						2.8x	2.5x

Source: Merrill Lynch & Co.

EXHIBIT 12.30 AdvancePCS: Forecast Assumptions

	Q2 02E 9/30/01	Q3 02E 12/31/01	Q4 02E 3/31/02	Full Year 02E 3/31/02	Q1 03E 6/30/02	Q2 03E 9/30/02	Q3 03E 12/31/02	Q4 03E 3/31/03	Full Year 03E 3/31/03
Revenue Drivers									
Pharmacy network claims	113.1	113.1	113.3	452.5	113.50	113.70	114.20	114.40	455.8
Mail pharmacy scripts filled	2.6	2.7	2.8	10.7	2.88	2.98	3.23	3.33	12.4
Total adjusted claims	121.0	121.1	121.6	484.4	122.1	122.6	123.9	124.4	493.0
Revenue per claim	$26.08	$26.10	$27.93	$27.93	$27.93	$29.32	$29.32	$30.79	$30.79
EBITDA/adjusted claim	$ 0.59	$ 0.60	$ 0.60	$ 0.59	$ 0.62	$ 0.62	$ 0.63	$ 0.63	$ 0.63
Sequential claims growth									
Pharmacy	0.1%	0.0%	0.2%		0.2%	0.2%	0.4%	0.2%	
Mail	1.9%	1.9%	3.7%		3.6%	3.5%	8.4%	3.1%	
Total	0.2%	0.1%	0.4%		0.4%	0.4%	1.0%	0.4%	
Sequential per claim growth	$—	$0.02	$1.83		$ —	$1.40	$ —	$1.47	
Revenue/claim	$—	$0.01	$ —		$0.02	$ —	$0.01	$ —	
Margins									
Cost of revenue/revenue	96.6%	96.5%	96.7%	96.6%	96.6%	96.8%	96.8%	96.9%	96.8%
S&GA/revenue	1.5%	1.5%	1.5%	1.5%	1.5%	1.4%	1.4%	1.3%	1.4%
Revenue by division (pro forma)									
Revenue									
Data services									
Mail services									
Clinical and other services									
Total revenue									
Operating margin	2.0%	2.0%	1.8%	1.9%	1.9%	1.8%	1.8%	1.7%	1.8%
D&A/revenue	0.3%	0.3%	0.3%	0.3%	0.3%	0.3%	0.3%	0.3%	0.3%
EBITDA margin	2.3%	2.3%	2.1%	2.2%	2.2%	2.1%	2.1%	2.0%	2.1%
Tax rate	39.5%	39.5%	39.5%	39.5%	39.5%	39.5%	39.5%	39.5%	39.5%

Source: Merrill Lynch & Co.

EXHIBIT 12.31 AdvancePCS: Debt Service Projection

	12/31/00	3/31/01	Q1 02 6/30/01	Q2 02 9/30/01	Q3 02 12/31/01	Q4 02 3/31/02	Full Year 02 3/31/02	Full Year 03 3/31/03	3/31/04	3/31/05	3/31/06
Cash	124.35	100	150				100	100	100	100	100
Revolving credit	60	95.0	88.56	83.47	77.70	71.75	71.75	50	50	50	50
Bank debt	550	550.0	542.4	534.88	527.31	519.75	519.75	485.75			
Senior notes	200	200.0	200	200	200	200	200	200	200	200	200
Total debt	810	845.0	831	818.3	805.0	791.5	791.495153	735.75	250	250	250
Total equity	393.226										
Term A	150										
Term B	400										
Amortization											
Term A			6.5625	6.5625	6.5625	6.5625	26.3	30.3	37.5	45.0	
Term B			1.0	1.0	1.0	1.0	4.0	4.0	4.0	4.0	
Total amortization			7.6	7.6	7.6	7.6	30.3	34.0	41.5	49.0	
Interest rates											
R/C (L + 3)	8.25%	8.25%	8.25%	8.25%	8.25%	8.25%	8.25%	8.25%	8.25%	8.25%	8.25%
Bank debt (estimate blended)	8.25%	8.25%	8.25%	8.38%	8.38%	8.38%	8.38%	8.38%	8.38%	8.38%	8.38%
Senior notes	8.50%	8.50%	8.50%	8.50%	8.50%	8.50%	8.50%	8.50%	8.50%	8.50%	8.50%
Interest expense											
Revolving credit		7.8375	3.77				3	3			
Bank debt			11.28	11.28	11.12	10.96	44.64	42.11			
Senior notes			4.25	4.25	4.25	4.25	17	17			
Total interest expense			19.299	18	18	18	64.6374414	62.1053125			
Interest income	0.03						3				
Net interest expense							61.6374414				

Source: Merrill Lynch & Co.

AdvancePCS

AdvancePCS provides a variety of health improvement services, including integrated mail service, retail pharmacy networks, clinical services, customized disease management programs, research on clinical trials and outcomes, prescription drug service for the uninsured, and an Internet pharmacy. As a service provider, the company does not have substantial working capital requirements, unlike manufacturers and retailers that must carry large inventories.

Analyst Gray's forecasting task is consequently less complex than in the case of Select Medical. The company's historical and projected revenue (Exhibit 12.29) is largely a function of pharmacy network claims and prescriptions filled by mail (Exhibit 12.30). Gray projects rising revenue per claim, based largely on continued escalation in the price of prescription drugs. Also contributing to the expected rise in revenue per claim is growth in the mail order business, which tends to fill larger orders (three-month, as opposed to one-month prescriptions) than the other pharmacy operations. Again in contrast to Select Medical, AdvancePCS enjoys extremely stable margins. Exhibit 12.31 rounds out the story with a projection of debt service requirements.

CONCLUSION

Of the various types of analysis of financial statements, projecting future results and ratios requires the greatest skill and produces the most valuable findings. Looking forward is also the riskiest form of analysis, since there are no correct answers until the future statements appear. Totally unforeseeable events may invalidate the assumptions underlying the forecast; economic shocks or unexpected changes in a company's financial strategies may knock all calculations into a cocked hat.

The prominence of the chance element in the forecasting process means that analysts should not be disheartened if their predictions miss the mark, even widely on occasion. They should aim not for absolute prescience but rather for a sound probabilistic model of the future. The model should logically incorporate all significant evidence, both within, and external to, the historical statements. An analyst can then judge whether a company's prevailing valuations (e.g., stock price, credit rating) are consistent with the possible scenarios and their respective probabilities.

By tracking the after-the-fact accuracy of a number of projections, an analyst can gauge the effectiveness of these methods. Invariably, there will be room for further refinement, particularly in the area of gathering information on industry conditions. No matter how refined the methods are, however, perfection will always elude the modeler since no business cycle precisely recapitulates its predecessor. That is what ultimately makes looking forward with financial statements such a challenging task. The lack of a predictable, recurring pattern is also what makes financial forecasting so valuable. When betting huge sums in the face of massive uncertainty, it is essential that investors understand the odds as fully as they possibly can.

QUESTIONS

1. Are financial projections mere guesswork?
2. Are the effects of divesture more easily captured by pro forma statements than the effects of acquisitions? Explain.
3. Can a company reduce its credit risk, measured by the ratio of long-term debt to the sum of long-term debt and shareholders' equity, by acquiring other companies for stock? Explain.
4. Can sensitivity analysis enable the analyst to gauge the relative impact of changing the various assumptions in a projection?
5. Do all industries lend themselves to this macroeconomic approach to forecasting?
6. Do analysts forecast figures to the first decimal place? Why or why not?
7. Elaborate on two ways investors use sensitivity analysis.
8. For what industries is the projected capacity utilization a key variable?
9. From where does the analyst obtain the forecast of the repayment of current maturities of long-term debt?
10. How are key macroeconomic indicators used in forecasting shipments and price changes for a company's various business segments?
11. How can an increase in sales be achieved?
12. How can analysts anticipate loss of financial flexibility?
13. How can the analyst look forward with financial statements?
14. How can the bottom-up approach be used to forecast cost of goods sold?
15. How can the techniques studied in Chapters 2 through 4, discussed in conjunction with the historical statements, be used with the projected financial statements?
16. How does a history of sales by geographic area provide an input into the sales projection?
17. How does capacity utilization affect cost of goods sold?
18. How is a company's embedded cost of debt calculated?

19. How is the accuracy of macroeconomic forecasting related to the uses of projected financial statements?
20. How should the analyst verify this assumption?
21. How would the analyst obtain the forecast of an increase in notes payable of $21 million in Exhibit 12.7? What assumptions are implicit in the forecast?
22. If the company does not publish this information, what should the analyst do?
23. In which ways are electronic spreadsheets useful for multiyear projections?
24. Is interest expense on short-term debt included in the calculation above?
25. Is it safe to forecast the provision for income taxes at the statutory tax rate (34%)?
26. Is macroeconomic forecasting an exact science?
27. Over a normal business cycle, do dividends fluctuate to the same extent as earnings?
28. Under what circumstances are investors interested in multiyear projections?
29. Under what circumstances are multiyear projections essential?
30. Under what circumstances should the analyst change the assumption of a stable relationship between sales and SG&A expense?
31. Under what circumstances should the analyst forecast depreciation amounts that are different from their historical patterns?
32. Under what circumstances will the R&D expenditures vary from their historical pattern?
33. Using Colossal Chemical's capital spending, demonstrate how assumptions can be modified by recognizing the interaction among the various accounts.
34. Using Exhibits 12.10, 12.11, and 12.12, explain how an investor or lender may use a three-scenario sensitivity analysis.
35. Were there substantial variances between the actual and forecast in the key financial ratios of Jostens? Why or why not?
36. What additional assumptions are required to construct the projected balance sheet beyond those made in projecting the income statement and statement of cash flows?
37. What are some of the contentious issues in the recognition of the cost of employee stock options?
38. What are some of the discontinuities that have forced companies to revise their long-range plans?
39. What are the two factors that determine the amount of depreciation expense?

40. What assumption drives the numerical calculation of working capital changes in Exhibit 12.7?
41. What causes the figure for deferred income taxes to vary somewhat unpredictably from year to year?
42. What determines credit quality?
43. What determines the extent to which financial projections will correspond to actual future results?
44. What determines the value of a company's stock?
45. What does the analyst gain from tracking the after-the-fact accuracy of a number of projections?
46. What does the projected gross margin reflect?
47. What factors contributed to the variance between actual and forecast figures for Jostens?
48. What factors that affect companies' valuations are not captured in pro forma statements?
49. What information from the income statement supplies the first two lines of the projected statement of cash flows?
50. What is a "point forecast"? How do investors and lenders use point forecasts?
51. What is sensitivity analysis? How do analysts use sensitivity analysis?
52. What is the best way to affirm the reasonableness of assumptions about future financial performance?
53. What is the best way to appreciate the interrelatedness of the income statement, the balance sheet, and the statement of cash flows?
54. What is the difference between the statutory tax rate and the effective tax rate?
55. What is the first step taken to project the income statement?
56. What is the important aspect of financial flexibility for which projections are indispensable? Explain.
57. What is the largest use of cash for Colossal Chemical Corporation (Exhibit 12.7)?
58. What kind of observations do pro forma statements enable analysts to make?
59. What makes looking forward with financial statements such a challenging task?
60. What maneuver, demonstrated in the Cabot example, is often advocated by market participants?
61. What must the financial analyst do to capture fundamental value that is not already reflected in securities prices?
62. What other assumptions might be more appropriate in other circumstances?

63. What should be the aim of the analyst engaged in financial forecasting?
64. What should the analyst do if the calculations above, when applied retroactively, do not produce the precise interest expense shown in the financial statements?
65. What two expenditures are typically budgeted as a percent of sales?
66. What type of analysis of financial statements requires the greatest skill? Explain.
67. Where would the analyst obtain the figures needed to complete the projection of long-term debt?
68. Why must sensitivity analysis be used with caution?

Credit Analysis

Credit analysis is one of the most common uses of financial statements, reflecting the many forms of debt that are essential to the operation of a modern economy. Merchants who exchange goods for promises to pay need to evaluate the reliability of those promises. Commercial banks that lend the merchants the funds to finance their inventories likewise need to calculate the probability of being repaid in full and on time. The banks must in turn demonstrate their creditworthiness to other financial institutions that lend to them by purchasing their certificates of deposit and bonds. In all of these cases, financial statement analysis can significantly influence a decision to extend or not to extend credit.

As important as financial statements are to the evaluation of credit risk, however, the analyst must bear in mind that other procedures also play a role. Financial statements tell much about a borrower's *ability to* repay a loan, but disclose little about the equally important *willingness* to repay. Accordingly, a thorough credit analysis may have to include a check of the subject's past record of repayment, which is not part of a standard financial statement. Moreover, to assess the creditworthiness of the merchant in this example, the bank must consider along with his balance sheet and income statement the competitive environment and strength of the local economy in which the borrower operates. Lenders to the bank will in turn consider not only the bank's financial position, but also public policy. Believing that a sound banking system benefits the economy as a whole, national governments empower central banks to act as lenders of last resort. As a result, fewer bank failures occur than would be the case under pure, unrestrained competition.

An even more basic reason why analyzing a company's financial statements may not be sufficient for determining its credit quality is that the borrower's credit may be supported, formally or informally, by another entity. Many municipalities obtain cost savings on their financings by having their debt payments guaranteed by bond insurers with premier credit ratings. For holders of these municipal bonds, the insurer's creditworthiness, not the municipality's financial condition, is the basis for determining the likelihood of repayment. Corporations, too, sometimes guarantee the debt of weaker credits. Even when the stronger company does not take on a legal obligation to pay if the weaker company fails on its debt, "implicit support" may affect the latter's credit quality. If a company is dependent on raw materials provided by a subsidiary, there may be a reasonable presumption that it will stand behind the subsidiary's debt, even in the absence of a formal guarantee.

Keeping in mind that the final judgment may be influenced by other information as well, the analyst can begin to extract from the financial statements the data that bear on credit risk. Each of the basic statements—the balance sheet, income statement, and statement of cash flows—yields valuable insights when studied through ratio analysis techniques, as well as when used in the evaluation of fixed-income securities. In each case, the analyst must temper any enthusiasm generated by a review of historical statements with caution based on a consideration of financial ratios derived from projected statements for future years.

BALANCE SHEET RATIOS

The most immediate danger faced by a lender is the risk that the borrower will suffer illiquidity—an inability to raise cash to pay its obligations. This condition can arise for many reasons, one of which is a loss of ability to borrow new funds to pay off existing creditors. Whatever the underlying cause, however, illiquidity manifests itself as an excess of current cash payments due, over cash currently available. The current ratio gauges the risk of this occurring by comparing the claims against the company that will become payable during the current operating cycle (current liabilities) with the assets that are already in the form of cash or that will be converted to cash during the current operating cycle (current assets). Referring to Johnson & Johnson's balance sheet (Exhibit 13.1), the company's current ratio as of December 31, 2000, was 2.16 (dollar figures are in millions):

$$\text{Current ratio} = \frac{\text{Current assets}}{\text{Current liabilities}} = \frac{\$15,450}{\$7,140} = 2.16$$

Analysts also apply a more stringent test of liquidity by calculating the quick ratio, or acid test, which considers only cash and current assets that

EXHIBIT 13.1   Johnson & Johnson

Consolidated Balance Sheets
at December 31, 2000
($000 omitted)

Assets

Current assets

Cash and cash equivalents	$ 3,411
Marketable securities	2,333
Accounts receivable trade, less allowances $411 (1999, $389)	4,464
Inventories	2,842
Deferred taxes on income	1,151
Prepaid expenses and other receivables	1,249
Total current assets	15,450
Marketable securities, noncurrent	269
Property, plant and equipment, net	6,971
Intangible assets, net	7,256
Deferred taxes on income	54
Other assets	1,321
Total assets	$31,321

Liabilities and Shareowners' Equity

Current liabilities

Loans and notes payable	$ 1,479
Accounts payable	2,083
Accrued liabilities	2,776
Accrued salaries, wages and commissions	488
Taxes on income	314
Total current liabilities	7,140
Long-term debt	2,037
Deferred tax liability	255
Employee related obligations	1,753
Other liabilities	1,328
Shareowners' equity	
Preferred stock—without par value (authorized and unissued 2,000,000 shares)	—
Common stock—par value $1.00 per share (authorized 2,160,000,000 shares; issued 1,534,921,000 and 1,534,916,000 shares)	1,535
Note receivable from employee stock ownership plan	(35)
Accumulated other comprehensive income	(470)
Retained earnings	18,812
	19,842
Less: common stock held in treasury, at cost (143,984,000 and 145,233,000)	1,034
Total shareowners' equity	18,808
Total liabilities and shareowners' equity	$31,321

Source: 10-K405 March 30, 2001.

can be most quickly converted to cash (marketable securities and receivables). Johnson & Johnson's quick ratio on December 31, 2000, was 1.43:

$$\text{Quick ratio} = \frac{\text{Quick assets}}{\text{Current liabilities}} = \frac{\$10,208}{\$7,140} = 1.43$$

Besides looking at the ratio between current assets and current liabilities, it is also useful, when assessing a company's ability to meet its near-term obligations, to consider the difference between the two, which is termed working capital. Referring once again to Exhibit 13.1, working capital is $8.31 billion.

$$\text{Working capital} = \text{Current assets} - \text{Current liabilities}$$

$$\$8,310 = \$15,450 - \$7,140$$

Analysis of current assets and current liabilities provides warnings about impending illiquidity, but lenders nevertheless periodically find themselves saddled with loans to borrowers who are unable to continue meeting their obligations and are therefore forced to file for bankruptcy. Recognizing that they may one day find themselves holding defaulted obligations, creditors wish to know how much asset value will be available for liquidation to pay off their claims.[1] The various ratios that address this issue can be grouped as measures of financial leverage.

A direct measure of asset protection is the ratio of total assets to total liabilities, which in the example shown in Exhibit 13.1 comes to:

$$\frac{\text{Total assets}}{\text{Total liabilities}} = \frac{\$31,321}{\$12,513} = 2.50$$

(Total liabilities can be derived quickly by subtracting stockholders' equity from total assets.)

Put another way, Johnson & Johnson's assets of $31,321 billion could decline in value by 60% before proceeds of a liquidation would be insufficient to satisfy lenders' $12,531 billion of claims. The greater the amount by which asset values could deteriorate, the greater the "equity cushion" (equity is by definition total assets minus total liabilities), and the greater the creditor's sense of being protected.

Lenders also gauge the amount of equity "beneath" them (junior to them in the event of liquidation) by comparing it with the amount of debt outstanding. For finance companies, where the ratio is typically greater than 1.0, it is convenient to express the relationship as a debt-equity ratio:

$$\frac{\text{Total debt}}{\text{Total equity}}$$

Conventionally capitalized industrial corporations (as opposed to companies that have undergone *leveraged buyouts)*, generally have debt-equity ratios of less than 1.0. The usual practice is to express their financial leverage in terms of a total-debt-to-total-capital ratio:

$$\frac{\text{Total debt}}{\text{Total debt} + \text{Minority interest} + \text{Total equity}}$$

Banks' "capital adequacy" is commonly measured by the ratio of equity to total assets:

$$\frac{\text{Total equity}}{\text{Total assets}}$$

Many pages of elaboration could follow on the last few ratios mentioned. Their calculation is rather less simple than it might appear. The reason is that aggressive borrowers frequently try to satisfy the letter of a maximum leverage limit imposed by lenders, without fulfilling the conservative spirit behind it. The following discussion of definitions of leverage ratios addresses the major issues without laying down absolute rules about "correct" calculations. As explained later in the chapter, ratios are most meaningful when compared across time and across borrower. Consequently, the precise method of calculation is less important than the consistency of calculation throughout the sample being compared.

What Constitutes Total Debt?

At one time, it was appropriate to consider only long-term debt in leverage calculations for industrial companies, since short-term debt was generally used for seasonal purposes, such as financing Christmas-related inventory. A company might draw down bank lines or issue commercial paper to meet these funding requirements, then completely pay off the interim borrowings when it sold the inventory. Even today, a firm that "zeros out" its short-term debt at some point in each operating cycle can legitimately argue that its true leverage is represented by the permanent (long-term) debt on its balance sheet. Many borrowers have long since subverted this principle, however, by relying heavily on short-term debt that they neither repay on an interim basis nor fund (replace with long-term debt) when it grows to sufficient size to make a bond offering cost-effective. Such short-term debt must be viewed as permanent and included in the leverage calculation. (Current maturities of long-term debt should also enter into the calculation of total debt, based on a conservative assumption that the company will replace maturing debt with new long-term borrowings.)

As an aside, the just-described reliance on short-term debt is not necessarily as dangerous a practice as in years past, although it should still raise a caution flag for the credit analyst. Two risks are inherent in depending on debt with maturities of less than one year. The first is potential illiquidity. If substantial debt comes due at a time when lenders are either unable to renew their loans (because credit is tight) or unwilling to renew (because they perceive the borrower as less creditworthy than formerly), the borrower may be unable to meet its near-term obligations. This risk may be mitigated, however, if the borrower has a revolving credit agreement, which is a longer-term commitment by the lender to lend (subject to certain conditions such as maintaining prescribed financial ratios and refraining from significant changes in the business). The second risk of relying on short-term borrowings is exposure to interest-rate fluctuations. If a substantial amount of debt is about to come due, and interest rates have risen sharply since the debt was incurred, the borrower's cost of staying in business may skyrocket overnight.

Note that exposure to interest rate fluctuations can also arise from long-term **floating-rate debt.** Companies can limit this risk by using **financial derivatives.** One approach is to cap the borrower's interest rate; that is, set a maximum rate that will prevail, no matter how high the market rate against which it is pegged may rise. Alternatively, the borrower can convert the floating-rate debt to fixed-rate debt through a derivative known as an interest-rate swap. (The forces of supply and demand may make it more economical for the company to issue floating-rate debt and incur the cost of the swap than to take the more direct route to the same net effect, that is, to issue floating-rate debt.) Public financial statements typically provide only general information about the extent to which the issuer has limited its exposure to interest rate fluctuations through derivatives.

Borrowers sometimes argue that the total debt calculation should exclude debt that is convertible, at the lender's option, into common equity. Hardliners on the credit analysis side respond: "It's equity when the holders convert it to equity. Until then, it's debt." Realistically, though, if the conversion value of the bond rises sufficiently, most holders will in fact convert their securities to common stock. This is particularly true if the issuer has the option of calling the bonds for early retirement, which results in a loss for holders who fail to convert. Analysts should remember that the ultimate objective is not to calculate ratios but to assess credit risk. Therefore, the best practice is to count convertible debt in total debt, but to consider the possibility of conversion when comparing the borrower's leverage with that of its peer group.

Preferred stock[2] is a security that further complicates the leverage calculation. From a legal standpoint, preferred stock is clearly equity; in liquidation, it ranks junior to debt. Preferred stock pays a dividend rather than interest, and failure to pay the dividend does not constitute a default. On the other hand, preferred dividends, unlike common dividends, are contractually fixed in amount. An issuer can omit its preferred dividend, but not without also omitting its common dividend. Furthermore, a preferred dividend is typically cumulative, meaning that the issuer must repay all preferred dividend arrearages before resuming common stock dividends. Furthermore, not all preferred issues have the permanent character of common stock. A preferred stock may have a sinking fund provision, much like the provision typically found in bonds, that requires redemption of a substantial portion of the outstanding par amount prior to final maturity. Such a provision implies less financial flexibility than is the case for a perpetual preferred stock, which requires no principal repayment at any time. Another preferred security, exchangeable preferred stock, can be transformed into debt at the issuer's option. Treating it purely as equity for credit analysis purposes would understate financial risk. In general, the credit analyst must recognize the heightened level of risk implied by the presence of preferred stock in the capital structure. A formal way to take this risk into account is to calculate the ratio of total fixed obligations to total capital:[3]

$$\frac{\text{Total debt} + \text{Preferred stock} + \text{Preference stock}}{\text{Total debt} + \text{Minority interest} + \text{Preferred stock} + \text{Preference stock} + \text{Common equity}}$$

Off-balance-sheet lease obligations, like preferred stock, enable companies to obtain many of the benefits of debt financing without violating covenanted limitations on debt incurrence. Accounting standards have partially brought these debtlike obligations out of hiding by requiring capital leases to appear on the balance sheet, either separately or as part of long-term debt. Credit analysts should complete the job. In addition to including capital leases in the total debt calculation, they should also take into account the off-balance-sheet liabilities represented by contractual payments on operating leases, which are reported (as "rental expense") in the Notes to Financial Statements. The rationale is that although the accounting rules distinguish between capital and operating leases, the two financing vehicles frequently differ little in economic terms. Indeed, borrowers have used considerable ingenuity in structuring capital leases to qualify as operating leases under GAAP, the benefit being that they will consequently be excluded from the balance sheet and, it is hoped, from credit analysts' scrutiny. Analysts should not fall for this ruse, but should instead capitalize the current year rental payments shown in the Notes to Financial Statements. The most common method is to multiply the payments by seven or eight, a calculation that has been found to be reasonably accurate when actual figures on capitalized value of leases have been available for comparison.

Other Off-Balance-Sheet Liabilities

In their quest for methods of obtaining the benefits of debt without suffering the associated penalties imposed by credit analysts, corporations have by no means limited themselves to the use of leases. Like leases, the other popular devices may provide genuine business benefits, as well as the cosmetic benefit of disguising debt. In all cases, the focus of credit-quality determination must be economic impact, which may or may not be reflected in the accounting treatment.

A corporation can employ leverage yet avoid showing debt on its consolidated balance sheet by entering joint ventures or forming partially owned subsidiaries. At a minimum, the analyst should attribute to the corporation its proportionate liability for the debt of such ventures, thereby "matching" the cash flow benefits derived from the affiliates. (Note that cash flow is generally reduced by unremitted earnings—the portion not received in dividends—of non-fully-consolidated affiliates.) In some cases, the affiliate's operations are critical to the parent's operations, as in the case of a jointly owned pulp plant that supplies a paper plant wholly owned by the parent. There is a strong incentive, in such instances, for the parent to keep the jointly owned operation running by picking up the debt service commitments of a partner that becomes financially incapacitated, even though it may have no legal obligation to do so. (In legal parlance, this arrangement is known as a *several* obligation, in contrast to a *joint* obligation in which each partner is compelled to back up the other's commitment.) Depending on the particular circumstances, it may be appropriate to attribute to the parent more than its proportionate share—up to 100%—of the debt of the joint venture or unconsolidated subsidiary.

Surely one of the most ingenious devices for obtaining the benefits of debt without incurring balance sheet recognition was described by *The Independent* in 1992. According to the British newspaper, the Faisal Islamic Bank of Cairo had provided $250 million of funding to a troubled real estate developer, Olympia & York. As an institution committed to Islamic religious principles, however, the bank was not allowed to charge interest. Instead, claimed *The Independent,* Faisal Islamic Bank in effect had acquired a building from Olympia & York, along with an option to sell it back. The option was reportedly exercisable at $250 million plus an amount equivalent to the market rate of interest for the option period. Because the excess was not officially classified as interest, said *The Independent,* the $250 million of funding did not show up as a loan on Olympia & York's balance sheet.

The Independent noted a denial by an Olympia & York spokesperson that "any such *loan* existed" (emphasis added). If, however, the account was substantially correct, then the religious-prohibition-of-interest gambit succeeded spectacularly in diverting attention from a transaction that had all the trappings of a loan. Barclays Bank, one of Olympia & York's most important lenders, commented that it had never heard of the Faisal Islamic Bank transaction.[4]

Of a somewhat different character within the broad category of off-balance-sheet liabilities are employee benefit obligations. Under SFAS 87, balance sheet recognition is now given to pension liabilities related to employees' service to date. Similarly, SFAS 106 requires recognition of postretirement health care benefits as an on-balance-sheet liability. Projected future wage increases are still not recognized, however, although they affect the calculation of pension expense for income statement purposes. Unlike some other kinds of hidden liabilities, these items arise exclusively in furtherance of a business objective (attracting and retaining capable employees), rather than as a surreptitious means of leveraging shareholders' equity.

Generally speaking, pension obligations that have been fully funded (provided for with investment assets set aside for the purpose) present few credit worries for a going concern. Likewise, a modest underfunding that is in the process of being remediated by an essentially sound company is no more than a small qualitative factor on the negative side. On the other hand, a large or growing underfunded liability can be a significantly negative consideration—albeit one that is hard to quantify explicitly— in assessing a deteriorating credit. In bankruptcy, it becomes essential to monitor details of the Pension Benefit Guaranty Corporation's efforts to assert its claim to the company's assets, which, if successful, reduce the settlement amounts available to other creditors.

Are Deferred Taxes Part of Capital?

Near the equity account on many companies' balance sheets appears an account labeled "Deferred Income Taxes." This item represents the cumulative difference between taxes calculated at the statutory rate and taxes actually paid. The difference reflects the tax consequences, for future years, of the differences between the tax bases of assets and liabilities and their carrying amounts for financial reporting purposes.

Many analysts argue that net worth is understated by the amount of the deferred tax liability, since it will in all likelihood never come due and is therefore not really a liability at all. (As long as the company continues to pay taxes at less than the statutory rate, the deferred tax account will continue to grow.) Proponents of this view adjust for the alleged understatement of net worth by adding deferred taxes to the denominator in the total-debt-to-total-capital calculation, thus:

$$\frac{\text{Total debt}}{\text{Total debt} + \text{Deferred taxes} + \text{Minority interest} + \text{Total equity}}$$

In general, this practice is sound. Analysts must, however, keep in mind that the precise formula for calculating a ratio is less important than the assurance that it is calculated consistently for all companies being evaluated. The caveat is that many factors can contribute to deferred taxes, and not all of them imply a permanent deferral. A defense contractor, for example, can defer payment of taxes related to a specific contract until the contract is completed. The analyst would not want to add to equity the taxes deferred on a contract that is about to be completed, although in such situations specific figures may be hard to obtain.

The Importance of Management's Attitude toward Debt

As the preceding discussion has established, companies use numerous gambits in their quest to enjoy the benefits of aggressive financial leverage without suffering the consequences of low credit ratings and high borrowing costs. Analysts should note that corporations' bag of tricks is not confined to accounting gimmicks. Some management teams also rely on a bait-and-switch technique.

The ploy consists of announcing that management has learned the hard way that conservative financial policies serve shareholders best in the long run. Never again, vows the chief executive officer, will the company undergo the financial strain that it recently endured as a result of excessive borrowing a few years earlier. To demonstrate that they truly have gotten religion, the managers institute new policies aimed at improving cash flow and pay down a slug of short-term borrowings. On the strength of the favorable impression that these actions create among credit analysts who rely heavily on trends in financial ratios, the company floats new long-term bonds at an attractive rate. Once the cash is in the coffers, management loses its motivation to present a conservative face to lenders and reverts to the aggressive financial policies that so recently got the company into trouble.

Not everybody is taken in by this ruse. Moody's and Standard & Poor's place heavy emphasis on management's attitude toward debt when assigning bond ratings (see "Relating Ratios to Credit Risk" later in this chapter). They strive to avoid upgrading companies in response to balance sheet improvements that are unlikely to last much beyond the completion of the next public offering. In reward for such vigilance, the agencies are routinely accused of being backward-looking. The corporations complain that the bond raters are dwelling unduly on past, weaker financial ratios. In reality, the agencies are thinking ahead. Based on their experience with management, they are inferring that the recent reduction in financial leverage reflects expediency, rather than a long-term shift in debt policy. As evidence that the rating agencies have good reason to take corporate managers' assurances with a grain of salt, consider Viacom International's long-run record on stated objectives and actual financial practices.

Since 1987, Standard & Poor's has raised and lowered the diversified media company's rating several times (see Exhibit 13.2). The graph tracks the company's **subordinated debt** rating because for much of the period, the company had no public, rated **senior debt** outstanding. A leveraged buyout precipitated a downgrading from BB- to B- in early 1987. The rating rebounded to B in 1989 on the strength of strong operating performance and, with the additional help of a stock offering, to B+ in 1991.

Viacom president and chief executive officer Frank J. Biondi enunciated a corporate drive toward further improvements in July 1992, when he commented on the company's plans to redeem an issue of high-cost debentures:

> *The expense associated with the debt redemption represents a one-time investment which will have a quick payback in subsequent quarters as Viacom continues to achieve a lower cost of borrowing.*[5]

EXHIBIT 13.2   Rating History: Viacom International.

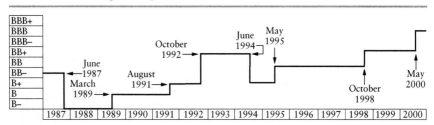

Credit Watch Listings:

January	to	June 1987	Negative
August	to	October 1992	Positive
September	to	October 1993	Positive
November 1993			Developing
December 1993	to	June 1994	Negative
October 1994	to	May 1995	Positive
July 1995	to	September 1996	Positive
January 1998	to	October 1998	Positive
September 1999	to	May 2000	Positive

Sources: Standard & Poor's.

Based on Biondi's statement that the corporation's objective was to continue reducing its cost of borrowing, a logical inference was that Viacom would strive to raise its debt rating. After all, a higher rating would signify lower credit risk and enable the company to borrow at lower interest rates. Viacom did, in fact, achieve an upgrade to BB+ at the subordinated level in October 1992. Less than two years later, however, Viacom acquired another media giant, Paramount. The resulting increase in Viacom's ratio of debt to capital precipitated a June 1994 downgrade back to the previous B+ subordinated rating. Evidently, the company's stated objective of continuing to reduce its borrowing cost did not necessarily mean that management would continue in that direction for very long.

In fairly short order, however, the picture improved once again. Viacom merged with the video store operator Blockbuster, which had a moderately leveraged balance sheet and a lot of cash. The combined company not only had a strong financial position, but also declared that it would liquidate debt by selling both its cable television operations and its partial ownership of Spelling Entertainment Group. On the strength of these developments, Standard & Poor's watchlisted Viacom for possible upgrading in August 1994. The subordinated rating climbed to BB– in May 1995 as the cable television sale was completed and S&P said that a further boost would follow the completion of the planned Spelling transaction.

Once again, though, Viacom's upward progress was interrupted. President Biondi, who had a reputation as a good financial manager, abruptly resigned in January 1996. The trade press claimed that he was forced out. Chairman Sumner Redstone took over the chief executive officer duties and announced that the company would adopt a more "entrepreneurial, aggressive" management style. To Moody's, which had watchlisted Viacom for upgrading in July 1995, this suggested a possible sidetracking of the company's debt-reduction plans.

Redstone sought to allay such concerns, which were likely to cool investors' enthusiasm for Viacom's bonds. "Viacom has been and will remain absolutely committed to strengthening its capital structure," he said, adding that further upgrading would remain a major corporate priority. He repeated that pledge on February 21, 1996, as speculation began to mount that the company would repurchase shares, an action at variance with the goal of reducing the debt-to-equity ratio.

Investors did not have an inordinately long wait to learn how Viacom would reconcile management's stated objective of boosting credit quality with the securities analysts' claims that management was hinting at a stock buyback. In May 1996, the company abandoned its plan to sell Spelling, the transaction on which further upgrading by Standard & Poor's hinged, saying that the offers it had received were inadequate. Then, in September 1996, Viacom and Redstone's investment firm announced plans to repurchase 5.2% of the company's shares. Even as the price of the company's bond fell in the secondary market, the company once again insisted that it remained committed to achieving further upgrading. Standard & Poor's nevertheless removed Viacom from its upgrade watchlist.

Credit analysts were rewarded for being skeptical about Viacom's dogged insistence, from late 1992 through 1996, that reduction of financial leverage was a top priority. Not until October 1998 did the company's subordinated debt rating recover to the BB+ perch from which it fell in June 1994. The rating continued to rise thereafter, suggesting that at some level, management truly did see it as important to move in the direction of lower debt to capital. Along the way, however, Viacom was willing to take a few steps back, in the form of strategic acquisitions and share-boosting stock repurchases, before moving forward.

In general, credit analysts should assume that the achievement of higher bond ratings is a secondary goal of corporate management. If a company's stock has been languishing for a while, management will not ordinarily feel any urgency about eliminating debt from the capital structure, an action that reduces return on shareholders' equity (see Chapter 14). Similarly, the typical chief executive officer, being only human, finds it difficult to resist a chance to run a substantially bigger company. Therefore, if a mammoth acquisition opportunity comes along, the CEO is likely to pursue it, even if it means borrowing huge amounts of money and precipitating a rating downgrade, rather than the hoped-for upgrade.

Like other types of financial statement analysis, finding meaning in a company's balance sheet requires the analyst to look ahead. When management's probable future actions are taken into account, the company's prospects for repaying its debts on schedule may be better or worse than the ratios imply. The credit analyst cannot afford to take management's representations at face value, however. When a chief executive officer claims that obtaining a higher bond rating is the corporation's overriding objective, it is essential to ask for specifics: What are the elements of the company's action plan for achieving that goal? Which of the steps have been achieved so far?

Above all, the credit analyst must listen closely for an escape clause, typically uttered while the company is engaged in a debt offering. It can be heard when a prospective buyer asks whether management will stay on course for a rating upgrade come hell or high water. The CEO casually replies, "Of course, if a once-in-a-lifetime major acquisition opportunity were to come along, and it required us to borrow, we would have to delay our plans for debt reduction temporarily." The credit analyst can generally assume that shortly after the bond deal closes, the once-in-a-lifetime opportunity will materialize.

INCOME STATEMENT RATIOS

Although an older approach to credit analysis places primary emphasis on liquidity and asset protection, both of which are measured by balance-sheet ratios, the more contemporary view is that profits are ultimately what sustain liquidity and asset values. High profits keep plenty of cash flowing through the system and confirm the value of productive assets such as plant and equipment. In line with this latter view, the income statement is no longer of interest mainly to the equity analyst, but is essential to credit analysis as well.

A key income statement focus for credit analysis is the borrower's profit margin (profit as a percentage of sales). The narrower the margin, the greater is the danger that a modest decline in selling prices or a modest increase in costs will produce losses, which will in turn begin to erode such balance sheet measures as total-debt-to-total-capital by reducing equity.

Profit can be measured at several levels of the income statement, either before or after deducting various expenses to get to the bottom line, net income. The most commonly used profit margins are the following:

$$\text{Gross margin} = \frac{\text{Sales} - \text{Cost of goods sold}}{\text{Sales}}$$

$$\text{Operating margin} = \frac{\text{Operating income}}{\text{Sales}}$$

$$\frac{\text{Net income} + \text{Income taxes}}{+ \text{Interest expense}} = \frac{\text{Interest income} - \text{Other income}}{\text{Sales}}$$

$$\text{Pretax margin} = \frac{\text{Net income} + \text{Income taxes}}{\text{Sales}}$$

$$\text{Net margin} = \frac{\text{Net income}}{\text{Sales}}$$

Applying these definitions to Johnson & Johnson's income statement (Exhibit 13.3), the company's profit margins in 2000 were:

$$\text{Gross margin} = \frac{\$29,139 - 8,861}{\$29,139} = 69.6\%$$

$$\text{Operating margin} = \frac{\$4,800 + 1,822 + 146 - 379 + 67}{\$29,139} = 22.2\%$$

$$\text{Pretax margin} = \frac{\$4,800 + 1,822}{29,139} = 22.7\%$$

$$\text{Net margin} = \frac{\$4,800}{\$29,139} = 16.5\%$$

Johnson & Johnson's profit margins are atypically high, relative to industrial companies in general, but less exceptional compared with its peers in the pharmaceutical business. Observe also that in the operating margin calculation, the deduction of other income called for by the formula becomes an addback of a negative figure, since other expenses exceeded other income. Finally, note that the formula does not call for adding back the $33 million restructuring charge, which does not qualify for aftertax treatment as an *extraordinary item* (see Chapter 3). Analysts should nevertheless be cognizant of such nonrecurring charges when forming an impression of a company's bona fide profitability.

In some instances, an aftertax nonoperating item can produce a disparity between the numerators in the pretax and operating margins, as calculated from the bottom up in accordance with the formula, and the

EXHIBIT 13.3 Johnson & Johnson

Income Statement
at December 31, 2000
($000 omitted)

Sales to customers	$29,139
Cost of products sold (1998 includes $60 of inventory write-offs for restructuring)	8,861
Gross profit	20,278
Selling, marketing, and administrative expenses	10,875
Research expense	2,926
Purchased in-process research and development	54
Interest income	(379)
Interest expense, net of portion capitalized	146
Other expense, net	67
Restructuring charge	(33)
	13,656
Earnings before provision for taxes on income	6,622
Provision for taxes on income	1,822
Net earnings	$ 4,800
Basic net earnings per share	$3.45
Diluted net earnings per share	$3.40

Source: 10-K405 March 30, 2001.

corresponding figure derived by working from the top down. For example, the cumulative effect of a change in accounting procedures will appear below the line, or after income taxes have already been deducted. The sum of net income and provision for income taxes will then differ from the pretax income figure that appears in the income statement. To ensure comparability across companies, analysts should take care to follow identical procedures in calculating each company's margins, rather than adopting shortcuts that may introduce distortion.

The various margin measures reflect different aspects of management's effectiveness. Gross margin, which is particularly important in analyzing retailers, measures management's skill in buying and selling at advantageous prices. Operating margin shows how well management has run the business—buying and selling wisely, and controlling selling and administrative expenses—before taking into account financial policies (which largely determine interest expense) and the tax rate (which is outside management's control).[6] These last two factors are sequentially added to the picture by calculating pretax margin and net margin, with the latter ratio reflecting all factors, whether under management's control or not, that influence profitability.

In calculating profit margins, analysts should eliminate the effect of extraordinary gains and losses to determine the level of profitability that is likely to be sustainable in the future.

Fixed-charge coverage is the other income statement ratio of major interest to credit analysts. It measures the ability of a company's earnings to meet the interest payments on its debt, the lender's most direct concern. In its simplest form, the fixed-charge coverage ratio indicates the multiple by which operating earnings suffice to pay interest charges:

$$\text{Fixed-charge coverage} = \frac{\text{Net income} + \text{Income taxes} + \text{Interest expense}}{\text{Interest expense}}$$

This basic formula requires several refinements, however. As with profit margins, extraordinary items should be eliminated from the calculation to arrive at a sustainable level of coverage. The other main adjustments involve capitalized interest and payments on operating leases.

Capitalized Interest

Under SFAS 34, companies may be required to capitalize, rather than expense, a portion of their interest costs. The underlying notion is that like the actual bricks and mortar purchased to construct a plant, the cost of the money borrowed to finance the purchase provides benefits in future periods and therefore should not be entirely written off in the first year. Whether it is expensed or capitalized, however, all interest accrued must be covered by earnings and should therefore appear in the denominator of the fixed-charge coverage calculation. Accordingly, the basic formula can be rewritten to include not only the interest expense shown on the income statement, but also capitalized interest, which may appear either on the income statement or else in the Note to Financial Statements. (If the amount is immaterial, capitalized interest will not be shown at all, and the analyst can skip this adjustment.) The numerator should not include capitalized interest, however, for the amount is a reduction to total expenses and consequently reflected in net income. Including capitalized interest in the numerator would therefore constitute double counting:

$$\begin{pmatrix} \text{Fixed-charge coverage} \\ \text{(adjusted for capitalized interest)} \end{pmatrix} = \frac{\text{Net income} + \text{Income taxes} + \text{Income expense}}{\text{Interest expense} + \text{Capitalized interest}}$$

Lease Expense

As mentioned, off-balance-sheet operating leases have virtually the same economic impact as on-balance-sheet debt. Just as credit analysts should take into account the liabilities represented by these leases, they should also factor into coverage calculations the annual fixed charges associated with them. One approach simply adds the total current-year rental expense from Notes to Financial Statements to both the numerator and denominator of the fixed-charge coverage calculation. An alternate method includes one-third of rentals (as shown in the following calculation) on the theory that one-third of a lease payment typically represents interest that would be paid if the assets had been purchased with borrowed money, and two-thirds is equivalent to principal repayment:

$$\begin{matrix} \text{Fixed-charge coverage} \\ \text{(adjusted for capitalized interest} = \\ \text{and operating leases)} \end{matrix} \frac{\begin{matrix} \text{Net income} + \text{Income taxes} \\ + \text{Income expense} + \frac{1}{3}\text{Rentals} \end{matrix}}{\begin{matrix} \text{Interest expense} + \text{Capitalized interest} \\ + \frac{1}{3}\text{Rentals} \end{matrix}}$$

Two complications arise in connection with incorporating operating lease payment into the fixed-charge coverage calculation. First, the SEC does not require companies to report rental expense in quarterly statements. The analyst can therefore only estimate where a company's fully adjusted coverage stands, on an interim basis, in relation to its most recent full-year level. (Capitalized interest, by the way, presents the same problem, although a few companies voluntarily report capitalized interest on an interim basis.) Second, retailers in particular often negotiate leases with rents that are semi-fixed, tied in part to revenues of the leased stores. Some argue that the variable portion—contingent rentals—should be excluded from the fixed-charge coverage calculation. That approach, however, results in a numerator that includes income derived from revenues in excess of the threshold level, while omitting from the denominator charges that were automatically incurred when the threshold was reached. A better way to recognize the possible avoidance of contingent lease payments is by capitalizing only the mandatory portion when calculating the balance sheet ratio of total-debt-to-total-capital.

Interest Income

A final issue related to fixed-charge coverage involves interest income. Companies sometimes argue that the denominator should include only net interest expense; the difference between interest expense and income derived from interest-bearing assets, generally consisting of marketable securities. They portray the two items as offsetting, with operating earnings having to cover only the portion of interest expense not "automatically" paid for by interest income. Such treatment can be deceptive, however, when a company holds a large but temporary portfolio of marketable securities. In this situation, fixed-charge coverage based on net interest expense in the current year can greatly overstate the level of protection that may be expected in the succeeding year, after the company has invested its funds in operating assets. If, however, a company's strategy is to invest a substantial portion of its assets indefinitely in marketable securities (as some pharmaceutical manufacturers do, to capture certain tax benefits), analysts should consider the associated liquidity as a positive factor in their analysis.

STATEMENT OF CASH FLOWS RATIOS

Ratios related to sources and uses of funds measure credit quality at the most elemental level—a company's ability to generate sufficient cash to pay its bills. These ratios also disclose a great deal about financial flexibility; a company that does not have to rely on external financing can take greater operating risks than one that would be forced to retrench if new capital suddenly became scarce or prohibitively expensive. In addition, trends in sources-and-uses ratios can anticipate changes in balance-sheet ratios. Given corporations' general reluctance to sell new equity, which may dilute existing shareholders' interest, a recurrent cash shortfall is likely to be made up with debt financing, leading to a rise in the total-debt-to-total-capital ratio.

For capital-intensive manufacturers and utilities, a key ratio is cash flow to capital expenditures:

$$\frac{\text{Cash flow from operations}}{\text{Capital expenditures}}$$

The higher this ratio, the greater the financial flexibility implied. It is important, though, to examine the reasons underlying a change in the relationship between internal funds and capital outlays. It is normal for a capital-intensive industry to go through a capital-spending cycle, adding capacity by constructing large-scale plants that require several years to complete. Once the new capacity is in place, capital expenditures ease for a few years until demand growth catches up and another round of spending begins. Over the cycle, the industry's ratio of cash falls. By definition, the downleg of this cycle does not imply long-term deterioration in credit quality. In contrast, a company that suffers a prolonged downtrend in its ratio of cash flow to capital expenditures is likely to get more deeply into debt, and therefore become financially riskier with each succeeding year. Likewise, a rising ratio may require interpretation. A company that sharply reduces its capital budget will appear to increase its financial flexibility, based on the cash-flow-to-capital-expenditures ratio. Cutting back on outlays, however, may impair the company's long-run competitiveness by sacrificing market share or by causing the company to fall behind in technological terms.

Although the most recent period's ratio of cash flow to capital expenditures is a useful measure, the credit analyst is always more interested in the future than in the past. One good way of assessing a company's ability to sustain its existing level of cash adequacy is to calculate depreciation as a percentage of cash flow:

$$\frac{\text{Depreciation}}{\text{Cash flow from operations}}$$

Unlike earnings, depreciation is essentially a programmed item, a cash flow assured by the accounting rules. The higher the percentage of cash flow derived from depreciation, the higher is the predictability of a company's cash flow, and the less dependent its financial flexibility on the vagaries of the marketplace.

Finally, among the ratios derived from the statement of cash flows is the ratio of capital expenditures to depreciation:

$$\frac{\text{Capital expenditures}}{\text{Depreciation}}$$

A ratio of less than 1.0 over a period of several years raises a red flag, since it suggests that the company is failing to replace its plant and equipment. Underspending on capital replacement amounts to gradual liquidation of the firm. By the same token, though, the analyst cannot necessarily assume that all is well simply because capital expenditures consistently exceed depreciation. For one thing, persistent inflation means that a nominal dollar spent on plant and equipment today will not buy as much capacity as it did when the depreciating asset was acquired. (Technological advances in production processes may mitigate this problem because the cost in real terms of producing one unit may have declined since the company purchased the equipment now being replaced.) A second reason to avoid complacency over a seemingly strong ratio of capital expenditures to depreciation is that the depreciation may be understated with respect either to wear and tear or to obsolescence. If so, the adequacy of capital spending will be overstated by the ratio of capital spending to depreciation. Finally, capital outlays may be too low even if they match in every sense the depreciation of existing plant and equipment. In a growth industry, a company that fails to expand its capacity at roughly the same rate as its competitors may lose essential economies of scale and fall victim to a shakeout.

COMBINATION RATIOS

Each of the financial ratios discussed so far in this chapter is derived from numbers collected from just one of the three basic financial statements. In financial analysis, these rudimentary tools are analogous to the simple machines—the wedge, the lever, the wheel, and the screw—that greatly increased the productivity of their prehistoric inventors. How much more remarkable an advance it was, however, when an anonymous Chinese combined two simple machines, a lever and a wheel, to create a wheelbarrow! In similar fashion, combining numbers from different financial statements unleashes vast new analytical power.

Rate-of-Return Measures

One of the most valuable types of combination ratios combines earnings with balance sheet figures. Such ratios measure the profit that an enterprise is generating relative to the assets employed or the capital invested in it. This kind of measure provides a link between credit analysis and the economic concept of productivity of capital.

To illustrate, consider Companies A, B, and C, all of which are debt-free. If we look only at net margin, a ratio derived solely from the income statement, Company A is superior to both its direct competitor, Company B, and Company C, which is in a different business. Looking at the combination ratio of return on equity, however, we find that Company C ranks highest, notwithstanding that sales margins tend to be narrower in its industry:

	Company A	Company B	Company C
Sales	$1,000,000	$1,000,000	$2,000,000
Net income	50,000	40,000	60,000
Equity	500,000	500,000	500,000
Net margin	5.0%	4.0%	3.0%
$\left(\dfrac{\text{Net Income}}{\text{Net Sales}}\right)$			
Return on equity	10.0%	8.0%	12.0%
$\left(\dfrac{\text{Net Income}}{\text{Equity}}\right)$			

To an economist, this result suggests that investors earning 8% to 10% in Company A and Company B's industry will seek to shift their capital to Company C's industry, where 12% returns are available. The credit implication of this migration of capital is that Companies A and B will have greater difficulty raising funds and therefore less financial flexibility. The credit impact on Company C, conversely, is favorable.

There are several variants of the rate-of-return combination ratio, each with a specific analytical application. Return on equity, which has already been alluded to, measures a firm's productivity of equity and therefore provides an indication of its ability to attract a form of capital that provides an important cushion for the debtholders:

$$\text{Return on equity} = \frac{\text{Net income}}{\text{Common equity} + \text{Preferred equity}}$$

In calculating this ratio, analysts most commonly use as the denominator equity as of the final day of the year in which the company earned the income shown in the numerator. This method may sometimes produce distortions. A company might raise a substantial amount of new equity near the end of the year. The denominator in the return-on-equity calculation would consequently be increased, but the numerator would not reflect the benefit of a full year's earnings on the new equity because it was employed in the business for only a few days. Under these circumstances, return on equity will compare unfavorably (and unfairly) with that of a company that did not abruptly expand its equity base.

The potential for distortion in the return-on-equity calculation can be reduced somewhat by substituting for end-of-year equity so-called average equity:

$$\text{Return on average equity} = \frac{\text{Net income}}{\dfrac{\left(\text{Equity at beginning of year} + \text{Equity at end of year}\right)}{2}}$$

(Some analysts prefer this method to the year-end-based calculation, even when sudden changes in the equity account are not an issue.)

Another limitation of combination ratios that incorporate balance-sheet figures is that they have little meaning if calculated for portions of years. Suppose that in 2001 a company earns $6 million on year-end equity of $80 million, for a return on equity of 7.5%. During the first half of 2002, its net income is $4 million, of which it pays out $2 million in dividends, leaving it $82 million in equity at June 30, 2002. With the company having earned in half a year two-thirds as much as it did during all of 2001, it is illogical to conclude that its return on equity has fallen from 7.5% to 4.9% ($4 million ÷ $82 million).

To derive a proper return on equity, it is necessary to annualize the earnings figure. Merely doubling the first half results can introduce some distortion, though, since the company's earnings may be seasonal. Even if not, there is no assurance that the first-half rate of profitability will be sustained in the second half. Accordingly, the best way to annualize earnings is to calculate a trailing 12-months' figure:

$$\frac{\text{Net income for second half of 2001} + \text{Net income for first half of 2002}}{\text{Equity at June 30, 2002}}$$

If the analyst is working with the company's 2001 annual report and 2002 second-quarter statement, 2001 second-half earnings will not be available without some backing out of numbers. For ease of calculation, the numerator in the preceding ratio can be derived as follows:

Net income for full year 2001

Less: Net income for first half of 2001

Plus: Net income for first half of 2002

For the credit analyst, return on equity alone may be an insufficient, or even a misleading, measure. The reason is that a company can raise its return on equity by increasing the proportion of debt in its capital structure, a change that reduces credit quality. In Exhibit 13.4, Company Y produces a higher return on equity than the more conservatively capitalized Company X, even though both have equivalent operating margins.

Note that Company Y enjoys its edge despite having to pay a higher interest rate on account of its riskier financial structure.

Income statement ratios such as net margin and fixed-charge coverage, which point to higher credit quality at Company X, serve as a check against return on equity, which ranks Company Y higher. A later section of this chapter explores systematic approaches to reconciling financial ratios that give contradictory indications about the relative credit quality of two or more

EXHIBIT 13.4 Effect of Debt on Return on Equity ($000 omitted)

	Company X				Company Y			
	12/31/01		12/31/02		12/31/01		12/31/02	
Total debt	$25.0	25.0%	$25.0	23.5%	$50.0	50.0%	$50.0	47.5%
Total equity	75.0	75.0%	81.4	76.5%	50.0	50.0%	55.3	52.5%
Total capital	$100.0	100.0%	$106.4	100.0%	$100.0	100.0%	$105.3	100.0%

2002 Results	Company X	Company Y
Sales	$125	$125.0
Operating expenses	108.5	108.5
Operating income	16.5	16.5
Interest expense	2.0*	4.5
Pretax income	14.5	12.0[†]
Income taxes	4.9	4.1
Net income	9.6	7.9
Dividends	3.2	2.6
Additions to retained earnings	6.4	5.3
Operating margin	16.5/125.0 = 13.2%	16.5/125.0 = 13.2%
Net margin	9.6/125.0 = 7.7%	7.9/125.0 = 6.3%
Return on equity	9.6/81.4 = 11.8%	7.9/55.3 = 14.3%
Fixed-charge coverage	(9.6 + 4.9 + 2.0)/2.0 = 8.25 X	(7.9 + 4.1 + 4.5)/4.5 = 3.7 X

*At 8%.
[†]At 9%.

companies. The more immediately relevant point, however, is that other combination ratios can also be used as checks against an artificially heightened return on equity. Using the same figures for Companies X and Y, the analyst can calculate return on total capital, which equalizes for differences in capital structure. On this basis, Company Y enjoys only a negligible advantage related to its slower growth in retained earnings (and hence in capital):

$$\text{Return on total capital} = \frac{\text{Net income} + \text{Income taxes} + \text{Interest expense}}{\text{Total debt} + \text{Total equity}}$$

Company X

Company Y

$$\frac{9.6 + 4.9 + 2.0}{25.0 + 81.4} = \frac{16.5}{106.4} = 15.5\% \qquad \frac{7.9 + 4.1 + 4.5}{50.0 + 55.3} = \frac{16.5}{105.3} = 15.7\%$$

Total debt in this calculation includes short-term debt, current maturities of long-term debt, and long-term debt, for reasons described earlier under "What Constitutes Total Debt?" Similarly, total equity includes both preferred and preference stock. If there is a minority interest, the associated income statement item should appear in the numerator, and the balance sheet amount in the denominator.

Turnover Measures

In addition to measuring return on investment, a particular type of combination ratio known as a turnover ratio can provide valuable information about asset quality. The underlying notion of a turnover ratio is that a company requires a certain level of receivables and inventory to support a given volume of sales. For example, if a manufacturer sells its goods on terms that require payment within 30 days, and all customers pay exactly on time, accounts receivable on any given day (barring seasonality in sales) will be 30 ÷ 365 or 8.2% of annual sales. Coming at the question from the opposite direction, the analyst can calculate the average length of time that a receivable remains outstanding before it is paid (the calculation uses the average amount of receivables outstanding during the year):

$$\text{Average days of receivables} = \frac{\dfrac{\left(\text{A/R beginning of year} + \text{A/R end of year}\right)}{2}}{\times 365 \text{ Annual sales}}$$

This ratio enables the analyst to learn the company's true average collection period, which may differ significantly from its stated collection period.

By inverting the first portion of the average days of receivables calculation, one can determine how many times per year the company turns over its receivables:

$$\text{Receivables turnover} = \frac{\text{Annual sales}}{\dfrac{(\text{ARBY} + \text{AREY})}{2}}$$

where ARBY = Accounts receivable at beginning of year
AREY = Accounts receivable at the end of year

As long as a company continues to sell on the same terms, its required receivables level will rise as its sales rise, but the ratio between the two should not change. A decline in the ratio may signal that the company's customers are paying more slowly because they are encountering financial difficulties. Alternatively, the company may be trying to increase its sales by liberalizing its credit standards, allowing its salespeople to do more business with less financially capable customers. Either way, the ultimate collectibility of the accounts receivable shown on the balance sheet has become less certain. Unless the company has reflected this fact by increasing its allowance for doubtful receivables, it may have to write off a portion of receivables against income at some point in the future. The analyst should therefore adjust the company's total-debt-to-total-capital ratio for the implicit overstatement of equity.

Another asset quality problem that can be detected with a combination ratio involves unsalable inventory. A fashion retailer's leftover garments from the preceding season or an electronics manufacturer's obsolete finished goods can be worth far less than their balance sheet values (historical cost). If the company is postponing an inevitable write-off, it may become apparent through a rise in inventory without a commensurate rise in sales, resulting in a decline in inventory turnover:

$$\text{Inventory turnover} = \frac{\text{Annual sales}}{\dfrac{(\text{IBY} + \text{IEY})}{2}}$$

where IBY = Inventory at beginning of year
IEY = Inventory at end of year

A drop in sales is another possible explanation of declining inventory turnover. In this case, the inventory may not have suffered a severe reduction in value, but there are nevertheless unfavorable implications for credit quality. Until the inventory glut can be worked off by cutting back production to match the lower sales volume, the company may have to borrow to finance its unusually high working capital, thereby increasing its financial leverage. Profitability may also suffer as the company cuts its selling prices, accepting a lower margin to eliminate excess inventory.

One objection to the preceding inventory-turnover calculation involves the variability of selling prices. Suppose that the price of a commodity chemical suddenly shoots up as the result of a temporary shortage. A chemical producer's annual sales—and hence its inventory turnover—may rise, yet the company may not be physically moving its inventory any faster than before. Conversely, a retailer may respond to a drop in consumer demand and cut its prices to avoid a buildup of inventory. The shelves and back room have no more product than previously, yet the ratio based on annual sales indicates that turnover has declined.

To prevent such distortions, the analyst can use the following variant ratio:

$$\text{Inventory turnover} = \frac{\text{Annual cost of goods sold}}{\dfrac{(\text{IBY} + \text{IEY})}{2}}$$

This version should more closely capture the reality of a company's physical turnover. Cost of goods sold and inventory are both based on historical cost, whereas selling prices fluctuate with market conditions, causing a mismatch between the numerator and denominator of the turnover calculation.

Total-Debt-to-Cash-Flow Ratio

A final combination ratio that is invaluable in credit analysis is the ratio of total debt to cash flow:

$$\text{Total debt to cash flow} = \frac{\text{Short-term debt} + \text{Current maturities} + \text{Long-term debt}}{\text{Cash flow from operations}}$$

This ratio expresses a company's financial flexibility in a most interesting way. If, for the sake of illustration, a company has total debt of $60 million and cash flow from operations of $20 million, it has the ability to liquidate all its debt in three years by dedicating 100% of its cash flow to that purpose. This company clearly has greater financial flexibility than a company with $80 million of debt and a $10-million annual cash flow, for an eight-year debt-payback period. In the latter case, flexibility would be particularly limited if the company's debt had an average maturity of significantly less than eight years, implying the possibility of significant refinancing pressure under tight credit conditions.

All very interesting, one might say, but in reality how many companies dedicate 100% of their cash flow to debt retirement? The answer is "very few," but total debt to cash flow is still a good ratio to monitor for credit quality. It enjoys distinct advantages over some of the more frequently invoked credit-quality measures, which are derived from the balance sheet or income statement alone. The total-debt-to-total-capital ratio has the inherent flaw that equity may be understated or overstated relative to its economic value. After all, the accounting rules do not permit a writeup of assets unless they are sold, nor do the rules require a writedown until someone makes the often subjective determination that the assets have fallen in value. In comparison, total debt is an objective number, a dollar amount that must contractually be repaid. Fixed-charge coverage, too, has a weakness, for it is based on earnings, which are subject to considerable manipulation. Cash flow eliminates one major opportunity for manipulation: underdepreciation. If a company inflates its reported earnings by writing down its fixed assets more slowly than economic reality dictates, it is merely taking money out of one cash flow pocket and putting it into the other. Cash flow, then, puts companies on equal footing, whatever their depreciation policies.

Built from two comparatively hard numbers, the ratio of total debt to cash flow provides one of the best single measures of credit quality. Analysts should not worry about whether its literal interpretation—the period required for a total liquidation of debt—is realistic, but instead focus on its analytical value.

RELATING RATIOS TO CREDIT RISK

The discussion of financial ratios up to this point has sidestepped an obvious and critical question: How does an analyst who has calculated a ratio know whether it represents good, bad, or indifferent credit quality? Somehow, the analyst must relate the ratio to the likelihood that the borrower will satisfy all scheduled interest and principal payments in full and on time. In practice, this is accomplished by testing financial ratios as predictors of the borrower's propensity not to pay (to default). For example, a company with high financial leverage is statistically more likely to default than one with low leverage, all other things being equal. Similarly, high fixed-charge coverage implies less default risk than low coverage. After identifying the factors that create high default risk, the analyst can use ratios to rank all borrowers on a relative scale of propensity to default.

Many credit analysts conduct their ratio analyses within ranking frameworks established by their employers. Individuals engaged in processing loan applications may use criteria derived from the lending institution's experience over many years in recognizing the financial characteristics that lead to timely payment or to default. In the securities field, bond ratings provide a structure for analysis. Exhibits 13.5 and 13.6 show the rating definitions of two leading bond rating agencies, Moody's Investors Service and Standard & Poor's. (The following discussion uses the rating notations and their corresponding "spoken equivalents" interchangeably—AAA and Triple-A, AA and Double-A, etc.)

Because much credit work is done in the context of established standards, the next order of business is to explain how companies can be ranked by ratios on a relative scale of credit quality. Bond ratings are the standard on which the discussion focuses, but the principles are applicable to in-house credit-ranking schemes that analysts may encounter. Following a demonstration of the use of credit rating standards, the chapter concludes with an examination of the methods underlying the construction of standards to show readers how financial ratios are linked to default risk.

The analysis in this section focuses primarily on determining the probability that a borrower will pay interest and principal in full and on time. It does not address the percentage of principal that the lender is likely to recover in the event of default. Certainly, expected recoveries have an important bearing on the decision to extend or deny credit, as well as on the valuation of debt securities. Bankruptcy analysis, however, is a huge topic in its own right. Its proper practice depends on a detailed knowledge of the relevant legislation and a thorough understanding of the dynamics of the negotiations between creditors and the management of a company in Chapter 11 reorganization proceedings. Such matters are beyond the scope of the present work. For the securities of highly rated companies, moreover, the potential percentage recovery of principal tends to be a comparatively minor valuation factor. Over the short to intermediate term, the probability of a bankruptcy filing by such a company is small.

Although the reader will not find a complete guide to bankruptcy analysis in these pages, Chapter 14 is relevant from the standpoint of determining

EXHIBIT 13.5 Moody's Bond Ratings (Definitions) Debt Ratings

Aaa

Bonds and preferred stock which are rated Aaa are judged to be of the best quality. They carry the smallest degree of investment risk and are generally referred to as "gilt edged." Interest payments are protected by a large or by an exceptionally stable margin and principal is secure. While the various protective elements are likely to change, such changes as can be visualized are most unlikely to impair the fundamentally strong position of such issues.

Aa

Bonds and preferred stock which are rated Aa are judged to be of high quality by all standards. Together with the Aaa group they comprise what are generally known as high-grade bonds. They are rated lower than the best bonds because margins of protection may not be as large as in Aaa securities or fluctuation of protective elements may be of greater amplitude or there may be other elements present which make the long-term risk appear somewhat larger than the Aaa securities.

A

Bonds and preferred stock which are rated A possess many favorable investment attributes and are to be considered as upper-medium-grade obligations. Factors giving security to principal and interest are considered adequate, but elements may be present which suggest a susceptibility to impairment some time in the future.

Baa

Bonds and preferred stock which are rated Baa are considered as medium-grade obligations (i.e., they are neither highly protected nor poorly secured). Interest payments and principal security appear adequate for the present but certain protective elements may be lacking or may be characteristically unreliable over any great length of time. Such bonds lack outstanding investment characteristics and in fact have speculative characteristics as well.

Ba

Bonds and preferred stock which are rated Ba are judged to have speculative elements; their future cannot be considered as well-assured. Often the protection of interest and principal payments may be very moderate, and thereby not well safeguarded during both good and bad times over the future. Uncertainty of position characterizes bonds in this class.

B

Bonds and preferred stock which are rated B generally lack characteristics of the desirable investment. Assurance of interest and principal payments or of maintenance of other terms of the contract over any long period of time may be small.

Caa

Bonds and preferred stock which are rated Caa are of poor standing. Such issues may be in default or there may be present elements of danger with respect to principal or interest.

EXHIBIT 13.5 *Continued*

Ca

Bonds and preferred stock which are rated Ca represent obligations which are speculative in a high degree. Such issues are often in default or have other marked shortcomings.

C

Bonds and preferred stock which are rated C are the lowest rated class of bonds, and issues so rated can be regarded as having extremely poor prospects of ever attaining any real investment standing.

Moody's assigns ratings to individual debt securities issued from medium-term note (MTN) programs, in addition to indicating ratings to MTN programs themselves. Notes issued under MTN programs with such indicated ratings are rated at issuance at the rating applicable to all pari passu notes issued under the same program, at the program's relevant indicated rating, provided such notes do not exhibit any of the characteristics listed below. For notes with any of the following characteristics, the rating of the individual note may differ from the indicated rating of the program:

1) Notes containing features which link the cash flow and/or market value to the credit performance of any third party or parties.
2) Notes allowing for negative coupons, or negative principal.
3) Notes containing any provision which could obligate the investor to make any additional payments.

Market participants must determine whether any particular note is rated, and if so, at what rating level. Moody's encourages market participants to contact Moody's Ratings Desks directly if they have questions regarding ratings for specific notes issued under a medium-term note program.

Note: Moody's applies numerical modifiers 1, 2, and 3 in each generic rating classification from Aa through Caa. The modifier 1 indicates that the obligation ranks in the higher end of its generic rating category; the modifier 2 indicates a mid-range ranking; and the modifier 3 indicates a ranking in the lower end of that generic rating category.

Source: Reprinted with permission from Moody's Investors Service.

EXHIBIT 13.6 Standard & Poor's Bond Ratings (definitions)

Issue Credit Rating Definitions

A Standard & Poor's issue credit rating is a current opinion of the creditworthiness of an obligor with respect to a specific financial obligation, a specific class of financial obligations, or a specific financial program (including ratings on medium term note programs and commercial paper programs). It takes into consideration the creditworthiness of guarantors, insurers, or other forms of credit enhancement on the obligation and takes into account the currency in which the obligation is denominated. The issue credit rating is not a recommendation to purchase, sell, or hold a financial obligation, inasmuch as it does not comment as to market price or suitability for a particular investor. Issue credit ratings are based on current information furnished by the obligors or obtained by Standard & Poor's from other sources it considers reliable. Standard & Poor's does not perform an audit in connection with any credit rating and may, on occasion, rely on unaudited financial information. Credit ratings may be changed, suspended, or withdrawn as a result of changes in, or unavailability of, such information, or based on other circumstances. Issue credit ratings can be either long-term or short-term. Short-term ratings are generally assigned to those obligations considered short-term in the relevant market. In the U.S., for example, that means obligations with an original maturity of no more than 365 days—including commercial paper. Short-term ratings are also used to indicate the creditworthiness of an obligor with respect to put features on long-term obligations. The result is a dual rating, in which the short-term rating addresses the put feature, in addition to the usual long-term rating. Medium-term notes are assigned long-term ratings.

Long-term issue credit ratings

Issue credit ratings are based, in varying degrees, on the following considerations:

- Likelihood of payment-capacity and willingness of the obligor to meet its financial commitment on an obligation in accordance with the terms of the obligation;
- Nature of and provisions of the obligation;
- Protection afforded by, and relative position of, the obligation in the event of bankruptcy, reorganization, or other arrangement under the laws of bankruptcy and other laws affecting creditors' rights.

The issue rating definitions are expressed in terms of default risk. As such, they pertain to senior obligations of an entity. Junior obligations are typically rated lower than senior obligations, to reflect the lower priority in bankruptcy, as noted above. (Such differentiation applies when an entity has both senior and subordinated obligations, secured and unsecured obligations, or operating company and holding company obligations.) Accordingly, in the case of junior debt, the rating may not conform exactly with the category definition.

EXHIBIT 13.6 *Continued*

AAA

An obligation rated "AAA" has the highest rating assigned by Standard & Poor's. The obligor's capacity to meet its financial commitment on the obligation is extremely strong.

AA

An obligation rated "AA" differs from the highest rated obligations only in small degree. The obligor's capacity to meet its financial commitment on the obligation is very strong.

A

An obligation rated "A" is somewhat more susceptible to the adverse effects of changes in circumstances and economic conditions than obligations in higher rated categories. However, the obligor's capacity to meet its financial commitment on the obligation is still strong.

BBB

An obligation rated "BBB" exhibits adequate protection parameters. However, adverse economic conditions or changing circumstances are more likely to lead to a weakened capacity of the obligor to meet its financial commitment on the obligation. Obligations rated "BB," "B," "CCC," "CC," and "C" are regarded as having significant speculative characteristics. "BB" indicates the least degree of speculation and "C" the highest. While such obligations will likely have some quality and protective characteristics, these may be outweighed by large uncertainties or major exposures to adverse conditions.

BB

An obligation rated "BB" is less vulnerable to nonpayment than other speculative issues. However, it faces major ongoing uncertainties or exposure to adverse business, financial, or economic conditions which could lead to the obligor's inadequate capacity to meet its financial commitment on the obligation.

B

An obligation rated "B" is more vulnerable to nonpayment than obligations rated "BB," but the obligor currently has the capacity to meet its financial commitment on the obligation. Adverse business, financial, or economic conditions will likely impair the obligor's capacity or willingness to meet its financial commitment on the obligation.

CCC

An obligation rated "CCC" is currently vulnerable to nonpayment, and is dependent upon favorable business, financial, and economic conditions for the obligor to meet its financial commitment on the obligation. In the event of adverse business, financial, or economic conditions, the obligor is not likely to have the capacity to meet its financial commitment on the obligation.

(continued)

EXHIBIT 13.6 *Continued*

CC

An obligation rated "CC" is currently highly vulnerable to nonpayment.

C

A subordinated debt or preferred stock obligation rated "C" is CURRENTLY HIGHLY VULNERABLE to nonpayment. The "C" rating may be used to cover a situation where a bankruptcy petition has been filed or similar action taken, but payments on this obligation are being continued. A "C" also will be assigned to a preferred stock issue in arrears on dividends or sinking fund payments, but that is currently paying.

D

An obligation rated "D" is in payment default. The "D" rating category is used when payments on an obligation are not made on the date due even if the applicable grace period has not expired, unless Standard & Poor's believes that such payments will be made during such grace period. The "D" rating also will be used upon the filing of a bankruptcy petition or the taking of a similar action if payments on an obligation are jeopardized.

Plus (+) or minus (−)

The ratings from "AA" to "CCC" may be modified by the addition of a plus or minus sign to show relative standing within the major rating categories.

r

This symbol is attached to the ratings of instruments with significant noncredit risks. It highlights risks to principal or volatility of expected returns which are not addressed in the credit rating.

N.R.

This indicates that no rating has been requested, that there is insufficient information on which to base a rating, or that Standard & Poor's does not rate a particular obligation as a matter of policy.

Short-term issue credit ratings

A-1

A short-term obligation rated "A-1" is rated in the highest category by Standard & Poor's. The obligor's capacity to meet its financial commitment on the obligation is strong. Within this category, certain obligations are designated with a plus sign (+). This indicates that the obligor's capacity to meet its financial commitment on these obligations is extremely strong.

A-2

A short-term obligation rated "A-2" is somewhat more susceptible to the adverse effects of changes in circumstances and economic conditions than obligations in higher rating categories. However, the obligor's capacity to meet its financial commitment on the obligation is satisfactory.

EXHIBIT 13.6 *Continued*

A-3

A short-term obligation rated "A-3" exhibits adequate protection parameters. However, adverse economic conditions or changing circumstances are more likely to lead to a weakened capacity of the obligor to meet its financial commitment on the obligation.

B

A short-term obligation rated "B" is regarded as having significant speculative characteristics. The obligor currently has the capacity to meet its financial commitment on the obligation; however, it faces major ongoing uncertainties which could lead to the obligor's inadequate capacity to meet its financial commitment on the obligation.

C

A short-term obligation rated "C" is currently vulnerable to nonpayment and is dependent upon favorable business, financial, and economic conditions for the obligor to meet its financial commitment on the obligation.

D

A short-term obligation rated "D" is in payment default. The "D" rating category is used when payments on an obligation are not made on the date due even if the applicable grace period has not expired, unless Standard & Poor's believes that such payments will be made during such grace period. The "D" rating also will be used upon the filing of a bankruptcy petition or the taking of a similar action if payments on an obligation are jeopardized.

Local currency and foreign currency risks

Country risk considerations are a standard part of Standard & Poor's analysis for credit ratings on any issuer or issue. Currency of repayment is a key factor in this analysis. An obligor's capacity to repay foreign currency obligations may be lower than its capacity to repay obligations in its local currency due to the sovereign government's own relatively lower capacity to repay external versus domestic debt. These sovereign risk considerations are incorporated in the debt ratings assigned to specific issues. Foreign currency issuer ratings are also distinguished from local currency issuer ratings to identify those instances where sovereign risks make them different for the same issuer.

Source: Used with permission from sandp.com, a website from Standard & Poor's (www.standardpoor.com/ResourceCenter/RatingsDefinitions.html).

the failed firm's equity value, a key step in the reorganization or liquidation of the company. In addition, the Bibliography includes books that discuss bankruptcy in extensive detail.

Comparative Ratio Analysis

The basic technique in assigning a relative credit ranking is to compare a company's ratio with those of a peer group. Size and line of business are the key criteria for identifying a company's peers.

On the matter of size, a manufacturer with $5 billion in annual sales will ordinarily be a better credit risk than one with similar financial ratios but only $5 million in sales. As a generalization, bigger companies enjoy economies of scale and have greater leverage with suppliers by virtue of their larger purchasing power. A big company can spread the risks of obsolescence and competitive challenges over a wide range of products and customers, whereas a smaller competitor's sales are likely to be concentrated on a few products and customers. Particularly vulnerable is a company with just a single manufacturing facility. An unexpected loss of production could prove fatal to such an enterprise. Lack of depth in management is another problem commonly associated with smaller companies.

Unquestionably, some very large companies have failed in the past. There is ample evidence, as well, of inefficiency in many large, bureaucratic organizations. The point, however, is not to debate whether big corporations are invincible or nimble, but to determine whether they meet their obligations with greater regularity, on average, than their pint-sized peers. Statistical models of default risk confirm that they do. Therefore, the bond rating agencies are following sound methodology when they create size-based peer groups.

A survey of Standard & Poor's Compustat database in 2001 identified 452 companies with ratings on their senior debt and shareholders' equity of less than $200 million. Of that total, only 40 were rated in the investment grade category, defined as BBB- or higher and just 11 were rated A- or higher. The concentration of smaller companies in the speculative grade category, defined as BB+ or lower, supports a strong presumption on S&P's part that size is inversely correlated with propensity to default.

Line of business is another basis for defining a peer group. Because different industries have different financial characteristics, ratio comparisons across industry lines may not be valid. A machinery manufacturer's sales may fluctuate substantially over the capital goods cycle. In contrast, a packaged food company derives its revenues from essential products that are in demand year in and year out. The food processor therefore has greater predictability of earnings and cash flow. It can tolerate a higher level of fixed charges, implying a larger proportion of debt in its capital structure, than the machinery manufacturer. The rating agencies may assign Double-A ratings to a food company with a 35% ratio of total debt to total capital, whereas a machinery maker with a similar ratio might be rated no higher than Single-A.

A ratio comparison between a packaged food producer and a machinery manufacturer sheds little light. The latter company can look good in comparison with the former, yet still be too highly leveraged in view of the operating risks in its industry. Comparability problems become even more pronounced when ratio analysis crosses boundaries of broadly defined sectors of the economy (e.g., industrial, financial, utility, and transportation).

Carrying this principle to its logical conclusion, however, requires a peer group consisting of companies with virtually identical product lines. Operating risk varies to some extent even among closely allied businesses. Strictly speaking, a producer of coated white paper is not comparable to a producer of kraft linerboard, nor a producer of facial tissue to a producer of fine writing paper.

Too zealous an effort to create homogeneous peer groups, though, narrows the field to such an extent that ratio comparisons begin to suffer from having too few data points. At the extreme, a comparison with only one other peer company is not terribly informative. The company being evaluated may rank above its lone peer, but the analyst does not know whether the peer is strong or weak.

Suppose, on the other hand, that with respect to a particular financial ratio a company ranks fourth among a peer group of ten companies, with eight in the group tightly distributed around the median and with one outlier each at the high and low ends. It is valid to say that the company has average risk within its peer group, at least in terms of one particular ratio.

There are two techniques for resolving the trade-off between strict comparability and adequate sample size. By employing both, the analyst can achieve a satisfactory assessment of relative credit risk.

The first technique is to compare the company against a narrowly defined industry peer group, as in Exhibit 13.7. The credit analyst can use this type of analysis to "slot" a company within its industry. The ratios in the sample comparison are averages, computed over three years. Averaging minimizes the impact of unrepresentative results that any company may report in a single year. Observe as well that the eight-member peer group includes only oil companies and is further restricted to the integrated competitors. (An integrated company produces, transports, refines, and

EXHIBIT 13.7 Comparative Ratio Analysis of Integrated Oil and Gas Companies Annual Average 1998–2000

Rank	Standard & Poor's Rating	Company	Times
Pretax Interest Coverage			
1	AAA	Exxon Mobil	12.0
2	AA	Chevron	9.8
3	AAA	Shell Oil	6.4
4	A+	Texaco	5.3
5	A−	Conoco	4.9
6	BBB	Phillips Petroleum	4.4
7	BBB+	Amerada Hess	3.2
8	BBB−	Occidental Petroleum	3.1
Funds Flow as a Percentage of Total Debt			
1	AAA	Exxon Mobil	108.7
2	AA	Chevron	69.8
3	AAA	Shell Oil	64.3
4	BBB+	Amerada Hess	55.9
5	A+	Texaco	46.3
6	A−	Conoco	46.0
7	BBB	Phillips Petroleum	36.3
8	BBB−	Occidental Petroleum	23.6
Total Debt as a Percentage of Capital			
1	AAA	Exxon Mobil	21.7
2	AA	Chevron	31.5
3	AAA	Shell Oil	32.2
4	A+	Texaco	38.1
5	BBB+	Amerada Hess	48.9
6	A−	Conoco	52.4
7	BBB	Phillips Petroleum	52.7
8	BBB−	Occidental Petroleum	61.3

markets petroleum. An independent company, on the other hand, typically performs only one of those functions.)

ExxonMobil ranks well ahead of all its competitors on each of the three financial ratios. It deserves to carry the peer group's highest rating, which is also the highest on Standard & Poor's scale, AAA. Similarly, Occidental Petroleum ranks eighth on each financial measure and carries the group's lowest rating, BBB−.

Among the remaining members of the integrated oil peer group, the correspondence between ranking and rating is less exact. The companies in slots 4 through 7 trade places from one ratio to the next. Other considerations by which the rating agencies establish a pecking order under such circumstances include subjective assessments of competitive position, management quality, and the like. Observe also that Chevron outranks Shell Oil by every measure shown, yet is rated lower (AA versus AAA). This seeming anomaly is explained by Shell Oil's position as a key subsidiary of a vast multinational enterprise, Royal Dutch/Shell Group of Companies. Although the parent company does not formally guarantee the subsidiary's debt, Standard & Poor's awards Shell Oil the AAA rating of Royal Dutch/Shell on the basis of implicit credit support.

Exhibit 13.7 also brings out an important characteristic of financial ratios—their interrelatedness. Except for Amerada Hess, no company ranks further than one slot away from where it ranks on the other measures. This is not a chance result. It would be difficult for a company to have (as an example), both a comparatively high ratio of debt to capital and comparatively high interest coverage. A combination of unusually low-interest-rate debt and exceptionally high return on capital could produce such a result, but it is hardly a common occurrence.

An important implication of this observation is that beyond a certain point, calculating and comparing companies on the basis of additional financial ratios contributes little incremental insight. Each additional ratio merely represents a new way of expressing information already contained in the analysis. Accordingly, analysts rely on a limited number of ratios to extract the bulk of the information obtainable through this mode of analysis. They can put their remaining time and energy to best use by searching for other pertinent facts, both inside and outside the financial statements.

The second technique of comparative ratio analysis is to rank a company within a rating peer group. As noted, it is not appropriate to compare companies in disparate sectors of the economy, such as industrials and utilities. A rating peer group can, however, legitimately include a variety of industries within a broadly defined economic sector. The expanded sample available under this approach enables the analyst to fine-tune the slotting achieved via the industry peer group comparisons.

Instead of displaying ratios for all 151 industrial companies rated Single-A by Standard & Poor's, Exhibit 13.8 lists the medians for the Single-A group. As a further aid in slotting companies, the table includes the cutoff points for the upper and lower quartiles in the rankings of Single-A companies.

Texaco's rating at the high end (A+) of the Single-A peer group appears generous, relative to its ranking within the rating peer group. The company's statistics approximately match the medians for funds flow as a percentage of

EXHIBIT 13.8   Average Ratios for Standard & Poor's Single-A Industrials 1998–2000

	Pretax Interest Coverage	Funds Flow as a Percentage of Total Debt	Total Debt as a Percentage of Capital
Best quartile	9.1	63.6	30.6
Median	6.8	46.1	40.1
Worst quartile	4.9	34.3	50.4

Source: Standard & Poor's.

total debt and total debt as a percentage of capital. As for pretax interest coverage, Texaco's ratio is closer to the worst quartile than the median.

Does Texaco's overall showing, as of 2000, imply an overrating of the company by Standard & Poor's? Based solely on the financial ratios, that would be a reasonable inference. Far from being in imminent danger of a rating reduction, however, Texaco was on S&P's watchlist for possible upgrading as it reported its year-end results.

Several factors explained this seeming paradox. To begin with, S&P attributed great significance to Texaco's strong competitive position. In addition to its strong brand names, the company boasted an excellent record of replacing its oil production with new discoveries at a comparatively low cost. Financial flexibility was another of the company's strong suits. Texaco could fund its exploration and production budget from internally generated funds, precluding any need to borrow. The final factor that supported a rating somewhat higher than the company's financial ratios implied was management's credibility with S&P's analysts. Having committed themselves to capping the company's total debt at 40% of capital, Texaco's senior managers kept their word. In one instance, that required the funding of a major acquisition with equity, a financing strategy ordinarily not calculated to win the applause of shareholders. As for S&P's watchlisting of the company for an even higher rating, there was another critical factor not visible in Exhibit 13.7. Chevron, a more highly rated peer, had made an offer to acquire Texaco.

The lesson is that although comparative ratio analysis plays a large role in the bond rating process, Moody's and Standard & Poor's also consider factors outside the financial statements. Therefore, analysts working outside the rating agencies must be cautious about concluding that a company is rated incorrectly. If they make such an inference without exploring the possibility of extenuating circumstances, they may recommend buying or selling a bond in expectation of an upgrade or downgrade that has little chance of materializing.

With that proviso, analysts can derive considerable value from comparative ratio analysis. It is helpful to determine that a company not rated by

Moody's or Standard & Poor's most closely resembles the companies in a particular rating category. In assigning a nonrated company to a rating category based on ratio comparisons, analysts should keep in mind the size criterion, previously discussed, for creation of peer groups.

Comparative ratio analysis is also useful in assessing the credit impact of a major transaction, such as a debt-financed acquisition or a major stock repurchase. The analyst can calculate ratios based on pro forma financial statements (see Chapter 12) and slot the company in a grid of median ratios by rating category (see Exhibit 13.9). In view of changes in the peer group ratios that arise from fluctuations in business conditions, it is important to use data that is as up-to-date as possible for the exercise.

Analysts should also bear in mind that a company can potentially avert a downgrade implied by the pro forma ratios, provided management's credibility with the rating agencies is high. The key is to present a plausible plan for restoring financial leverage to its pretransaction level within a few years. Note, however, that the company will merely delay the downgrade if it does not begin fairly quickly to make palpable progress toward the long-range target. The rating agencies tend to be skeptical about a company's ability to implement a three-year plan entirely in the third year.

Ratio Trend Analysis

Comparative ratio analysis is an effective technique for assessing relative credit risk, yet it leaves the analyst exposed to a major source of error. Suppose two companies in the same industry posted an identical fixed-charge coverage of 3.5 times last year. On a ratio comparison, the two appear to be equally risky. Suppose, however, that one company had coverage of 5.0 times five years ago and has steadily declined to 3.5 times. Imagine, as well,

EXHIBIT 13.9 Median Ratios by Bond Rating Category (Industrials, 1997–1999)

	AAA	AA	A	BBB	BB	B	CCC
EBIT interest coverage (x)	17.5	10.8	6.8	3.9	2.1	1.0	0.2
EBITDA interest coverage (x)	21.8	14.6	9.6	6.1	3.5	2.0	1.4
Funds flow/total debt (%)	105.8	55.8	46.1	30.5	18.4	9.4	5.8
Free operating cash flow/ total debt (%)	55.4	24.6	15.6	6.6	3.1	(4.5)	(14.0)
Return on capital (%)	28.2	22.9	19.9	14.0	11.7	7.2	0.5
Operating income/sales (%)	29.2	21.3	18.3	15.3	15.6	11.2	13.6
Long-term debt/total capital (%)	15.2	26.4	32.5	41.0	59.0	70.7	80.3
Total debt/capital (%)	26.9	35.6	40.1	47.4	63.9	74.6	89.4

that the other company's coverage has improved over the same period from 2.0 times to 3.5 times. If the two companies' trends appear likely to continue, based on analysis, then the happenstance that both covered their interest by 3.5 times last year should have little bearing on the credit assessment. The company that will have stronger coverage in the future is the better risk.

A further complication is that improving or deteriorating financial ratios can have different implications for different companies. In some cases, a declining trend over several years signals that a company has genuinely fallen to a new, lower level of credit quality. For other companies, negative year-over-year comparisons merely represent the downlegs of their normal operating cycles.

Certain industries enjoy fairly stable demand, year in and year out. Small-ticket nondurables such as food, beverages, and beauty aids are not items that consumers cease to buy during recessions. At worst, people trade down to cheaper products within the same categories. In contrast, consumers tend to postpone purchases of big-ticket durable goods when credit is tight or when they have misgivings about economic conditions. Producers of automobiles, houses, and major appliances are among the businesses that experience wide swings in demand between peaks and troughs in the economy. Profits typically fluctuate even more dramatically in these industries, due to the high fixed costs entailed in capital-intensive production methods.

In evaluating the long-range creditworthiness of cyclical companies, the bond rating agencies historically focused on cycle-to-cycle, rather than year-to-year trends. Their notion was that a cycle-to-cycle pattern of similar highs and similar lows (Exhibit 13.10) did not imply a true impairment of financial strength. Deterioration was indicated only when a company displayed a trend of successively lower highs and lower lows (Exhibit 13.11).

Moody's and Standard & Poor's label this traditional approach "rating through the cycle." Although it still influences the agencies' analysis, they have deemphasized the concept somewhat in recent years. The evolution reflects, in part, a perception that although business activity still fluctuates from year to year, the United States economy no longer undergoes the classic business cycles of former decades. By implication, an extended upturn or downtrend in a company's ratios is more likely than in bygone times to represent a longer-lived shift.

Even in years past, when the agencies adhered more closely to the doctrine of rating through the cycle, it was often difficult to distinguish a normal, cyclical decline from more permanent deterioration, without the benefit of hindsight. There was always a danger that a company's management was portraying a permanent reduction in profitability as a routine

EXHIBIT 13.10   Cycle-to-Cycle Stability
(Similar highs and lows)

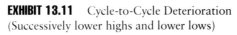

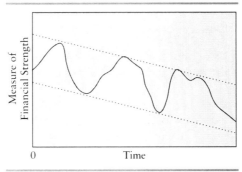

*Examples: Operating margin, fixed charge cover-
age, ratio of cash flow to total debt.

cyclical slump. Then, as now, an analyst had to look beyond the financial
statements to make an informed judgment about the likely persistence of an
improvement or deterioration in financial measures.

Default Risk Models

As noted, comparative ratio analysis and ratio trend analysis are techniques
for placing companies on a relative scale of credit quality. Many analysts
have no need to look more deeply into the matter, but it is impossible to

EXHIBIT 13.11   Cycle-to-Cycle Deterioration
(Successively lower highs and lower lows)

cover the topic of credit analysis satisfactorily without discussing two more fundamental issues. First, there is the question of how to set up a ranking scheme such as bond ratings in the first place. Second, there is the problem of conflicting indicators. How, for example, should an analyst evaluate a company that ranks well on fixed-charge coverage but poorly on financial leverage? A rigorous approach demands something more scientific than an individual analyst's subjective opinion that coverage should be weighted twice as heavily as leverage, or vice versa.

The solution to both of these problems lies in establishing a statistical relationship between financial ratios and default. This requires, first of all, collecting data on the default experience in a given population. Next, statistical methods are employed to determine which financial ratios have historically predicted defaults most reliably. Using a model derived from the best predictors, the analyst can then rank companies on the basis of how closely their financial profiles resemble the profiles of companies that defaulted.

One example of the various models that have been devised to predict defaults is Edward I. Altman's Z-Score model, which takes the following form:

$$Z = 1.2x_1 + 1.4x_2 + 3.3x_3 + 0.6x_4 + 1.0x_5$$

where: x_1 = Working capital/Total assets (%, e.g., .20, or 20%)
x_2 = Retained earnings/Total assets (%)
x_3 = Earnings before interest and taxes/Total assets (%)
x_4 = Market value of equity/Total liabilities (%)
x_5 = Sales/Total assets (number of times, e.g., 2.0 times)

In this model, scores below 1.81 signify serious credit problems, whereas a score above 3.0 indicates a healthy firm.

A refinement of the Z-Score model, the Zeta model developed by Altman and his colleagues,[7] achieved greater predictive accuracy by using the following variables:

x_1 = Earnings before interest and taxes (EBIT)/Total assets
x_2 = Standard error of estimate of EBIT/Total assets (normalized) for 10 years
x_3 = EBIT/interest charges
x_4 = Retained earnings/Total assets
x_5 = Current assets/Current liabilities
x_6 = Five-year average market value of equity/Total capitalization
x_7 = Total tangible assets, normalized

Quantitative models such as Zeta, as well as others that have been devised using various mathematical techniques, have several distinct benefits. First, they are developed by objectively correlating financial variables with defaults. They consequently avoid guesswork in assigning relative weights to the variables. Second, the record of quantitative models is excellent from the standpoint of classifying as troubled credits most companies that subsequently defaulted. In addition, the scores assigned to nondefaulted companies by these models correlate fairly well with bond ratings. This suggests that although Moody's and Standard & Poor's originally developed their rating methods along more subjective lines, their conclusions are at least partially vindicated by statistical measures of default risk. Therefore, the credit analyst can feel comfortable about using methods such as ratio trend analysis to slot companies within the ratings framework. Although one can quarrel with the rating agencies' assessments of particular companies or particular industries, there is strong statistical support for the notion that in the aggregate, ratings provide a valid, if rough, assessment of default risk. The lower a company's present rating, the higher is its probability of defaulting over the next year, next 2 years, and so on up to 20 years.[8]

Useful as they are, though, quantitative default models cannot entirely replace human judgment in credit analysis.

For one thing, quantitative models tend to classify as troubled credits not only most of the companies that eventually default, but also many that do not default.[9] Often, firms that fall into financial peril bring in new management and are revitalized without ever failing in their debt service. If faced with a huge capital loss on the bonds of a financially distressed company, an institutional investor might wish to assess the probability of a turnaround—an inherently difficult-to-quantify prospect—instead of selling purely on the basis of a default model.

The credit analyst must also bear in mind that companies can default for reasons that a model based solely on reported financial data cannot pick up. For example, U.S. Brass entered Chapter 11 proceedings in 1994 in an effort to resolve litigation involving defective plastic-plumbing systems that it had manufactured. Dow Corning's 1995 bankruptcy filing offered a possible means of resolving massive litigation arising from silicone gel breast implants sold by the company, which were alleged to cause autoimmune disease and other maladies. In 1999, Gulf States Steel, Inc. of Alabama filed for bankruptcy to address, among other matters, pending litigation with the Environmental Protection Agency and other potential environmentally related claims.[10] Typically, in such cases, neither the company's balance sheet nor its income statement signals an impending collapse. U.S. Brass's parent company, Eljer Industries, specifically indicated that the bankruptcy filing did not result from a cash flow shortfall. The problems were apparent in the company's Notes to Financial Statements, but default models based entirely on financial statement data do not deal with contingent liabilities.

In the case of the Zeta model, the default hazard posed by a company's environmental or product liability litigation may be picked up, at least in part, by the ratio of market value of equity to total capitalization. Stock market investors consider such risks in determining share prices.

Some default risk models dispense with statement data altogether in favor of complete reliance on the equity market's wisdom. The best-known are marketed by KMV and Helix Investment Partners, L.P. Underlying these models is the observation that a company's debt and equity both derive their value from the same assets. Equity holders have only a residual claim after bondholders have been paid. Therefore, if the market value of a company's assets falls below the value of its liabilities, the stock becomes worthless. At the same time, the company becomes bankrupt; its liabilities exceed its assets. Extending the logic, a declining stock price indicates that the company is getting closer to bankruptcy. In theory, then, credit analysts can skip the financial statement work and monitor companies' default risk simply by watching their stock prices.

Like the quantitative models consisting of financial ratios, the default risk models based on stock prices provide useful, but not infallible, signals. For example, when a company dramatically increases its total-debt-to-total-capital ratio by borrowing money to repurchase stock, its default risk clearly rises. At the same time, its stock price may also rise, reflecting the positive impact on earnings per share of increased financial leverage and a reduction in the number of shares outstanding. According to the theory underlying the stock-based default risk models, however, a rising share price indicates declining default risk. This is one of several caveats typically accompanying credit opinions derived from stock-based models.

Even if share prices were perfect indicators of credit risk, credit analysts would not escape the rigors of tearing apart financial statements. To begin with, not every company's shares trade in the public market. The producers of stock-based models attempt to get around this problem by using share prices of industry peers to create surrogates for private companies' unobservable equity values. This method, however, cannot capture the sort of company-specific risks that led to the bankruptcies of U.S. Brass, Dow Corning, and Gulf States Steel Inc. of Alabama. Neither can stock-based default risk models relieve the analyst of such tasks as creating pro forma financial statements to gauge the impact of a potential merger or major asset sale. At most, incorporating stock prices into credit analysis is a useful complement to plumbing the financial statements for meaning with time-tested ratio calculations.

CONCLUSION

Default risk models can provide a solid foundation for credit analysis but must be complemented by the analyst's judgment on matters too complex to be modeled. Much the same applies to all of the quantitative techniques discussed in this chapter. A lender should not provide credit before first "running the numbers." By the same token, it is a mistake to rely solely on the numbers in order to sidestep a difficult decision. This can take the form either of rejecting a reasonable risk by inflexibly applying quantitative criteria, or of approving a credit against one's better judgment while counting on financial ratios that are technically satisfactory as a defense against criticism if the loan goes bad.

As other chapters in this book demonstrate, financial statements are vulnerable to manipulation, much of which is perfectly legal. Often, the specific aim of the manipulators is to outfox credit analysts who mechanically calculate ratios without pausing to consider whether accounting ruses have defeated the purpose. Another danger in relying too heavily on quantitative analysis is that a company may unexpectedly and radically alter its capital structure to finance an acquisition or to defend itself against a hostile takeover. Such action can render ratio analysis on even the most recent financial statements largely irrelevant. In the end, credit analysts must equip themselves with all the tools described in this chapter, yet not be made complacent by them.

QUESTIONS

1. Accounting rules distinguish between capital and operating leases. Should the user of financial statements be satisfied with this treatment?
2. Do improving or deteriorating financial ratios always have the same implications for different companies?
3. Do the rating agencies consider management attitude toward debt when assigning bond ratings? Explain.
4. Given the balance sheet of Johnson and Johnson, (Exhibit 13.1) calculate its current ratio, quick ratio, and its working capital.
5. How can seasonality introduce a distortion when using financial ratios that combine balance sheet and income statement figures?

6. How can the financial analyst detect an asset quality problem related to inventory?

7. How did Viacom's management respond to the price drop in the secondary market for its bonds?

8. How do analysts relate financial ratios to the borrower's propensity to pay interest and principal in full and on schedule?

9. How do changes in unit sales and the variability of selling prices affect the usefulness of the inventory turnover ratio? How can the analyst prevent such distortions?

10. How do the figures in Exhibit 13.6 bring out the interrelatedness of financial ratios?

11. How does size (as measured by annual sales) affect the placement of a company in a credit quality peer group?

12. How is line of business used to define a peer group?

13. How is this ratio related to financial flexibility? How does it vary with the capital-spending cycle?

14. How is total debt-to-cash flow calculated? How does it reflect financial flexibility?

15. How is total debt-to-cash flow superior to total debt-to-total capital and fixed-charge coverage?

16. Is achieving higher bond ratings a primary goal of corporate management? Explain.

17. Is it always better to calculate and compare a still greater number of financial ratios?

18. Other than leases, what are the ways corporations try to obtain the benefits of debt without suffering the associated penalties imposed by credit analysts?

19. Under what circumstances does a long-term floating-rate insulate the borrower from interest rate fluctuations?

20. Under what conditions can the use of net interest expense in the denominator of fixed-charge coverage overstate the level of protection implied by the coverage?

21. What are cycle-to-cycle comparisons and why would they be used instead of year-to-year comparisons?

22. What are financial leverage ratios and why would a creditor calculate them?

23. What are some of the complications that preferred stock introduces in the leverage calculation?

24. What are some of the issues associated with size?

25. What are some of the reasons why analyzing a company's financial statements may not be sufficient to determine its credit quality?

26. What are some of the reasons why companies default that are not captured in reported financial data?
27. What are the consequences of the fact that financial statements are vulnerable to manipulation, much of which is perfectly legal?
28. What are the dangers of attempting to create homogeneous peer groups?
29. What are the distinct benefits of quantitative models of credit quality? Can they replace human judgment in credit analysis?
30. What are the most commonly used profit margins?
31. What are the two fundamental issues the credit analyst must face? How are those two issues addressed by, for example, Altman's Z-score model?
32. What are the two risks inherent in depending on debt with maturities of less than one year?
33. What are two techniques used to resolve the tradeoff between strict comparability and sufficient sample size?
34. What do financial statements tell about a borrower's ability and willingness to repay a loan?
35. How does "bait and switch" play a role in financial statement analysis?
36. What does return on equity measure and how may distortions be introduced in calculating this ratio? How can the distortion above be mitigated?
37. What does the account labeled "Deferred Income Taxes" represent? What does it reflect?
38. What does the ratio of capital expenditures to depreciation capture? What needs to be considered in the analysis, even if this ratio consistently exceeds one?
39. What does the wheelbarrow have to do with financial ratio analysis?
40. What does a total assets to total liabilities ratio of 1.63 mean?
41. What is fixed-charge coverage? What does it measure? Why is it of major interest to credit analysts?
42. What is SFAS No. 34 and what refinement in fixed-charged coverage is required by it?
43. What is the aspect of management's effectiveness that each profit margin reflects?
44. What is the basic technique in assigning a relative credit ranking to a company?
45. What is the major opportunity for earnings manipulation that cash flow eliminates?
46. What is the most immediate danger faced by a lender and how can this condition arise?
47. What is the total-debt-to-total-capital ratio? Why do credit analysts put less emphasis on it than in the past?

48. What is the ultimate objective of the credit analyst? How does convertible debt figure in this issue?
49. What may a decline in the receivables turnover signal to the financial analyst?
50. What measure provides a link between credit analysis and the economic concept of the productivity of capital?
51. What other combination ratios can be used as checks against an artificially heightened return on equity?
52. What ratios measure credit quality at the most elemental level?
53. What refinement in fixed-charge coverage is required by the existence of operating leases?
54. What risk does the ratio of total fixed obligations to total capital take into account?
55. What two complications arise in connection with incorporating operating lease payments into a fixed-charge coverage calculation?
56. What types of off-balance sheet obligations do SFAS No. 87 and SFAS No. 106 cover? What distinguishes these liabilities from other kinds of hidden liabilities?
57. What impact did Viacom's merger with Blockbuster have on the combined companies' bond ratings?
58. What's the underlying notion of a turnover ratio?
59. When should short-term debt be viewed as permanent and included in the leverage calculations?
60. Why is cash flow from operations to capital expenditures a key ratio to watch for in capital-intensive manufacturers and utilities?
61. Why is it important to understand how companies can be ranked by ratios on a relative scale of credit quality?
62. Why is it no longer appropriate to consider only long-term debt in leverage calculations?
63. Why is it not useful to lay down absolute rules about "correct" calculations of leverage ratios?
64. Why is profit margin such an integral part of the contemporary view of credit analysis?
65. Why is the ratio of depreciation to cash flow from operations considered forward-looking?
66. Why should a financial analyst not use return on equity as the only measure of credit quality?

CHAPTER 14

Equity Analysis

Countless books have been written on the subject of "picking stocks." The approaches represented in their pages cover a vast range. Some focus on technical analysis, which seeks to establish the value of a common equity by studying its past price behavior. Others take as their starting point the Efficient Market Hypothesis, which in its purest form implies that no sort analysis can identify values not already recognized and properly discounted by the market.

This chapter does not attempt to summarize or criticize all the methods employed by the legions who "play the market." Rather, the discussion focuses primarily on the use of financial statements in **fundamental analysis.** This term refers to the attempt to determine whether a company's stock is fairly valued, based on its financial characteristics.

Certain elements of fundamental analysis do *not* use information found in the financial statements. For example, a company may seem like a good candidate for a "bust-up," or hostile takeover, premised on selling portions of the company to realize value not reflected in its stock price. As discussed later in this chapter, the analyst can estimate the firm's ostensible breakup value by studying its annual report. The feasibility of a hostile raid, however, may hinge on the pattern of share ownership, the availability of financing for a takeover, or laws applicable to tender offers. All these factors lie outside the realm of financial statement analysis, but may have a major bearing on the valuation process.

A final point regarding the following material is that it should be read in conjunction with Chapter 12 ("Forecasting Financial Statements"). A company's equity value lies wholly in its future performance, with historical financial statements aiding the analysis only to the extent that they provide a basis for projecting future results. Into the formulas detailed in this chapter, the analyst must plug earnings and cash flow forecasts derived by the techniques described in Chapter 12.

THE DIVIDEND DISCOUNT MODEL

Several methods of fundamental common stock analysis have been devised over the years, but few match the intuitive appeal of regarding the stock price as the discounted value of expected future dividends. This approach is analogous to the yield-to-maturity calculation for a bond and therefore facilitates the comparison of different securities of a single issuer. Additionally, the method permits the analyst to address the uncertainty inherent in forecasting a noncontractual flow[1] by varying the applicable discount rate.

To understand the relationship between future dividends and present stock price, consider the following fictitious example: Tarheel Tobacco's annual common dividend rate is currently $2.10 a share. Because the company's share of a nonexpanding market is neither increasing nor decreasing, it will probably generate flat sales and earnings for the indefinite future and continue the dividend at its current level. Tarheel's long-term debt currently offers a yield of 10%, reflecting the company's credit rating and the prevailing level of interest rates. Based on the greater uncertainty of the dividend stream relative to the contractual payments on Tarheel's debt, investors demand a risk premium of four percentage points—a return of 10% + 4% = 14%—to own the company's common stock rather than its bonds.

The stock price that should logically be observed in the market, given these facts, is the price at which Tarheel's annual $2.10 payout equates to a 14% yield, or algebraically:

$$P = \frac{D}{K}$$

$$P = \frac{\$2.10}{.14}$$

$$P = \$15.00$$

where P = Current stock price
D = Current dividend rate
K = Required rate of return

If the analyst agrees that 14% is an appropriate discount rate, based on a financial comparison between Tarheel and other companies with similar implicit discount rates, then any price less than $15 a share indicates that the stock is undervalued. Alternatively, suppose the analyst concludes that

Tarheel's future dividend stream is less secure than the dividend streams of other companies to which a 14% discount rate is being applied. The analyst might then discount Tarheel's stream at a higher rate, say 15%, and recalculate the appropriate share price as follows:

$$P = \frac{\$2.10}{.15}$$

$$P = \$14.00$$

A market price of $15 a share would then indicate an overvaluation of Tarheel Tobacco.

Dividends and Future Appreciation

When initially introduced to the dividend-discount model, many individuals respond by saying, "Dividends are not the only potential source of gain to the stockholder. The share price may rise as well. Shouldn't any evaluation reflect the potential for appreciation?" It is in responding to this objection that the dividend-discount model displays its elegance most fully. The answer is that there is no reason for the stock price to rise in the future unless the dividend rises. In a no-growth situation such as Tarheel Tobacco, the valuation will look the same five years hence (assuming no change in interest rates and risk premiums) as today. There is consequently no fundamental reason for a buyer to pay more for the stock at that point. If, on the other hand, the dividend payout rises over time (the case that immediately follows), the stock *will* be worth more in the future than it is today. The analyst can, however, incorporate the expected dividend increases directly into the present-value calculation to derive the current stock price, without bothering to determine and discount back the associated future price appreciation. By thinking through the logic of the discounting method, the analyst will find that value always comes back to dividends.

Valuing a Growing Company

No-growth companies are simple to analyze, but in practice most public corporations strive for growth in earnings per share, which, as the ensuing discussion demonstrates, will lead to gains for shareholders. In analyzing growing companies, a somewhat more complex formula must be used to equate future dividends to the present stock price:

$$P = \frac{D(1+g)^1}{(1+K)^1} + \frac{D(1+g)^2}{(1+K)^2} + \cdots \frac{D(1+g)^n}{(1+K)^n}$$

where P = Current stock price
       D = Current dividend rate
       K = Required rate of return
       g = Growth rate

    A number of dollars equivalent to P, if invested at an interest rate equivalent to K, will be equal, after n periods, to the cumulative value of dividends paid over the same interval, assuming the payout is initially an amount equivalent to D and increases in each period at a rate equivalent to g.

    Fortunately, from the standpoint of ease of calculation, if n, the number of periods considered, is infinite, the preceding formula reduces to the simpler form:

$$P = \frac{D}{K-g}$$

In practice, this is the form ordinarily used in analysis, since companies are presumed to continue to operate as going concerns, rather than to liquidate at some arbitrary future date.

    Figures projected from the financial statements of the fictitious Wolfe Food Company (Exhibit 14.1) illustrate the application of the dividend-discount model. Observe that the company is expected to pay out 33 1/3% of its earnings to shareholders in the current year:

$$\text{Dividend} - \text{payout ratio} = \frac{\text{Dividends to common shareholders}}{\text{Net income available to common shareholders}}$$

$$= \frac{\$15,000,000}{\$45,000,000}$$

$$= 33\tfrac{1}{3}\%$$

If Wolfe maintains a constant dividend-payout ratio, it follows that the growth rate of dividends will equal the growth rate of earnings, which is

EXHIBIT 14.1   Selected Financial Data for Wolfe Food Company

Net income available to common shareholders	$45,000,000
Dividends to common shareholders	$15,000,000
Common shares outstanding	10,000,000
Expected annual growth in earnings	10%
Investors' required rate of return, given predictability of Wolfe's earnings	13%

expected to be 10% annually. On a per share basis, the initial dividend comes to $1.50:

$$\text{Dividend rate} = \frac{\text{Dividends to common shareholders}}{\text{Common shares outstanding}}$$

$$= \frac{\$15,000,000}{10,000,000}$$

$$= \$1.50 \text{ per share}$$

With these numbers, the analyst can now use the valuation formula to derive a share price of $50 for Wolfe:

$$P = \frac{D}{K - g}$$

$$P = \frac{\$1.50}{.13 - .10}$$

$$P = \frac{\$1.50}{.03}$$

$$P = \$50$$

The execution of this model rests heavily on the assumptions underlying the company's projected financial statements. To estimate the future growth rate of earnings, the analyst must make informed judgments both about the growth of the company's markets and about the company's ability to maintain or increase its share of those markets. Furthermore, the company's earnings growth rate may diverge from its sales growth due to changes in its operating margins that may or may not reflect industrywide trends.

Because of the uncertainties affecting such projections, the analyst should apply to equity valuation the same sort of sensitivity analysis discussed in connection with financial forecasting (see Chapter 12). For instance, if Wolfe Foods ultimately falls short of the 10% growth rate previously projected, then the $50 valuation will prove in retrospect to have been $12.50 too high:

$$P = \frac{D}{K - g}$$

$$P = \frac{\$1.50}{.13 - .09}$$

$$P = \$37.50$$

Therefore, an analyst whose forecast of earnings growth has a margin of error of one percentage point should not put a strong "Buy" recommendation on Wolfe when it is trading at $45 a share. By the same token, a price of $25, which implies a 7% growth rate, can safely be regarded as an undervaluation, provided the other assumptions are valid.

Earnings or Cash Flow?

Intuitively appealing though it may be, the relating of share price to future dividends through projected earnings growth does not jibe perfectly with reality. In particular, highly cyclical companies do not produce steady earnings increases year in and year out, yet the formula $P = D/K{-}g$ demands a constant rate of growth. If, as assumed previously, the company's dividend-payout ratio remains constant, the pattern of its dividends will plainly fail to fit neatly into the formula.

What saves the dividend-discounting approach from irrelevance is that companies generally do not strive for a constant dividend-payout ratio at all costs. More typically, they attempt to avoid cutting the amount of the payout, notwithstanding declines in earnings. For example, a company that aims to pay out 25% of its earnings over a complete business cycle might record a payout ratio of 15% in a peak year and 90% or 100% in a trough year. Indeed, a company that records net losses may maintain its dividend at the established level, at least for a few years, resulting in a meaningless payout-ratio calculation. (If losses persist, financial prudence will usually dictate cutting or eliminating the dividend to conserve cash.) As a rule, a cyclical company will not increase its dividend on a regular, annual basis. Nevertheless, the board will ordinarily endeavor to raise the payout over the longer term. In all of these cases, the $P = D/K{-}g$ formula will work reasonably well as a valuation tool, with the irregular pattern of dividend increases recognized through adjustments to the discount rate (K).

Although the dividend-discount model can accommodate earnings' cyclicality, the analyst must pay close attention to the method by which a company finances the continuation of its dividend at the established rate. A chronically money-losing company that borrows to pay dividends is simply undergoing slow liquidation. (It is replacing its equity, 100% of it in time, with liabilities.) In such circumstances, the key assumption that dividends will continue for an infinite number of periods becomes unsustainable.

On the other hand, a cyclical company may sustain losses at the bottom of a business cycle but never reach the point at which its funds from operations, net of capital expenditures required to maintain long-term competitiveness, fail to cover the dividend. Maintaining the dividend under these circumstances poses no financial threat. Accordingly, many analysts argue that cash flow, rather than earnings, is the true determinant of dividend-paying capability. By extension, they contend that projected cash flow, rather than earnings-per-share forecasts, should be the main focus of equity analysis.

Certainly, analysts need to be acutely conscious of changes in a company's cash-generating capability that are not paralleled by changes in earnings. For example, a company may for a time maintain a given level of profitability even though its business is becoming more capital-intensive. Rising plant and equipment requirements might transform the company from a self-financing entity into one that is dependent on external financing. Return on equity will not reflect the change until, after several years, either the resulting escalation in borrowing costs or the increase in the equity base required to support a given level of operating earnings becomes material. Furthermore, as detailed in Chapters 6 and 7, reported earnings are subject to considerable manipulation. In fact, that is the flaw that helped to popularize the use of cash flow analysis in the first place. Cash generated from operations, which is generally more difficult for companies to manipulate than earnings, can legitimately be viewed as the preferred measure of future dividend-paying capability.

Notwithstanding these arguments, earnings per share forecasts remain the focal point of equity research on Wall Street and elsewhere. (As explained in Chapter 3, some companies have managed to shift analysts' focus from GAAP earnings to so-called pro forma earnings.) For many companies, the components of cash flow other than net income, especially depreciation, are highly predictable over the near term. By accurately forecasting the more variable component, earnings, an investor can get a fairly good handle on cash flow as well. To some extent, too, the unflagging focus on earnings probably reflects institutional inertia. Portfolio managers measure the accuracy of brokerage houses' equity analysis in terms of earnings per share forecasts and investment strategists rely on aggregate earnings per share forecasts to gauge the attractiveness of the stock market as a whole. Analysts who lack an EPS forecast simply have a hard time getting into the discussion. Despite the stranglehold of earnings forecasts, however, a mechanism is available for adjusting a stock evaluation when the quality of the forecasted earnings is questionable. Investors can reduce the earnings multiple, as explained in the following section.

THE PRICE-EARNINGS RATIO

Although the dividend-discount model is an intuitively satisfying approach to valuing a common stock, it is not the most convenient method of comparing one stock's value with another's. Better suited to that task is the price-earnings ratio, alternately known as the P/E ratio or earnings multiple:

$$\text{Price-earnings ratio} = \frac{\text{Stock price}}{\text{Earnings per share}}$$

Based on this formula, Wolfe Food Company (see preceding section) has a price-earnings ratio of:

$$\text{Stock price} = \$50$$

$$\text{Net income available to common shareholders} = \$45,000,000$$

$$\text{Common shares} = \$10,000,000$$

$$\text{Earnings per share} = \frac{\$45,000,000}{10,000,000}$$

$$= \$4.50$$

$$\text{Price-earnings ratio} = \frac{\$50}{\$4.50}$$

$$= 11.1X$$

To understand how the price-earnings ratio may be used to compare companies with one another, consider a competitor of Wolfe Food Company,

EXHIBIT 14.2   Selected Financial Data for Grubb & Chao

Net income available to common shareholders	$54,000,000
Dividends to common shareholders	$18,000,000
Common shares outstanding	15,000,000
Expected annual growth in earnings	10%
Investors' required rate of return, given predictability of company's earnings	13%
Current stock price	$48.75

Grubb & Chao (Exhibit 14.2). Grubb & Chao has the same expected earnings growth rate as Wolfe (10%) and is assigned the same required rate of return (13%). Its price-earnings ratio, however, is higher than Wolfe's (13.5X vs. 11.1X):

$$\text{Price-earnings ratio} = \frac{\text{Stock price}}{\text{Earnings per share}}$$

$$= \frac{\$48.75}{\left(\dfrac{\$54,000,000}{15,000,000}\right)}$$

$$= \frac{\$48.75}{\$3.60}$$

$$= 13.5X$$

Based on the information provided, an investor would regard Wolfe as a better value than Grubb & Chao. This conclusion proceeds from applying the dividend-discount model to the latter's numbers:

$$P = \frac{D}{K - g}$$

$$P = \frac{\left(\dfrac{\$18,000,000}{15,000,000}\right)}{.13 - .10}$$

$$P = \frac{\$1.20}{.03}$$

$$P = \$40$$

The price thus derived is lower than the actual price of $48.75, implying an overvaluation by the market. Observe as well that the "correct" price for Grubb & Chao produces the same price-earnings ratio as calculated for Wolfe Food Company:

$$\text{Price-earnings ratio} = \frac{\$40}{\$3.60}$$

$$= 11.1\text{X}$$

P/E-based value comparisons can go well beyond this sort of company-to-company matchup. The analyst can rank all the companies within an industry (Exhibit 14.3), then judge whether the variations in price-earnings ratios appear justified, or whether certain companies seem misranked. Note that the table ranks companies on the basis of actual earnings over the preceding four quarters, rather than estimated earnings for the coming year, another

EXHIBIT 14.3 Companies within an Industry Ranked by Price-Earnings Ratio: Cosmetics and Personal Care Industry—September 2001

Company	Share Price Divided by Estimated 2001 Earnings per Share
Colgate-Palmolive	29.06
Gillette	25.00
Estee Lauder	24.71
Avon Products	22.58
Chattem	19.37
Inter Parfums	18.75
Alberto-Culver A	17.47
Del Laboratories	16.27
DSG International	15.31
Paragon Trade	9.36
CCA Industrie	5.42
Parlux Fragrance	5.38
Oralabs Holding	4.35

Source: Bloomberg.

typical format employed in P/E ratio comparisons. Earnings exclude both extraordinary and nonrecurring items (see Chapter 3). Earnings per share are calculated on a diluted basis by taking into account the possibility that new shares will be created through conversion of outstanding **convertible** securities.

WHY P/E MULTIPLES VARY

Justifications for differences in earnings multiples derive from the variables of the preceding valuation formulas. Consider the following two equations:

$$P = \frac{D}{K - g} \text{ and } P/E = \frac{P}{EPS}$$

where
P = Current stock price
D = Current dividend rate
K = Required rate of return
g = Growth rate
P/E = Price-earnings ratio
EPS = Current earnings per share (annual)

Substituting $D/K - g$, which equals P, for the P in the other equation, produces the following expanded form:

$$P/E = \frac{\left(\frac{(D)}{(K - g)} \right)}{EPS}$$

Using this expanded equation permits the analyst to see quickly that an increase in the expected growth rate of earnings produces a premium multiple. For example, both Wolfe Food Company and Grubb & Chao have 10% growth factors, and both stocks currently trade at 11.1 times earnings. Suppose another competitor, Eatmore & Co., can be expected to enjoy 11% growth, by virtue of concentration in faster-growing segments of the food business. A substantially higher multiple results from this modest edge in earnings growth:

$$P/E = \frac{\left(\dfrac{D}{(K-g)}\right)}{EPS}$$

$$P/E = \frac{\left(\dfrac{\$1.60}{(.13-.11)}\right)}{\$4.80}$$

$$P/E = 16.7X$$

Eatmore & Co.'s earnings will not, however, command as big a premium (16.7X vs. 1.1X for its competitors) if the basis for its higher projected growth is subject to unusually high risks. For example, Eatmore's strategy may emphasize expansion in developing countries, where the rate of growth in personal income is higher than in the more mature economy of the United States. If so, Eatmore may be considerably more exposed than Wolfe or Grubb & Chao to the risks of nationalization, new restrictions on repatriation of earnings, protectionist trade policies, and adverse fluctuations in exchange rates. If so, the market will raise its discount rate (K) on Eatmore's earnings. An increase of just one-half percentage point (from 13.0% to 13.5%) wipes out more than half the premium in Eatmore's multiple, dropping it from 16.7X to 13.3X:

$$P/E = \frac{\left(\dfrac{D}{(K-g)}\right)}{EPS}$$

$$P/E = \frac{\left(\dfrac{\$1.60}{(.135-.11)}\right)}{\$4.80}$$

$$P/E = 13.3X$$

In effect, the ability to vary the discount rate, and therefore to assign a lower or higher multiple to a company's earnings, is the equity analyst's defense against the sort of earnings manipulation by management described in Chapter 3. A company may use liberal accounting practices and skimp on long-term investment spending, yet expect the resulting artificially inflated earnings per share to be valued at the same multiple as its competitor's more legitimately derived profits. Indeed, the heart of many management presentations to analysts is a table showing that the presenting company's multiple is low by comparison with its peers. Typically, the chief executive officer cites this table as proof that the company is undervalued. The natural corollary is that in time investors will become aware of the discrepancy and raise the multiple, and therefore the price of shares owned by those who are astute enough to buy in at today's dirt-cheap level.

These stories are sometimes persuasive, yet one must wonder whether such "discrepancies" in earnings multiples are truly the result of inattention by analysts. In the case of a large-capitalization company, hundreds of Wall Street and institutional analysts probably are making the comparison on their own. If so, they are fully aware of the below-average multiple but consider it justified for one or more reasons, including the following:

- The company's earnings are more cyclical than those of its peer group.
- The company has historically been prone to earnings "surprises," which raise suspicions that the reported results reflect an exceptionally large amount of "earnings management."
- Management has a reputation for erratic behavior (e.g., abrupt changes in strategy, ill-conceived acquisitions) that makes future results difficult to forecast.

Analysts may be mistaken in these perceptions, and may genuinely be undervaluing the stock. The low multiple is a conscious judgment, however, not a function of neglect. Even a small-capitalization company, which can more credibly claim that its stock is underfollowed by Wall Street, may have the multiple it deserves, although its competitors sport higher P/E ratios. It is appropriate to assign an above-average discount factor to the earnings of a company that competes against larger, better-capitalized firms. A small company may also suffer the disadvantages of lack of depth in management and concentration of its production in one or two plants.

Recognizing that qualitative factors may depress their multiples, companies often respond in kind, arguing that their low valuations are based on misperceptions. For example, a company in a notoriously cyclical industry may argue that it is an exception to the general pattern of its peer group. Thus, a manufacturer of automotive components may claim that its earnings are protected from fluctuations in new car sales by a heavy emphasis on selling replacement parts. Whether or not consumers are buying new cars, the reasoning goes, they must keep their existing vehicles in good repair. In fact, sales of replacement parts should rise if the existing fleet ages because fewer individuals buy new autos. Similarly, a building-materials manufacturer may claim to be cushioned against fluctuations in housing starts because of a strong emphasis in its product line on the remodeling and repair markets.

These arguments may contain a kernel of truth, but investors should not accept them on faith. Instead of latching on to the "concept" as a justification for immediately pronouncing the company's multiple too low, an analyst should independently establish whether an allegedly countercyclical business has in fact fit that description in past cycles. It is also important to determine whether the supposed source of earnings stability is truly large enough to offset a downturn of the magnitude that can realistically be expected in the other areas of the company's operations.

A good rule to remember is that a company can more easily create a new image than it can recast its operations. Analysts should be especially wary of companies that have tended to jump on the bandwagon of "concepts" associated with the hot stocks of the moment. During the late 1970s, skyrocketing oil prices led directly to higher expected earnings growth (g), and hence higher P/E multiples and stock prices for oil producers. Suddenly, chemical companies, capital-goods producers, and others began presenting themselves as "energy plays." Some did so by acquiring oil properties, but others simply began publicizing their existing, albeit tangential, links to the oil business in markets that might conceivably have benefited from rising petroleum prices. A few years later, when oil prices collapsed, these same companies deleted from their annual reports the glowing references and photographs playing up their energy-relatedness. Around the same time, as the economic boom ended in Houston and other cities that had benefited from surging oil prices, national retailing chains became less vocal about their concentration in the Sunbelt, which had for several years been synonymous with high growth and therefore high P/E ratios.

Normalizing Earnings

Companies have strong incentives to gain increases, however modest, in their earnings multiples, even at the cost of stretching the facts to the breaking point (or beyond). Accordingly, it is prudent to maintain a conservative bias in calculating appropriate multiples. In addition to upping the discount rate (K) when any question about the quality of earnings arises, the analyst should normalize the earnings per share trend when its sustainability is doubtful.

Suppose, for example, that the fictitious PPE Manufacturing Corporation's earnings per share over the past five years are as shown in Exhibit 14.4. PPE has customarily commanded a multiple in line with the overall market,

EXHIBIT 14.4   PPE Manufacturing
Corporation Earnings History Table

Year	Earnings per Share
2002	$1.52
2003	1.63
2004	1.86
2005	2.04
2006	2.67 (Estimated)

which is at present trading at 12 times estimated current-year earnings. By this logic, a price of 12 times $2.67, or approximately 32, seems warranted for PPE stock.

Exhibit 14.5 shows, however, that the current-year earnings estimate is well above PPE's historical trend line, making the sustainability of the

EXHIBIT 14.5   PPE Manufacturing Corporation Earnings
History Graph

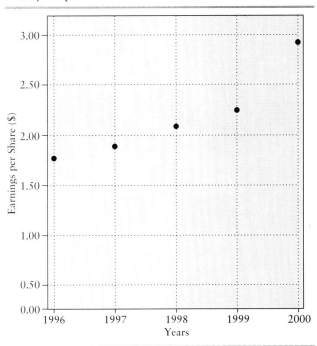

current level somewhat suspect. As it turns out, the $2.67 estimate is bloated by special conditions that will probably not recur in the near future. Specifically, the customers for PPE's major product are stepping up their purchases in anticipation of an industrywide strike later in the year. A temporary shortage has resulted, causing buyers to raise their bids. With its plants running flat out (reducing unit costs to the minimum) and its price realizations climbing, PPE is enjoying profit margins that it has never achieved before—and probably never will again.

It hardly seems appropriate to boost PPE's valuation from 24½ (12 times last year's earnings per share) to 32, a 31% increase, solely on the basis of an EPS hiccup that reflects no change in PPE's long-term earnings power. Accordingly, the analyst should normalize PPE's earnings by projecting the trend line established in preceding years. Exhibit 14.6 shows such a

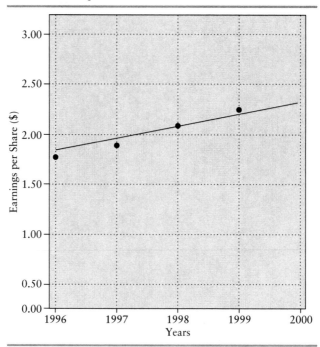

EXHIBIT 14.6   PPE Manufacturing Corporation Earnings Trend—Least-Squares Method

projection, using the least-squares method. The formula for this method is as follows:

$$y = a + m(x - \overline{x})$$

$$a = \overline{y}$$

$$m = \frac{\Sigma xy - n\overline{x}\,\overline{y}}{\Sigma x^2 - n\overline{x}^2}$$

$$\overline{x} = \frac{0 + 1 + 2 + 3}{4} = 1.5$$

$$\overline{y} = \frac{1.52 + 1.63 + 1.86 + 2.04}{4} = 1.7625$$

$$\Sigma xy = (0 \times 1.52) + (1 \times 1.63) + (2 \times 1.86) + (3 \times 2.04) = 11.47$$

$$n\overline{x}\,\overline{y} = 4 \times 1.5 \times 1.7625 = 10.575$$

$$\Sigma x^2 = 0^2 + 1^2 + 2^2 + 3^2 = 14$$

$$n\overline{x}^2 = (4) \times (1.5)^2 = 9$$

$$m = \frac{11.47 - 10.575}{14 - 9} = 0.179$$

$$y = 1.7625 + 0.179(x - 1.5)$$

Solving for $x = 4$, we derive a current-year trend-line value of $2.21. Applying the market multiple of 12 produces an indicated stock price of $26\frac{1}{2}$. Some modest upward revision from this point may be warranted, for if nothing else the company can reinvest its windfall profit in its business and generate a small, incremental earnings stream. By no means, though, should the company be evaluated on the basis of an earnings level that is not sustainable.

Sustainable Growth Rate

Sustainability is an issue not only in connection with unusual surges in earnings, but also when it comes to determining whether a company's historical rate of growth in earnings per share is likely to continue. The answer is probably "no" if the growth has been fueled by anything other than additions to retained earnings per share.

Consider the following derivation of earnings per share:

$$\frac{\text{Asset}}{\text{turnover}} \times \frac{\text{Return on}}{\text{sales}} \times \text{Leverage} \times \frac{\text{Book value}}{\text{per share}} = \text{Earnings per share}$$

Or:

$$\frac{\text{Sales}}{\text{Assets}} \times \frac{\text{Net income}}{\text{Sales}} \times \frac{\text{Assets}}{\text{Net worth}} \times \frac{\text{Net worth}}{\text{Shares outstanding}} = \frac{\text{Net income}}{\text{Shares outstanding}}$$

Earnings per share will not grow merely because sales increase. Any such increase will be canceled out in the preceding formula, since sales appears in the denominator of return on sales as well as in the numerator of asset turnover. Only by an increase in one of the four terms on the left side of the equation, or by a reduction in the number of shares outstanding, will the product (earnings per share) rise. Aggressive management may boost asset turnover, but eventually the assets will reach the limits of their productive capacity. Return on sales, likewise, cannot expand indefinitely because too-fat margins will invite competition. Leverage also reaches a limit because lenders will not continue advancing funds beyond a certain point as financial risk increases. This leaves only book value per share, which can rise unceasingly through additions to retained earnings, as a source of sustainable growth in earnings per share. As long as the amount of equity capital invested per share continues to rise, more income can be earned on that equity, and (as the reader can demonstrate by working through the preceding formula) earnings per share can increase.

A company's book value per share will not rise at all, however, if it distributes 100% of its earnings in dividends to shareholders. (This, by the way, is why an immediate increase in the dividend-payout ratio will not ordinarily cause a direct, proportionate rise in the stock price, as might appear to be the implication of the equation $P = D/K-g$.) Assuming the company can earn its customary return on equity on whatever profits it reinvests internally, raising its dividend-payout ratio reduces its growth in earnings per share (g). Such a move proves to be self-defeating as both the numerator and the denominator (D and $K-g$, respectively) rise and P remains unchanged.

To achieve sustainable growth in earnings per share, then, a company must retain a portion of its earnings. The higher the portion retained, the more book value is accumulated per share and the higher can be the EPS growth rate. By this reasoning, the following formula is derived:

$$\text{Substainable growth rate} = (\text{Return on equity}) \times (\text{Income reinvestment rate})$$

$$\text{where Income reinvestment rate} = 1 - \text{Dividend payout ratio}$$

As mentioned, the one remaining way to increase earnings per share, after exhausting the possibilities already discussed, is to reduce the number of shares outstanding. During the 1990s, a number of companies used stock buybacks to maintain EPS growth in the face of constrained opportunities for revenue growth. Between 1995 and 1999, International Business Machines spent $34.1 billion to repurchase shares, more than its cumulative net income for the period of $31.3 billion. By reducing its shareholders' equity through stock purchases, IBM increased its **leverage** and, therefore, its financial risk. Moreover, the company intensified this effect by adding to its debt. Financial commentator James Grant quipped that if IBM continued to buy in shares, it would undergo a slow-motion leveraged buyout.[2] Such EPS-boosting plans tend to be self-limiting, for as already noted, lenders refuse at some point to countenance increased indebtedness.

Analysts should note one subtlety in calculating the impact of stock repurchases on earnings per share. To the extent that the company funds the buybacks with idle cash, the increase in EPS is offset by a reduction arising from forgone income on investments. If a company has far more cash on its balance sheet than it can employ profitably in its operations, it is unfair to accuse management of deceitfully inflating its per share income by buying in stock.

THE DU PONT FORMULA

The preceding discussion of sustainable growth introduced a formula that provided insight into earnings per share by disaggregating it into several simple financial ratios. Disaggregation can be applied in other beneficial ways in equity analysis, most notably in a technique known as the Du Pont Formula. (The idea is generally credited to Donaldson Brown, who developed the formula while at E. I. du Pont de Nemours, then applied it during the 1920s as vice president of finance at General Motors.) With the aid of the Du Pont Formula, the analyst can more readily perceive the sources of a firm's return on assets:

$$\text{Asset turnover} \times \text{Return on sales} = \text{Return on assets}$$

$$\frac{\text{Sales}}{\text{Assets}} \times \frac{\text{Income}}{\text{Sales}} = \frac{\text{Income}}{\text{Assets}}$$

Like most ratio analysis, the Du Pont Formula is valuable not only for the questions it answers but also for the new ones it raises. If a company raises its return on assets by finding ways to reduce working capital without impairing competitiveness (thereby improving asset turnover), then it is likely to be able to perform at the higher level. On the other hand, cutting back on necessary capital expenditures will also have a positive effect—in the short run—on return on assets. Not only will the denominator decline in the asset turnover factor as a result of depreciation, but return on sales will rise as future depreciation charges are reduced by lower capital outlays in the current year. Underspending will eventually hurt competitiveness, and therefore the company's long-run return on assets, so analysts must probe to determine the true nature of shifts in these ratios.

A Du Pont analysis of the food processing industry (Exhibit 14.7) confirms the value of examining the components of return on equity. Based on ROE alone, Conagra (13.93%) and Kraft Foods (14.24%) look very similar. They achieved those numbers by very different methods, however. Conagra, a more commodity-oriented company, worked on a narrower sales margin (1.63% vs. 7.54% for Kraft), but turned over its assets much more frequently

EXHIBIT 14.7 Du Pont Analysis of Food Processing Industry's 2000 Results*

Company Name	Asset Turnover (x)	×	Return on Sales (%)	=	Return on Assets (%)	×	Financial Leverage (x)	=	Return on Equity
Conagra	2.06		1.63%		3.36%		4.15		13.93%
Dole Food	1.67		1.42		2.38		5.13		12.19
Heinz (H J)	1.06		9.47		10.06		5.55		55.80
Hershey Foods	1.22		7.93		9.70		2.93		28.47
Hormel Foods	2.24		4.63		10.37		1.88		19.48
Kellogg	1.42		8.45		12.00		5.46		65.48
Kraft Foods	0.51		7.54		3.84		3.71		14.24
McCormick	1.28		6.48		8.28		4.62		38.27
Ralston Purina	0.94		19.19		18.02		6.71		120.93
Sara Lee	1.51		6.98		10.52		9.22		97.06

*Calculations are subject to rounding error.

(2.06 X vs. 1.28 X). McCormick appears to be far more profitable than Hershey Foods, based on the companies' respective returns on equity of 38.27% and 28.47%. That advantage resulted entirely from more aggressive financial leverage (4.62 X for McCormick vs. Hershey's 2.93 X, the second most conservative ratio in the industry). Hershey's return on sales and, consequently, its return on assets were substantially higher than McCormick's corresponding figures. The analysis shows investors that to benefit from McCormick's higher return on equity, they must assume more financial risk than they would expose themselves to by owning the stock of Hershey Foods.

Some of the companies in Exhibit 14.7 achieved returns on equity that seem absurdly high, with Sara Lee at 97.06% and Ralston Purina at 120.93%. In part, those results reflected the two companies' employment of the highest financial leverage within the industry. In addition, the extremely high ROEs derived from the companies' very low levels of book value. As producers of branded food products, Sara Lee and Ralston Purina derive their equity value primarily from the consumer acceptance of well-known brands, rather than the physical plants in which they produce their goods. On June 30, 2001, Ralston Purina's stock closed at $30.02 a share, yet its book value was only $2.36 a share. The company's return on equity looks less stratospheric when equity is viewed in terms of market capitalization rather than historical cost (see "Pros and Cons of a Market-Based Equity Figure" in Chapter 2).

The Modified Du Pont Formula

Carrying the disaggregation technique a step further, the Modified Du Pont Formula analyzes the sources of return on shareholders' investment:

$$\text{Return on assets} \times \text{Financial leverage} = \text{Return on equity}$$

$$\frac{\text{Income}}{\text{Equity}} \times \frac{\text{Assets}}{\text{Equity}} = \frac{\text{Income}}{\text{Equity}}$$

As noted, the stock market will ordinarily value earnings at lower multiples than they would otherwise command if the earnings were subject to unusual risks. Financial risk, as signified by financial leverage, is one consideration that may penalize a company's P/E ratio. Generally speaking, an analyst will respond more favorably to a firm that raises its return on equity by increasing its return on assets than one that does so by leveraging its equity more aggressively. Besides introducing greater volatility into the rate of return, adding debt to the balance sheet demonstrates no management skill in improving operations. Furthermore, a company that has already fully utilized its debt capacity has no additional potential for increasing its return on equity by the same means. A somewhat underborrowed company, on the other hand, has hidden profitability potential that may be exploited (with concomitant benefits to shareholders) at a later point. The Modified Du Pont Formula enables investors to judge the quality of a company's return on equity in much the same way that other financial tests can be applied to the quality of earnings.

VALUATION THROUGH RESTRUCTURING POTENTIAL

A more subtle benefit of the Du Pont analysis is the insight it can provide into companies' potential for enhancing value through corporate restructuring. Whether initiated internally or imposed from outside, major revisions in operating and financial strategies can dramatically increase the price of a corporation's common shares. The analysis illustrated in Exhibit 14.7 helps to identify the type of restructuring that can unlock hidden value in a particular instance. Some companies have the potential to raise their share prices by utilizing their assets more efficiently, whereas others can increase their value by increasing their financial leverage.[3]

By way of background, corporate managers frequently find themselves at odds with stock market investors and speculators over issues of corporate policy. In general, managers prefer to maintain a certain amount of slack in their organizations, that is, a reserve capacity to deal with crises and opportunities. They tend to be less troubled than investors if their companies generate excess cash that remains on the balance sheet earning the modest returns available on low-risk, short-dated financial instruments. That cash may come in handy, they argue, if earnings and cash flow unexpectedly turn down or if an outstanding acquisition opportunity suddenly presents itself. Investors and speculators, in contrast, prefer to see the cash used to repurchase stock or else returned to shareholders. Managers also tend to be more inclined than shareholders to believe that underperforming units can be rehabilitated. Their judgment is sometimes influenced by reluctance to admit that acquisitions in which they had a hand have worked out poorly.

Over the years, management-shareholder disputes over such operating- and financial-policy issues have featured a variety of tactics. As far back as 1927 and 1928, pioneer securities analyst Benjamin Graham waged a successful campaign to persuade the management of Northern Pipeline to liquidate certain assets that were not essential to the company's crude oil transportation business and distribute the proceeds to shareholders. Graham enlisted pivotal support for his effort from a major institutional holder, the Rockefeller Foundation. The outcome was unusual, as institutional investors generally sided with management, both at the time and for many years afterward. At most, institutions sold their shares if they became thoroughly dissatisfied with the way a company was being run. Trying to bring about change was not a widespread institutional practice, even in the 1980s. Therefore, management's main adversaries in battles over corporate governance were aggressive financial operators. During the 1950s, these swashbucklers attracted considerable attention by pushing for strategic redirection through proxy battles. Their modus operandi consisted of striving to obtain majority control of the board through the election of directors at the annual meeting of shareholders.

The 1970s brought the tactical shift to hostile takeovers, a type of transaction previously regarded as unsavory by the investment banks that acted as intermediaries in mergers and acquisitions. Hostile takeovers became especially prominent in the 1980s, fueled in part by the greatly increased availability of high-yield debt (informally referred to as "junk bond") financing. High-yield bonds also financed scores of leveraged buyouts. LBO sponsors defended these controversial transactions in part by arguing that corporations could improve their long-run performance if they were taken private and thereby shielded from the public market's insatiable demand for short-run profit increases.

In the 1990s, institutional investors finally began to understand the influence they could wield in corporate boardrooms by virtue of their vast share holdings. Large institutional shareholders began to prod corporations to increase their share prices by such measures as streamlining operations, divesting unprofitable units, and using excess cash to repurchase shares. In some instances, where merely making their collective voice heard had no discernible effect, the institutions precipitated the ouster of senior management.

The shareholder activism of the 1990s flourished in an environment of comparatively high price-earnings ratios. Additionally, the period was characterized by a backlash against the previous decade's trend toward increased financial leverage. Conditions were not conducive to the sort of borrow-and-acquire transactions that drove much of the corporate restructurings of the 1980s.

In that era, the prototypical deal consisted of gaining control of a company by buying its stock at a depressed price, then adding a large amount of debt to the capital structure. Opportunities of this sort were abundant, not only because of low prevailing price-earnings ratios, but also because many corporations carried far less debt than their cash flows could support. At least in the early stages, before some raiders became overly aggressive in their financial forecast assumptions, it was feasible to extract value without creating undue bankruptcy risk, simply by increasing the ratio of debt to equity. The hostile takeover artists focused on the second factor in the Modified Du Pont Formula—financial leverage.

By releasing the potential embedded in a relatively debt-free balance sheet, the corporate raiders of the 1980s did more than pursue large profits. More important to the subject at hand (although not to the raiders), their activities seriously undermined the earnings multiple as a basis for valuing companies.

Consider the fictitious Sitting Duck Corporation (Exhibit 14.8). Under conventional assumptions, and given a prevailing earnings multiple of 11 on similar companies, Sitting Duck's equity will be valued at $715 million, about 1.7 times its book value of $413 million.

EXHIBIT 14.8   Sitting Duck Corporation

Year Ended December 31, 2001
($000,000 omitted)

Balance Sheet		Statement of Cash Flows	
Current assets	$ 594	Net income	$ 65
Property, plant, and equipment	406	Depreciation	38
Total assets	$1,000	Cash generated by operations	103
Current liabilities	$ 350	Dividends	22
Long-term debt	237	Capital expenditures	41
Shareholders' equity	413	Increase in working capital	10
Total liabilities and equity	$1,000	Cash used in operations	73
		Net cash available	30
Income Statement		Reduction of long-term debt	25
Sales	$1,253	Increase in cash and equivalents	$ 5
Cost of goods sold	972		
Selling, general, and administrative expense	95		
Operating income	186		
Interest expense	19		
Pretax income	167		
Income taxes	102		
Net income	$ 65		

Corporate raiders, however, would approach the valuation much differently. Their focus would not be on earnings, but on cash flow. After paying out approximately one-third of its earnings in dividends and more than offsetting depreciation through new expenditures for plant and equipment, Sitting Duck generated $30 million of cash in 2001. The incumbent management group used this cash to reduce an already conservative (36%) total-debt-to-total-capital ratio and to add to the company's existing portfolio of marketable securities. To a takeover artist, a more appropriate use would be to finance a premium bid for the company.

The arithmetic goes as follows: Assume commercial banks are currently willing to lend to sound leveraged buyout projects that can demonstrate EBITDA coverage of 1.5 times. (The lenders do not care about the company's book profits, but rather about its ability to repay debt. Cash generation is a key determinant of that ability.) Sitting Duck's operating income of $186 million, with $38 million of depreciation added back, produces EBITDA of $224 million. The amount of interest that $224 million can cover by 1.5 times is $149 million, an increase of $130 million over Sitting Duck's present interest expense. Assuming a blended borrowing cost of 13% on the LBO financing, a raider can add $1 billion of debt to the existing balance sheet. If prevailing lending standards require equity of at least 10% in the transaction, the raider must put up an additional $111 million, for a total capitalization of $1.1 billion. By this arithmetic, the takeover artist can pay a premium of 55% ($1.111 billion ÷ $715 million = 1.55) over Sitting Duck's present market capitalization. The purchase price equates to a multiple of 17 times earnings, rather than the 11X figure currently assigned by the market. The raider got to this number, however, through a measure of cash flow, rather than earnings. The EBITDA multiple of the bid is 5.0 times, a moderate level by the standards of LBO specialists. (As explained in Chapter 8, EBITDA is by no means the *best* measure of cash flow, but it can be fairly described as the standard in leveraged finance circles.)

Stepping back from these calculations, one is bound to wonder whether the raider can truly expect to earn a high return on investment after paying 55% above the prevailing price for Sitting Duck's shares. In actuality, many comparably high-priced takeovers of the 1980s proved quite remunerative for the equity investors. Some of the cycle's early deals benefited from asset values that could not be discerned from even a thorough review of the financial statements. For example, companies owned real estate bought decades earlier and carried at historical cost. These assets were salable at substantially higher prices than their balance sheet values. Armed with such information, managers led buyouts of their own companies, knowing that they were not taking on inordinately large debt *relative to the market value of the acquired assets.* Naturally, transactions in which the managers had an informational advantage over the shareholders, who were in principle their ultimate employers, prompted complaints of conflicts of interest. As the LBO cycle of the 1980s progressed, boards of directors took greater care to arrange competitive auctions for their companies, lest they be accused of obtaining inadequate value for selling shareholders through "sweetheart" deals with management. The opportunities for LBO sponsors and management teams to buy companies on the cheap consequently diminished. Purchasers could no longer be confident that the economic value of the acquired assets exceeded the amount of debt they were taking on. Many bonds connected with these late-cycle LBOs went into default in 1990 and 1991.

Leveraged buyouts became a less prominent feature of the financial landscape during the 1990s. Transactions continued to occur, although with less highly leveraged capital structures than investors countenanced in the late 1980s. In future bear markets, when stocks again sell at depressed price-earnings multiples, investors will probably renew their focus on companies' values as LBO candidates. Equity analysts will need to understand how those values are determined to assess the upside potential in stocks. In addition, lenders, bondholders, and purchasers of LBO equity can be expected to call on analysts of financial statements to judge the likelihood that particular deals will prove profitable. The answers will lie partly in ability of the companies to emulate the strategies employed by leveraged buyouts of the past that succeeded in paying off their debts and providing satisfactory risk-adjusted returns to their equity investors. Typically, the LBO world's winners have achieved their gains through one or both of the following means:

1. *Profit Margin Improvement.* A leveraged buyout can bring about improved profitability for either of two reasons. First, a change in ownership results in a fresh look at the company's operations. The newcomers typically have less sentimental attachment to product lines that are long on tradition but are no longer profitable. In addition, they can more easily take the emotionally difficult, but necessary, steps to restore competitiveness, such as reducing the work force and outsourcing production. Second, management may obtain a significantly enlarged stake in the firm's success as the result of a buyout. In lieu of stock options that could leave them comfortably provided for in their retirement, senior and even middle-level executives may receive equity interests that can potentially make them immensely wealthy within a few years. The change in incentives can reduce managers' zeal for maintaining slack in their operations and cause them instead to squeeze every possible dollar of profit out of their company's assets. With an enhanced opportunity to participate in the benefits, the managers may crack down on unnecessary costs that they formerly tolerated and pursue potential new markets more aggressively than in the past. Regardless of how it comes about, however, improvement in profit margins means higher EBITDA. That, in turn, leads to a higher valuation and generates a profit for the LBO's equity investors.

As a caveat, analysts must watch out for improvements in reported profit margins that represent nothing more than reductions in investment spending. Following an LBO, a company can report an immediate improvement in earnings by cutting back expenditures on advertising and research and development. Even though the accounting rules do not permit these items to be capitalized, the outlays provide benefits in future periods. Sharply reducing such outlays, or delaying capital expenditures to conserve cash, can impair a company's future competitiveness, making the increase in current-period earnings illusory. Invariably, LBO organizers either deny that such cutbacks will occur or maintain that before the buyout, the company was plowing more into these categories than the associated benefits justified. In light of the high LBO failure rate of 1980s-vintage LBOs in 1990 and 1991, however, a prudent analyst will be skeptical about such arguments. Today's profit improvement may be a precursor of tomorrow's bankruptcy by a company that has economized its way to an uncompetitive state.

Regrettably, the income statement may provide too little detail to determine whether specific kinds of investment spending have been curtailed. Analysts must therefore query industry sources for evidence regarding the adequacy of the company's investment spending. If the company's customers report a drop in the quality of service following a leveraged buyout, it may indicate that important sales support functions have been eviscerated. Earnings may rise in the short run, but suffer in the only slightly long term as customers switch to other providers.

2. *Asset Sales.* As a function of the stock market's primary focus on earnings, a company's market capitalization may be far less than the aggregate value of its assets. For example, a subsidiary that contributes little to net income, but generates substantial cash flow from depreciation, has potentially large value in the private market. In that realm, the unit would be priced on a multiple of EBITDA. Alternatively, a subsidiary might be unprofitable only because its scale is insufficient. A competitor might be willing to buy the unit and consolidate it with its own operations. The result would be higher combined earnings than the two operations were able to generate independently. An LBO sponsor who spies this sort of opportunity within a company may invest a small amount of equity and borrow the greater part of the purchase price, then liquidate the low-net-income operations to repay the borrowings. If carried out as planned, the asset sales will

leave the acquirer debt-free and in possession of the remainder of the company, that is, the operations that previously contributed almost all of the net income. In the P/E-multiple-oriented stock market, that portion of the company will be worth as much as the entire company was previously. The LBO sponsor may then cash out by taking it public again. After all the dust has settled, the sponsor should have cleared more than enough to cover the premium paid to original shareholders who sold into the buyout.

Unrealized earnings potential and EBITDA multiples are by no means the only valuation factors that come into play in corporate governance controversies. Proponents of policy changes in pursuit of enhanced shareholder value sometimes focus on the values of specific assets identified in the financial statements. For example, oil companies disclose the size of their reserves in their annual reports. Because energy companies frequently buy and sell reserves, and because the prices of larger transactions are widely reported, current market valuations are always readily at hand. If recent sales of reserves in the ground have occurred at prices that equate to $10 a barrel, then a company with 25 million barrels of reserves could theoretically liquidate those assets for $250 million.[4] It may be that the sum of $250 million and a P/E-multiple-based price for the company's refining, marketing, and transportation assets substantially exceeds the company's current market capitalization. If so, the "unrecognized" value of the oil reserves can be the basis of an alternative method of evaluating the company's stock.

Would-be corporate restructurers also seek unrecognized value in other types of minerals, real estate, and long-term investments unrelated to a company's core business. Methods of realizing the value of such an asset include:

- Selling the asset for cash.
- Placing it in a separate subsidiary, then taking a portion of the subsidiary public to establish a market value for the company's residual interest.
- Placing the asset in a master limited partnership, interests in which are distributed to shareholders.

The key message to take away from this overview of valuation via restructuring potential is that a focus on price-earnings multiples, the best-known form of fundamental analysis, is not the investor's sole alternative to relying on technicians' stock charts. There are in fact several approaches to fundamental analysis. A solid understanding of financial statements is essential to all of them, even though factors outside the financial statements also play a role in fundamental valuation.

CONCLUSION

As noted at the outset of this chapter, valuations derived from financial statements represent only a portion of the analyses being conducted by millions of stock buyers and sellers during each trading session. Indeed, the split-second decision making of traders on the exchange floors can scarcely be described as analysis of any kind. Rather, it amounts to a highly intuitive response to momentary shifts in the balance of supply and demand.

For the investor who takes a longer view, however, financial statement analysis provides an invaluable reference point for valuation. A stock may temporarily soar or plummet in frenzied reaction to a development of little ultimate consequence. Eventually, however, rationality usually reasserts itself. The share price then returns to a level that is justifiable on the basis of the company's long-range capacity to generate earnings and cash. Focusing on breakup values, as well as P/E and EBITDA multiples, is consistent with this thesis. Ultimately, the value of previously "unrecognized" assets likewise rests on their potential to generate cash, which must be measured in the context of previous performance. By studying the company's historical financial statements to forecast its future results, the analyst can derive an intrinsic value for a stock that is unaffected by the market's transitory mood.

QUESTIONS

1. "The unflagging focus on earnings probably reflects institutional inertia." True, or False? Explain.
2. Earnings per share can be derived as the product of asset turnover times return on sales times leverage times book value per share. How can an increase in one (or more) of the four terms lead to a sustainable increase in earnings per share?
3. How are equity valuation models analogous to the yield-to-maturity calculation for a bond?
4. How are these adjustments related to the time companies are presumed to operate as going concerns?
5. How can the "unrecognized" value of specific assets identified in the financial statements be the basis of a method of evaluating a company's stock? Illustrate using the example of oil reserves.
6. How can the modified Du Pont formula be used to analyze the focus of the hostile takeover artists?
7. How can the modified Du Pont formula help identify the type of restructuring that can unlock hidden value?

8. How can the recent focus on breakup values be consistent with the thesis that financial statement analysis constitutes a solid foundation for valuation for the long-term investor?

9. How can the stock price rise in the future while the dividend remains constant?

10. How does breakup analysis work? Has it supplanted the dividend discount and PIE methods of stock valuation?

11. How is the 14% required rate of return used to value Tarheel Tobacco determined?

12. How is the dividend-discount formula adjusted to value a growing company?

13. How is the execution of this model related to the company's projected financial statements?

14. How is the forecasting of financial statements related to equity analysis?

15. How should the analyst deal with the uncertainties affecting such projections?

16. In addition to upping the discount rate (K) when any question about the quality of earnings arises, what else can the analyst do?

17. Is all fundamental analysis based on information found in financial statements?

18. Show how you can combine the dividend discount and the price-earnings valuation formulas into an equation that permits the analyst to see quickly that an increase in the expected growth rate of earnings produces a premium multiple.

19. Sitting Duck Corporation currently sells for 11 times earnings. How can a raider pay a multiple of 17 times earnings and still expect to earn a high return on investment?

20. Under what conditions is a below average earnings multiple for a company justified?

21. Use the information of Exhibits 14.1 and 14.2 to illustrate how the price-earnings ratio may be used to compare one company with another.

22. What are some examples of how a company can more easily create a new image than it can recast its operations?

23. What are some of the questions the Du Pont formula raises? Do these questions nullify its validity?

24. What assumption of the dividend-discount model does not jibe perfectly with the earnings pattern of highly cyclical companies?

25. What did the activities of the hostile takeover artists seriously undermine?

26. What is the Du Pont formula and how can it be used to perceive the sources of a firm's return on assets?

27. What is the equity analyst's defense against earnings manipulation by management?
28. What is the main lesson of the numerical example of the PPE Manufacturing Corporation?
29. What is the modified Du Pont formula? What does it enable investors to judge?
30. What is the most convenient method of comparing one stock's value with another's?
31. What is the primary focus of this chapter and how is it related to "picking stocks"?
32. What must a company do to achieve sustainable growth in earnings per share?
33. What saves the dividend-discount model from irrelevance in these circumstances?
34. What strategies worked well and allowed takeover artists to pay a premium above the prevailing prices for their acquisitions?
35. Why do analysts need to be acutely conscious of changes in a company's cash-generating capability that are not paralleled by changes in earnings?
36. Why should the analyst pay close attention to the method by which a company finances the maintenance of its dividend at an established rate?
37. Will earnings per share grow merely because sales increase?
38. Would corporate raiders focus on earnings or cash flow?

bibliography

BOOKS

Browne, Lynn E., and Eric S. Rosengren (Editors), *The Merger Boom: Proceedings of a Conference Held in October 1987* (Boston: Federal Reserve Bank of Boston, 1988).

Fabozzi, Frank J., and T. Dessa Fabozzi (Editors), *The Handbook of Fixed Income Securities,* Fourth Edition (Burr Ridge, Illinois: Irwin Professional Publishing, 1995).

Fridson, Martin S., *High Yield Bonds: Identifying Value and Assessing Risk of Speculative-Grade Securities* (Chicago: Probus Publishing, 1989).

Gitman, Lawrence J., *Principles of Managerial Finance,* Seventh Edition (New York: HarperCollins Financial Publishers, 1994).

Hale, Roger H., *Credit Analysis: A Complete Guide* (New York: John Wiley & Sons, 1983).

Levine, Sumner N. (Editor), *Handbook of Turnaround & Bankruptcy Investing* (New York: Harper & Row Publishers, 1991).

Maginn, John L., and Donald L. Tuttle (Editors), *Managing Investment Portfolios: A Dynamic Process,* Second Edition (Boston: Warren, Gorham & Lamont, 1989).

Malonis, Jane A. (Editor), *Encyclopedia of Business,* Second Edition (Detroit: Gale Group, 1999).

McConnell, Campbell R., *Economics: Principles, Problems and Policies,* Tenth Edition (New York: McGraw-Hill Book Company, 1987).

Mosteller, Frederick, Robert K. E. Rourke, and George B. Thomas, Jr., *Probability with Statistical Applications,* Second Edition (Reading, Mass.: Addison-Wesley Publishing Company, 1970).

Pass, Christopher, Bryan Lowes, Leslie Davis, and Sidney J. Kronish (Editors), *The HarperCollins Dictionary of Economics* (New York: HarperCollins Publishers, 1991).

Prochnow, Herbert V. (Editor), *Bank Credit* (New York: Harper & Row Publishers, 1981).

Reilly, Frank K., *Investment Analysis and Portfolio Management,* Third Edition (Orlando, Florida: The Dryden Press, 1989).

Siegel, Joel G. and Jae K. Shim, *Dictionary of Accounting Terms* (New York: Barron's Educational Series, 1987).

Standard & Poor's Municipal Finance Criteria (New York: Standard & Poor's Corporation, 1989).

White, Gerald I., and Ashwinpaul C. Sondhi (Editors), *CFA Readings in Financial Statement Analysis* (Charlottesville, Virginia: The Institute of Chartered Financial Analysts, 1985).

PERIODICALS

CreditWeek (New York: Standard & Poor's, Weekly).

Moody's Bond Record (New York: Moody's Investors Service, Monthly).

Moody's Bond Survey (New York: Moody's Investors Service, Weekly).

Schilit's Shenanigan Busters (Rockville, Maryland: Center for Financial Research and Analysis).

Standard & Poor's Bond Guide (New York: Standard & Poor's, Monthly).

accelerate   To demand immediate repayment of debt in default, exercising thereby a right specified in the loan contract.

Accounting Principles Board (APB)   Formerly, a rule-making body of the American Institute of Certified Public Accountants. Predecessor of the Financial Accounting Standards Board (see).

accrual accounting   An accounting system in which revenue is recognized during the period in which it is earned and expenses are recognized during the period in which they are incurred, whether or not cash is received or disbursed.

actuarial assumptions   Forecasts of the rates of phenomena such as mortality and retirements, used to determine funding requirements for pension funds and insurance policies.

APB   Accounting Principles Board (see).

book value   The amount at which an asset is carried on the balance sheet. Book value consists of the asset's construction or acquisition cost, less depreciation (see) and subsequent impairment of value, if applicable. An asset's book value does not rise as a function of an increase in its market value or inflation. (See also *historical cost accounting*.)

breakeven rate   The production volume at which contribution (see) is equivalent to fixed costs (see), resulting in a pretax profit of zero.

Example:

$$\text{Price per unit} = \$2.50$$

$$\text{Variable cost per unit} = \$1.00$$

$$\text{Fixed costs} = \$600$$

To calculate breakeven: $\left[(\$2.50 - \$1.00) \times B\right] - \$600 = 0$

$$(\$1.50 \times B) = \$600$$

$$B = 400 \text{ units}$$

Definitions of cash balance plan and defined benefit plan are adapted from descriptions provided by the Pension Benefit Guaranty Corporation.

bridge loan   A temporary loan made in the expectation that it will subsequently be repaid with the proceeds of permanent financing.

business cycle   Periodic fluctuations in economic growth, employment, and price levels. Phases of the classic cycle, in sequence, are peak, recession, trough, and recovery.

CAGR   Compound annual growth rate (see).

capital-intensive   Characterized by a comparatively large proportion of plant and equipment in asset base. The heavy depreciation charges that arise from capital intensity create a high level of fixed costs and volatile earnings.

capitalization (of an expenditure)   The recording of an expenditure as an asset, to be written off over future periods, on the grounds that the outlay produces benefits beyond the current accounting cycle.

cash balance plan   In the field of pensions, a type of defined benefit plan (see) in which each participant's benefit is defined in terms of a hypothetical account balance. Each year, the account is credited with a pay credit and an interest credit specified by the plan. The interest credit may be fixed or based on a variable index such as the yield on 30-year Treasury bonds.

cash-on-cash profit   In real estate, the cash flow from a property divided by the cash equity invested. Unlike conventional rate-of-return measures calculated in accordance with accrual accounting (see), cash-on-cash profit is not reduced by noncash charges such as depreciation (see). This reflects a presumption that land and buildings tend to increase in value over time, rather than lose value through wear-and-tear, as in the case of plant and equipment.

Chapter 11   Under the 1978 Bankruptcy Reform Act, a method of resolving bankruptcy that provides for reorganization of the failed firm as an alternative to liquidating it.

class-action suit   A type of lawsuit filed under Federal Rule of Civil Procedure 23, which allows one member of a large group of plaintiffs with similar claims to sue on behalf of the entire class, provided certain conditions are met. Damages awarded in certain class-action suits have been large enough to compromise the solvency of corporate defendants.

comparability   In accounting, the objective of facilitating financial comparisons of a group of companies, achieved by requiring them to use similar reporting practices.

compound annual growth rate (CAGR)   The level, annual rate of increase that results in a stated beginning value rising to a stated terminal value.

Example:

Year	Value of Asset ($)
0	377
1	421
2	414
3	487
4	541
5	596

The year-to-year increase in the asset's value has been uneven, ranging from −1.7% in Year 2 to 17.6% in Year 4. If the increase had been 9.6% in each year, however, the value would have grown from the beginning figure of $377 to the terminal figure of $596. Computation of the compound annual growth rate is a standard function on sophisticated hand-held calculators. CAGRs can also be derived from compound interest tables.

consolidation (of an industry)   A reduction in the number of competitors in an industry through business combinations.

contribution   Revenue per unit minus variable cost (see) per unit.

convertible   With reference to bonds or preferred stock, redeemable at the holder's option for common stock of the issuer, based on a specified ratio of bonds or preferred shares to common shares. (See also *exchangeable.*)

cost of capital   The rate of return that investors require for providing capital to a company. A company's cost of capital consists of the cost of capital for a risk-free borrower, a premium for business risk (the risk of becoming unable to continue to cover operating costs), and a premium for financial risk (the risk of becoming unable to continue covering financial costs, such as interest). The risk-free cost of capital is commonly equated with the prevailing interest rate on U.S. Treasury obligations.

cumulative dividend   A characteristic of most preferred stocks whereby any preferred dividends in arrears must be paid before dividends may be paid to common shareholders.

default   The failure of a debt obligor to make a scheduled interest or principal payment on time. A defaulting issuer becomes subject to claims against its assets, possibly including a demand by creditors for full and immediate repayment of principal.

defined benefit plan   A type of pension plan in which the level of beneficiaries' retirement income is established contractually, generally based on such factors as age, earnings, and years of service. The pension plan sponsor bears the risk of earning a return on investment assets sufficient to meet the contractual payments. (See also *cash balance plan, defined contribution plan.*)

defined contribution plan   A type of pension plan in which the amounts contributed to the plan by its sponsor are established contractually. The retirement income paid to the beneficiaries is determined by the investment returns on the pension assets. (See also *defined benefit plan.*)

depreciation   A noncash expense meant to represent the amount of capital equipment consumed through wear and tear during the period.

dilution   A reduction in present shareholders' proportional claim on earnings. Dilution can occur through the issuance of new shares in an acquisition if the earnings generated by the acquired assets are insufficient to maintain the level of earnings per share previously recorded by the acquiring company. Existing shareholders' interest is likewise diluted if the company issues new stock at a price below book value. In this circumstance, a dollar invested by a new shareholder purchases a larger percentage of the company than is represented by a dollar of net worth held by an old shareholder.

discount rate   The interest rate used to equate future value (see) with present value (see). Also referred to as cost of capital (see).

discounted cash flow   A technique for equating future cash flows to a present sum of money, based on an assumed interest rate. For example, $100 compounded annually at 8% over three years will cumulate to a sum of $125.97, ignoring the effect of taxes. This figure can be calculated via the equation

$$P \times (1 + r)^n = F$$

where P = Principal value at beginning of period (Present value)
   r = Interest rate
   n = Number of periods
   F = Principal value at end of period (Future value)

In this case, $100 \times (1.08)^3 = \$125.97$. (Note that this formula implicitly assumes reinvestment of cash interest received at the original rate of interest throughout the period.)

   If $125.97 three years hence is equivalent to $100 today—given the assumed discount rate (see) of 8% per annum—then the ratio $100.00/$125.97, or 0.794, can be used to determine the present value (see) of any other amount discounted back from the same date and at the same rate.

By using the same general formula, it is possible to assign a value to an asset, based on a series of cash flows it is expected to generate. By way of illustration, suppose the right to distribute a particular product is expected to generate cash flow of $5,000 a year for four years, then expire, leaving no terminal value. At a discount rate of 15%, the distribution rights would be valued at $14,820, derived as follows:

Year	Expected Cash Flow	Discount Factor	Present Value
1	$5,000	.870	$ 4,350
2	5,000	.756	3,780
3	5,000	.658	3,290
4	5,000	.572	2,860
			Total: $14, 280

discretionary cash flow   Cash flow that remains available to a company after it has funded its basic operating requirements. There is no universally accepted, precise definition of discretionary cash flow, but conceptually it includes funds from operations less required new investment in working capital and nondiscretionary capital expenditures. The latter figure is difficult to quantify with precision, but it exceeds the required "maintenance" level required to keep existing plant and equipment in good working order. Ordinarily, some additional expenditures, which may be designated "semidiscretionary," are necessary to keep a company competitive with respect to capacity, costs, and technology. Only a portion of the total capital budget, including expansion-oriented outlays that can be deferred in the event of slower-than-expected growth in demand, can truly be considered discretionary. In a similar vein, mandatory principal repayments of debt, by definition, cannot be regarded as discretionary. Still, a company with strong cash flow and the assurance, as a practical matter, of being able to refinance its maturing debt, has considerable freedom in the disposition even of amounts that would appear to be earmarked for debt retirement.

diversification   In portfolio management, the technique of reducing risk by dividing one's assets among a number of different securities or types of investments. Applied to corporate strategy, the term refers to participation in several unrelated businesses. The underlying premise is often countercyclicality, or the stabilization of earnings over time through the tendency of profits in certain business segments to be rising at times when they are falling in others.

double-entry bookkeeping A system of keeping accounts in which each entry requires an offsetting entry. For example, a payment to a trade creditor causes both cash and accounts payable to decline.

Dow Jones Industrial Average A widely followed index of the U.S. stock market composed of the common stocks of 30 major industrial corporations.

EBIT Earnings before deduction of interest expense and income taxes.

EBITDA Earnings before deduction of interest expense, income taxes, depreciation, and amortization. (Also referred to as EBDIT, an acronym for "earnings before depreciation, interest, and taxes.")

economies of scale Reductions in per unit cost that arise from large-volume production. The reductions result in large measure from the spreading of fixed costs (i.e., those that do not vary directly with production volume) over a larger number of units than is possible for a smaller producer.

economies of scope Reductions in per unit cost that arise from applying knowledge or technology to related products.

exchangeable In reference to a security, subject to mandatory replacement by another type of security, at the issuer's option. (See also *convertible*.)

external growth Revenue growth achieved by a company through acquisition of other companies.

externally generated funds Cash obtained through financing activities such as borrowing or the flotation of equity. (See also *internally generated funds*.)

factor A financial institution that provides financing to companies by buying accounts receivable at a discount.

FASB Financial Accounting Standards Board (see).

Financial Accounting Standards Board (FASB) A rule-making body for the accounting profession. Its members are appointed by a foundation, the members of which are selected by the directors of the American Institute of Certified Public Accountants.

financial derivative A financial instrument with a return linked to the performance of an underlying asset, such as a bond or a currency.

financial flexibility The ability, achieved through such means as a strong capital structure and a high degree of liquidity, to continue to invest in maintaining growth and competitiveness despite business downturns and other financial strains.

financial leverage   (See *leverage (financial)*.)

fixed costs   Costs that do not vary with the volume of production. Examples include rent, interest expense, senior management salaries and, unless calculated by the units-of-production method, depreciation (see).

fixed-rate debt   A debt obligation on which the interest rate remains at a stated level until the loan has been liquidated. (Compare *floating-rate debt*.)

floating-rate debt   A debt obligation on which the interest rate fluctuates with changes in market rates of interest, according to a specified formula. (Compare *fixed-rate debt*.)

fundamental analysis   A form of security analysis aimed at determining a stock or bond's intrinsic value, based on such factors as the issuer's expected earnings and financial risk. In contrast, technical analysis aims to predict a security's future value based on its past price changes.

funding   Replacement of short-term debt with long-term debt. Funding increases a company's financial flexibility by reducing the near-term risk of insolvency through inability to roll over or replace maturing debt.

future value   The amount to which a known sum of money will accumulate by a specified future date, given a stated rate of interest. For example, $100 compounded annually at 8% over three years will cumulate to a sum of $125.97, ignoring the effect of taxes. This figure can be calculated via the formula

$$P \times (1 + r)^n$$

where P = Principal at beginning of period
  r = Interest rate
  n = Number of periods

In this case, $100 \times (1.08)^3 = \$125.97$. (This formula implicitly assumes that cash interest received will be reinvested at the original rate of interest throughout the period.)

(See also *discounted cash flow, net present value*, and *present value*.)

GAAP   Generally Accepted Accounting Principles (see).

GDP   Gross Domestic Product (see).

Generally Accepted Accounting Principles   Rules that govern the preparation of financial statements, based on pronouncements of authoritative accounting organizations such as the Financial Accounting Standards Board, industry practice, and the accounting literature (including books and articles).

goodwill   A balance sheet item arising from purchase method (see) accounting for a business combination, representing the excess of the purchase price over the acquired company's tangible asset value.

Gross Domestic Product   The value of all goods and services that residents and nonresidents provide in a country.

historical cost accounting   An accounting system in which assets are recorded at their original value (less any applicable depreciation or other impairment of value), notwithstanding that the nominal dollar value of the assets may rise through some cause such as inflation or increased scarcity. (See also *book value.*)

hostile takeover   An acquisition of a corporation by another corporation or by a group of investors, typically through a tender for outstanding shares, in the face of initial opposition by the acquired corporation's board of directors.

internal growth   Revenue growth achieved by a company through capital investment in its existing business.

internally generated funds   Cash obtained through operations, including net income, depreciation, deferred taxes, and reductions in working capital. (See also *externally generated funds.*)

investor-relations officer   An individual designated by a corporation to handle communications with securities analysts.

involuntary inventory accumulation   An unintended increase in a company's inventory levels, resulting from a slowdown in sales that is not offset by a reduced rate of production.

LBO   Leveraged buyout (see).

leverage (financial)   The use of debt financing in hopes of increasing the rate of return on equity. In the following example, the unleveraged company, with no debt in its capital structure, generates operating income of $30.0 million, pays taxes of $10.2 million, and nets $19.8 million for a return on equity (net income divided by shareholders' equity) of 13.2%. The leveraged company, with an equivalent amount of operating income, relies on long-term debt (at an interest rate of 12%) for one-third of its capital. Interest expense causes its net income before taxes to be lower ($24 million) than the unleveraged company's ($30 million). After taxes, the leveraged company earns less (15.8 million) than the unleveraged company ($19.8 million), but on a smaller equity base ($100 million vs. $150 million) provides shareholders a higher rate of return ($15.8% vs. 13.2%).

Note, however, that leverage works in reverse as well. In the following scenario operating income declines by two-thirds (to $10 million) at both companies. With no interest expense, the unleveraged company

($ Million)

	Unleveraged Company	Leveraged Company
Operating income	$ 30.0	$ 30.0
Interest expense	0.0	6.0
Net income before taxes	30.0	24.0
Taxes	10.2	8.2
Net income	$ 19.8	$ 15.8
Long-term debt	0	$ 50
Shareholders' equity	150	100
Total capital	$150	$150
Net Income / Shareholders' Equity	13.2%	15.8%

manages to net $6.6 million for a 4.4% return on equity. The leveraged company, obliged to pay out 60% of its operating income in interest expense, suffers a sharper decline in return on equity (to 2.6%). Incurring financial leverage increases the risk to equity holders, whose returns become more subject to fluctuations. The greater the percentage of the capital structure that consists of debt, the greater is the potential for such fluctuations.

($ Million)

	Unleveraged Company	Leveraged Company
Operating income	$ 10.0	$ 10.0
Interest expense	0.0	6.0
Net income before taxes	10.0	4.0
Taxes	3.4	1.4
Net income	$ 6.6	$ 2.6
Long-term debt	$ 0	$ 50
Shareholders' equity	150	100
Total capital	$150	$150
Net Income / Shareholders' Equity	4.4%	2.6%

leverage (operating) The substitution of fixed costs (see) for variable costs (see) in hopes of increasing return on equity. In the following example, Company A's cost structure is dominated by variable expenses, of which labor represents a substantial portion. A 5% increase in sales volume (from 500,000 to 525,000 units) raises the rate of return on shareholders' equity from 11.0% to 13.7%. Company B, on the other hand, has installed labor-saving equipment that sharply reduces man-hours per unit of production. Its variable costs are lower than Company A's ($50.00 versus $30.00 per unit), but as a function of its greater depreciation (see) charges, its fixed costs are higher ($30 million versus $25 million per annum). The benefit of Company B's higher operating leverage is that a 5% increase in its unit sales raises its return on shareholders' equity from 11.0% to 14.7%, a larger boost than Company A receives from a comparable rise in volume. By the same token, Company B's return on shareholders' equity will fall more sharply than Company A's if unit volume at both companies subsequently recedes from 525,000 to 500,000 units.

	Company A		Company B	
Sales (units)	500,000	525,000	500,000	525,000
Price per unit	$100.00	$100.00	$100.00	$100.00
Fixed costs ($ million)	$25.0	$25.0	$30.0	$30.0
Variable cost per unit	$50.0	$50.0	$30.0	$30.0
	($ Million)			
Sales	$50.0	$52.5	$50.0	$52.5
Fixed costs	25.0	25.0	30.0	30.0
Variable costs	25.0	26.3	15.0	15.8
Income before taxes	5.0	6.2	5.0	6.7
Taxes	1.7	2.1	1.7	2.3
Net income	$ 3.3	$ 4.1	$ 3.3	$ 4.4
Shareholders' equity	$30.0	$30.0	$30.0	$30.0
$\frac{\text{Net Income}}{\text{Shareholders' Equity}}$	11.0%	13.7%	11.0%	14.7%

leveraged buyout (LBO) An acquisition of a company or a division, financed primarily with borrowed funds. Equity investors typically hope to profit by repaying debt through cash generated by operations (and possibly from proceeds of asset sales), thereby increasing the net value of their stake.

leveraged recapitalization   A corporate strategy involving the payment of a large, debt-financed cash dividend. The strategy is often employed as a defense against an attempted hostile takeover, for two reasons. First, by increasing the company's financial leverage (see), the transaction reduces the potential for a raider to use borrowed funds, lest the post-takeover company become excessively debt-laden. Second, the recapitalization increases the concentration of ownership in the hands of those attempting to retain control.

liquidity   The ability of a company to meet its near-term obligations when due.

macroeconomic   Pertaining to the economy as a whole or its major subdivisions, e.g., the manufacturing sector, the agricultural sector, the government. (See also *microeconomic.*)

market capitalization   The aggregate market value of all of a company's outstanding equity and debt securities. Also used loosely to represent the product of a company's share price and number of shares outstanding. (See also *total enterprise value.*)

mature   With respect to a product, firm, or industry, at a stage of development at which the rate of sales growth remains positive but no longer exceeds the general growth rate of the economy.

microeconomic   Pertaining to a small segment of the economy, e.g., an individual industry, a particular firm. (See also *macroeconomic.*)

multiple   With respect to a common stock, the ratio of the share price to earnings per share. Similarly, the price paid in an acquisition can be viewed as a multiple of the acquired company's earnings, cash flow, or EBITDA (see).

multivariate   In the field of quantitative modeling, having the characteristic of employing more than one explanatory factor.

mutual fund   An investment vehicle consisting of a portfolio of securities, shares of which are sold to investors. The firm that organizes the fund collects a fee for managing the portfolio, while shareholders enjoy a diversification (see) benefit that would be more costly to obtain via direct purchase of individual securities.

net present value   The present value (see) of a stream of future cash inflows, less the present value of an associated stream of current or future cash outflows. This calculation is useful for comparing the attractiveness of alternative investments, as shown in the following example. Both proposed capital projects require an expenditure of $60 million during the first year. Project A generates a higher cash flow, without trailing off in the latter years as Project B is projected to do. Residual value in year 10 is likewise superior in Project A. Even so, Project B is the more profitable investment, based on a higher net present value ($17.7 million vs. $14.3 million for Project A).

Net Present Value Illustration
(Presumed Discount Rate = 20%)
($000,000 omitted)

| | Year | | | | | | | | | | | Net Present Value |
	0	1	2	3	4	5	6	7	8	9	10	
Project A												
Cash flow*	(40)	(20)	16	18	21	24	24	26	26	26	20	
Discount factor	1.000	.833	.694	.579	.482	.402	.335	.279	.233	.194	.162	
Present value	(40.00) + (16.66) + 11.10 + 10.42 + 10.12 + 9.65 + 8.04 + 7.25 + 6.06 +											
	5.04 + 3.24											= 14.26
Project B												
Cash flow*	(10)	(50)	17	20	22	23	23	23	22	21	17	
Discount factor	1.000	.833	.694	.579	.482	.402	.335	.279	.233	.194	.162	
Present value	(10.00) + (41.65) + 11.80 + 11.58 + 10.60 + 9.25 + 7.71 + 6.42 + 5.13 +											
	4.07 + 2.75											= 17.66

*Figures in parentheses represent projected outflows, i.e., construction costs. Figures for years 2–9 represent projected inflows, i.e., net income plus noncash expenses. Year 10 figure represents expected residual value of equipment.

nominal dollar   A monetary sum expressed in terms of its currency face amount, unadjusted for changes in purchasing power from a designated base period. (See also *real dollar*.)

operating leverage   (See *leverage (operating)*.)

payment-in-kind security (PIK)   A security (generally a bond or preferred stock) that gives the issuer an option to pay interest or dividends in the form of additional fractional bonds or shares, in lieu of cash.

payout ratio   Dividends per share divided by earnings per share. In financial theory, a low payout ratio (other than as a result of a dividend reduction forced on the company by financial distress) is generally viewed as a sign that the company has many opportunities to reinvest in its business at attractive returns. A high payout ratio, in contrast, is appropriate for a company with limited internal reinvestment opportunities. By distributing a large percentage of earnings to shareholders, the company enables them to seek more attractive returns by investing elsewhere.

PIK Payment-in-kind security (see).

pooling-of-interests method A method of accounting for a business combination accomplished through an exchange of stock. No goodwill (see) is created in accounting for the transaction, even if the price paid for one of the parties exceeds its tangible asset value. In 2001, the Financial Accounting Standards Board forbade the further use of pooling-of-interests accounting, leaving the purchase method (see) as the only acceptable approach to business combinations.

portfolio A group of securities. Barring the unlikely circumstance that all securities contained in a portfolio produce identical returns in all periods, it generally produces a steadier return than a single security. The comparative stability arises from the tendency of declines in the prices of certain securities to be offset by rises in the prices of others during the same period. (See *diversification*.)

present value The sum that, if compounded at a specified rate of interest, or discount rate (see), will accumulate to a particular value at a stated future date. For example: To calculate the present value of $500, five years hence at a discount rate of 7%, solve the equation.

$$\frac{F}{\left(1+r\right)^{n}}$$

where F = Future value
r = Interest rate
n = Number of periods
p = Present value

In this case $500/(1.07)^5 = $356.49.

(See also *discounted cash flow, future value, and net present value*.)

pro forma Describes a financial statement constructed on the basis of specified assumptions. For example, if a company made an acquisition halfway through its fiscal year, it might present an income statement intended to show what the combined companies' full-year sales, costs, and net income would have been, assuming that the acquisition had been in effect when the year began.

purchase method A method of accounting for business combinations in which goodwill (see) is created if the acquisition price exceeds the tangible asset value of the acquired company.

rationalization In reference to a business or an industry, the process of eliminating excess capacity and other inefficiencies in production.

real dollar   A monetary sum expressed in terms of its purchasing-power equivalent, relative to a designated base period. For example, at the end of the third quarter of 2001, $500 (face amount) had only 56.1% of the purchasing power that $500 had in the base period 1982–1984. The erosion reflected price inflation during the intervening years. The real value of $500 in September 2001 was therefore $280.50 in 1982–1984 dollars. This calculation employs a series of the purchasing power of the consumer dollar, published by the United States Bureau of Labor Statistics. See the Bureau's Web site, www.bls.gov. (See also *nominal dollar.*)

reinsurance   A transaction whereby one insurance company takes over the risk of a policy originally issued by another company.

reorganization proceedings   A procedure under Chapter 11 of the Bankruptcy Reform Act that permits a bankrupt company to continue in operation, instead of liquidating, while restructuring its liabilities with an aim toward ensuring its future financial viability.

reported earnings   A company's profit or loss for a specified period, as stated in its income statement. The figure may differ from the company's true economic gain or loss for the period for such reasons as delayed recognition of items affecting income, changes in accounting practices, and discrepancies between accruals and actual changes in asset values.

    Disparities between reported and economic earnings can also arise from certain nuances of inventory accounting. For example, under the last-in, first-out (LIFO) method, a company's inventory account may include the historical acquisition costs of goods purchased several years earlier and unaffected (for book purposes) by inflation in the interim period. To the extent that a surge in sales causes a company to recognize the liquidation of older inventories during the current period, revenues will reflect post-inflation (i.e., higher) values but expenses will not. The mismatch will produce unusually wide reported profit margins in the current period, even though the nominal dollar (see) gains arising from inflation are in reality benefits that accumulated over several preceding periods.

sale-leaseback   A transaction in which a company sells an asset and immediately leases it back. The lessee thereby obtains cash while retaining use of the asset. An additional motivation for the transaction may be a difference in the marginal tax rates of the lessee and lessor. The tax shelter provided by depreciation charges on the asset are more valuable to the party paying the higher tax rate.

scale economies   (See *economies of scale.*)

SEC   Securities and Exchange Commission (see).

Securities and Exchange Commission (SEC) An agency of the federal government that regulates the issuance and trading of securities, the activities of investment companies and investment advisers, and standards for financial reporting by securities issuers.

senior debt Borrowings that have preference in liquidation over subordinated debt (see). In the event of a bankruptcy, senior lenders' claims must be satisfied before consideration can be given to subordinated lenders or equity investors.

sensitivity analysis The testing of "what-if" scenarios in financial statement analysis. Typically, sensitivity analysis measures the potential impact (on earnings, cash flow, etc.) of a change of a stated amount in another variable (sales, profit margins, etc.). In connection with financial forecasting, sensitivity analysis may be used to gauge the variation in projected figures that will occur if a particular assumption proves either too optimistic or too pessimistic by a given amount.

SFAS Statement of Financial Accounting Standards. Designation for a numbered series of statements of accounting rules promulgated by the Financial Accounting Standards Board (see).

shakeout A reduction in the number of competitors (through failures or through mergers) that typically occurs as a rapidly growing industry begins to mature. Factors that may contribute to a firm's survival during a shakeout include advantages in raising new capital, economies of scale (see), and superior management.

short interest ratio The ratio between the number of a company's shares that are sold short and remain uncovered and the stock's average daily trading volume. A high ratio indicates a widespread expectation that the stock's price will decline.

slack Unutilized productive capability within a company. Although the term ordinarily connotes inefficiency, management may have a conscious strategy of maintaining a certain amount of slack. For example, a company may benefit from keeping skilled employees on the payroll during recessions, when demand can be met with a reduced workforce. The cost savings entailed in laying off the workers may be offset by the costs of replacing them with equally skilled employees during the next boom. Another example is a backup trading floor maintained by a company engaged in trading securities or commodities. The associated cost may be justified by the potentially devastating loss of business that could result in a shutdown of the primary trading floor because of a natural disaster or civil disturbance.

standard error of estimate A measure of the scatter of the observations in a regression analysis. In statistical terms, the standard error of the estimate is equivalent to the standard deviation of the vertical deviations from the least-squares line.

statement of stockholders' equity   A financial statement that details changes in components of stockholders' equity, including capital stock, paid-in capital, retained earnings, treasury stock, unrealized loss on long-term investments, and gains and losses on foreign-currency translation. The basic problem addressed by the statement of stockholders' equity is that it may not be possible to reconcile one year's equity account with the next year's using only the income statement and statement of cash flows. Certain adjustments to equity are included neither in earnings nor in cash flows from financing activities.

statutory tax rate   The percentage of pretax income that would be recorded as income tax if all of a company's reported income were subject to the corporate tax rate specified by federal law. Disparities between the statutory rate and the effective rate (that which is actually recorded) arise from such reasons as tax credits and differences between U.S. and foreign tax rates.

straight-line method   A depreciation method that charges off an equivalent portion of the asset in each period. During inflationary periods, straight-line depreciation may understate the true economic impact of capital consumption. That is, as the replacement cost of the asset rises in nominal terms, the dollar amount required to offset wear and tear during a period grows to exceed a pro rata write-off based on the original acquisition cost. In these circumstances, accelerated methods of depreciation, which result in larger amounts being written off in earlier than in later years, represent more conservative reporting of expenses.

subordinated debt   Borrowings that have a lesser preference in liquidation vis-à-vis other, senior, debt (see). In the event of a bankruptcy, subordinated lenders' claims cannot be provided for until senior claims have been satisfied.

synergy   An increase in profitability arising from a merger or acquisition, relative to the stand-alone profitability of the companies involved. Synergy may result from economies of scale (see) or economies of scope (see).

total enterprise value   The value that a business would fetch if put up for sale, commonly estimated as a multiple of its sales, earnings, or EBITDA (see). (See also *market capitalization*.)

units-of-production method   A depreciation method that is based on the estimated total output of an asset over its entire life. The asset's cost is divided by the estimated number of units to be produced. Depreciation for the period is then calculated by multiplying the cost per unit by the number of units produced during the period. The units-of-production method appears, on its face, to match revenues and expenses rather precisely. While a piece of equipment sits idle, however, it generates no depreciation expense—even though its value may be decreasing as a result of the introduction of technologically more advanced, lower-cost equipment by competing firms. In this light, adoption of the units-of-production method by a firm that formerly employed a straight-line or accelerated method should generally be viewed as a switch to a more liberal accounting practice.

variable costs   Costs that increase as the volume of production rises. Examples include materials, fuel, power, and wages.

working capital   Current assets minus current liabilities. Working capital is commonly employed as an indicator of liquidity, but care must be taken in interpreting the number. The balance sheets of some corporations that are strong credits by all other methods ordinarily have little (or even negative) working capital. These companies manage inventories closely and extract generous terms from creditors, including long payment periods, which result in chronically high trade payable balances. In such cases, no threat of illiquidity is implied by the fact that more liabilities than assets will be liquidated during the current operating cycle.

notes

Chapter 1   The Adversial Nature of Financial Reporting

1. Howard M. Schilit, *Financial Shenanigans: How to Detect Accounting Gimmicks and Fraud in Financial Reports* (New York: McGraw Hill, 1993), p. 153.
2. Although this book focuses on for-profit companies, nonprofit companies and governmental entities also produce financial statements. Readers should not presume that those entities invariably eschew reporting trickery. Like their for-profit counterparts, nonprofit organizations seek to raise capital. They have incentives to portray their financial positions in as favorable a light as possible, when trying to borrow or to demonstrate their financial viability to providers of grants. On the other hand, nonprofits sometimes strive to make themselves appear less flush than they really are, to impress on donors the urgency of their appeal for funds. Governmental units sometimes resort to disingenuous reporting to avoid political fallout from the consequences of unsound fiscal policies. Anticapitalist ideologues cannot truthfully contend that the profit motive alone leads to devious financial reporting.
3. Floyd Norris, "Auto Lender's Finance Chief Disappears; Profits Are Cut," *New York Times*, January 30, 1997, pp. D1, D5.
4. "Mercury Finance Company Announces Discovery of Accounting Irregularities," *PRNewswire*, January 29, 1997.
5. Jeff Bailey, "Mercury Finance's Controller Denies He Inflated Firm's Profit Statements," *Wall Street Journal*, January 31, 1997, pp. A3, A6.
6. Norris, "Auto Lender's Finance Chief," p. D5.
7. Arthur Goldgaber, "Life after Mercury," *Financial World*, May 20, 1997, pp. 40–44.
8. Nick Wingfield and Paul Beckett, "MicroStrategy, Results Restated, Is Macro-Loser," *Wall Street Journal*, March 21, 2000, pp. B1, B4.
9. Floyd Norris, "A Hard Fall as Highflier Revises Figures," *New York Times*, March 21, 2000, pp. C1, C16.
10. Floyd Norris, "Failed Audit: The Humiliation of Pricewaterhouse Coopers," *New York Times*, March 24, 2000, p. C1.
11. Alan Abelson, "Up & Down Wall Street: Way to Go," *Barron's*, July 19, 1999, p. 5. The $59 million purchase price that Lernout & Hauspie paid for Brussels Translation Group was neither a revenue nor an expense, but an exchange of one asset (cash) for another (BTG's stock).

12. John Carreyrou and Mark Maremont, "Lernout Files for Bankruptcy Protection," *Wall Street Journal,* November 30, 2000, pp. A3, A6.

13. Randall Smith, Steven Lipin, and Amal Kumar Naj, "Managing Profits: How General Electric Damps Fluctuations in Its Annual Earnings," *Wall Street Journal,* November 3, 1994, pp. A1, A6.

14. In financial statements prepared for tax purposes, the corporation minimizes its taxable income by writing off fixed assets over the shortest allowable period. This is both a lawful and a customary practice. Companies are permitted to prepare separate sets of accounts for tax and financial reporting purposes. In the latter, they can make choices on discretionary accounting items that result in lower profits than shown in the former.

15. Senior executives typically own stock in their corporations, so to some extent they penalize their wealth by undercutting quality of earnings. Unless their stock holdings are very large, however, the direct benefits of increased bonuses more than fully offset the impact of reduced valuations on their shares.

16. Richard Zeckhauser, Jayendu Patel, Francois Degeorge, and John Pratt, "Reported and Predicted Earnings: An Empirical Investigation Using Prospect Theory." Project for David Dreman Foundation (1994).

17. *Ibid.*

18. As December 31, 1999, approached, economic pundits warned of massive dislocations arising from a programming quirk whereby many computer systems would interpret the following date to be January 1, 1900. Many corporations attributed sluggish sales during the latter part of 1999 to customers' unwillingness to make major commitments in advance of impending chaos, fears of which proved to be greatly overstated.

19. See, for example, Michael C. Jensen and William H. Meckling, "Theory of the Firm: Managerial Behavior, Agency Costs and Ownership Structure," *Journal of Financial Economics* (1976:3), pp. 305–60.

Chapter 2   The Balance Sheet

1. For the record, the accounting profession defines assets as "probable future economic benefits obtained or controlled by a particular entity as a result of past transactions or events" (Statement of Financial Accounting Concepts No. 6, Financial Accounting Standards Board, Stamford, Connecticut, December 1985, p. 10).

2. Barry Libert and Barbara Sayre Casey, "Accounting for Value" (letter to editor), *Barron's,* December 11, 2000, p. 65.

3. Jonathan R. Laing, "The New Math: Why an Accounting Guru Wants to Shake Up Some Basic Tenets of His Profession," *Barron's,* November 20, 2000, pp. 31–36.

4. Barnaby J. Feder, "JDS Uniphase Will Write Down $44.8 Billion in Assets," *New York Times,* July 27, 2001, pp. C1–C2.

5. *Advances in Behavioral Finance*, Richard H. Thaler, ed. (New York, Russell Sage Foundation, 1993).

Chapter 3   The Income Statement

1. Strictly speaking, Boston Beer has no *direct* exposure to interest rate fluctuations. Like any other company, the brewer's earnings are sensitive to swings in the general level of economic activity, which are in turn sensitive to changes in the level of interest rates. As it happens, demand for beer (and for consumer nondurables generally) is less sensitive to variations in the level of economic activity than demand for many other types of goods.

2. There are a few exceptions to this generalization. Tax collectors, for example, examine a company's income statement to determine its tax liability. For them, *next* year is irrelevant because they can assess a tax only on what has already been earned.

3. Financial Accounting Standards: Original Pronouncements, as of June 1, 1980, Financial Accounting Standards Board, Stamford, Connecticut, pp. 371–373. The APB opinion covering the issue became effective on October 1, 1973.

4. Floyd Norris, "No Special Accounting Breaks for Recent Corporate Setbacks," *New York Times*, October 2, 2001, p. C9.

5. Source: J. Douglas Hanna, University of Chicago. Cited in Nelson, "P&G" (n. 6).

6. Emily Nelson, "P&G's One-Time Charges Make Critics Look Twice at Earnings," *Wall Street Journal*, April 4, 2001, pp. C1–C2.

7. Roger Lowenstein, "Sipping the Fizz in Coca-Cola's Profit," *Wall Street Journal*, May 1, 1997, p. C1.

8. Patrick McGeehan, "Gabelli Asset Management Earnings Release Accentuates the Positive, Bottom Line Aside," *Wall Street Journal*, May 25, 1999, p. C4.

9. Bill Alpert, "The Numbers Game: Reporting of Pro Forma Earnings Is Rising, and So Is the Debate about It," *Barron's*, September 11, 2000, pp. 22, 24.

10. Edward Wyatt, "Putting on a Happier Profit Face," *New York Times*, May 16, 1999, Sec.3, p. 6.

11. Elizabeth MacDonald, "Varied Profit Reports by Firms Create Confusion," *Wall Street Journal*, August 24, 1999, p. C1.

12. Randall Smith, with Henry Sender, Gasten Ceron, and Greg Ip, "Bids and Offers," *Wall Street Journal*, November 2, 2001, p. C13.

13. McGeehan, "Gabelli Asset Management," p. C4.

14. Steve Liesman and Jonathan Weil, "Two Profit Calculations for S&P 500 Differ," *Wall Street Journal*, August 24, 2001, pp. A2, A4. As the authors explain, the year-over-year declines were preliminary figures, subject to adjustment during the third quarter.

15. Alpert, "The Numbers Game," p. 24.

16. Gretchen Morgenson, "In an Effort to Placate Investors, Some Results too Good to Be True," *New York Times*, December 21, 1999, p. A1.

17. Messod D. Beneish, "The Detection of Earnings Manipulation," *Financial Analysts Journal*, September/October 1999, pp. 24–36.

Chapter 4   The Statement of Cash Flows

1. Exhibit 4.2 and the accompanying narrative simplify the concept of cash flow to introduce it to the reader. Only the two major sources of cash, net income and depreciation, appear here, leaving to subsequent exhibits refinements such as deferred taxes, which arise from timing differences between the recognition and payment of taxes. Similarly, the uses of cash exclude a working capital factor, which is discussed in connection with Exhibit 4.9.
2. For a detailed rationale for the use of the EBITDA multiple to evaluate a firm, see "Valuation via Restructuring Potential" in Chapter 14. See also "The Applications and Limitations of EBITDA" in Chapter 8.
3. In large measure, the high failure rate of the late-1990s dot-com public companies is attributable to premature IPOs. During less exuberant stock markets, new ventures go through longer gestation periods before going public. A large proportion of them fail while still in the hands of the venture capitalists, rather than under the glare of the financial media.
4. Amortization of debt discount arises from bonds issued at a discount to face value. Buyers of such a security receive a portion of their interest (all of it, in the case of zero-coupon bonds) through price appreciation over the life of the bond, rather than in the form of semiannual cash payments. The issuer recognizes the noncash interest expense in annual installments between issuance and maturity, rather than in a lump sum at maturity.
5. James Bandler and Mitchell Pacelle, "Polaroid Is Using Chapter 11 to Seek a Buyer," *Wall Street Journal*, October 15, 2001, p. B9.
6. Claudia H. Deutsch, "Market Place: For Polaroid, the Bad News Seems to Be the Only News," *New York Times*, October 4, 2001, p. C7.
7. Michael C. Jensen, "The Free Cash Flow Theory of Takeovers: A Financial Perspective on Mergers and Acquisitions and the Economy," in *The Merger Boom*, Proceedings of a Conference Held in October 1978, edited by Lynn E. Browne and Eric S. Rosengren, Federal Reserve Bank of Boston, pp. 102–37. This article provides the basis for the synopsis of the free cash flow argument described here, as well as the definition quoted.
8. *Ibid.*

Chapter 5   What Is Profit?

1. John Francis Fowler, Jr., *Introduction to Wall Street: A Practical Guide Book for the Investor or Speculator* (New York: Harper & Brothers Publishers, 1930), p. 76.
2. This was probably even truer in 1930 than today, for it was only with the passage of the Securities Act of 1933 that it became a requirement for most United

States public companies to have their financial statements audited by independent public accountants. Even then, financial reporting rules remained fairly loose while the federal government and accounting profession wrestled with the question of how best to establish standards.

3. *Ninotchka:* The MGM Library of Film Scripts (New York: Viking Press, 1972), p. 13.

Chapter 6   Revenue Recognition

1. David Bank, "Informix Reveals More Severe Accounting Errors," *Wall Street Journal,* September 23, 1997, p. B10.
2. Don Clark, "Informix Hurt by Results, Resignation; Accounting, Sales Strategy Play Rose," *Wall Street Journal Europe,* May 5, 1997, p. 12.
3. Mark Boslet, "Revenue Recognition Violations behind Informix Restatement," *Dow Jones News Service,* August 7, 1997.
4. Bank, "Informix Reveals," p. B10.
5. Informix Corporation, *Form 10-K: Annual Report for the Fiscal Year Ended December 13, 1997,* Disclosure, p. 110.
6. Michael Schroeder, "Informix Settles Allegations by SEC of Accounting Fraud Tied to Deficits," *Wall Street Journal,* January 12, 2000, p. B6.
7. Informix Corporation, *Form 10-K: Annual Report for the Fiscal Year Ended December 31, 1999,* Disclosure, p. 58.
8. Tom Steinert-Threlkeld, "KnowledgeWare Stock Decline Imperils Sale to Sterling," *The Dallas Morning News,* August 2, 1994, p. 1D.
9. Melinda-Carol Ballou, "Sterling Attempts KnowledgeWare Rescue," *Computerworld,* August 8, 1994, p. 32.
10. Alison Eastwood, "KnowledgeWare Acquisition Could Benefit Canadian User Base; Company to Be Bought by Sterling Software, Inc.," *Computing Canada,* August 17, 1994, p. 1.
11. Mary Welch, "KnowledgeWare Retries: Sterling Reduces Offer for Struggling Software Business," *Advertising Age,* September 26, 1994, p. 28.
12. Bill Husted, "KnowledgeWare Okays Merger with Sterling," *Atlanta Constitution,* December 1, 1994, sec. F, p. 3.
13. Floyd Norris, "SEC Charges 68 Companies and Individuals with Accounting Fraud," *New York Times,* September 29, 1999, p. C2.
14. Liz Skinner, "Former NFL Star Tarkenton among 68 Charged by SEC," *Bloomberg News,* September 28, 1999.
15. Steinert-Threlkeld, "KnowledgeWare Stock Decline," p. 1D.
16. The account of Kendall Square's revenue recognition controversies draws on the following articles: Dorfman, John R., and William M. Bulkeley, "Supercomputer Maker Kendall Square's Effort to Crack Business Market Has Some Skeptics," *Wall Street Journal* (October 11, 1993), p. C2; Gallese, Liz Roman, "Kendall Square Fires Founder Burkhardt, Two Demoted Executives," *Bloomberg News* (October 26, 1993); "Kendall Square Closes Down 32%,"

Bloomberg Business News (October 29, 1993); Zielenziger, David, "Kendall Square Drops 21% after Auditors Withdraw Backing," *Bloomberg News*, (November 29, 1993).

17. Chip Cummins, "Wal-Mart's Net Income Increases 28%, but Accounting Change Worries Investors," *Wall Street Journal*, August 10, 2000, p. A6.

18. Heather Landy, "Wal-Mart 2nd-Quarter Net to Miss Forecasts," *Bloomberg*, August 9, 2000.

19. Linda Sandler, "Bally Total Fitness's Accounting Procedures Are Getting Some Skeptical Investors Exercised," *Wall Street Journal*, August 26, 1998, p. C2.

20. Eric Matejevich, "Bally Total Fitness: Flexing Its Muscles; Buy Reiterated," *Merrill Lynch HYLights*, September 2, 1999, pp. 18–24.

21. Sandler, "Bally," p. C2.

22. "BJ's Wholesale Club, Inc. Says Membership Income Accounting Complies with All Applicable Standards," *Business Wire*, September 3, 1998.

23. Elizabeth MacDonald, Laura Johannes, and Emily Nelson, "Discount-Club Retailers Shift Accounting," *Wall Street Journal*, October 28, 1998, p. B4.

24. "MemberWorks Reports Record Fiscal 2000 Fourth Quarter Financial Results," *Business Wire*, July 28, 2000.

25. Elizabeth MacDonald, "Are Those Revenues for Real?" *Forbes*, May 29, 2000, pp. 108–110. The author credits Bear Stearns & Co. with identifying 120 companies that announced they had changed or would change their revenue recognition policies in recent months.

26. "Sequoia, Ex-Officials Settle SEC Charges of Inflating Results," *Wall Street Journal*, February 17, 1996, p. B6.

27. Mark Maremont, "Numbers Game at Bausch & Lomb?" *Business Week*, December 19, 1994, pp. 108–110.

28. Maremont, "Numbers Game," p. 109.

29. "Bausch & Lomb Responds to Article in *Business Week Magazine*," *Business Wire*, December 9, 1994. Note that the issue of *Business Week* in which Mark Maremont's Bausch & Lomb article appeared was published several days before the newsstand date of December 19, 1994.

30. "Bausch & Lomb Announces Results for 1994 Fourth Quarter and Full Year Earnings Impacted by Charge to Write Off Goodwill in Oral Care Business," *Business Wire*, January 25, 1995.

31. Ben Dobbin, "Bausch & Lomb Posts $3.36 Million Loss, Restates Past Earnings," *Associated Press*, January 24, 1996.

32. Louis Hau, "Bausch & Lomb CEO Resignation Blamed on Poor Earnings," *Dow Jones News*, December 13, 1995.

33. "Panel at Bausch & Lomb Releases Results of Probe," *Wall Street Journal*, April 24, 1996, p. B5.

34. Reed Abelson, "Not Quite the Last Word: Gary Lynch, Defender of Companies, Has His Critics," *New York Times*, September 3, 1996, p. D1.

35. "Bausch & Lomb Responds."

36. Joseph B. White, "GM Shifts to Reverse on December Data for Cadillac Sales," *Wall Street Journal*, May 6, 1999, pp. A3, A6.

37. Melody Peterson, "S.E.C. Charges Grace and 6 Former Executives with Fraud," *New York Times*, December 23, 1998, pp. C1, C6.

38. Ann Davis, "SEC Claims Profit 'Management' by Grace," *Wall Street Journal*, April 7, 1999, p. C1, C20.

39. Davis, "SEC Case," p. C20.

40. *Ibid.*

41. Peter Ramjug, "W.R. Grace Settles SEC Income Manipulation Case," *Reuters*, June 30, 1999.

42. Michael C. Jensen, "Why Pay People to Lie?" *Wall Street Journal*, January 8, 2001, p. A32.

43. Elizabeth MacDonald and Daniel Kruger, "Aiding and Abetting," *Forbes*, April 2, 2001, pp. 82–84.

44. MacDonald and Kruger, "Aiding," p. 84.

45. Davis, "SEC Case," p. C1.

46. Lipin, Steven, "Citicorp Unit's Top Officials Are Dismissed." *Wall Street Journal* (November 11, 1991), p. A4.

47. "Cincinnati Milacron Overstated Earnings by $300,000 for Half," *Wall Street Journal* (August 4, 1993), p. C9.

48. "Net of First Financial Management Corp. Restated for 3 Periods," *Wall Street Journal* (December 30, 1991), p. B7.

49. The account of T2 Medical is drawn from the following articles: Krensavage, Mike, "T2 Medical 3rd-Quarter Net Falls 40%; Company Restates 1st Half," *Bloomberg News* (August 23, 1993); Pauly, David, "Ways of Wall Street: T2 Medical's Numbers Aren't Right," *Bloomberg News* (August 13, 1993); Quinson, Tim, "T2 Medical Says Management Group May Make Buyout Offer," *Bloomberg News* (May 25, 1993); "T2 Medical Net Fell 40% in 3rd Period: Company Restates Profit for First Half," *New York Times* (August 24, 1993), p. B4.

Chapter 7   Expense Recognition

1. Gary Samuels, "What Profits?" *Forbes*, October 24, 1994, p. 74.

2. "Prodigy Management to Unveil Buyout Plan," *Financial Post*, May 9, 1996, p. 14. (Originally reported by *Bloomberg News*.)

3. Roger Lowenstein, "Did AOL Succeed in Spinning the Street?" *Wall Street Journal*, November 7, 1996, p. C1.

4. Floyd Norris, "AOL Pays Fine to Settle a Charge That It Inflated Profits," *New York Times*, May 16, 2000, p. C6.

5. David S. Hilzenrath and Jill Dutt, "Looking for the AOL Numbers That Count," *Washington Post*, February 23, 1997, pp. H1, H7.

6. Linda Sandler, "America Online's Fancy Accounting Methods Once Again Are Raising Red Flags for Some," *Wall Street Journal*, June 3, 1998, p. C4.

7. Jon G. Auerbach, "IBM's Accounting Method Faces Scrutiny," *Wall Street Journal*, November 24, 1999, pp. C1-C2.

8. Auerbach, "IBM's Accounting," p. C2.

9. *Ibid.*

10. "Wickes PLC Discovers Accounting Problems; '95 Profit Overstated," *Dow Jones and Company*, June 25, 1996.
11. Nigel Cope, "Accounting Problems Ravage Wickes," *The Independent* (London), June 26, 1996, p. 17.
12. Paul Farrelly, "'Dirty Tricks' at Wickes; Internal Inquiry Looks at Sweetbaum's Management," *The Independent* (London), August 4, 1996, p. B3.
13. Andrew Sawers, "SFO Puts FDS in the Dock over Wickes 'Pyramid Buying' Scandal," *Financial Director*, August 1, 1999, p. 8.
14. Edward Orlebar, "Wickes Says Profit Overstated by 51 Million Pounds," *Bloomberg*, October 16, 2001.
15. Nigel Cope, "Senior Wickes Management Was Aware of Bogus Profits 6 Months before Disclosure," *The Independent* (London), October 17, 1996, p. 22.
16. "Wickes PLC Discovers Accounting Problems; '95 Profit Overstated," *Dow Jones and Company*, June 25, 1996.
17. Ron Winslow and Scot J. Paltrow, "At Oxford Health, Financial 'Controls' Were out of Control," *Wall Street Journal*, April 29, 1998, pp. A1, A14.
18. Ron Winslow, "A Few Securities Analysts Spotted Problems at Oxford Health Plans," *Wall Street Journal*, April 29, 1998, p. A14.

Chapter 8   The Applications and Limitations of EBITDA

1. Failures by leveraged buyouts largely accounted for the escalation in the default rate on speculative grade bond issuers, as reported by Moody's Investors Service, from 3.5% in 1988 to a peak of 10.5% in 1991.
2. William H. Beaver, "Financial Ratios as Predictors of Failure," *Journal of Accounting Research* (Supplement 1966), pp. 71–111.
3. The development of this tradition is more fully explored in Martin S. Fridson, "EBITDA Is *Not* King," *Journal of Financial Statement Analysis*, Spring 1998, pp. 59–62.
4. Edward I. Altman, "Financial Ratios, Discriminant Analysis, and the Prediction of Corporate Bankruptcy," *Journal of Finance*, September 1968, pp. 589–609.
5. Richard Bernstein, "An Analysis of Low EV/EBITDA," Merrill Lynch & Co., September 4, 2001.
6. Defined as Equity Market Capitalization + Long-Term Debt + Short-Term Debt + Preferred Stock + Minority Interest − (Cash + Cash Equivalents).

Chapter 9   The Reliability of Disclosure and Audits

1. James Bandler, "Computer Associates Says Error Boosted Annual Earnings," *Wall Street Journal*, May 7, 2001, p. B9.
2. Jacqueline Doherty, "Fuzzy Numbers from Mr. Trump," *Barron's*, November 1, 1999, p. MW16.

3. "Trump Hotels & Casino Resorts Third Quarter Results," *Business Wire*, October 25, 1999.

4. Christina Binkley, "Trump Hotels Failed to Disclose Gain, So Firm Appeared to Beat Estimates," *Wall Street Journal*, November 8, 1999, p. B12.

5. Binkley, "Trump Hotels," p. B12.

6. Doherty, "Fuzzy Numbers," p. MW16.

7. Steve Lohr, "Trump Hotels Settles Case Accusing It of Misleading Investors," *New York Times*, January 17, 2002, p. C4.

8. Adam Steinhauer, "Park Place CEO Goldberg Is out of Hospital," *Bloomberg News*, July 7, 2001.

9. Jeannine DeFoe, "Park Place Taps Hilton Exec to Succeed Goldberg," *Bloomberg News*, October 23, 2000.

10. Shawn Tully, "The New King of Casinos," *Fortune*, September 18, 2000, p. 156.

11. Judy DeHaven, "What Now for Park Place?" *The Star-Ledger*, October 20, 2000, p. 53.

12. John A. Byrne, "Chainsaw," *Business Week*, October 18, 1999, pp. 128–149.

13. John A. Byrne, "How Al Dunlap Self-Destructed," *Business Week*, July 6, 1998, pp. 58–65.

14. Jonathan R. Laing, "SEC vs. Chainsaw Al," *Barron's*, May 21, 2001, p. 13.

15. ". . . And Take the Chainsaw with You!" *Barron's*, June 22, 1998, p. 13.

16. Jonathan R. Laing, "Dangerous Games: Did 'Chainsaw Al' Manufacture Sunbeam's Earnings Last Year?" *Barron's*, June 8, 1998, p. 17.

17. Laing, "Dangerous Games," p. 17.

18. Martha Brannigan, "Sunbeam Slashes Its 1997 Earnings in Restatement," *Wall Street Journal*, October 21, 1998, p. B6.

19. Byrne, "Chainsaw," p. 142.

20. Jonathan R. Laing, "High Noon at Sunbeam," *Barron's*, June 16, 1997, p. 29.

21. Floyd Norris, "They Noticed the Fraud but Figured It Was Not Important," *New York Times*, May 18, 2001, p. C1.

22. Floyd Norris, "An Executive's Missing Years: Papering Over Past Problems," *New York Times*, July 16, 2001, p. A1.

23. Stephanie Strom, "Woolworth's Treasurer Blew Whistle," *New York Times*, May 20, 1994, p. D4.

24. Patrick M. Reilly, "Woolworth Executives Faulted in Probe, but Lavin Reinstated as Chief Executive," *Wall Street Journal*, May 19, 1994, pp. A3, A6.

25. Floyd Norris, "Sometimes, Safeguards Protect Nobody," *New York Times*, March 22, 1998, Sec. 3, p. 1.

26. Elizabeth MacDonald, "Auditors Miss a Fraud and SEC Tries to Put Them out of Business," *Wall Street Journal*, November 6, 2000, pp. A1, A8.

27. Jeanne Patterson and Nell Minow, "Blame Directors for Accounting Practices, Managing Earnings," *Pensions & Investments*, May 28, 2001, p. 12.

Chapter 10   Mergers-and-Acquisitions Accounting

1. Reed Abelson, "Market Place: A Candidate Weighs in on an Accounting Rule Change," *New York Times*, October 17, 2000, p. C16.

2. See Abraham J. Briloff, "Pooling and Fooling: A Critic Draws a Bead on Cisco's Accounting Policies," *Barron's*, October 23, 2000, pp. 26–29.

3. Greg Hitt, "Cisco's Chambers Revs Up Political-Contribution Engine," *Wall Street Journal*, June 8, 2000, p. A26.

4. Jonathan Weil, "FASB Backs Down on Goodwill-Accounting Rules," *Wall Street Journal*, December 7, 2000, pp. A1, A6.

5. Jonathan Weil, "Goodwill Hunting: Accounting Change May Lift Profits, but Stock Prices May Not Follow Suit," *Wall Street Journal*, January 25, 2001, pp. C1–C2.

6. Michael Davis, "Roiling the Waters: Why the Case for Pooling-of-Interests Accounting Is All Wet," *Barron's*, October 23, 2000, p. 73.

7. Bill Alpert, "The Numbers Game," *Barron's*, September 11, 2000, pp. 22, 24.

8. Floyd Norris, "At Tyco, Accounting 'Baths' Begin before the Deals Close," *New York Times*, October 29, 1999, p. C1.

9. Thatcher Thompson, "Navigant: Downgrading NCI Shares," Merrill Lynch & Co. Research Comment, November 5, 1999.

10. Barry Henderson, "Number Theory: Navigant's Growth Rate May Not Be What It Seems," *Barron's*, October 25, 1999, p. 24.

11. Barry Henderson, "Follow the Money," *Barron's*, November 29, 1999, pp. 15–17.

12. James P. Miller, "Navigant CEO Resigns, Two Officials Are Fired over Stock-Purchase Deals," *Wall Street Journal*, November 23, 1999, p. A4.

13. A month later, when Navigant announced that it was not for sale, the stock receded to $41.44.

Chapter 11   Profits in Pensions

1. Gretchen Morgenson noted this contrast between the 1999 IBM and GE annual reports in "What's Hiding in Big Blue's Small Print," *New York Times*, June 4, 2000, sec. 3, p. 1.

2. General Electric 1999 Annual Report, p. 42.

3. Pat McConnell, Janet Pegg, and David Zion, "Retirement Benefits Impact Operating Income," Bear Stearns & Co. September 17, 1999, p. 55.

4. Vineeta Anand, "SEC Tells Companies to Explain Earnings' Origin," *Pensions & Investments*, December 25, 2000, pp. 4, 43.

Chapter 12   Forecasting Financial Statements

1. A less restrictive type of covenant merely prohibits incurrence of new debt or payment of dividends that would cause financial measures to deteriorate below a targeted level. No violation occurs if, for example, net worth declines as a result of operating losses.

2. Cabot's chemical operations sold $20 million of products to the LNG and CMC units during fiscal 1999. In preparing a consolidated statement for

Cabot, these intercompany sales were eliminated, in accordance with GAAP. If the accounting rules did not require such elimination, a multidivisional company could create the illusion of dramatic increases in sales and earnings by trading goods back and forth among its various business units. Taking money out of one pocket and putting it into another would not represent a wealth increase (income) for the combined enterprise.

3. Gretchen Morgenson, "Time to Look at Stock Options' Real Cost," *New York Times,* October 21, 2001, Sec. 3, p. 1.

Chapter 13   Credit Analysis

1. In practice, the United States Bankruptcy Code encourages companies to reorganize, rather than simply liquidate, if they become insolvent. Typically, a reorganization results in settlement of creditors' claims via distribution of securities of a firm that has been rehabilitated through forgiveness of a portion of its debt. Determination of the value of securities awarded to each class of creditor is related to asset protection, however, so the analysis that follows applies equally to reorganization and liquidation.

2. The comments on preferred stock in this paragraph also apply generally to preference stock, which is similar to preferred stock in form but junior to it in the capital structure.

3. In this and subsequent definitions of total capital, minority interest is included. This item should be viewed as equity in leverage calculations because it involves no contractual payment and ranks junior to debt.

4. Nick Fielding, Richard Thomson, and Larry Black, "Undisclosed Debt Worries Hang over O&Y," *The Independent,* May 10, 1992, Business on Sunday Section, p. 1.

5. All quotations in the discussion of Viacom, except where otherwise noted, are from Martin S. Fridson, "Crossover Dreams versus Crossover Reality," *This Week in High Yield,* published by Merrill Lynch & Co., October 4, 1996, pp. 1–8.

6. Technically speaking, the effective tax rate is somewhat manageable, even though the statutory rate is not. It is nevertheless useful to calculate the operating margin separately from the pretax margin, to measure management's operating prowess separately from its financial acumen.

7. See Edward I. Altman, Robert G. Haldeman, and Paul Narayanan, "Zeta Analysis: A New Model to Identify Bankruptcy Risk of Corporations," *Journal of Banking and Finance,* June 1977, pp. 29–54.

8. See, for example, David T. Hamilton, Greg Gupton, and Alexandra Berthault, *Default and Recovery Rates of Corporate Bond Issuers: 2000,* Moody's Investors Service, February 2001. The tables in this report relating ratings to multiyear, cumulative default rates show just one small discrepancy. According to the statistics, companies rated AA are more prone to default within one year than companies rated A, an aberration undoubtedly attributable to the tiny

sample of companies that have ever fallen from such high ratings to default within the space of a year.

9. Altman, Haldeman, and Narayanan set the Zeta model's cutoff score (the level at which a loan request is rejected on grounds of excessive default risk) with an explicit goal of achieving the optimal tradeoff between the costs of making loans that default and rejecting loans that do not default.

10. *The 2000 Bankruptcy Yearbook & Almanac*, Christopher M. McHugh, ed. (Boston: New Generation Research, Inc., 2000), pp. 187–190.

Chapter 14   Equity Analysis

1. Dividends, unlike interest payments on debt, are payable at the discretion of the board of directors, rather than in fulfillment of a contractual obligation. They are consequently subject to greater variability—through reduction, increase, or suspension—than bond coupons or scheduled principal repayments.

2. Bethany McLean, "Hocus-Pocus: How IBM Grew 27% a Year," *Fortune*, June 26, 2000, p. 165.

3. The notion that a company can increase its market capitalization by boosting its financial leverage appears to fly in the face of a fundamental tenet of modern finance. Nobel economics laureates Franco Modigliani and Merton Miller demonstrated that under certain critical assumptions, a company's stock market value was insensitive to the proportions of debt and equity in its capital structure. Modigliani and Miller followed up on this pioneering work, however, by exploring what happened when the assumptions were relaxed to reflect real-world conditions. In particular, they and subsequent researchers found that the company's stock market value could in fact rise as a result of boosting financial leverage to take fuller advantage of the tax shield provided by debt. Interest on borrowings is a tax-deductible expense, whereas dividends on stock are not.

4. Note, however, the uncertainties associated with reserve valuations, discussed in Chapter 2 under the heading "The Value Problem."

index